Political Control of the Soviet Armed Forces

Michael J. Deane

Crane, Russak & Company, Inc.

NEW YORK

Political Control of the Soviet Armed Forces

Published in the United States by
Crane, Russak & Company, Inc.
347 Madison Avenue
New York, New York 10017

Published in Great Britain by
Macdonald and Jane's Publishers Ltd.
Paulton House 8 Shepherdess Walk
London N1 7LW

Copyright © 1977 Stanford Research Institute, Inc.

Crane Russak ISBN 0-8448-1055-x
Macdonald and Jane's ISBN 0354-01129-4
LC 76-49751

PRINTED IN THE UNITED STATES OF AMERICA

Contents

Commentary

The formulation and implementation of Soviet domestic and foreign policy has long been subject to the scrutiny of Western scholars and government experts, yet little real consensus exists today as to the nature of high-level decision-making in the USSR and the role of various "groups" in that process. Along with such generalizations as a "monolithic" CPSU, absolute in its control over all Soviet institutions, or hypothesized conflict and cleavages among supposed "interest groups," Western discussion on this subject is often characterized by a plethora of dichotomous concepts (hawks v. doves, hardliners v. softliners, party v. state, bureaucrats v. idealogues) derived for the most part from the Western political context, whose utility for analyses of the Soviet leadership is tenuous at best.

This well-researched and careful study of the Main Political Administration (MPA) and political control of the Soviet Armed Forces provides original and thoughtful insights into the relationship of the CPSU and the professional military in the decisionmaking process. Not only does it offer a much-needed illumination of the MPA (a unique organization whose important role in Soviet policy has long been underestimated or overlooked) but it also serves to enlighten our understanding of "conflict" and "debate" within and among the main institutions of Soviet state and society. The author persuasively argues that the evidence of debate is not a sign that the Soviet military is "challenging" the political authority of the CPSU, but rather that these "debates" occur within well-defined and sanctioned limits, both as to the issues involved and scope of discussion.

Dr. Michael J. Deane until recently served as a member of the Soviet

i

Research Staff at Stanford Research Institute's Strategic Studies Center, which has for many years devoted its attention to the study of Soviet political and military affairs, national strategy, and foreign policy. With this publication, Dr. Deane has made an important contribution to the existing body of knowledge on the USSR in general and its armed forces in particular. Such efforts are essential steps in the ongoing process of developing a deeper understanding of the Soviet Union — a process fundamental to the task of meeting the challenge posed to the West by the USSR.

Richard B. Foster
Director, Strategic Studies Center

Preface

Under the totalitarian model, which until recent years dominated much of Western analysis of Soviet processes and behavior, the Soviet Union was viewed as a system free from the struggles of ideas and interests below the leadership level and especially from the conflicts of rival interest groups. It was conceived that only the Communist Party of the Soviet Union (CPSU), and most particularly the Party's uppermost leadership, raised issues and influenced decisions. The values, influence, and interests of other groups were considered to be of little importance. As H. Gordon Skilling pointed out, "the monolithic party was regarded as the only interest group, not itself differentiated in its thinking or behavior."[1]

One of the first attempts to counteract the totalitarian school of thought and to describe more accurately the growing complexity of Soviet politics emerged as the school of "Kremlinology" pioneered by Boris I. Nicolaevsky.[2] Searching Soviet publications for signs of struggle and factionalism, this group basically sought to illustrate the perpetual conflict that emerged from the monolithic façade of the Stalinist years. As Nicolaevsky once observed:

> Disagreements on what is desirable and what is possible at any given moment are the determining factor in the emergence of rival groups in the Party leadership. Even in Lenin's days, Party factions had been forbidden — and this applied

[1] H. Gordon Skilling, "Interest Groups and Communist Politics," in H. Gordon Skilling and Franklyn Griffiths, eds., *Interest Groups in Soviet Politics* (Princeton, N.J.: Princeton University Press, 1971), p. 8.

[2] Carl A. Linden, *Khrushchev and the Soviet Leadership, 1957–1964* (Baltimore: The Johns Hopkins University Press, 1966), p. 5.

iv   *Preface*

to the leaders as well. But it has always been difficult for the leaders to prevent
the rise of factions, for in the process of working together, members of the
Soviet elite develop ideas and arrive at conclusions concerning the desirable
and the possible which necessarily lead to the creation of more or less stable
groupings. While Stalin was alive, this process continued at a slower pace. . . .
But Stalin could only slow down this process of group formation; he could not
eliminate it altogether. For the emergence of cliques among the top leadership
is a reflection of the emergence of different social groups within the ruling
classes.[3]

Similarly, in the view of Robert Conquest, "intense struggle is the primary condition of Soviet politics."[4]

Fundamentally, the types of power struggles and factional alignments described by the Kremlinologists were based on personal followings as well as career
and associated groupings.[5] The methodology of the Kremlinologists employed
a type of analysis "which lays great stress on a careful study of the promotion,
demotion, and interaction of personalities, and also on the exact wording of
pronouncements of certain conventional or formal kinds."[6]

Moving beyond the mere description of struggle, there arose a second school,
known as the conflict school. According to Linden:

. . . the adherents of the conflict school have turned to the general conceptional
device of conventional political science, where attempts are made to define
change in terms analogous to left-wing or conservative-reforming tendencies
in other political systems. They have seen the post-Stalin period as one in which
the normal dualisms of politics have increasingly influenced contemporary
Soviet leadership politics.[7]

One general difference between the schools of Kremlinology and conflict is that
the former seeks to describe the existing struggles and the groups involved,
whereas the latter school wants to explain the purposes and effects these phenomena have on Soviet policy issues. A second difference is that the Kremlin-
ologist's method stressed personal rivalries among elites, while the conflict

[3] Janet D. Zagoria, ed., *Power and the Soviet Elite, "The Letter of an Old Bolshevik" and
Other Essays by Boris I. Nicolaevsky* (New York: Praeger, 1965), pp. 131–32.

[4] Robert Conquest, *Power and Policy in the USSR: The Struggle for Stalin's Succession,
1945–1960* (New York: Harper & Row, 1967), p. viii.

[5] Linden, p. 6.

[6] Alec Nove, "The Uses and Abuses of Kremlinology," *Survey, No. 50* (January 1964), p. 174.

[7] Linden, p. 6.

school emphasized constant strife arising from continuous disagreements on policy issues.[8]

As a consequence of the evolution in Western analyses and building on the two previous models, there arose a third model. This model emphasized the formation and influence of various groups in Soviet political affairs. According to one of the leading Western observers of the groups in Soviet politics, H. Gordon Skilling:

> . . . since Stalin's death the Soviet political system has been passing through a period of transition, characterized among other things by the increased activity of political interest groups and the presence of group conflict. Although decision-making in its final stage still remains in the hands of a relatively small group at the top of the party hierarchy, there has been . . . a broadening of group participation in the crucial preliminary stages of policy deliberation and in the subsequent phase of implementation.[9]

At present, interest group theorists agree that the Party maintains a dominant position in Soviet politics, but they also recognize the growing importance of other groups. The observer just cited, for example, has noted that in the making of its decisions the Party must take various group interests into account and that "the party increasingly performs the role of an aggregator of conflicting interests."[10] Moreover, one predictor of "drastic institutional changes" in the USSR maintains that "these changes will be facilitated by the declining hold of the party on the various interest groups."[11]

Soviet Interest Group Theory

According to Soviet theoreticians, Soviet institutions cannot conflict with one

[8] Joel J. Schwartz and William R. Kreech, "Group Influence and the Policy Process in the Soviet Union," *American Political Science Review*. LXII, No. 3 (September 1968), 845–46; and Arthur E. Adams, "The Hybrid Art of Sovietology," *Survey*, No. 50 (January 1964), p. 160.

[9] H. Gordon Skilling, "Groups in Soviet Politics: Some Hypotheses," in Skilling and Griffiths, p. 19.

[10] H. Gordon Skilling, "The Party, Opposition, and Interest Groups in Communist Politics: Fifty Years of Continuity and Change," in Kurt London, ed., *The Soviet Union: A Half-Century of Communism* (Baltimore: The Johns Hopkins University Press, 1968), pp. 122–23.

[11] Jayantanuja Bandyopadhyaya, "The Changes Ahead," *Problems of Communism*, XVI, No. 1 (January–February 1967), 43.

another because they exist only as reflections on the division of labor.[12] Moreover as Roman Kolkowicz has pointed out:

> Communist theoreticians tend to view articulated group interests as a sign of anti-systemic alienation from society and state, as a remnant of the bourgeois past, and such dissent, unless it can be directed and usefully channeled, must be eradicated. Institutional or particularist group loyalties and objectives which significantly depart from those of the party are viewed as being "pathological." The only "interest groups" Soviet theoreticians recognize are the economically and historically conditioned social classes; the proletariat, the peasantry, and the intelligentsia.[13]

Indeed the CPSU's party program adopted in 1961 notes that "under [the stage of full] communism there will be no classes, and the socioeconomic conditions between town and countryside will disappear," and that only after the victory of communism will the intelligentsia "no longer be a distinct social stratum."[14] However, since Soviet theory maintains that these groups are not antagonistic, Soviet institutions cannot be competitive or antagonistic.

Despite these Soviet assertions that interest groups and conflicts of interest cannot exist within a socialist state, Western observers generally classify Soviet interest groups as falling into two types: (1) institutional or occupational and (2) opinion or issue.[15] If it is acceptable to define a political interest group as any group with a commonly shared outlook, direction, and goal, then an institutional or occupational interest group is one which derives its commonality from a particular organization or type of employment. For example, the Party, the military, industrial managers, urban workers, and similar groups would constitute this type.

The second type of interest group arises, as pointed out by Skilling, from the fact that institutional and occupational groups are characterized by "both substantial cohesion and marked internal differentiation." Skilling further sug-

[12] Vernon V. Aspaturian, "The Soviet Military-Industrial Complex — Does It Exist?" *Journal of International Affairs*, XXVI, No. 1 (1972), 2.

[13] Roman Kolkowicz, "The Military," in Skilling and Griffiths, p. 131.

[14] *The Road to Communism. Documents of the 22nd Congress of the Communist Party of the Soviet Union* (Moscow: Foreign Language Publishing House, 1961), p. 510.

[15] Skilling, "Groups in Soviet Politics: Some Hypotheses," in Skilling and Griffiths, p. 25; and Philip D. Stewart, "Soviet Interest Groups and the Policy Process: The Repeal of Production Education,"*World Politics*, XXII, No. 1 (October 1969), 30. Both sources note additionally the existence of personal leadership factions, but strictly speaking these do not constitute political interest groups.

gests that "in almost all groups there is, at the same time, some community of interest on certain issues and sharp clashes of opinion on others. The balance of unity and disunity varies according to the group and changes with the issue involved."[16] Consequently, there develop interest groups which share opinions and stands on a given issue and, thus, aggregate "cutting across institutional and functional lines in which subgroups as well as the larger groups make informal alliances with one another in opposition to similar formations on the opposite side."[17] An examination of the Soviet armed forces, itself an occupational interest group, on the basis of opinions and issues appears to demonstrate that the military is less than a homogeneous interest group. It is possible to show that subgroups of the military align themselves with other subgroups in order to assert pressure for the fulfillment of their views on an issue. Some of the more important issues producing such issue-oriented cleavages include: resource allocation, disarmament, relations with other Communist countries, especially military relations with Warsaw Pact countries, education, and arts and culture. One source also points out that some of the factors which might prompt military men to seek alliances across institutional lines include: present position of command, wartime experience, age, training, and educational background.[18]

Soviet Interest Group Theory and the Soviet Armed Forces

Originally, the Main Political Administration of the Soviet Army and Navy (Glavnoye polititcheskoye upravleniye Sovetskoy Armii i Voyenno-Morskogo Flota, herein abbreviated as MPA) was an instrument of the Bolshevik Government, whose duty it was to ensure the loyalty of the many ex-tsarist officers employed in the new Red Army. In the mid-1920's, the MPA passed under the direct subordination of the Party and became officially designated as an agent of the Party Central Committee in the armed forces. Since then the MPA has generally been regarded as the means by which the Party dominates the professional military members of the armed forces.

This has not always been the case in practice, however. During some periods,

16 H. Gordon Skilling, "Group Conflict in Soviet Politics: Some Conclusions," in Skilling and Griffiths, p. 384.

17 Aspaturian, "The Soviet Military-Industrial Complex," p. 3.

18 John R. Thomas, "The Soviet Military as a Force for Change," in Norton T. Dodge, ed., *Analysis of the USSR's 24th Party Congress and 9th Five-Year Plan* (Mechanicsville, Md.: Cremona Foundation, 1971), p. 23.

as in the 1930's when Yan Gamarnik headed the MPA, the MPA was criticized (and purged) for its inclination to side with the military rather than the party viewpoint. In the 1950's, Minister of Defense Marshal Zhukov severely restricted the MPA's ability to represent the Party. More recent evidence suggests that the relationship of the MPA to the military and the role of the MPA are becoming less clear.

This study will analyze the evolving character of political control, evaluate the changing relationship among the MPA, the Party, and the professional military, examine the political-military policies advocated by these three groups, and assess the future significance of political control in Soviet party-military affairs. The purpose of this analysis is to define types of interest groups represented by the MPA, the Party, and the professional military. For example, is the MPA an occupational or institutional interest group which can be demonstrated to represent the interests of either the Party or the professional military leadership? Is the MPA an issue or opinion group with subgroup cleavages in which some MPA members lean relatively more toward representing the interests of the Party and others lean relatively more toward representing the interests of the armed forces? It will be a major objective of this study, therefore, to relate these models to the MPA, the Party, and the professional military.

One important factor in examining Soviet institutions is the struggle for power and position among elites. It was noted earlier that one of the major contributions of the Kremlinological and conflict schools was to illustrate the existence of perpetual power struggles among the Soviet leadership. It will also be an objective of this study to scrutinize debates on political-military affairs for any evidence of struggles for political control over the armed forces or internal political power.

Methodology

Two methods of analysis will be used in this study: (1) policy and content analysis based on Soviet and non-Soviet sources and (2) analysis of the careers and backgrounds of major political and military leaders, especially MPA officials.

Policy and content analysis relies primarily on open Communist communications, particularly on speeches, journal and newspaper articles, and broadcasts by major spokesmen. By these and other means, interest groups are able to express their views. As Barbara B. Green has noted:

> In order to have group politics it is necessary not only to have groups, but for

the groups to have access to the means of influencing government policy. Such means too are not totally lacking in the Soviet Union, although they are far fewer in number and importance than those existing in the United States. Groups attempt to influence policy through articulation of their views at professional meetings. Newspapers and journals express the vital concerns of various organized groups and even reflect differences of opinion within groups. In recent years it has become possible to speak of liberal and conservative journals, liberal and conservative editors.[19]

In a similar assessment, Robert C. Angell raised a basic question for anyone attempting to analyze Soviet material. He notes:

Everyone knows that the Communist Party exercises a close surveillance over Soviet periodicals. Is there any point, then, in analyzing the contents of Soviet newspapers and journals in the hope of finding any differences among elites? Is it not a case of one voice speaking through a hundred mouths?[20]

Like Green, however, Angell also finds justification for analysis of Soviet material. With a mixture of certitude and caution, Angell suggests that "enough free play has developed near the top of Soviet society since the death of Stalin for elite differences of value to come to light in Soviet periodicals. It is true that the explicit differences on the Soviet side are not striking but in a good many of our value dimensions they are real."[21] Writing with particular regard to Soviet military publications, Kolkowicz reaches the same conclusions. He points out that military spokesmen frequently present their opinions publicly in speeches and articles, but he also emphasizes that this is often done "in a veiled and esoteric way."[22]

In his survey of elite attitudes since the death of Stalin, Milton Lodge has given succinct insight into the limits and reason for the emergence of divergent expressions in Soviet communications. It is Lodge's position that:

In sum, although specialist journals are rarely vehicles for an open and direct confrontation within the Party, specialist attitudes are articulated through instrumental proposals and criticsms — within the Party's espoused values of produc-

---

[19] Barbara B. Green, "Soviet Politics and Interest Groups," *Current History*, LI, No. 302 (October 1966), 215–16.

[20] Robert C. Angell, "Content Analysis of Elite Media," *Journal of Conflict Resolution*, VIII, No. 4 (December 1964), 334.

[21] *Ibid.*, p. 335.

[22] Kolkowicz, "The Military," in Skilling and Griffiths, p. 135.

tivity, efficiency, and "communism" — without overtly challenging the Party's role in policy integration. In the Soviet context, elite participation in the formulation and implementation of specific policies is politics. Direct opposition is rare, politics is ubiquitous. With the decline of terror in the post-Stalin period controversies are no longer zero-sum games.[23]

In what "veiled and esoteric way" are these views expressed? Sidney I. Ploss has suggested that the expression of divergent opinion, or, in his term, the "language of conflict," is a compound of several principal elements: "(1) statements which tend to legitimate political argument; (2) rebukes of anonymous personalities for dissidence; (3) shadings of textual emphasis; (4) modifications of standard terminology; and (5) a leader's reticence about some question which his associates have commented on."[24] Two additional aspects, noted by Donald S. Zagoria in his analysis of the Sino-Soviet debates, should be added to this list. Along with those mentioned by Ploss, Zagoria points out that omissions and distortions may sometimes be means for Soviet spokesmen to carry on their dialogues.[25]

In this study, a frequently encountered problem concerns the questions "Who is an MPA official?" and "Who is an MPA spokesman?" Although *Kommunist Vooruzhennykh Sil (Communist of the Armed Forces)* is the official organ of the MPA, articles in this biweekly journal are sometimes authored by non-MPA members. Thus, a particular article might be authored by a professional military man or by a civilian economist or historian. Those authors who are clearly labeled by *Kommunist Vooruzhennykh Sil* as instructors at a military-political academy can be designated as MPA officials and spokesmen, because such academies are under the control of the MPA. More often, however, authors are identified only by a military rank and/or an academic degree in the social sciences. It is a general assumption of this study that an individual identified by both a military rank and an academic degree in the social sciences is an MPA official or spokesman.

Organization of the Study

This study basically follows a chronogical pattern. Chapters 1 and 2 examine

[23] Milton Lodge, "Soviet Elite Participatory Attitudes in the Post-Stalin Period," *American Political Science Review*, LXIII, No. 3 (September 1968), 829.

[24] Sidney I. Ploss, *Conflict and Decision-Making in Soviet Russia: A Case Study of Agricultural Policy, 1953–1963* (Princeton, N.J.: Princeton University Press, 1965), pp. 10–11.

[25] Donald S. Zagoria, *The Sino-Soviet Conflict, 1956–61* (New York: Atheneum, 1967), pp. 30–34, esp. p. 32.

the theoretical and historical evolution of the political administration of the Soviet armed forces. Chapters 3 through 9 concentrate on the major political-military issues of the 1960's and 1970's.

1

Origins of the Political Administration in the Soviet Armed Forces

The purpose of this chapter is to illustrate the pre-1917 socialist concept of the military in a proletarian society and the impact which this concept had on the origin and early evolution of the political administration in the Soviet armed forces. As in the case of other Soviet institutions, the political administration of the Soviet armed forces has over the years been constantly reshaped to meet the political demands of the moment according to the designs of the faction having ascendance at that time. It is expected that this and the following chapter will provide the background and a survey of the major military-political issues which the Soviet armed forces have had to face during its formative years. In this way it will be easier to understand the problems and issues presently confronted by the political administration.

Socialist Views of the Military Before the Bolshevik Revolution

Soviet writers of the present day admit that at the time of the Bolshevik Revolution in 1917 "Lenin and the Communist Party did not yet have a thoroughly formulated view of the methods and forms of the military organization of the proletarian state and of the principles of its military structure."[1] They also ac-

[1] Quoted in Roman Kolkowicz, *The Soviet Army and the Communist Party: Institutions in Conflict* (Sonta Monica, Calif.: Rand, 1966), p. 57.

1

knowledge that "formulating a thesis on the possibility of the victory of socialism simultaneously in all or in a majority of developed capitalist countries, Marx and Engels did not elaborate the issue of the armed defense of isolated socialist states."[2] A major reason for this lack of foresight was the fact that most of the early socialists held a very simplistic view of the military and its role. Their concept was succinctly expressed by Friedrich Engels in 1845 when he said, "In a Communist society no one will even think about a standing army. Why would one need it?"[3] In sum, the regular or standing army was considered to be completely contrary to socialist principles and, therefore, would cease to exist with the onset of the revolution. According to Engels, for example, proletarian socialism based on popular will "will mean the bursting asunder *from within* of militarism and with it of all standing armies."[4]

Marx similarly maintained a simplistic view of the future military establishment. In "Demands of the Communist Party in Germany," written in joint authorship with Engels during the Year of Revolution, 1848, Marx demanded the general arming of the people. He also advocated the institution of "working armies," a theme which would again arise in Russia after 1917. Marx asserted that "in the future, the armies are to be at the same time working armies, so that the troops are no longer, as hitherto, consumers but, rather, producers of more than their maintenance."[5] In a March 1850 leaflet, Marx gave an even more detailed projection of the proletarian army following a petty-bourgeois democratic revolution. Noting that the workers must ally themselves with the petty bourgeoisie in the first stage of the revolution, Marx observed that the workers would immediately after victory turn upon their former ally. A major role in this struggle would be played by the armed masses. As Marx stated:

> In a word, from the first moment of victory, mistrust must be directed no longer against the conquered reactionary party, but against the workers' previous allies, against the party that wishes to exploit the common victory for itself alone.
>
> But in order to be able energetically and threateningly to oppose this party,

---

[2] General Major Ye. Nikitin and Lieutenant Colonel V. Tret'yakov, "Historical Experience of Party Leadership for Soviet Military Construction," *Voyenno-Istoricheskiy Zhurnal*, No. 8 (August 1973), p. 3.

[3] Quoted in Roman Kolkowicz, *War, Revolution, Army: Communist Theory and Reality* (Arlington, Va.: Institute for Defense Analyses, 1968), p. 1, n. 1.

[4] Friedrich Engels, *Anti-Dühring: Herr Eugene Dühring's Revolution in Science* (Moscow: Foreign Language Publishing House, 1959), p. 236. Italics in original.

[5] Karl Marx and Friedrich Engels, "Demands of the Communist Party in Germany," in Saul K. Padover, ed. and trans., *Karl Marx on Revolution* (New York: McGraw-Hill, 1971), p. 108.

whose treachery to the workers will begin from the first hour of victory, the workers must be armed and organized. The arming of the whole proletariat with rifles, muskets, cannon, and munitions must be put through at once; the revival of the old Citizens' Guard directed against the workers must be resisted. However, where the latter is not feasible the workers must attempt to organize themselves independently as a proletarian guard with commanders elected by themselves and with a general staff of their own choosing, and to put themselves in command not of the state authority but of the revolutionary community councils which the workers will have managed to get adopted. Where workers are employed at the expense of the state they must see that they are armed and organized in a separate corps with commanders of their own choosing or as part of the proletarian guard. Arms and ammunition must not be surrendered on any pretext; any attempt at disarming must be frustrated, if necessary by force.[6]

As Marx indicates, the early socialists foresaw the replacement of regular armies by the masses organized into proletarian-controlled militia groups. Since the early socialists believed wholeheartedly that the proletariat would be capable of instituting and maintaining their own administration, it was a small step to declaring that the proletariat would also control its own military establishment. In part the rationale for this view was supplied by Engels. In *Anti-Dühring*, he noted the extremely close relationship between the level of military affairs and the level of economic development. It is the level of production and communications, he said, which will determine the armaments, composition and organization. tactics, and strategy of the armed forces. He was quite emphatic that the command element had only minor significance in these matters. He declared:

> It is not the "free creation of the mind" or generals of genius that have had a revolutionary effect here, but the invention of better weapons and the change in the human material, the soldier; at the very most, the part played by generals of genius is limited to adopting methods of fighting to the new weapons and combatants.[7]

The primary factor in military affairs, then, was the economic one. According to Engels, the producer of less perfect arms could not defeat the producer of more perfect arms.[8] He summarized his argument in saying that "the triumph

6 Karl Marx, "Address of the Central Committee to the Communist League," in *ibid.*, p. 116.
8 *Ibid.*, pp. 229–30.
7 Engels, p. 230.

of force is based on the production of arms, and this in turn on production in general — therefore, on 'economic power,' on the 'economic situation,' on the *material* means which force has at its disposal."[9] In his view, if there is to be an improvement in military affairs, it would have to come from the improvement of either the soldier or the economic-armaments base.

Quite dogmatically, however, despite even the evidence cited here, Engels denied the possibility of producing better armaments. He argued that the Franco-German War of 1870 had marked a turning point in military affairs. In this war, arms had reached such a devastating level that no further significant improvements were possible. In the words of Engels:

> The Franco-German War marked a turning point of entirely new implications. In the first place weapons used have reached such a stage of perfection that further progress which would have any revolutionizing influence is no longer possible. Once armies have guns which can hit a battalion at any range at which it can be distinguished, and rifles which are equally effective for hitting individual men, while loading them takes less time than aiming, then all further improvements are of minor importance for field warfare. The era of evolution is therefore, in essentials, closed in this direction.[10]

In short, only the soldier — that is, the proletarian — was capable of further improvement. Herein would be the superiority of military developments controlled by the masses as opposed to those exploited by the bourgeoisie. The early socialists consequently viewed the mass militia, which was to be proletarian based and commanded, as the superior type of military formation for the future.

Early in his political career, V. I. Lenin expressed views on the military which were consistent with those held by most of the early socialists. In a 1905 article in *Proletary,* entitled "The Revolutionary Army and the Revolutionary Government," Lenin declared that a revolutionary army and government "are two institutions equally necessary for the success of the uprising and for the consolidation of its results."[11] The need for a revolutionary army, stated Lenin, derives from the fact that "great historical issues can be resolved only *by force,* and, in modern struggle, the *organization of force* means military organization."[12] This did not imply, however, an approval of the regular standing army.

Like earlier socialists, Lenin uncompromisingly denounced the concept of

[9] *Ibid.,* p. 230. Italics in original.

[10] *Ibid.,* p. 235.

[11] V. I. Lenin, *Collected Works,* VIII (Moscow: Foreign Language Publishing House, 1962), 568.

[12] *Ibid.,* p. 653. Italics in original.

the standing army in his early writings. In a January 1905 article, entitled "The Beginning of the Revolution in Russia," he insisted that "only an armed people can be the real bulwark of popular liberty."[13] A May 1903 pamphlet, entitled *To the Rural Poor: An Explanation for the Peasants of What the Social Democrats Want*, asserted that the standing army is an unnecessary burden upon the masses. Lenin wrote:

> The Social Democrats demand that the standing army be abolished and that a militia be established in its stead, that all the people be armed. A standing army is an army that is divorced from the people and trained to shoot down the people. If the soldier were not locked up for years in barracks and inhumanly drilled there, would he ever agree to shoot down his brothers, the workers and peasants? Would he go against the starving peasants? A standing army is not needed in the least to protect the country from attack by an enemy; a people's militia is sufficient. If every citizen is armed, Russia need fear no enemy. And the people would be relieved of the yoke of the military clique. The upkeep of this clique costs *hundreds of millions of rubles a year*, and all this money is collected from the people; that is why the taxes are so heavy and why it becomes increasingly difficult to live.[14]

In a November 1905 article in *Novaya Zhizn*, entitled "The Armed Forces and the Revolution," Lenin again stressed the two themes that the standing army is a bourgeois instrument for internal oppression and that it is unnecessary for external defense. According to Lenin's article:

> Everywhere, in all countries, the standing army is used not so much against the external enemy as against the internal enemy. Everywhere the standing army has become the weapon of reaction, the servant of capital in its struggle against labour, the executioner of the people's liberty. Let us not, therefore, stop short of mere partial demands in our great liberating revolution. Let us tear the evil up by the roots. Let us do away with the standing army altogether. Let the army merge with the armed people, let the soldiers bring to their people their military knowledge, let the barracks disappear to be replaced by free military schools. No power on earth will dare to encroach upon free Russia, if the bulwark of her liberty is an armed people which has destroyed the military caste, which has made all soldiers citizens and all citizens capable of bearing arms, soldiers.
>
> The experience of Western Europe has shown how utterly reactionary the standing army is. Military science has proven that a people's militia is quite

---

13 *Ibid.*, p. 99.

14 *Ibid.*, VI, 401–2. Italics in original.

practicable, that it can rise to the military tasks presented by a war both of defense and attack.[15]

In an article published in *Ekho* in July 1906, entitled "The Army and the People," Lenin argued that soldiers ought to be permitted to elect their own leaders. Commenting on the demand of an infantry regiment in St. Petersburg to be allowed to elect its own representatives to the State Duma, Lenin said:

> The soldiers do not want to keep out of politics. The soldiers do not agree with the Cadets. The soldiers are advancing a demand that obviously amounts to the abolition of the caste army, of the army that is isolated from the people, and its replacement by an army of free and equal citizens. Now this is exactly the same things as the abolition of the standing army and the arming of the people.[16]

It appears that Lenin's concept of proletarian military needs underwent little, if any, modification from this period until the outbreak of the Bolshevik Revolution in 1917. In a pamphlet published in September 1917, entitled *The Tasks of the Proletariat in Our Revolution: Draft Platform for the Proletarian Party*, Lenin noted that the two most important tasks for the safeguard, consolidation, and development of the proletarian revolution were the destruction of the police apparatus and the formation of a people's militia.[17] During this period, Lenin was quite clear that the people's militia would be different from not only the standing army but also a bourgeois militia.[18]

Twice in mid-1917 alone, Lenin wrote extensive monographs on the militia idea. In the third of his *Letters from Afar*, written shortly before his return to Russia, Lenin declared that the proletarist must now smash the bourgeois state together with its instruments of force, the police and the standing army. Based on the experience of the Paris Commune of 1871 and the Russian Revolution of 1905, he said "the proletariat must organize and arm *all* the poor, exploited sections of the population in order that they *themselves* should take the organs of state power directly into their own hands, in order that they *themselves should constitute* these organs of state power."[19] But, asks Lenin, what is a genuine people's militia? In answer, he notes that it is a militia that would include two

[15] *Ibid.*, X, 56–57.
[16] *Ibid.*, XI, 86–87.
[17] *Ibid.*, XIV, 71.
[18] *Ibid.*, XXII, 101.
[19] *Ibid.*, XXIII, 326. Italics in original.

elements: "one that, first, consists of the *entire* population, of all adult citizens of both sexes; and second, one that combines the functions of the people's army with police functions, with the functions of the chief and fundamental organ of public order and public administration."[20]

In a *Pravda* article written shortly after his return to Russia, entitled "A Proletarian Militia," Lenin again proclaimed the need for establishing people's militias. He maintained that "the people must learn, one and all, how to use arms, they must belong, one and all, to the militia which is to replace the police and standing army," and that "the workers do not want an army standing apart from the people; what they want is that the workers and soldiers should *merge* into a single militia consisting of all the people."[21]

Furthermore, in this article written six months before the Bolshevik Revolution, Lenin went on to describe several items which would cause heated debate after November 1917, especially the election and recall of officers. Lenin stated in the article:

> Public service through a really universal people's militia, composed of men and women, a militia capable partly of replacing the bureaucrats — this, combined with the principle of elective office and displaceability of all public officers, with payment for their work according to proletarian, not "master-class," bourgeois standards, is the ideal of the working class.[22]

Again, on the very eve of the Bolshevik Revolution, Lenin asserted the all-round superiority of the militia. In his article "Can the Bolsheviks Retain State Power?" Lenin observed that the militia created by the Soviets, unlike the old standing army, was "very closely bound up with the people." Consequently, "from the military point of view this force is incomparably more powerful than previous forces; from the revolutionary point of view, it cannot be replaced by anything else."[23]

Based on socialist tradition and Lenin's own views, then, the concept of the superiority of the militia system held a primary position at the time of the Bolshevik Revolution. There does not appear to be even one major socialist thinker who believed it necessary to draw up plans for an organized armed force. As Lenin pointed out at the 8th Party Congress in March 1919, "the organization of a Red Army was an entirely new question which had never been dealt with

20 *Ibid.*, pp. 327–28. Italics in original.
21 *Ibid.*, XXIV, 180. Italics in original.
22 *Ibid.*, p. 181.
23 *Ibid.*, XXVI, 103.

before, even theoretically."[24] Indeed, it was only after much agonizing debate within the Communist Party, lasting almost a full decade after the Bolshevik Revolution, that the utopian idea of a mass people's militia was laid to rest.

This section is not intended to ridicule the almost blind faith of the pre-Revolution socialists in the militia system or to deride the Russian Communists for abandoning it after the Revolution. Rather its purpose is to illustrate and emphasize the evolution in military thought, which took place in light of the actual post-Revolutionary situation. Moreover, it is within the context of the militia-standing army debates that the political administration of the Red Army had its origin and evolution. The next section of this study will examine these early debates and their influence on the political administration of the Red Army.

Early Attempts to Create Military and Political-Military Organs in the Soviet Armed Forces

In an article written during World War I, entitled "The Question of Peace," Lenin asserted that lasting peace among capitalist countries is impossible. Such peace as from time to time may exist is temporary and illusionary. Moreover, he observed that periods of peace are harmful for the socialist movement because they lull the proletarist into forgetting about the deep contradictions between socialism and capitalism.[25]

Despite this attitude on Lenin's part, the first state paper issued by the new Bolshevik Government was the "Decree on Peace" (November 8, 1917), which proposed immediate negotiations among the World War I belligerents toward a "just, democratic peace."[26] A close inspection of the document indicates, however, that the Decree had more than one purpose: first, it was a call for peace; and second, it was a call for revolution aimed at the proletariat of non-Russian countries.[27] Obviously, for Lenin, the second did not contradict the first. Now that the initial breach in the capitalist system had been made, the other advanced states would in theory follow within a short time. Until then it was necessary to protect the one socialist stronghold. Knowing the great popular hostility toward

[24] *Ibid.,* XXIX, 152.

[25] *Ibid.,* X, 57.

[26] *Ibid.,* XXVI, 249.

[27] Cf. Adam B. Ulam, *Expansion and Coexistence: The History of Soviet Foreign Policy, 1917–67* (New York: Praeger, 1968), pp. 52–53.

the war policy of the Kerensky government, Lenin realized that protection of socialism in Russia meant that Russia would have to withdraw from the war at all costs. Similarly, it meant that Russian Communists would have to refrain from militarily intervening in Europe for the purpose of spreading revolution, despite Lenin's belief that the success of the Russian Revolution was absolutely dependent on a successful German revolution.[28] He attacked, therefore, those Leftists who wanted to wage a revolutionary war against imperialism. An article of early January 1918, entitled "Theses on the Question of the Immediate Conclusion of a Separate and Annexationist Peace," declared:

> If the German revolution were to break out and triumph in the coming three or four months, the tactics of an immediate revolutionary war might perhaps not ruin our socialist revolution.
>
> If, however, the German revolution does not occur in the next few months, the course of events, if the war is continued, will inevitably be such that grave defeats will compel Russia to conclude an even more disadvantageous separate peace, a peace, moreover, which would be concluded, not by a socialist government, but by some other (for example, a bloc of the bourgeois Rada and Chernov's followers, or something similar). For the peasant army, which is exhausted to the limit by the war, will after the very first defeats — and very likely within a matter of weeks, and not of months — overthrow the socialist workers' government.[29]

Again in a *Pravda* article of February 21, 1918, Lenin countered the Leftist call for transforming the imperialist war into a revolutionary war. As in the previous statement, Lenin reiterated that the weakness of the Soviet forces was a prime factor inhibiting the launching of a revolutionary war. He noted that Russia had two alternatives: (1) propaganda, agitation, and fraternization or (2) revolutionary war. In regard to the latter he stated:

> It is clear to everyone (except those intoxicated with empty phrases) that to undertake a serious insurrectionary or military clashing *knowing* that we have no forces, *knowing* that we have no army, is a gamble that will not help the German workers but will make their struggle more difficult and make matters easier for their enemy and for our enemy.[30]

An essential factor to be noted here is Lenin's recognition of the weakness

[28] Lenin, XXVII, 98.
[29] *Ibid.*, XXVI, 448.
[30] *Ibid.*, XXVII, 25. Italics in original.

of Communist forces, and the resultant belief that this weakness made the Bolshevik regime extremely vulnerable to internal and external enemies. This weakness was derived from two pre-Revolution tenets. First, the Bolsheviks were the victims of their own pre-Revolution propaganda, which advocated the total destruction of the imperial army. They had advocated insubordination, extremist demands, and even desertion from the front. As will be shown later, this anarchistic tradition was difficult to overcome after the Bolshevik Revolution when the new regime attempted to create a regular army.

A second major factor contributing to the weakness of the Bolshevik forces was the numerical composition of the Party itself. According to one source, the Bolshevik Party of January 1, 1917, had only 23,600 members, and by January 1, 1918, had 115,000 members.[31] The size of the Party had been restricted before the Revolution by Lenin's insistence on a small, elite party. Now its smallness was a detriment. If further military defeats were to be encountered, the overthrow of this authoritarian elite group would not be difficult. Yet to abandon this elitism with too much speed — either by enlarging the Party or by coalition with other major elements — would mean in reality the abandoning of the dictatorship of the proletariat.[32]

In some respects, then, a major cause of Bolshevik military weakness immediately after the Revolution can be traced to the pre-Revolution anarchistic line of the Party itself. An immediate return to a regular army was both theoretically and practically impossible. Still, in order to provide some defense for the new regime, the Bolsheviks instituted two policies. First, the new regime established several military bodies, whose function it was to provide at least a minimum of centralized direction to military affairs. Second, it promoted the erection of the militia system advocated by the early socialists and Lenin.

On November 11, 1917, the first Bolshevik organ for the central direction of military affairs was created by a decree of the 2nd All-Russian Congress of Soviets. This decree, which also established the Council of People's Commissars, created the Committee for Military and Naval Affairs, composed of three veteran Bolsheviks — N. V. Krylenko, P. Ye. Dybenko, and V. A. Antonov-Ovseyenko.[33] On December 6, this committee was replaced by an enlarged People's Commissariat for Military and Naval Affairs (Narkomvoen) The Collegium of the

[31] D. Fedotoff White, *The Growth of the Red Army* (Princeton, N.J.: Princeton University Press, 1944), p. 32.

[32] *Ibid.*

[33] Lieutenant Colonel Yu. I. Korablev and Colonel M. I. Loginov, *KPSS i stroitel'stvo Vooruzhennykh Sil SSSR (1918–iyun' 1941) (The CPSU and Construction of the Armed Forces of the USSR [1918–June 1941])* (Moscow: Voyenizdat, 1959), p. 34.

Narkomvoen was headed by N. I. Podvoyskiy and its membership included V. A. Antonov-Ovseyenko, P. Ye. Dybenko, V. N. Vasil'yevskiy, K. S. Yeremeyev, M. S. Kedrov, N. V. Krylenko, K. A. Mekhanoshin, T. S. Lazimir, B. V. Legran, A. D. Sadovskiy, E. M. Sklyanskiy, and Leon Trotsky.[34] On December 19, the Narkomvoen formed the All-Russian Collegium for the Organization and Administration of the Workers-Peasant Red Army, staffed by N. V. Krylenko, K. A. Mekhanoshin, N. I. Podvoyskiy, E. M. Sklyanskiy, and V. A. Trifonov.[35]

Concurrently with these moves, the Bolshevik regime set out to smash the remnants of the imperial army and to institute a proletarian mass militia. On November 10, 1917, a decree of the People's Commissariat for the Interior signed by A. I. Rykov stated:

> 1. All the Soviets of Workmen's and Soldiers' Deputies shall form a workers' militia.
> 2. The workers' militia shall be fully and exclusively under the orders of the Soviet of Workmen's and Soldiers' Delegates.
> 3. The military and civil authorities are bound to render assistance in arming the workers' militia and to supply it with the technical means even up to providing it with the arms belonging to the war department of the government.[36]

Later in the same month, the government enacted a decree for the gradual demobilization of the old army.[37] In early December, the Military Affairs Commissariat published a draft decree calling for "a free army of armed citizens, an army of workers and peasants with broad self-government of elected soldiers organizations."[38] Shortly this principle was enacted into law and followed in late December by another law abolishing all military ranks and titles. This decree stated:

> All titles and stations in the army, starting with that of corporal and ending

[34] General Major N. M. Kiryayev *et al.*, eds., *KPSS i stroitel'stvo Sovetskykh Vooruzhennykh Sil (The CPSU and the Construction of the Soviet Armed Forces)* (2nd ed.; Moscow: Voyenizdat, 1967), p. 20.

[35] Korablev and Loginov, p. 45.

[36] A. I. Rykov, "Workers' Militia," in James H. Meisel and Edward S. Kozera, eds., *Materials for the Study of the Soviet System* (Ann Arbor, Mich.: George Wahr Publishing Co., 1950), Document 19, p. 24.

[37] Kolkowicz, *The Soviet Army and the Communist Party*, p. 58.

[38] Quoted in John Erickson, "The Origins of the Red Army," in Richard Pipes, ed., *Revolutionary Russia: A Symposium* (Garden City, N.Y.: Doubleday, 1969), p. 294.

with that of general, are abolished. The army of the Russian Republic from now on consists of free and equal-to-one-another citizens, holding the honorable stations of Soldiers of the Revolutionary Army.[39]

Almost from the start, however, there were some Bolshevik leaders who argued that the militia system might temporarily be unsuitable for the needs of the regime. This is not to say that even this segment totally abandoned the militia concept, but rather they maintained that the militia system would have to await more favorable circumstances. Under the pressure of this group, an All-Russian Committee for the organization of the army was appointed on December 20, 1917, to study the possibilities of creating a more centralized military force.[40]

On January 28, 1918, a decree of the Soviet of People's Commissars, signed by Lenin, Krylenko (now Supreme Commander-in-Chief), Dybenko and Podvoyskiy (now People's Commissars of War and Naval Affairs), and others, resolved to organize a new army to be called the Workers-Peasants Red Army (Raboche-Krest'yanskaya Krasnaya Armiya, or RKKA). According to the provisions of the decree, the new army was to consist of only "the more class-conscious and organized elements of the toiling masses."[41] In sum, the RKKA was to be an all-volunteer, professional, class-based army drawn solely from the workers and peasants. In order to be admitted into the RKKA, a soldier candidate had to secure recommendations from an army committee or any of the other Bolshevik-controlled government, party, or labor organizations.[42] It has been estimated that Bolshevik military forces drawn from all sources amounted to between 50,000 and 60,000 men.[43]

Although accepted on January 28, the officially celebrated day for the founding of the RKKH is February 23. On this latter date, a group of Red Guards and volunteers were alleged to have temporarily checked the advance of a German

[39] Cited in Meisel and Kozera, Document 31, p. 37.

[40] Michel Berchin and Eliahu Ben-Horin, *The Red Army* (New York: W. W. Norton, 1942), p. 45.

[41] *KPSS o Vooruzhennykh Silakh Sovetskogo Soyuza. Dokumenty 1917–1968 (The CPSU on the Armed Forces of the Soviet Union. Documents 1917–1968)* (Moscow: Voyenizdat, 1969), p. 19.

[42] *Ibid.*

[43] John Erickson, *The Soviet High Command: A Military-Political History, 1918–1941* (London: Macmillan, 1962), p. 19.

column near Pskov.[44] Thus, it was considered to be a good occasion to commemorate the beginning of the Soviet armed forces.

Under renewed German attack, the Soviet Government created on March 4 the Higher Military Council, led by a former tsarist officer, General M. D. Bronch-Bruyevich, and two political commissars, P. P. Prosh'yan and K. I. Shutko.[45] Later in the month, the Council was enlarged to include N. I. Podvoyskiy, K. A. Mekhanoshin, and E. M. Sklyanskiy, as well as several "military" and "naval" specialists.[46]

On May 8, 1918, the All-Russian Main Staff was created and charged with responsibility for the formation and training of the Red Army, as well as the elaboration of regulations, instructions, and directions.[47] In assuming control of the highest military organs, the All-Russian Main Staff replaced the All-Russian Collegium for the Organization and Administration of the Workers-Peasants Red Army. From the end of March to the beginning of May, the country was divided into thirteen military districts. On July 8, a Field Staff, headed by a Commander-in-Chief, was established to command all the armed forces. In September, the Revolutionary Military Council (Revvoensovet) of the Republic was created under the chairmanship of Trotsky. Its function was to coordinate all military operations, administration, and supply work at the front and throughout the country.[48] In addition, revvoensovets, consisting of a commander (i.e., a military specialist) and two political commissars, were established at the head of fronts and armies.[49]

In effect, these events were the initial steps in propelling the Red Army toward a highly disciplined and centrally controlled standing army. At the time, most proponents argued, however, that they were only temporary expedients to meet the immediate external threat.[50] It was within this context also that the office and functions of the political commissar were first defined in April 1918.

[44] Edgar O'Ballance, *The Red Army: A Short History* (New York: Praeger, 1964), p. 23.

[45] Colonel Ya. Zimin, "V. I. Lenin and the Beginning of the Construction of the Higher Military Organs of the Soviet State," *Voyenno-Istoricheskiy Zhurnal*, No. 11 (November 1969), p. 4. Between March 18 and April 10, Prosh'yan, a member of the Left Social Revolutionaries, withdrew from the Council.

[46] *Ibid.*, p. 5: and Colonel (Reserves) A. Popov, "From the History of the Creation of the Revvoensovet of the Republic," *Voyenno-Istoricheskiy Zhurnal*, No. 2 (February 1967), p. 96.

[47] Korablev and Loginov, p. 71.

[48] Fedotoff White, *Growth of the Red Army*, p. 38.

[49] Korablev and Loginov, p. 108.

[50] Erickson, *Soviet High Command*, p. 27.

Actually, the office of political commissar was not the invention of the Bolsheviks. As early as June 1917, commissars had been appointed in the army in the field by the Provisional Government under Alexander Kerensky[51] in an attempt to lessen desertions from the war front. The first use of military commissars as representatives of the Communist Party in the armed forces occurred in October 1917, when the Military-Revolutionary Committee dispatched them into the Petrograd garrison in order to isolate the reactionary officers and to mobilize soldiers in the overthrow of the Provisional Government.[52] After the Revolution, the Bolsheviks also employed political commissars but their number was few and their functions vague. Generally, their responsibilities were of several types: to agitate and spread propaganda among enemy troops,[53] to win support for the Bolshevik regime among the numerous groups of anarchistic Russian partisans,[54] to ensure discipline within newly formed army units, and to oversee the activities of military specialists enlisted from the old army.[55] Furthermore, it was not an early requirement that political commissars had to be Bolsheviks. The only standard was that the commissar had to be "an irreproachable revolutionary."[56]

On April 6, 1918, the Bolshevik regime attempted to structure and define the office of political commissar. In accordance with an order of the People's

[51] L. Gavrilov, "The First Commissars of Soviet Authority in the Army in the Field," *Voyenno-Istoricheskiy Zhurnal*, No. 11 (November 1974), p. 69, n. 5.

[52] Korablev and Loginov, p. 76.

[53] Agitation among the enemy was initially assigned to the All-Russian Bureau of Military Commissars and later to the Political Section of the Revvoensovet. In 1919, the Political Administration of the Republic set up a special group for the writing and dissemination of agitation literature in foreign languages. In addition, political sections of fronts and armies established departments to agitate among the specific nationalities within the enemy camp. These agitation sections generally worked in close connection with the Central Bureau of Communist Organizations of Occupied Areas, created by the CC RKP(b) in September 1918; the Section of Soviet Propaganda of the VTsIK, formed on December 5, 1918, in place of the Section of International Revolutionary Propaganda; the Polish Bureau of the CC RKP(b); the Central Federation of Foreign Groups of the RKP(b); local party organs; and various bureaus on the war fronts. (Colonel V. Kolychev, "Political Work on the Demoralization of the Troops of the Enemy in the Years of the Civil War," *Voyenno-Istoricheskiy Zhurnal*, No. 7 [July 1971], p. 13.)

[54] Nikolaus Basseches, *The Unknown Army: The Nature and History of the Russian Military Forces*, trans. Marion Saerchinger (New York: Viking Press, 1943), p. 108.

[55] S. Klyatskin, "The Institute of Military Commissars," *Voyenno-Istoricheskiy Zhurnal*, No. 4 (April 1968), pp. 123–24.

[56] Littleton B. Atkinson, *Dual Command in the Red Army, 1918–1942* (Montgomery, Ala.: Air University, 1950), p. 12.

Commissar for War, political commissars, appointed from among "irreproachable revolutionaries" as earlier, were henceforth to be considered the immediate political arm of the Bolshevik Government in the Red Army.[57] Among their duties, the political commissars were to ensure the loyalty of the soldiers, to inhibit any development of counterrevolutionary forces in the armed forces, to supervise the political activities of commanders, to countersign all of the commander's orders, and to provide for the prompt execution of all orders.[58] Two days later, on April 8, the All-Russian Bureau of Military Commissars, the first centrally controlled organization of political commissars in the Red Army, was created under the chairmanship of K. K. Yurenev.[59] The new importance ascribed to the political commissars was recognized in the resolution of the 5th Congress of Soviets (July 10, 1918), which, in addition to calling for an even further strengthening of the office, stated:

> The military commissars are the guardians of the close and inviolable inner bond between the Red Army and the workers' and peasants' regime as a whole. Only irreproachable revolutionaries, staunch champions of the proletariat and the village poor, should be appointed to the posts of military commissars, to whom is handed over the fate of the Army.[60]

[57] A. Geronimus, "Fundamental Points of the Development of the Party-Political Apparatus of the Red Army in 1918–1920," in A. S. Bubnov, S. S. Kamenev, and R. P. Eydeman, *Grazhdanskaya voyna, 1918–1921 (The Civil War, 1918–1921),* II (Moscow: Military Herald Publishing House, 1928), 113.

[58] Fedotoff White, *Growth of the Red Army,* pp. 74–75; and Berchin and Ben-Horin, p. 47.

[59] Kiryayev p. 100. At this time, several other military-political organs arose or already existed which would soon be incorporated into the All-Russian Bureau of Military Commissars: the Agitation — Enlightenment Compartment of the Organization — Agitation Section of the All-Russian Collegium for the Organization of the Red Army (incorporated into the All-Russian Bureau at the end of April 1918), the Military-Political Section of the Operations Section of the People's Commissariat for Military Affairs (in October 1917), the Political Section of the Higher Military Inspectorate (in November 1917), and the All-Russian Agitation Bureau of the Red Army (in November 1917). Briefly during October–November 1918, the functions of the All-Russian Bureau were divided so that the All-Russian Bureau took responsibility for the leadership of political activity in the army in the rear and the Political Section of the Revvoensovet of the Republic was responsible for the leadership of political activity in the army in the field. By the end of November, the arrangement had proved so unsuitable that the Political Section of the Revvoensovet was subsumed by the All-Russian Bureau. See Yu. P. Petrov, *Stroitel'stvo politorganov, partiynykhi komsomal'skikh organizatsiy armii i flota (1918–1968) (The Construction of Political Organs and Party and Komsomol Organizations in the Army and Navy [1918–1968])* (Moscow: Voyenizdat, 1968), p. 50.

[60] Quoted in Zbigniew Brzezinski, ed., *Political Controls in the Soviet Army* (New York: Research Program on the USSR, 1954), p. 5.

In many instances, the political commissar came to share authority with the commander. This did not mean, however, that the commisar had an easy job, for he also shared the dangers of the position. On September 30, 1918, Trotsky ordered the arrest of the families of officers who betrayed the Red Army, as a measure to ensure the officers' loyalty.[61] Just as the family was to be held responsible for the actions of the officer, the commissar was to be held responsible for the actions of the soldiers. During the battle at Svyazhsk in 1918 against the Czech Legion, a particular regiment withdrew without authorization. Trotsky had both the commissar and the commander court-martialed and shot. Commenting on the event, Trotsky noted that the Red Army soldiers

> . . . are neither cowards nor scoundrels. They want to fight for the freedom of the working class. If they retreat or fight poorly, commanders and commissars are guilty. I issue this warning: if any detachment retreats without orders, the first to be shot will be the commissar, the next the commander.[62]

It would appear from the beginning that not even the proponents of the political commissar system envisioned it as more than a temporary measure. It was argued that the commissar's main duty was to watch over the commanders, most of whom in the early years were ex-tsarist officers.[63] Later as more proletarian officers took over command, there would be less need for commissars. At the same time it was believed that the principle of *yedinonachaliye*, unified or one-man command — a principle still debated and never fully achieved — would soon replace the dual control system. As Trotsky noted at the end of 1918:

> The more the commissar begins to penetrate into combatant work, and the commander to assimilate the political work, the nearer we are getting to unified command, where the person placed at the head of a unit will be both commander and commissar.[64]

Similarly, in a speech on Red Officers' Day, November 24, 1918, Lenin asserted

[61] Merle Fainsod, *How Russia Is Ruled* (Cambridge, Mass.: Harvard University Press, 1963), p. 468.

[62] Quoted in Isaac Deutscher, *The Prophet Armed: Trotsky, 1879–1921* (New York: Vintage Books, 1954), pp. 420–21.

[63] For a discussion of the role of ex-tsarist officers, especially those who went on to prominent careers in the Red Army, see S. Fedyukin, "On the Use of Military Specialists in the Red Army," *Voyenno-Istoricheskiy Zhurnal*, No. 6 (June 1962), pp. 32–44.

[64] Quoted in Leonard Schapiro, *The Origin of the Communist Autocracy* (Cambridge, Mass.: Harvard University Press, 1956), p. 241.

that most of the tsarist officers had been "the spoiled and depraved darling sons of capitalists." Conversely, since "only Red officers will have any respect among the soldiers and be able to strengthen socialism in our army," Lenin contended that "we must draw our officers solely from among the people."[65]

In practice, the Bolsheviks found it necessary to use more and more former imperial officers, first under the pressure of a German attack and then under the pressures of civil war and Allied intervention. It followed that the employment of political commissars likewise increased. On December 15, 1918, by Order No. 337 of the Revvoensovet, political organs were formed in all fronts, armies, and divisions.[66] During the same month, Soviet calculations show, 6,389 military commissars were at work among the troops.[67] Moreover, of the 501 commissars sent out from June to December 10, 1918, only 60 percent were Communists. In this particular group, political affiliations were as follows:[68]

Number	
300	Communists
93	Communist "sympathizers"
35	Left Social Revolutionaries
3	"Internationalists"
1	Anarchist
1	SR-Maximalist
68	No party affiliation

The number of non-Bolshevik military commissars assigned thereafter rapidly declined. From 1918 to May 1919, only 11.2 percent of the newly appointed commissars were non-party men or representatives of other parties.[69]

Transformation to Permanent, Centralized Military and Political-Military Organs

When the 8th Congress of the Russian Communist Party convened in March

[65] Lenin, XXVIII, 195.

[66] Kolkowicz, *The Soviet Army and the Communist Party*, p. 132.

[67] General of the Army A. A. Yepishev, *Partiyno-politicheskaya rabota v Vooruzhennykh Silakh SSSR, 1918–1973 gg: Istoricheskiy ocherk (Party-Political Work in the Armed Forces of the USSR, 1918–1973: Historical Essay)* (Moscow: Voyenizdat, 1974), p. 38.

[68] *Ibid.*, p. 85.

[69] *Ibid.*

1919, the character of the Red Army and the office of the political commissar were two topics of heated discussion. On the character of the Red Army, a compromise was reached which maintained a present need for a regular army but pointed to the militia as a future objective. The party program, adopted at the 8th Congress, declared:

> In this epoch of rotting imperialism and spreading civil war, it is not possible either to preserve the old army or to construct a new army on a so-called classless or national basis. The Red Army, as an instrument of the proletarian dictatorship, must necessarily have an overt class character, i.e., it should be formed exclusively from the proletarians and the closely related semi-proletarian stratum of the peasants. Only in connection with the annihilation of classes will such a class army be transformed into a national socialist army.[70]

The program also proclaimed the objective of raising the most energetic and capable Communist soldiers to the position of commanders, but it recognized that there was an immediate need to attract military specialists from the tsarist army.[71] These specialists were to be employed only under the condition that political guidance of the army and control over the military officials would be retained by the working class, that is, by the Bolsheviks.[72] In one further significant step, the program abolished the principle of the election of officers, which supposedly had no meaning for a socialist army.[73]

The role of the political commissar was also debated at the 8th Party Congress. The question was whether to lessen or strengthen the commissars' authority. At one extreme, it was proposed that the commissar be given authority over actual military operations in addition to his purely administrative work.[74] At

[70] *KPSS o Vooruzhennykh Silakh Sovetskogo Soyuza*, p. 37.

[71] Considerable opposition to the use of military specialists was put forth by the so-called "military opposition," including A. S. Aleksandrov, A. S. Bubnov, K. Ye. Voroshilov, F. I. Goloshchekin, R. S. Zemlyachka, S. K. Minin, A. F. Myasnikov, M. L. Rukhimovich, V. G. Sorin, N. G. Tolmachev, Ye. M. Yaroslavskiy, V. M. Smirnov, G. I. Safarov, and G. L. Pyatakov — the latter three being particularly vocal. See Colonel Yu. Korablev, "V. I. Lenin and the Questions of the Construction of a Regular Army at the 8th Party Congress," *Voyenno-Istoricheskiy Zhurnal* No. 2 (February 1969), pp. 4–5, esp. n. 6; General Major N. Kiryayev, "Party Congress of the Fiery Years," *Kommunist Vooruzhennykh Sil*, No. 5 (March 1969), pp. 11–13; and A. Danilevskiy, "The Struggle of V. I. Lenin with the 'Military Opposition' at the 8th Congress of the RKP(b)," *Voyenno-Istoricheskiy Zhurnal*, No. 4 (April 1961), pp. 3–11 *passim*.

[72] *KPSS o Vooruzhennykh Silakh Sovetskogo Soyuza*, p. 38.

[73] *Ibid.*

[74] Atkinson, p. 21.

the other extreme, it was argued that the office of commissar should be abolished or, at least, severely restricted.

Generally speaking, majority opinion appears to have rested with the need for a stronger political commissar. In the series of resolutions adopted by the 8th Party Congress, for example, it was declared:

> The commissars in the army are not only the direct and first-hand representative of the Soviet government, but also first and foremost the bearers of the spirit of our party, its discipline, its steadfastness and courage in the struggle for the implementation of its proposed goal. The party may with full satisfaction glance back on the heroic work of its commissars, who hand in hand with the best elements of the command structure in a brief space of time created a war fighting army.[75]

Subsequently, the resolutions went on to elaborate three significant changes which would affect the political organs in the armed forces. First, the commissars were instructed to compile periodically a file of attestations of command personnel. As time passed, these attestations would become extremely important for an officer's promotion and, in time of purges, for his very life.

Second, the 8th Party Congress reaffirmed the subordination of party cells in the army to the political commissars. Between the Bolshevik Revolution and the end of 1918, numerous party cells, often not under the central guidance of the Party, established themselves. Lacking any direction, these party cells in the armed forces defined their own functions and powers.[76] Because they were largely dependent on local initiative and circumstances, some cells supported the work of command and commissar personnel; some were equal members of a triad, instituting triple control in place of the more common dual control of the officer and commissar; and some even sought to dominate and supervise the work of the commander and commissar.[77]

In January 1919, the Party issued its "Instruction on Party Cells," which attempted for the first time to define the role of the party cells in the armed forces. As in the centralization of the command and commissar structures, the purpose of the Instruction was to inhibit tendencies toward decentralization. The election of independent party cells in the armed forces was banned, and those already in existence were either absorbed by political sections or made into

---

[75] *KPSS o Vooruzhennykh Silakh Sovetskogo Soyuza*, p. 43.

[76] Fedotoff White, *Growth of the Red Army*, p. 93.

[77] General Major V. Soshnev, "From the History of the Construction of the Party Organizations in the Soviet Armed Forces," *Voyenno-Istoricheskiy Zhurnal*, No. 6 (June 1973), p. 4.

political sections themselves.[78] In the future, party cells were to be concerned mostly with maintaining the morale of the soldiers. In reaffirming this principle, the resolutions of the 8th Party Congress stated that "membership in the communist cell not only gives the soldier no special rights, but only imposes on him the duty to be a better selfless and courageous soldier."[79]

In a third action, the 8th Party Congress approved a measure for abolishing the All-Russian Bureau of Military Commissars, which would be replaced by a political section under the Revvoensovet. As a sign of the increased prestige and significance of the political commissars, the Congress resolved that henceforth the Political Section of the Revvoensovet would be headed by a Central Committee member who would simultaneously retain membership in the Revvoensovet.[80] Dual leadership of the Political Section of the Revvoensovet was entrusted to I. T. Smilga and A. G. Beloborodov.[81]

On April 18, 1919, the All-Russian Bureau of Military Commissars was officially replaced by the Political Section of the Revvoensovet. A month later, on May 26, this organization was renamed the Political Administration of the Republic (PUR). As a rule, the PUR consisted of five basic sections: agitation-information, cultural-enlightenment, literature-publishing, inspector, and administrative-financial. In June 1919, the military section of the Publishing House of the VTsIK came under the PUR. Then, in the beginning of 1920, special sections for the East and Poland were established under the PUR.[82]

It is worthy of note that the Political Administration, while it was headed by a member of the Party Central Committee, was not directly subordinate to that body, and would not be until 1925. As already stated, the political commissars began as agents of the government and were originally drawn from diverse affiliations. As a result of the demands of Trotsky, an advocate of a professional army at this time, the political organs of the army remained free from civilian party control throughout the Civil War period.

On October 14, 1919, the Revvoensovet of the Republic created the post of *politruk* in every company, battery, naval squadron, and separate command to

[78] For an extensive Soviet discussion of the instruction, see *Ibid.*, pp. 4–5. See also Fedotoff White, *Growth of the Red Army*, p. 94.

[79] *KPSS o Vooruzhennykh Silakh Sovetskogo Soyuza*, p. 44.

[80] *Ibid.*, p. 48.

[81] S. V. Lepitskiy, *Voyennaya deyatel'nost TsK RKP(b), 1917–1920 (Military Activity of the CC RKP(b), 1917–1920)* (Moscow: Voyenizdat, 1973), p. 54, n. 2; and S. N. Krasil'nikov, "Armed Forces," in Robert Maxwell, ed., *Information USSR* (Oxford: Pergamon Press, 962), p. 427.

[82] Petrov, *Stroitel'stvo politorganov*, p. 81.

assist the commissar of the regiment. Within their sub-units, the *politruki* were responsible for participating in the comrade courts, the cultural-enlightenment commission, and the control-management commission, for organizing group readings of newspapers and proclamations, and for managing the unit's library.[83]

The first head of the PUR was Ivan Smilga, a staunch advocate of military professionalism.[84] Ironically, it was Smilga who spoke out as one of the strongest opponents of the political commissar system. In direct contradiction to the trend of the 8th Party Congress, Smilga took the platform at the 1st All-Russian Assembly of Political Workers in December 1919 to champion the abolition of dual command and "the reorganization of the Red Army on the principle of one-man command."[85] In units commanded by officers of already proven loyalty, the commander would assume responsibility for political work. In other units, the political commissar's authority would cover only the political department, military police, and military tribunals. In both instances, the commander alone would have the responsibility for issuing all operational orders.[86]

With the end of the Civil War in sight, Trotsky began in December 1919 to propose the gradual transformation of the socialist army into a militia, that is, a territorial force. Trotsky had been greatly influenced by Jean Jaurès's *L'Armée Nouvelle*, in which the prominent French socialist advocated socialist armies of local militias that could be organized around the production unit. In this way, the soldier could continue to work on the farm or in the factory, but would at the same time receive his military training.[87] A more extremist position was taken by Podvoyskiy, who argued in favor of the immediate demobilition of the regular army and a complete transition to a militia system.[88]

At the 9th Party Congress in April 1920, Trotsky again proposed the gradual transformation to a militia built around the economic unit. Trotsky recognized that there still existed a need for some organized units, but he argued that the beginning of the change to a militia could be carried out. Such a transformation

---

[83] Yepishev, ed., *Partiyno-politicheskaya rabota*, p. 29; and Petrov, *Stroitel'stvo politorganov*, pp. 86–87.

[84] According to one Soviet source, Smilga spent most of his time in the armies in the field and, consequently, the duties of the chief of the PUR were generally carried out by A. G. Beloborodov, L. P. Serebryakov, and Kh. G. Rakovskiy. (See Petrov, *Stroitel'stvo politorganov*, p. 81, n. 1.)

[85] Quoted in Edward Hallett Carr, *Socialism in One Country, 1924–1926*, II (New York; Macmillan, 1960), 379.

[86] Atkinson, p. 21; Erickson, *Soviet High Command*, pp. 81–82; and Fedotoff White, *Growth of the Red Army*, pp. 84–85.

[87] Carr, p. 380.

[88] *Ibid.*, p. 381.

would aid the faltering Communist economy in the era of War Communism. At the same time, it would not hinder the efficiency of the soldiers, because for Trotsky the socialist system as a whole (not the military barracks) would create the conditions needed to inspire the socialist soldier. As Trotsky retorted to one of his critics:

> If Professor Svechin thinks that the Communist Party has taken power in order to replace the three-colored (Tsarist) barracks by a red one, he is gravely mistaken . . . The objection that under a militia system the command would not enjoy proper authority strikes one with its political blindness. Has perhaps the authority of the present leadership of the Red Army been established in the barracks? . . . That authority is based not on the salutary hypnosis of the barracks but the appeal of the Soviet regime and the Communist Party.[89]

Although the 9th Party Congress substantially accepted Trotsky's proposal for an economic-based militia,[90] subsequent events prevented the transformation from being initiated. The Tambov peasant insurrection, the Kronstadt rebellion, and numerous peasant uprisings in the Ukraine were major factors inhibiting the creation of the militia.[91] From a military standpoint, one further inhibiting factor was the severe Russian defeat before Warsaw in August 1920, which was widely attributed to the lack of training among peasant army units.[92] The time was ripe for the advocates of a professional army.

Again, the chief spokesman for the professional army was the head of the PUR, Ivan Smilga. On at least two occasions in December 1920, Smilga went before Bolshevik assemblies to protest against the transformation to a militia system. In both instances, Smilga argued that the new Russian Republic lacked

---

[89] Deutscher, *Prophet Armed*, p. 479. Ellipses and parentheses by Deutscher.

[90] See the "Resolution on the Transition to a Militia System," adopted at the 9th Party Congress, in *KPSS o Vooruzhennykh Silakh Sovetskogo Soyuza*, pp. 127–29.

[91] Fedotoff White, *Growth of the Red Army*, p. 191.

[92] Carr, p. 382. In many respects, the importance of the Soviet defeat at Warsaw goes far beyond this one issue. It was significant for not only international communism, but also party-military relations. The Soviet Army at Warsaw was under the command of General Tukhachevskiy. According to one commonly held opinion, Tukhachevskiy "would undoubtedly have taken the city and the consequences for Europe and international communism might have been tremendous if Stalin, then Budennyy's commissar on the southern front, had not persisted in pursuing his own ambitions and marched on Lemberg despite the orders of the Supreme General Staff." In his report on the matter, Tukhachevskiy blamed Stalin for the Soviet defeat. It is claimed that Stalin never forgave Tukhachevskiy for this humiliation. See Victor Alexandrov, *The Tukachevskiy Affair*, trans. John Hewish (Englewood Cliffs, N.J.: Prentice-Hall, 1963), p. 45, n. 1.

a sufficient number of trained workers to ensure the workers' control of the militia and a communication system capable of providing a swift mobilization of widely-spread-out militia units. At the 8th All-Russian Congress of Soviets, for example, he maintained:

> The militia system, the essential mark of which is its territorial basis, encounters an insuperable obstacle to its introduction in Russia in the form of our political regime. Considering the small number of the proletariat in Russia, we cannot guarantee proletarian leadership in such units. . . . To return to this form of organization would be a crude and totally unjustfiable mistake.[93]

Smilga also contended that Russia lacked sufficient economic development to meet the army's needs during a defensive war, the type of war which a militia would be forced to fight.[94]

The 2nd All-Russian Conference of Political Workers, also held in December 1920, likewise reflected Smilga's position on a number of points. First, the Conference suggested the enactment of legislation to reduce the authority of the political commissar.[95] Second, it adopted a resolution opposing the militia concept and stating that "the most expedient form of army for the RSFSR is at present moment the standing army, not especially large in numbers, but well trained in military respects and politically prepared, made up of young men."[96]

Again, at a meeting of the Moscow party organization on January 18, 1921, Smilga presented his arguments and received wide support.[97]

Based on this support, Smilga prepared to take his case next to the 10th Party Congress to be held in March 1921. However, a party plenum convened at the end of January and, after discussing the resolution of the political workers' conference, laid down a series of measures for strengthening political controls in the armed forces.[98] In this light, the Party found it expedient to remove Smilga from his PUR position and replace him with S. I. Gusev.[99]

---

[93] Quoted in Carr, p. 382. Ellipses by Carr.

[94] Deutscher, *Prophet Armed*, p. 480.

[95] Petrov, *Stroitel'stvo politorganov*, p. 119, n. 2.

[96] Quoted in Erickson, *Soviet High Command*, p. 118.

[97] I. B. Berklin, *Voyennaya reforma v SSSR (1924–1925) (Military Reform in the USSR [1924–1925])* (Moscow: Voyenizdat, 1958), p. 33.

[98] Petrov, *Stroitel'stvo politorganov*, p. 119, n. 2.

[99] *Ibid.*

The Impact of the Early Stalinist Years on Political-Military Affairs

Gusev's revolutionary activity began in 1896, when he joined the Union of Struggle for the Emancipation of the Working Class. After the 2nd Party Congress, he became one of the organizers and members of the Bolshevik Committee. At the end of 1904, he became a secretary of the Petersburg Committee of the RSDRP and a secretary of the Bureau of the Bolshevik Committee. Subsequently, he worked as a secretary of the Odessa and then the Moscow Bolshevik Committee. He was a delegate to the 4th Party Congress in Stockholm. In 1917, Gusev, then a secretary of the Petrograd Military-Revolutionary Committee, took an active part in the Revolution. After August 1918, he successively served as member of the Revvoensovet of the 5th and 2nd armies, the Eastern Front, the Republic, the Southeastern and the Southern fronts. In 1921, Gusev was elected a candidate member of the Party Central Committee. In 1926, he became the head of the Ispart of the CC VKP(b), and in 1928 and 1929, the head of the press section of the Party CC. From 1923 to 1933, he was a member of the Presidium of the Comintern.[100]

The choice of Gusev was a controversial move, because Gusev, in league with M. V. Frunze, was at the time seeking to popularize what they described as a new proletarian concept of the science of warfare. In a series of twenty-one theses, endorsed first in January 1921 by the Central Committee of the Ukrainian Communist Party, they attempted to define a "single military doctrine" which aimed at the transformation of the armed forces into "a single organism, welded together from top to bottom not only by a common political ideology, but also by unity of views on the character of the military problems facing the republic, on the method of solving these problems, as well as on the system of combat and training."[101] Some of the major propositions of the theses were:

- In expectation of aid from proletariats of other countries, doctrine should emphasize the offensive.
- Maneuverability necessitates small units and a minimum of centralization.
- Preparations for guerrilla warfare should be made.

---

[100] S. I. Gusev, *Grazhdanskaya voyna i Krasnaya Armiya (The Civil War and the Red Army)*, ed. Colonel Ye. A. Fedoseyev (Moscow: Voyenizdat, 1958), pp. 216–21; and General Major (Reserves) M. Yeremin, "S. I. Gusev," *Voyenno-Istoricheskiy Zhurnal*, No. 1 (January 1964), pp. 123–25.

[101] Quoted in Carr, p. 384.

- The mobility of cavalry (and later, mechanical forces) gave it prime importance.
- The main danger was external, and counterrevolution was unlikely.
- In structure the armed forces should maintain both a standing army of cadres and a territorial militia of reserves.
- It was mandatory to retain the Civil War pattern at political controls the army.[102]

The major opponent of the "single military doctrine" was Leon Trotsky, then Commissar for War. According to Fedotoff White, Trotsky's views were based upon an assessment of declining fervor in Europe for world revolution and evaporating cooperation between the workers and peasants in Russia. From this, Trotsky concluded that only a defensive doctrine — that is, waging war for the protection of Russian territory — could sufficiently unite the workers and peasants again. Trotsky also ridiculed the view of Gusev and Frunze on the possibility of developing a purely "proletarian" military doctrine. He argued that military science was objective, and the proletariat should study and learn from traditional doctrine.[103]

The latter point was extremely significant for the political administration, as its implications went far beyond a merely theoretical discussion. Within it was a struggle for position and influence. To admit the importance of traditional doctrine and strategy implied a greater importance for the professional strategist — that is, the former tsarist officer. On the other hand, to reject the importance of traditional doctrine and strategy meant that the professional was unnecessary and that the young revolutionary, steeped in Marxism, should be granted the influence and position of the army commander.[104]

When the 10th Party Congress convened in March 1921, the issues of military doctrine and political control in the army were consequently topics of considerable debate. To the positions of Trotsky and the Gusev-Frunze group were added several more extreme proposals. Podvoyskiy, for example, suggested that a militia order be immediately created and that local civilian party organizations be given authority over military political work.[105] Rejecting institutionalized

---

[102] Kenneth R. Whiting, "The Past and Present of Soviet Military Doctrine," *Air University Quarterly Review*, XI, No. 1 (Spring 1959), 41; Michael Gardner, *A History of the Soviet Army* (London: Pall Mall Press, 1966), p. 59; and Erickson, *Soviet High Command*, p. 338.

[103] Fedotoff White, *Growth of the Red Army*, p. 175.

[104] *Ibid.*, pp. 179–80.

[105] Captain 1st Rank Z. Grebel'skiy, "10th Congress of the Party on the Further Construction of the Red Army," *Voyenno-Istoricheskiy Zhurnal*, No. 3 (March 1971), p. 6.

and centralized leadership as unappropriate for peacetime conditions, several delegates (especially delegations from the army party organization of the Ukraine and the Southwest Front) advocated the return to control by party cells in the armed forces and the election of commissars.[106] Even Smilga, the former head of the political administration, arose at the Congress to chastise the militia advocates. In some instances, the debate became so heated that the situation was saved only by the personal intervention of Lenin. Indeed, in order to prevent a severe split, Lenin was forced to ask Gusev and Frunze to withdraw their theses from the agenda.[107]

Faced with internal dissension and other external pressures,[108] the 10th Party Congress proscribed the more extremist demands of the delegates, such as the election of commissars. The Congress limited itself to urging an increase in the number of commissars transferred to command positions and the replacement of non-Communist officers with Communists as soon as possible.[109] One important move taken at the Congress was a decision to create the post of assistant chief for the fleet in the PUR with a small apparatus.[110]

After the 10th Party Congress, Gusev again sought to disseminate his theses on the "single military doctrine." Moreover, he attempted to formulate from these theses a program for political work in the armed forces, one of the first such programs to be drawn up for the political sections. In a 1921 issue of *Politrabotnik,* Gusev described his program to be: "(1) education in the spirit of internationalism; (2) education in the spirit of overcoming village cohesion and petty-bourgeois narrow-mindedness; (3) struggle with the restorationist tendencies of the peasant; (4) anti-religious propaganda."[111] He also wrote

---

[106] Petrov, *Stroitel'stvo politorganov*, p. 120.

[107] Carr, p. 387.

[108] On the very eve of the 10th Congress, Communist dictatorial rule was severely threatened by the Kronstadt rebellion, which began on March 2, 1921. Once staunch supporters of the regime, the Kronstadt sailors demanded greater freedoms and rights from the Communists, including: (1) immediate re-elections in all soviets to be conducted by a truly free and secret ballot, (2) freedom of speech, press, and assembly for workers, peasants, and opposing political parties, (3) the release of political prisoners, (4) the abolition of a privileged position for Communist Party members, (5) private land ownership for peasants, and (6) the end to discrimination in food rationing. Basil Dmytryshyn, *USSR: A Concise History* (2nd ed., New York: Charles Scribner's Sons, 1971), pp. 116–17.

[109] Atkinson, p. 22; and *KPSS o Vooruzhennykh Silakh Sovetskogo Soyuza*, p. 151.

[110] Petrov, *Stroitel'stvo politorganov*, pp. 125–26. As most of the sections of the PUR soon created special subsections to deal with fleet activities, it was shortly thereafter decided to create a Naval Section in the PUR, headed by an assistant chief of the PUR for the fleet.

[111] Quoted in Erickson, *Soviet High Command*, p. 130.

that the basic mission of political education work was "to turn a large portion of the peasants into international communists and the rest — or, at least, the younger generation — into sympathetic supporters of the idea of a revolutionary war of aggression."[112]

In late 1921, Gusev presided over a general review of the entire staff of political workers in the armed forces. As a result of this evaluation, a political worker was either (1) promoted to a higher post, (2) transferred to command work, (3) directed into study, or (4) demobilized.[113] Consequently, political workers in the armed forces, who numbered 27,429 on January 1, 1922, dipped to 19,000 in mid-1922 and then more than doubled to 39,599 by October 1, 1922.[114]

At the 11th Party Congress, convened in March 1922, Trotsky again debated the merits of the Gusev-Frunze plan for a "proletarian" military doctrine.[115] In his statement, which appears almost humorous in light of the later Stalinist years, Trotsky ridiculed the idea of applying Marxism to warfare. He said:

> How can one develop war practice on the basis of Marxian method? This would be similar to the evolving on Marxian lines of a theory of architecture or a veterinary textbook.[116]

Still Trotsky did agree with Gusev on the point that the office of political commissar could not, at least at this time, be abolished.[117] Generally speaking, the 11th Congress marked a slight shift toward the positions of Trotsky.

In the autumn of 1922, Gusev was removed as PUR head and replaced by V. A. Antonov-Ovseyenko. A graduate of the St. Petersbury Military School and tsarist officer, Antonov-Ovseyenko had joined the Menshevik Party in 1902 and had once been sentenced to death for organizing an anti-tsarist revolt in Sevastopol. But the sentence was reduced to hard labor and he was able to escape abroad. In 1916, Antonov-Oveyenko broke with the Mensheviks and

---

[112] Quoted in Erich Wollenberg, *The Red Army: A Study of the Growth of Soviet Imperialism* (London: Secker and Warburg, 1940), p. 184.

[113] Petrov, *Stroitel'stvo politorganov*, p. 132. A similar review of command staff of divisions and higher took place beginning with the creation of the Higher Attestation Commission (VAK) in May 1921. Gusev also served as a prominent member of VAK. (See Korablev and Loginov, p. 195.)

[114] Berklin, p. 381; and Petrov, *Stroitel'stvo politorganov*, p. 132.

[115] Captain 1st Rank Z. Grebel'skiy, "11th Party Congress and the Further Strengthening of the Red Army," *Voyenno-Istoricheskiy Zhurnal*, No. 3 (March 1972), p. 7.

[116] Quoted in D. Fedotoff White, "Soviet Philosophy of War," *Political Science Quarterly*, LI, No. 3 (September 1936), 339.

[117] Carr, p. 406.

joined the Bolsheviks. In July 1917, he was imprisoned with Trotsky in the Kresty Prison. During the Bolshevik Revolution, he led the Red Guards in the attack on the Winter Palace. Among his positions after the Revolution were: member of the Committee for Military and Naval Affairs, member of the Ukrainian Revvoensovet, commander of the Petrograd Military District, commander of the Ukrainian Front, and member of the NKVD administration.[118]

Clearly, the PUR now passed under the leadership of a man sympathetic to Trotsky and his policies.[119] Perhaps even more than Gusev, Antonov-Ovseyenko used his office to promote his particular political line. He also used his position to promote the personal power and influence of Trotsky in the latter's struggles against Gusev, Frunze, Stalin, and others. For example, on December 24, 1923, Antonov-Ovseyenko issued Circular No. 200, which urged all levels within the armed forces to take up a discussion of *all* problems related to party-political work in the military.[120] The effect of the circular was to encourage opposition to the new party ruling triumvirate of Stalin, Zinovyev, and Kamenev, which was then coming to power. Now the triumvirate was faced with the possibility that Trotsky, through Antonov-Ovseyenko, might win military support and challenge their positions. Conversely, one way to strike at Trotsky's influence would be to remove Antonov-Ovseyenko.

At a party conference in January 1924, Antonov-Ovseyenko was charged by Stalin with promoting factionalism in the armed forces and removed from his post in the PUR.[121] He was replaced by Andrey Sergeyevich Bubnov, an old Bolshevik and former Left Communist. Bubnov began his revolutionary activity at the age of seventeen. A delegate to the 5th Party Congress in 1907, he was appointed a candidate member of the Party CC in 1912. In 1912–13, he was a member of the *Pravda* editorial collective. In 1917, he became a member of the original Politburo created to direct the Bolshevik Revolution, and a year later, with Pyatakov, he organized the Ukrainian revolution. In August 1923, Bubnov had sided with the Democratic Centralist group and signed a petition advocating greater decentralization, but soon recanted. Between 1922 and 1925, Bubnov

118 (General Colonel) A. I. Bednyagin *et al., Kiyevskiy Krasnoznamennyy: Istoriya Krasnoznamennogo Kieyvskogo voyennogo okruga, 1919–1971 (The Kiev Red Banner: History of the Red Banner Kiev Military District, 1914–1972)*, (Moscow: Voyenizdat, 1974), p. 19; Deutscher, *Prophet Armed, p.* 221; and Heinrich E. Schulz, Paul K. Urban, and Andrew I. Lebed, eds., *Who Was Who in the USSR* (Metuchen, N.J.: Scarecrow Press, 1972), p. 24.
119 Erickson, *Soviet High Command*, p. 138.
120 *Ibid.,* p. 142; and Petrov, *Stroitel'stvo politorganov*, p. 144.
121 *The New York Times*, January 23, 1924.

worked first as the head of the agitation and propaganda section of the Party CC and then as a CC secretary. At the 13th Party Congress, he was made a member of the Party CC. In 1929, Bubnov became People's Commissar for Education.[122]

One of the first major acts of Bubnov's administration was to annul Circular No. 200 and to issue Circular No. 32 on February 3, 1924. According to the new circular, military discipline required a limitation of democracy in the army organization. It also firmly declared that party and political workers above the regimental level would henceforth be appointed by higher bodies, not elected as some suggested.[123] In the opinion of Fedotoff White, this act was a significant event in the evolution of the Soviet armed forces and political administration:

> The annulling of Circular No. 200 marked an important turn for the Red Army. It is, in a way, the end of the tendencies which survived in the armed forces of the USSR from the days of 1917. From then on, the army was supposed to carry out political directions received from above and even the communist element within it lost the right of developing lines of action apart from that laid down by the PUR.[124]

In a second significant step, the political leadership set out to purge the PUR of its Trotskyist elements. In a special recruitment drive to commemorate the death of Lenin, 4,000 officers and soldiers were brought into the Party and 800 into the Komsomol. The PUR staff was reduced by 40 percent and replaced by a staff with strong pre-Revolution ties. In divisions and detached brigades, young political workers were selectively replaced by older men from proletarian backgrounds.[125]

Within the military leadership of the armed forces, several other major changes occurred in the first quarter of 1924. The Central Committee plenum of January 14, 1924 appointed a special commission to examine shortcomings in the army and its supply apparatus. The commission included Frunze, Gusev, Stalin, K. Ye. Voroshilov, G. K. Ordzhonikidze, N. M. Shvernik, I. S. Unshlikht, E. M. Sklyanskiy, and others.[126] In a report of the commission delivered by Gusev to a Central Committee plenum on February 3, several reforms (including

[122] A. S. Bubnov, *O Krasnoy Armii (On the Red Army)*, ed. Colonel Ye. A. Fedoseyev (Moscow: Voyenizdat, 1958), pp. 235–38.

[123] Atkinson, p. 22.

[124] Fedotoff White, *Growth of the Red Army*, pp. 231–32.

[125] Erickson, *Soviet High Command*, pp. 231–32.

[126] Krasil'nikov, p. 428.

Circular No. 32) were decreed. On March 11, Frunze was appointed Deputy Chairman of the Revvoensovet and head of the Army Staff. Moreover, the tasks of the RKKA staffs were more clearly defined.[127]

In October 1924, the PUR drew up a new program for political instruction in the armed forces. The program included instruction on such topics as the Red Army and its soldier, the victory of the Bolshevik Revolution, the Civil War, Lenin and the Party, as well as information on capitalist states and foreign workers.[128] However, the program was revised in November by the All-Union Conference of Heads of Political Organs, which developed a two-year program emphasizing the history of the Communist Party, Soviet achievements, and internal and international political affairs.[129]

On December 20, 1924, a decree issued jointly by L. Kaganovich, then a Central Committee Secretary, and Bubnov instructed that party cells be organized in the army and navy company, squadron, battery, and vessel where there were three or more party members. Supervision of these cells was placed under the political commissars. In an attempt to proscribe conflicts between the cell and the commissar, the new instructions for cells declared that the commissar

> . . . is the official representative of the Party and is responsible to it for the status of Party work in the given unit. The regimental collective and the cell do not interfere in the orders of the commissar.[130]

While the cell, therefore, was obliged to implement orders of the commissar, the instructions did provide that the cell could at the same time appeal to the political section at the next higher level.

In January 1925, the undermining of Trotsky's position and influence in the armed forces, begun a year earlier with the removal of Antonov-Ovseyenko and Frunze's appointment in March 1925, was completed. On January 17, the Central Committee removed Trotsky from the Revvoensovet and six days later promoted Frunze to Commissar for War and head of the Revvoensovet.[131]

---

[127] For a detailed discussion of these staff reorganizations, see Colonel V. Danilov, "Construction of the Central Military Apparatus in 1924–1928." *Voyenno-Istoricheskiy Zhurnal*, No. 6 (June 1973), p. 81.

[128] Erickson, *Soviet High Command*, p. 703, n. 77.

[129] *Ibid.*, p. 188.

[130] Quoted in Merle Fainsod, *Smolensk Under Soviet Rule* (Cambridge, Mass.: Harvard University Press, 1958), p. 337.

[131] Among the members of the new Revvoensovet were K. Ye. Voroshilov, G. K. Ordzhonikidze, S. M. Budennyy, A. F. Myasnikov, I. S. Unshlikht, A. S. Bubnov, S. S. Kamenev, P. I.

Ironically, however, Frunze's appointment was a setback for the PUR and many of the schemes which he had previously advocated. Despite his earlier support for a proletarian-controlled armed forces and the commissar system, Frunze now became, in Carr's words, "the unhesitating champion of the rights and interests of the officer corps."[132] His appointment also marked a period in which the PUR evolved from an independent government organization under loose party supervision to a party organization subordinate to the Party Central Committee.

Three significant events during late February and early March 1925 exemplified the decline of the PUR's independent, non-party authority over the army political work. The first occasion was the 1st All-Army Assembly of Cell Secretaries between February 25 and March 3, held to discuss the strengthening of party work in the armed forces. Clearly, it was the Central Committee which was responsible for initiating and presiding over the Assembly, not the PUR.[133] Secondly, on March 2, the Revvoensovet issued Directive No. 234, over Frunze's signature, by which (except in naval forces and national formations) the commander was given sole authority over combat and administrative matters. Thirdly, on March 6, a Central Committee decree, entitled "On One-Man Command in the Red Army" and signed by then Central Committee Secretary A. Andreyev, reiterated the Revvoensovet directive.[134] According to the party decree, favorable conditions for the transition to one-man command had developed out of the previous good work of political personnel and the general strengthening of commanders. This necessitated a radical change in the tasks of the political commissars. Two new systems were described to meet diverse circumstances. The decree stated:

> Firstly, in the hands of the chief and unit commanders is completely concentrated the operational-unit, administrative, and economic functions.
>
> The commissar in this type, released from the responsibilities of daily control of unit, administrative, and economic activities of the commander, retains the leadership of political and party work in the unit and bears the responsibility for its moral-political condition. The military commissar attached to the commander, implementing personally all unit and administrative-economic func-

---

Baranov, A. I. Yegorov, and M. N. Tukhachevskiy. (Korablev and Loginov, p. 227; and Kiryayev *et al.*, p. 140.)

[132] Carr, p. 406.

[133] Erickson, *Soviet High Command*, p. 189.

[134] Colonel Yu. Petrov, "Activity of the Communist Party for Building One-Man Command in the Armed Forces (1925–1931)," *Voyenno-Istoricheskiy Zhurnal*, No. 5 (May 1963), p. 17.

tions, not taking direct participation in the discharge of the latter, with all his influence and authority assists the commander (the chief) in strengthening and improving the educational-unit (military) and economic-technical status of the unit.

Secondly, in respect to those party commanders, who satisfy the requirements of the party-political leadership (i.e., are capable of being at the same time commissars also) will combine in their person the functions of the unit, administrative-economic, and party-political leadership.[135]

As in the case of the Revvoensovet directive, however, the new system was limited to Red Army units only. In April 1925, 41.1 percent of commanders of corps, 14.3 percent of commanders of divisions, and 25.8 percent of commanders of regiments had full one-man command. Moreover, three quarters of the first commanders with full one-man command were higher military commissars.[136] In the navy and national formations, one-man command was to be applied at a greatly decelerated pace or, "as a general rule," not at all.[137]

On June 30, 1925, the Revvoensovet adopted the Temporary Thesis on Military Commissars of the RKKA and the RKKF. Unlike earlier theses which had defined the purposes of the commissars as political control and direct supervision of former tsarist officers, the Temporary Thesis now declared that "commissars are appointed first of all for the *leadership and direct conducting* of party-political work and securing the training and education of the personnel of the Red Army and Navy in the spirit of class unity and communist enlightenment."[138] With this Temporary Thesis, asserts one present-day Soviet writer, "the control functions of the commissar almost lost their importance."[139]

In September 1925, the last strand of PUR independence was cut when the new Instructions on the Political Administration of the Workers-Peasants Red Army were issued. Under its provisions, the political administration was detached from the Revvoensovet and placed directly under the supervision of the Party Central Committee. While attachment to the Central Committee increased the authoritativeness of decisions through the political administration of the armed forces, this move eradicated whatever potential that existed for the PUR to act independently of the Party. As an additional indication of the change, the PUR was renamed the Politicheskoye Upravleniye Raboche-Krest'yanskoy Kras-

---

[135] *KPSS o Vooruzhennykh Silakh Sovetskogo Soyuza*, pp. 228–29.

[136] *Petrov, Stroitel'stvo politorganov*, p. 163.

[137] *KPSS o Vooruzhennykh Silakh Sovetskogo Soyuza*, p. 229.

[138] Berklin, pp. 395–96.

[139] Petrov, *Stroitel'stvo politorganov*, p. 174.

noy Armii (Political Administration of the Workers-Peasants Red Army, or PURKKA).[140]

On October 31, 1925, Commissar for War Frunze was officially announced as having passed away. According to a contemporary report in the Western press, there were widespread rumors in Moscow that Frunze had been poisoned. These rumors also suggested that Bubnov was being considered among possible successors.[141] However, on November 6, K. Voroshilov, a close associate of Stalin during the Civil War, was named the new Commissar for War, with M. Lashevitsh as first deputy.[142]

At the 14th Party Congress in December 1925, the direct subordination of the PURKKA was again spelled out. The party regulation adopted at this Congress contained, for the first time, a special section on party organization in the armed forces.[143] The regulation also formulated the status of the new PURKKA as a party rule for the first time. It stated that "the general leadership of the party work in the Red Army and the Red Fleet is effected by the Political Administration of the Workers' and Peasants' Red Army as the military section of the Central Committee."[144]

The movement toward one-man command was slow, as the number of commanders considered capable of being both commander and commissar was quite low. On May 13, 1927, this movement received a major setback when the Revvoensovet under Voroshilov issued Circular No. 11. Except for those directly connected with political work, the political assistant (or *politruk*) was no longer required to sign orders.[145] While the commander retained general supervision of all military and political training, the *politruk* retained control in the daily practical political work. Despite the *politruk*'s apparent subordination to the commander, the *politruk* retained a direct relationship to higher political organs, and political disputes between the commander and *politruk* were referred to higher political, not military, organs.[146] In essence, this latter factor meant a major victory for the political workers, since the definition of what constituted

140 Erickson, *Soviet High Command*, p. 191.

141 *The New York Times*, November 1, 1925.

142 *Ibid.*, November 7, 1925.

143 Krasil'nikov, p. 428.

144 Quoted in Abdurakhman Avtorkhanov, *The Communist Party Apparatus* (Chicago: Henry Regnery, 1966), p. 294.

145 In the units where the commander held both military and political duties, the commissar was now called the political assistant or *politruk*.

146 Petrov, "Activity of the Communist Party for Building One-Man Command in the Armed Forces (1925–1931)," p. 20.

a "political" question, as opposed to a purely military question, was generally vague. Consequently, it differed with interpretation and in some units brought significant power back into the *politruk*'s hands.

Another indication of the retreat from the one-man command principle was marked by the Internal Service Regulations of 1928. The Regulations clearly made the political worker independent of the commander in political work regardless of the commander's political status.[147] They also gave the *politruk* equal responsibility in watching over all of the unit's training, in maintaining the standard of service, and in supervising the morale and well-being of the troops.[148]

Still, the retreat from one-man command did not go to the extreme considered necessary by some leading political workers in the armed forces. First the Military-Political Academy imeni N. G. Tolmachev[149] on March 15, 1928, and then the political staff of the Belorussian Military District on May 23, 1928, adopted resolutions disputing the political advisability of one-man command and calling for a return to local control.[150]

At the end of October 1928, the Temporary Thesis adopted in May 1927 was replaced by the New Thesis on Commissars, Commanders with Single Authority, and Assistants for Political Affairs. As explained by one Soviet source, "the commissar in political considerations was subordinated to higher political organs and in administrative-combat considerations to the commander of the higher formation; the commander with single authority in combat considerations was subordinated to the higher commander and in political considerations to the higher political organs."[151] The New Thesis was indeed a significant gain for the political workers, because (1) the commander could not impose disciplinary punishment on his assistant for political affairs, (2) the commander no longer had the opportunity to compile an attestation on the political assistant, and (3) disputes between commanders and commissars were submitted only to higher political organs.[152]

On September 13, 1929, Bubnov gave up his position as chief of the PURKKA

---

[147] Fedotoff White, *Growth of the Red Army*, p. 316.

[148] *Ibid.*, pp. 316–17.

[149] In January 1923, the Petrograd Teacher's Institute imeni N. G. Tolmachev and the Mogilev Red Army University imeni the 16th Army were combined to form the Military-Political Institute (reorganized in May 1925 as the Military-Political Academy) imeni N. G. Tolmachev. (Petrov, *Stroitel'stvo politorganov*, pp. 135, 175–76).

[150] Korablev and Loginov, p. 285.

[151] *Ibid.*, p. 294.

[152] Petrov, *Stroitel'stvo politorganov*, pp. 174–75.

and succeeded Anatole Lunacharskiy as the Commiessar of Education. In view of the increased emphasis on education under the 1st Five-Year Plan begun in 1929, this move does not appear to imply any dissatisfaction with the work of Bubnov in the political administration. Rather, the opposite is true. It was an attempt by Stalin to bring better organizational talents to the field of education.

2

The Vacillation between Professionalism and Political Control in the Stalinist and early Post-Stalinist Years

Concessions to Professionalism and the 1937 Purge: The Gamarnik Era

Bubnov's replacement was Yan Borisovich Gamarnik,[1] whose eight-year length of service (October 1, 1929–May 31, 1937) as head of the political administration is second only to that of A. A. Yepishev. A member of several student revolutionary groups, Gamarnik joined the Bolshevik Party in 1916 and served until the Revolution as a member and secretary of the Kiev RSDRP(b) Committee. After the Revolution, he served on the Odessa, Kharkov, and Crimean party committees, and during the Civil War as a military commissar and Revvoensovet member of the Southern Group. Between 1920 and 1923, he served as chairman of the Odessa and Kiev district party committees and chairman of the Kiev city executive committee. From 1923 to 1928, he held the posts of chairman of the Far Eastern Revolutionary Committee and a kray executive committee, and secretary of the Far Eastern kray party committee. In 1928, he became the secretary of the CC of the Belorussian CP.[2] According to one observer, "Gamarnik had every quality likely to render him unfit for the generation of communists which Stalin was seeking to elevate — Jewish origin, intelligence, internationalism, honesty, and sincere belief in the communist mission."[3] On the positive side, however, two factors were responsible for Gamarnik's appoint-

[1] *The New York Times*, September 14, 1929.

[2] A. M. Prokhorov, ed., *Bol'shaya sovetskaya entsiklopediya (The Great Soviet Encyclopedia)*, VI (3rd ed.; Moscow: Soviet Encyclopedia Publishing House, 1971), 237; and Major General A. Lobachev in *Krasnaya Zvezda*, April 13, 1962.

[3] Leonard Schapiro, *The Communist Party of the Soviet Union* (New York: Random House, 1960), p. 419.

ment. First, he was a close friend of Voroshilov. Second, he had previously demonstrated his willingness to purge officers hostile to Stalin's interests.[4]

The latter point was probably very significant in light of the unrest which developed out of the collectivization scheme of the 1st Five-Year Plan. In 1929, only 50 percent of the Soviet officers were Communists.[5] As late as 1930, ex-tsarist officers still accounted for about 11 percent of the Soviet's commissioned force,[6] and Stalin apparently feared that some of this number might use the unrest against the Communist regime. Indeed, on June 30, 1930, Unshlikht was removed from his post of Deputy Commissar for War and head of the Revvoen-sovet, and I. P. Uborevich and Gamarnik were appointed respectively to these posts. Rumors in Moscow suggested that Unshlikht was being made a scapegoat for unrest in the armed forces.[7] Again, in 1933, General Blyukher complained to Stalin that it was becoming impossible to construct an adequate defense against Japan because of the unrest caused by collectivization.[8] It is significant, however, that during these difficult years there was no organized military opposition against Stalin or his drastic policies.[9] In no small part, the credit for this fact lies in the tight controls which Gamarnik maintained through the political administration.

Yet there were several factors at work during the first half of the 1930's which fostered a trend toward greater independence for the commander and the armed forces. First, the political administration gradually evolved into an integral part of the armed forces and ceased to interfere directly in military affairs.[10] As one source correctly notes, a major cause was the improved abilities of the commanders:

> As officers improved their professional capabilities, they began to feel technically superior not only to their men, but also to their political commissars, who remained, on the whole, more backward. In many cases the commissars fell under

[4] Michael Berchin and Eliahu Ben-Horin, *The Red Army* (New York: W. W. Norton, 1942), p. 120.

[5] T. H. Rigby, *Communist Party Membership in the USSR, 1917–1967* (Princeton, N.J.: Princeton University Press, 1968), p. 244.

[6] Arthur W. Just, *The Red Army*, trans. W. M. Potter (London: Figurehead, 1936), p. 24.

[7] *The Times* (London), June 4, 1930.

[8] John A. Armstrong, *The Politics of Totalitarianism: The Communist Party of the Soviet Union from 1934 to the Present* (New York: Random House, 1961), p. 62.

[9] John Erickson, *The Soviet High Command: A Military-Political History, 1918–1941* (London: Macmillan, 1962), p. 392.

[10] Littleton B. Atkinson, *Dual Command in the Red Army, 1918–1942* (Montgomery, Ala.: Air University, 1950), p. 33.

the influence of their military colleagues, and in the years 1933–36 a gradual reversal of the previous trend in commander-commissar relations took place. In the 1920's the commissar had dominated the commander; now, thanks to better education and technical knowledge, the commander began to dominate the commissar.[11]

A second factor was the perception of a growing threat to the Soviet Union from Hitler's Nazi Germany. To meet this threat, Stalin made a number of reforms in and concessions to the military.

On June 20, 1934, the People's Commissariat for Military and Naval Affairs was reorganized and renamed the People's Commissariat for the Defense of the USSR, with K. Ye. Voroshilov as the head, Yan. B. Gamarnik as first deputy, and M. N. Tukhachevskiy as a deputy.[12] At the same time the Revvoensovet of the USSR and the revvoensovets of the districts, armies, fleets, and flotillas were abolished; with this, single command replaced the collegiate principle as the basis for military leadership.[13] On November 22, the Military Council, numbering eighty persons, was created under the People's Commissariat for Defense as a consultative organ. In 1935, "in connection with the significant increasing of its role," the Staff of the RKKA was transformed into the General Staff, with A. I. Yegorov as its chief.[14]

Major transformations also occurred in the organization of the PURKKA. In April 1933, the sectors of the political administration for work in aviation, tank, and mechanized troops and in fleets were reorganized into independent sections. In the navy and the air force were introduced assistant commanders for political affairs, who were simultaneously assistant chiefs of the PURKKA for work in aviation and the fleet.[15] In April 1934, within select military districts were introduced the special post of deputy chief of the political administration

---

[11] J. M. Mackintosh, "The Red Army, 1920–1936," in B. H. Liddell Hart, ed., *The Red Army* (Gloucester, Mass.: Peter Smith, 1968), p. 60.

[12] Yu. P. Petrov, *Stroitel'stvo politorganov, partiyykh i komsomol'skikh organizatsiy armii i flota (1918–1968) (The Construction of Political Organs and Party and Komsomol Organizations [1918–1968])* (Moscow: Voyenizdat, 1968), p. 229, n. 2.

[13] D. Fedotoff White, *The Growth of the Red Army* (Princeton, N.J.: Princeton University Press, 1944), p. 358.

[14] Lieutenant Colonel Yu. I Korablev and Colonel M. L. Loginov, *KPSS i stroitel'stvo Vooruzhennykh Sil SSSR (1918–iyun' 1941) (The CPSU and Construction of the Armed Forces of the USSR [1918–June 1941])* (Moscow: Voyenizdat, 1959), p. 344.

[15] General of the Army A. A. Yepishev, *Partiyno-politicheskaya rabota v Vooruzhennykh Silakh SSSR, 1918–1973 gg: Istoricheskiy ocherk (Party-Political Work in the Armed Forces of the USSR, 1918–1973: Historical Essay)* (Moscow: Voyenizdat, 1974), pp. 152–53.

for leadership of party-political work among aviation, tank, and mechanized troops. In 1931, the first political sections of corps were created and within a year there were nineteen of them.[16] On every command level, the commander assumed responsibility for all military and political work. The political commissar was reduced in all instances to an adviser and supporter of the commander. One reason it was believed this change could be made was that under Gamarnik the number of "proletarian" commanders increased by 50 percent between 1930 and 1934, from 31 percent of command personnel to 46 percent.[17]

A second major concession to the professionalist element in the armed forces was the introduction in September 1935 of ranks for military and political officers. The corresponding ranks were:

Military: (1) Red Army man (i.e., private), (2) section commander, (3) platoon commander, (4) senior platoon commander (i.e., sergeant), (5) lieutenant, (6) senior lieutenant, (7) captain, (8) major, (9) colonel, (10) brigade commander, (11) corps commander, 12) army commander 2nd grade, (13) army commander 1st grade, and (14) marshal of the Soviet Union.[18]

Political: (1) junior political instructor, (2) political instructor, (3) senior political instructor, (4) battalion commissar, (5) senior battalion commissar, (6) regimental commissar, (7) brigade commissar, (8) divisional commissar, (9) corps commissar, (10) army commissar 2nd grade, and (11) army commissar 1st grade.[19]

With the introduction of ranks, five distinguished military, figures were appointed marshals of the Soviet Union: K. Ye. Voroshilov, S. M. Budennyy, V. K. Blyukher, A. I. Yegorov, and M. N. Tukhachevskiy. To the rank of commanders 1st grade were appointed S. S. Kamenev, I. E. Yakir, I. P. Uborevich, I. P. Belov, B. M. Shaposhnikov, and to commanders 2nd grade were appointed P. Ye. Dybenko, M. K. Levandovskiy, I. N. Dubovoy, I. F. Fed'ko, A. I. Kork, N. D. Kashirin, A. I. Sedyakin, Ya. I. Alksnis, I. A. Khalepskiy, and I. I. Vatsetis. Ya. B. Gamarnik was appointed commissar 1st grade.[20]

A third major concession concerned the upgrading of military schools. In

---

[16] Petrov, *Stroitel'stvo politorganov*, p. 230.

[17] J. M. Mackintosh, *Juggernaut: A History of the Soviet Armed Forces* (New York: Macmillan, 1967), p. 76.

[18] Erickson, *Soviet High Command*, pp. 391–92.

[19] Abdurakhman Avtorkhanov, *The Communist Party Apparatus* (Chicago: Henry Regnery, 1966), p. 292.

[20] Korablev and Loginov, pp. 354–55.

the early 1930's, several new military academies were created. Consequently, by the late 1930's there were 13 military academies, one military institute, and 5 military departments in civilian institutions, and 75 military schools.[21]

In addition, the officers of the armed forces were granted numerous minor concessions. It is true that soldiers in general were greatly favored in pay scales, but officers (and, among them, senior officers) were even more favored. Moreover, hundreds of special stores, theaters, and clubs were constructed for the use of officers only.[22]

At the beginning of the second half of the 1930's, the Red Army was well on the way to becoming a highly efficient, technical, and professional standing army. Then, most unexpectedly, the trend was reversed. In January 1937, during the show trials of Stalin's last political opponents, Radek let it "slip out" that Tukhachevskiy and Putna had been in contact with agents of Trotsky.[23] Then, in a speech of March 3, Stalin himself asserted that people in "certain responsible posts" were carrying out treasonous activities.[24]

On May 10, 1937, the principle of one-man command instituted so recently in March 1934 was abolished and the dual command principle was re-established. Authority in military districts, fleets, and armies was reinvested in a three-man military council consisting of the commander and two political workers. "In other words," points out Fedotoff White, "all functions of direction and supervision of military activity, as well as civilian work pertaining to defense, were placed in the hands of a collegium of three persons, of whom only one was necessarily a trained military man."[25] At the same time, military commissars were introduced in all troop units, formations, staffs, administrations, and institutions of the People's Commissariat for Defense; *politruki* were introduced on the comany level.[26]

Although orders were to be issued in the name of the commander, they

---

21 Colonel ·M. Lisenkov, "The Armed Forces of the USSR in the Years of Peaceful Socialist Construction (1921–1941)," *Kommunist Vooruzhennykh Sil,* No. 10 (May 1968) p. 71.

22 Raymond L. Garthoff, "The Military as a Social Force," in Cyril E. Black, ed., *The Transformation of Russian Society* (Cambridge, Mass.: Harvard University Press, 1960), p. 331.

23 John Erickson, "The Soviet Military Purge: 1937–1957," *Twentieth Century,* CLXII, No. 965 (July 1957), 31.

24 *Ibid.*

25 D. Fedotoff White, *Growth of the Red Army,* p. 394.

26 Petrov, *Stroitel'stvo politorganov,* p. 238. See also "Creation and Strengthening of Political Organs and Party Organizations in the Army and Fleet, 1921–1941," *Kommunist Vooruzhennykh Sil,* No. 1 (January 1966), p. 30.

were now required to bear the signature of both the commander and the commissar. The new statute emphasized the equal responsibilities of the commander and the commissar.

> The military commissar equally with the commander shall be responsible for the political-moral condition of the unit, for the fulfillment of the military duty and the execution of military discipline by all personnel of the unit from top to bottom, for preparedness for combat, operations, and mobilization, for the condition of the armament and military economy of the unit (command, administrative headquarters, installations, etc.)[27]

Clearly, these were signs of an imminent crisis. Other signs also existed. In later May, I. A. Bulin, deputy chief of the political administration, mysteriously disappeared. Then the head of the Volga Military District political administration, Orlov, and General Yakir's former political chief in Kiev, Amelin, were removed without apparent cause.[28] Numerous transfers were made of leading military figures and some were even arrested before they could reach their posts. But these were only minor acts compared to the first weeks of June 1937.

In early June, it was announced that eight of the Red Army's leading military officers had been arrested and sent to trial, and that the head of the political administration, Jan Gamarnik, had committed suicide because he feared an imminent arrest.[29] The eight officers now put on trial were: Marshal Tukhachevskiy, Vice-Commissar for Defense; General A. I. Kork, director of the Red Army War College; General I. E. Yakir, commander of the Leningrad Military District; General I. F. Uborevich, Assistant Commissar for War and vice-president of the Revvoensovet; General R. P. Eydemann, chief of the Home Defense Organization; General B. M. Feldman, chief of personnel of the General Staff; General V. M. Primkov, deputy commander of the Leningrad Military District; and General V. M. Putna, a former military attaché in London, who had been arrested in August 1936.[30]

On June 9, *Pravda* announced that the trial of the eight officers was to be

---

[27] "Statute on Military Commissars of the Worker-Peasant Red Army," in Harold J. Berman and Miroslav Kerner, eds. and trans., *Documents on Soviet Military Law and Administration* (Cambridge, Mass.: Harvard University Press, 1958), p. 13. Although passed on May 10, the decree was not issued until August 15.

[28] Erickson, *Soviet High Command*, pp. 460–61.

[29] Robert Conquest, *The Great Terror: Stalin's Purge of the Thirties* (New York: Macmillan, 1968), p. 221.

[30] Balticus, "The Russian Mystery Behind the Tukhachevskiy Plot," *Foreign Affairs*, XVI, No. 3 (October 1936), 47, n. 4.

transferred to a special military tribunal of eight judges.[31] Shortly thereafter, it was announced that all eight of the military officers were shot. As in the case of the eight military leaders, Gamarnik was accused of being a foreign spy. In an article entitled "We Do Not Permit the Enemies of the People to Live" (June 6), *Krasnaya Zvezda* declared:

> Events show that the enemy has succeeded in penetrating into the midst of our army. The accursed enemy of the people, the Trotskist dreg Gamarnik . . . using the most atrocious methods to disguise his double dealing for a long time carried on the black counterrevolutionary activity of a spy and Fascist bandit.[32]

In the military field, the purge that followed was almost beyond belief. Three of the five marshals of the Soviet Union were executed, along with 75 of the 80-odd members of the Supreme Military Council and 11 of the Vice-Commissars for Defense.[33] It has also been estimated that approximately 90 percent of the general officers and 80 percent of the colonels were removed by execution or imprisonment.[34] The navy was no less drastically affected by the purge than the army. In August 1938, Western sources reported that all eight of the Soviet naval officers of the rank of admiral had disappeared or been shot. Several professors of Leningrad's Naval Academy had also been executed.[35] In the air force, four successive chiefs were purged: Ya. I. Alksnis, A. D. Loktionov, Ya. V. Smushkevich, A. V. Rychagov, as well as deputy chief V. V. Khripin, chief of staff Lavrov, and all the chiefs of aviation of military districts.[36]

The political administration was also severely hit by the purge. According to information compiled by one Western writer, in addition to Gamarnik's suicide, his two deputies, A. S. Bulin and G. A. Osepyan, were arrested. The heads of all the political sections and most of the members of the military districts were also arrested. In addition, all 17 army commissars, 25 of 28 corps commissars, and 34 of 36 brigade commissars were removed.[37]

The very thoroughness of the purges appears to contradict the opinion of

---

[31] Ironically, five of the eight judges were themselves to die before firing squads.

[32] Quoted by Harold Denny in *The New York Times*, June 7, 1937.

[33] Edgar O'Ballance, *The Red Army: A Short History* (New York: Praeger, 1964), p. 131.

[34] *Ibid.*

[35] *The Times* (London), August 31, 1938.

[36] General Major N. M. Kiryayev *et al.*, eds. *KPSS i stroitel'stvo Sovetskykh Vooruzennykh Sil (The CPSU and the Construction of the Soviet Armed Forces)* (2nd ed.: Moscow: Voyenizdat, 1967), p. 206.

[37] Conquest, *Great Terror*, pp. 227-28.

those, such as Isaac Deutscher, who argue that the purges were the result of an anti-Stalinist conspiracy of Gamarnik and the generals.[38] Instead, the major cause of the purges seems to lay in the greater professionalization and, therewith, greater independence of the armed forces. The shortcomings of the political administration of the armed forces lay in its inability or unwillingness to restrict this trend. Therefore, in order to reassert leadership over the military, it was necessary to restaff all of the political organs of the armed forces.[39]

Gamarnik's successor as chief of the political administration was P. A. Smirnov, a Communist since May 1917. In 1926, Smirnov had been appointed chief of the political administration of the Baltic Fleet and member of the Revvoensovet. From late 1935 to June 1937, he headed the political administration of the Leningrad Military District.[40] He served only a brief term, however, before being promoted to head of the Red Navy. Outside of this brief stint, no other navy man has ever occupied the highest post within the political administration.

On December 31, 1937, the Red Navy was detached from the Commissariat for Defense and established as the Commissariat for Naval Affairs. Smirnov was appointed the new Naval Commissar. Simultaneously, the political administration for the navy was separated from the PURKKA and established as the Political Administration of the Workers-Peasants Red Navy (PURKKF), with M. R. Shaposhnikov as its chief. The PURKKF set up four political administrations of fleets (Black Sea, Baltic, Northern, and Pacific), four political sections of flotillas (Amur, Dnepr, Caspian, and North Pacific), and forty-five political sections of formations.[41]

Later, in March 1938, under the People's Commissariat for Defense was created the Main Military Council of the RKKA, "a collegial organ for putting into practice the resolutions of the Party in the area of the defense of the country."[42] The Main Military Council consisted of several secretaries of the CC VKP(b), the People's Commissars of Defense and of the Navy, the Chief of the General Staff of the Red Army, the chief of the political administration, and the remaining, unpurged marshals of the Soviet Union.[43]

When the political administration was split, Lev Zakharovich Mekhlis was

---

[38] Isaac Deutscher, *Stalin: A Political Biography* (2nd ed.; New York: Oxford University Press, 1966), p. 379.

[39] Atkinson, p. 37.

[40] *The New York Times*, January 1, 1938.

[41] Petrov, *Stroitel'stvo politorganov*, pp. 240–41.

[42] Kiryayev *et al.*, eds., pp. 229–30.

[43] Korablev and Loginov, pp. 379–80.

appointed the new head of the PURKKA and a Vice-Commissar for Defense.[44] Mekhlis, the son of a Jewish office worker, joined the Bolshevik Party in March 1918. During the Civil War Mekhlis served as a political commissar on the Southern Front against Wrangel. From 1922 to 1927, he worked for the Central Committee Secretariat and was "one of Stalin's special personnel entrusted with duties in the political apparatus."[45] In May 1930, Mekhlis became chief editor of *Pravda* and later in 1937 was made head of the Press and Publication Department of the Party Central Committee.[46] Clearly, Mekhlis' appointment was based on his political background and personal loyalty to Stalin. It is true that during the Civil War he had been the victorious commander and hero of the battle of Kakhovka, "one of the brilliant feats of the war,"[47] but his recent experience had been purely political.

Mekhlis' major duty during his first year as head of the political administration was to carry out the purge of the armed forces and the political administration begun in 1937. In addition to statistics previously cited.[48] it has been estimated by Conquest that by the end of 1938 at least 20,000 political workers in the military had been removed. He also estimates that one third of the 10,500 active political workers in the armed forces in 1938 had no political education at all.[49] In order to justify the purge and win the support of new political workers, Mekhlis charged at the 18th Party Congress in March 1939:

> Where the Gamarnik-Bulin gang of spies did the greatest damage to the political apparatus was in the sphere of its leading personnel. They promoted to the most important posts enemies of the people, incompetents, utter degenerates, who had sold their souls to foreign secret service agents. They held down the best commissars and political workers, capable and efficient people who were loyal to the Party of Lenin and Stalin, kept them in minor ranks and in relatively unimportant posts. They did their best to save their accomplices who were in danger of imminent exposure by transferring this scum to other posts.[50]

In 1940, komsomol members accounted for about 15,000 of the political workers in the armed forces. Thus, in the Russo-Finnish War, it sometimes

44 *The New York Times*, January 1, 1938.

45 Erickson, *Soviet High Command*, p. 840.

46 Heinrich E. Schulz, Paul K. Urban, and Andrew I. Lebed, eds., *Who Was Who in the USSR* (Metuchen, N.J.: Scarecrow Press, 1972), p. 378.

47 *The New York Times*, January 1, 1938.

48 See above, p. 43.

49 Conquest, *Great Terror*, p. 228.

50 Quoted in Atkinson, p. 38.

happened that an inexperienced young commissar shared equal responsibility and authority[51] with a company commander.[52] The dangers of such a situation were obvious and worked to the detriment of Soviet forces in combat with the Finns.

Under the pressures of Commander-in-Chief Marshal S. K. Timoshenko, the political leadership agreed to some modifications of this imbalance favoring the political administration. On May 16, 1940, Order No. 160 introduced a new training program for the armed forces. The program emphasized preparations for combat, somewhat at the expense of political education. Day and night military training left little time for political training.[53]

The next step toward increased professionalization of the armed forces occurred on August 12. On the recommendation of Timoshenko, the system of commissars and the office PURKKA head were simultaneously abolished.[54] An edict of the Presidium of the USSR Supreme Soviet, entitled "On Strengthening Unity of Command in the Red Army and Navy," declared:

> In connection with the fact that the institution of commissars has already fulfilled its principal aims, and that the command cadres of the Red Army and Navy in recent years have in reality gotten stronger, and as well for the purpose of realizing in units both joint full unity of command and a further increase in the authority of the commander — the absolute director of troops, bearing full responsibility as well for the political work in the units — the Presidium of the Supreme Soviet of the USSR decrees:
>
> 1. To annul "The Statute on Military Commissars of the Worker-Peasant Red Army," issued by the Central Executive Committee and the Council of People's Commissars of the USSR on August 15, 1937, No. 105/1387.[55]
>
> 2. To introduce into the joint (corps, divisions, brigades) units, vessels, subunits, military education institutions, and installations of the Red Army and Navy, an institution of deputy commanders (chiefs) for political affairs.
>
> 3. To oblige the military councils of districts, fronts, and armies to carry out daily active control over the political work in corps, divisions, and brigades.[56]

In sum, the new role of the deputy commander for political affairs, or the

---

[51] See the Statute of May 10, 1937.

[52] Fedotoff White, *Growth of the Red Army*, pp. 399–400.

[53] Erickson, *Soviet High Command*, p. 554.

[54] Louis B. Ely, *The Red Army Today* (Harrisburg, Pa.: Military Service Publishing Co., 1949), p. 127.

[55] See above, p. 42, and n. 27.

[56] *KPSS o Vooruzhennykh Silakh Sovetskogo Soyuza Dokumety 1917–1968 (The CPSU on the Armed Forces of the Soviet Union. Documents 1917–1968)* (Moscow: Voyenizdat, 1969), p. 298.

zampolit, was greatly restricted. While the commander was responsible for military and political training, the *zampolit* was limited to propaganda, morale building, and indoctrination.[57]

Political Control During World War II

On June 22, 1941, Germany launched a surprise attack against the Soviet Union. This move necessitated several changes in the military-related leadership apparatus. As early as May 6, Stalin had for the first time in Soviet history assumed official control over both the Party and the state by combining the role of Party CC Secretary and Chairman of the Council of People's Commissars.[58] On June 23, the Stavka of the High Command, the equivalent of a general headquarters, was created. It consisted of the People's Commissar of Defense, Marshal of the Soviet Union S. K. Timoshenko (chairman); the Chief of the General Staff, General of the Army G. K. Zhukov; J. V. Stalin; Marshals of the Soviet Union K. Ye. Voroshilov and S. M. Budennyy; and the People's Commissar of the Navy, N. G. Kuznetsov.[59] On June 30, the State Defense Committee, or GKO, replaced the Council of People's Commissars as the absolute authority in government, military, and administrative matters.[60] GKO originally consisted of Stalin, Molotov, Voroshilov, Bulganin, Kaganovich, Malenkov, and Mikoyan. On July 10, the Stavka of the High Command was reorganized and replaced by the Stavka of the Supreme Command. It now consisted of Stalin (chairman), V. M. Molotov, Marshals Timoshenko, Budennyy, Voroshilov, and Shaposhnikov, and General Zhukov.[61] Nine days later, Stalin appointed himself People's Commissar of Defense, and on August 8 officially became the Commander-in-Chief.[62]

The initial phase of the war found the Soviet Union unprepared militarily

[57] Mackintosh, *Juggernaut*, p. 127.

[58] Schapiro, *Communist Party of the Soviet Union*, p. 493.

[59] S. M. Klyutskin and A. M. Sinitsin, ed., *SSSR v Velikoy Otchestvennoy voyne 1941–1945 gg. (Kratkaya khronika) (The USSR in the Great Patriotic War 1941–1945 [A Short Chronicle])* (Moscow: Voyenizdat, 1970), pp. 14–15.

[60] For the text of the decree "The Organization of the State Committee of Defense, June 30, 1941," see V. B. Kalinin, V. I. Nechipurenko, and V. M. Savel'yev, *Kommunisticheskaya partiya v Velikoy Otchestvennoy voyne (iyun' 1941–1945): Dokumenty i materialy (The Communist Party in the Great Fatherland War [June 1941–1945]: Documents and Materials)* (Moscow: State Publishing House for Political Literature, 1970), p. 43.

[61] Marshal of the Soviet Union M. V. Zakharov *et al.*, eds., *50 let Vooruzhennykh Sil SSSR (50 Years of the USSR Armed Forces)* (Moscow: Voyenizdat, 1968), p. 267.

[62] *Ibid.*

and psychologically. In addition to several disastrous setbacks, some two million Red Army soldiers surrendered to the advancing Germans. Under these conditions, Mekhlis was able to convince the political leadership to reintroduce the system of political commissars under his command. A Supreme Soviet decree of July 16 asserted:

> The war, which was thrust on us, has basically changed the conditions of work in the Red Army. The war has undone the scope of political work in our army and demands that the political workers do not confine their work to propaganda, but take upon themselves responsibility also for military work at the fronts.
>
> On the other side, the war has complicated the work of the commanders in the regiment and division, and requires that to the commander of the regiment and division be rendered the complete assistance from the side of the political workers, not only in the sphere of political work, but also in the sphere of military work. All of these new circumstances in the work of the political workers, connected with the transition from peace time to war time, requires that the role and responsibility of the political workers be increased, as took place in the period of the civil war against the foreign military intervention.[63]

Another Supreme Soviet directive, entitled "Theses on Military Commissars of the Workers-Peasants Red Army," was also issued on July 16 to define further the duties and character of the new commissars. In the second of its eleven points, the directive noted:

> The military commissar is the representative of the Party and Government in the Red Army and equally with the commander bears full responsibility for the fulfillment of military tasks by the army unit, for its steadfastness in battle and readiness with firmness to fight to the last drop of blood with the enemies of our homeland and defend with honor every inch of Soviet earth.[64]

On July 20, 1941, these resolutions were extended to apply to the navy. In August, military commissars were introduced into all battalions and companies of tank troops and into artillery battalions and batteries of artillery units. In September, all divisions received commissars of staffs. Then, at the beginning of December, military commissars were introduced into battalions of rifle units and formations.[65] Consequently, the number of political workers in the armed forces rose within a year from 95,815 (89,282 in the Red Army and 6,533 in the

63 *KPSS o Vooruzhennykh Silakh Sovetskogo Soyuza*, p. 305.

64 *Ibid.*, p. 307.

65 Yepishev, ed., *Partiyno-politicheskaya rabota*, p. 204.

Red Navy) on June 22, 1941, to include about 100,000 full-time political workers, more than 70,000 members of party bureaus of primary party organizations, 73,000 party organizers of companies and equivalent party organizations, and 500,000 Communists from command and political leadership staffs.[66] It is also significant that numerous high-ranking party officials, including 54 members and candidate members of the CC VKP(b) and 13 members of the auditing commission, were transferred to political work in the armed forces within the first few days of the war.[67]

Once the tide of defeat in the early phase of the war was turned, the leadership took time to re-evaluate the system of commissars. It has already been observed that many of the experienced commissars had been removed by the purges of 1937–38 and replaced by younger, inexperienced personnel. Moreover, many of the best commissars, who had put themselves in posts near the fighting, were captured by the swiftly advancing German troops. Under a special "Commissar Order" issued by the German military command, these captured commissars were not to be considered prisoners of war, but rather were to be shot immediately.[68] Consequently, it was often the youngest and least experienced of the political workers who shared equal authority with the commander under the directives of July 1941. In such a situation, the commissar system was viewed extremely unfavorably by professional military leaders.

The stand of the military leaders received indirect support when Mekhlis, the head of the political administration in the armed forces, fell into disgrace for a blunder he committed while exercising command authority. Mekhlis had been sent by Stalin as a Stavka representative to the Crimean Front. Under urgings from Mekhlis, the Kerch Army Group set out in May 1942 to recapture the Kerch Peninsula from the Germans. A victory would have given the Russians a strong foothold in the Crimea and would have afforded significant relief to besieged Sevastopol.[69] Despite some initial Red Army successes, the Germans regrouped and inflicted a disastrous defeat on the Soviet troops. When the Germans entered the town of Kerch on May 15, they found that the Russians had fled, abandoning all their equipment. Whereas German casualties totaled only 7,500 men, Soviet losses totaled 170,000 in prisoners, 1,100 guns, 250 tanks, 3,800 motor vehicles, and 300 aircraft.[70] For his part, Mekhlis was demoted to the rank of corps commissar.

[66] Kiryayev *et als.*, eds., p. 317.

[67] *Ibid.*, p. 250.

[68] Alexander Werth, *Russia at War, 1941–1945* (New York: Avon, 1964), p. 641.

[69] *Ibid.*, p. 364.

[70] Albert Seaton, *The Russo-German War, 1941–45* (New York: Praeger, 1971), p. 259.

The new head of the political administration appointed in June 1942 was A. S. Shcherbakov, then a candidate member of the Politburo and a Secretary of the Party Central Committee. Once a printer's apprentice, Shcherbakov joined the Red Guards in 1917 and then the Bolshevik Party in 1918. Initially involved in komsomol work in 1918–21, Shcherbakov went on to membership in various rayon and oblast committees until 1934, when he was selected secretary of the USSR Writers' Union. Between 1936 and 1938, he served as a secretary in the Leningrad Oblast, the Irkutsk Oblast, the Donetsk Oblast, and the Stalino Oblast party committees. From 1938 to 1945, in addition to his other offices, he was first secretary of the Moscow City and Oblast Party Committee.[71]

Under the orders of Stalin, Shcherbakov presided over a thorough purging of the political administration and greatly curtailed the authority of the political worker over the commander. Not only were many political workers removed, but in October 1942 dual command was abolished.

An October 9 decree of the Supreme Soviet Presidium, entitled "On the Establishment of Full One-Man Command and the Abolition of the Institution of Military Commissars in the Red Army," declared that the political commissars were no longer needed to watch over the officers as in the time of the Civil War. It further stated:

> On the other side, military commissars and political workers have raised their military knowledge, have acquired rich experience in modern warfare, a part of these already put in command positions and successfully directing troops, many others may be of use in command positions either immediately or after certain military training.
>
> In all these new circumstances, combined with the growth of our command and political cadres, there is evidence that the ground for the existence of the system of political commissars has utterly fallen away.
>
> What is more, the further existence of the institution of military commissars may be a hindrance in improving the management of the troops, and for most commanders creates a false condition.
>
> Thus, the necessity to abolish the institution of military commissars in the Red Army ripened, to establish full one-man command and entrust completely in the commander the responsibility for all aspects of work with the troops.[72]

Under the provisions of the decree, the commissar was replaced by the sys-

---

[71] B. A. Vvedenskiy, ed., *Bol'shaya sovetskaya entsiklopediya (The Great Soviet Encyclopedia)*, XLVIII (2nd. ed.: Moscow: Great Soviet Encyclopedia State Scientific Publishing House, 1957), 262–63; and Colonel General I. Shikin, "Prominent Party, Government, and Military Figure," *Voyenno-Istoricheskiy Zhurnal*, No. 10 (October 1971), pp. 41–48.

[72] *KPSS o Vooruzhennykh Silakh Sovetskogo Soyuza*, pp. 318–19.

tem of political assistants (the *zampolit*), whose major concerns were now morale, propaganda, and education of the troops. Consequently, under battle-field conditions, the authority of the *zampolit* was greatly restricted.[73] Despite the high political status of its head and other political workers, such as N. S. Khrushchev, therefore, the political administration's role during World War II (or, as the Soviets call it, the Great Fatherland War) was subordinate to military requirements. Individual exceptions did exist, of course, where the commissar held an extremely high political rank outside of his position in the political administration.

In May 1943, the Central Committee of the Party again greatly curtailed the influence of the political workers when it issued its decision "On the Reorganization of the Structure of the Party and Komsomol Organizations in the Red Army and the Intensification of the Role of Front, Army, and Divisional Newspapers." In addition to calling for greater propaganda work from newspapers, the decree abolished the institute of deputy commanders for political affairs in companies and batteries. The battalion became the basic level for party-political work.[74] In connection with this reorganization, after appropriate military training, 122,000 released political workers were transferred to command pasts.[75]

Reassertion of Political Control over the Soviet Armed Forces in the Postwar Period

On May 11, 1945, Moscow radio reported that after a long illness Shcherbakov had died.[76] On the following day, Stalin and other leaders placed Shcherbakov's crematory urn in the Kremlin wall.[77]

The new chief of the political administration in the armed forces was Colonel General Iosif Vasil'yevich Shikin,[78] who had served under A. A. Zhdanov dur-

---

[73] Mackintosh, *Juggernaut*, p. 282.

[74] For the text of the decree, see Kalinin, Nechipurenko, and Savel'yev, pp. 98–99.

[75] General Major N. Bobkov, "Officer Training During the War," *Soviet Military Review*, No. 9 (September 1971), p. 35; see also Kirvayev *et al.*, eds., p. 304. According to one source, during the entire war more than 150,000 political workers were appointed to command posts; see "The Creation and Strengthening of Political Organs and Party Organizations in the Army and Fleet (1941–1945)," *Kommunist Vooruzhennykh Sil*, No. 2 (February 1968), p. 51.

[76] *The New York Times*, May 11, 1945.

[77] *Ibid.*, May 13, 1945.

[78] *Yezhegodnik bol'shoy sovetskoy entsiklopedii, 1971 (Annual of the Great Soviet Encyclopedia, 1971)* (Moscow: Soviet Encyclopedia Publishing House, 1971), p. 640.

ing the war. Shikin joined the Communist Party in 1927 and four years later graduated from the Academy of Communist Education imeni N. K. Krupskaya. From 1931 to 1934, he was director of studies at a factory training school and then director of the personnel training department at the Gorkiy Automobile Plant. In 1939, he joined the political administration of the armed forces and in 1941 was appointed by Zhdanov as the commissar to Major General A. M. Shilov, who commanded the supply route across Lake Ladoga to Leningrad during the German siege. In 1942, he was appointed deputy chief of the political administration and chief of the section for agitation and propaganda.[79]

The evidence clearly suggests that Shikin's rapid elevation was due in no small degree to his close relationship with Zhdanov, whose political influence also rose sharply during the war. In their respective fields — Zhdanov in the arts and sciences and Shikin in the armed forces — both sought to curtail the influence of non-party elites who had been allowed to assert some independence in the war years. In effect, as Kolkowicz has pointed out, the appointment of Shikin "signalled the end of the military's relative independence and ushered in another era of strong control and massive indoctrination by the Party."[80]

In September 1945, the State Defense Committee was abolished and the normal party organs (Politburo, Orgburo, and Secretariat) were restored. In January 1946, the People's Commissariat for Defense and the People's Commissariat of the Navy were again combined into the People's Commissariat of the USSR Armed Forces, renamed the Ministry of the Armed Forces on March 15. In February 1946, the functions of the wartime Stavka of the Supreme Command were taken over by the Higher Military Council, consisting of Politburo and CC members and military leaders.[81]

The political administration also experienced several changes. In February 1946, it was renamed the Main Political Administration of the Soviet Armed Forces. Political administrations were also appointed for the individual service branches, which had been reorganized in January. S. F. Galadzhev became chief of the political administration of the ground forces; P. T. Lukashin, of the air forces; and A. A. Murav'yev, of the navy.[82]

Shortly after the creation of the new Ministry of the Armed Forces, Chief Marshal of Aviation A. A. Novikov and several other leading air marshals were

---

[79] Petrov, *Stroitel'stvo organov*, p. 301.

[80] Roman Kolkowicz, *The Soviet Army and the Communist Party: Institutions in Conflict* (Santa Monica, Calif.: Rand, 1966), p. 118.

[81] Petrov, *Stroitel'stvo politorganov*, p. 391.

[82] *Ibid.*, p. 392.

removed from their posts.[83] In July, Marshal G. K. Zhukov, whose fame had grown widely during the war both at home and abroad,[84] was removed from his post as the Commander-in-Chief of Ground Forces and demoted to commander of the Odessa Military District. Commenting on the significance of these events, J. Malcolm Mackintosh has noted:

> It was a sharp lesson to the High Command: in dismissing the country's most popular soldier, Stalin demonstrated to his leading military advisers that any leanings they might have had toward building up the armed forces as an independent political force would be ruthlessly crushed. Coming so soon after the disgrace of Air Marshal Novikov — and there is some evidence that a group of senior naval officers were arrested and imprisoned at the same time — Marshal Zhukov's removal was designed to frighten the military leadership into absolute obedience.[85]

Then, in 1947, Chief Marshal of Aviation Ye. A. Golovanov, chief of the heavy-bomber force, and Admiral N. G. Kuznetsov, chief of the navy, were removed.[86]

Also, in the political affairs of the armed forces under Shikin, the *zampolit* regained some of the influence lost during the war. For example, the post of deputy commander of the company for political affairs was reintroduced.[87] Also, an officer's promotion again became highly dependent on his "political reliability," as opposed to his purely military expertise. Of course, the judge of the officer's reliability was the *zampolit*. Consequently, while the *zampolit* lacked direct authority over or equal to the commander, he had significant indirect influence over the commander's actions. Shikin also gave wide authority to the three new political sections for the army, navy, and air force, which he had created.

When Zhdanov died in 1948 many of his cronies found their fortunes swiftly declining. According to one Western report, Shikin and six other leaders closely related to Zhdanov were removed between January and March 1949.[88] The six

---

[83] Raymond L. Garthoff, "The Marshals and the Party: Soviet Civil-Military Relations in the Postwar Period," in Harry L. Coles, ed., *Total War and Cold War: Problems in Civilian Control of the Military* (Columbus, Ohio: Ohio State University Press, 1962), p. 243.

[84] P. Ruslanov, "Marshal Zhukov," *Russian Review*, XV (April 1956), 122.

[85] Mackintosh, *Juggernaut*, p. 216.

[86] Garthoff, "Marshals and the Party," p. 244.

[87] Colonel Yu. Petrov, "Construction of Party Organizations of the Soviet Armed Forces," *Voyenno-Istoricheskiy Zhurnal*, No. 3 (March 1968), p. 9.

[88] Subsequently, Shikin became the chief of the Military-Political Academy imeni V. I. Lenin (1949–50) and then entered into "responsible work" in the apparatus of the CC CPSU

were M. I. Rodionov, former chairman of the RSFSR Council of Ministers; N. A. Voznesenskiy, former Politburo member; A. A. Kuznetsov, a Central Committee secretary; Yuriy Zhdanov, son of A. A. Zhdanov; P. S. Popkov, a Supreme Soviet Presidium member; and I. T. Golyakov, former chief of the Soviet Supreme Court.[89] In addition, numerous officials in the Leningrad party machine, where Zhdanov had been first secretary until 1944, were dismissed.[90]

Shikin's replacement was Colonel General Fyodor Fedotovich Kuznetsov.[91] Born in 1904 in a peasant family, he worked his way up to deputy director of a Moscow factory. In 1931, he entered into party work, becoming the first secretary of a rayon in Moscow in 1937. Joining the Red Army in 1938, Kuznetsov was appointed chief of a section and deputy chief of the political administration. In 1942–43, he served as political member of the military council of the 60th Army and then the Front, which was under the command of F. I. Golikov, who was later also a political administration chief. In 1943, Kuznetsov became the chief of the Main Administration and deputy chief of the General Staff. From 1945 to 1949, he performed "responsible work" in the General Staff.

Under Kuznetsov there were several significant alterations in the structure of the political administration. First, in January 1950, the *zampolit* was reintroduced on the company level.[92] Second, in February 1950, when the Ministry of the Armed Forces was split into separate army and naval ministries, the political administration was similarly reorganized. While Kuznetsov was retained as chief of the army political administration, Admiral S. E. Zakharov was appointed chief of the naval political administration. Although the split may have resulted in an overall lessening of the political administration's authority and influence, it appears that Kuznetsov continued as the dominant figure.

On January 13, 1953, the Soviet press announced the arrest of nine physicians, six of whom were of Jewish background. The doctors were charged with having caused the death of A. A. Zhdanov and his brother-in-law,[93] A. S.

(1950–61). In 1962–63, he was Ambassador Extraordinary and Plenipotentiary of the USSR in NRA (People's Republic of Albania). From 1962 to 1965, he served as first deputy chairman of the Committee of Party-State Control. In 1965, he became the first deputy chairman of the Committee of People's Control. *(Yezhegodnik, 1971,* p. 640.)

[89] *The New York Times,* June 19, 1949.

[90] Robert Conquest, *Power and Policy in the USSR: The Struggle for Stalin's Succession, 1945–1960* (New York: Harper & Row, 1961), p. 97.

[91] Prokhorov, ed., *Bol'shaya sovetskaya entsiklopediya,* XIII, 563.

[92] Kolkowicz, *The Soviet Army and the Communist Party,* p. 205; and Yepishev, *Partiyno-politicheskaya rabota,* p. 282.

[93] Martin Ebon, *Malenkov: Stalin's Successor* (New York: McGraw-Hill, 1953), p. 99.

Shcherbakov, the former political administration chief. They were also accused of being foreign agents and plotting to kill Marshals A. M. Vasilevskiy, L. A. Govorov, I. S. Konev, General of the Army S. M. Shtemenko, and Admiral G. I. Levchenko.

The Doctors' Plot, as this case is usually referred to, was an extremely important event in the postwar struggles of the Soviet political leadership. It most likely was a step toward another major purge. Numerous scholarly works have sought to ascertain the ultimate victim of the new purge and L. P. Beria is generally considered to have been the target.[94] For present purposes, however, it is necessary only to consider the possible implications for the military leaders.[95]

Relatively speaking, the military men named as intended victims of the doctors were individuals who were unlikely to challenge strict party control over the armed forces. On the other hand, some of the more independent-minded military leaders were not listed. This includes Marshals Zhukov and Sokolovskiy and Admiral Kuznetsov.[96] Aside from this rather obscure point, there is no evidence that the armed forces were to be a major target of a future purge. Indeed, on February 21, 1953, Sokolovskiy replaced Shtemenko as Chief of Staff. Therefore, as Conquest notes, the inclusion of military figures was probably not a major factor:

> It is true that the selection of officers as potential Doctors' Plot victims was to some extent partial, and may be taken as the equivalent of a high award, from which pointed omission could be considered a mild rebuke of warning. Yet it has never been suggested, even by Khrushchev in the Secret Speech, when he was doing his utmost to emphasize Stalin's hostility to Zhukov and others, that the purge was to involve the army. Indeed, we may thing that the "army factor" aspect, though present, was minor, and the main aim of the inclusion of the military victims was to reassure the army leadership as a whole.[97]

---

94 For example, see Janet D. Zagoria, ed., *Power and the Soviet Elite, "The Letter of an Old Bolshevik" and Other Essays by Boris I. Nicolaevsky* (New York: Praeger, 1965), p. 114; and Bertram D. Wolfe, *Khrushchev and Stalin's Ghost* (New York: Praeger, 1957), p. 195. So far, available evidence does not suggest that the death in mid-February 1953 of Lev Mekhlis, the former PUR head and politically one of the highest-ranking Jewish figures within the Stalin administration, was connected with the intrigues of the Doctors' Plot. Indeed, the extensive coverage given to Mekhlis' death (*Pravda*, February 14–16, 1953) would appear to indicate that he died in good standing.

95 It will be necessary later to return to the issue of the Doctors' Plot, because at the time A. A. Yepishev was serving as USSR Deputy Minister of State Security.

96 Robert Conquest, *Power and Policy in the USSR: The Struggle for Stalin's Succession, 1945–1960* (New York: Harper & Row, 1967), p. 168.

97 *Ibid.*, p. 169.

Before the purge (whoever its intended victims might have been) could be carried out, Stalin died on March 5, 1953. Widespread changes in leadership assignments were immediately carried out by Stalin's successors. The Presidium and the Bureau of the Presidium of the CC CPSU were combined into the Presidium of the CC CPSU, consisting of ten members and four candidates. G. M. Malenkov became both the General Secretary of the Central Committee and the Chairman of the Council of Ministers. N. S. Khrushchev was relieved of his post as first secretary of the Moscow Committee of the CPSU, supposedly in conjunction with his heavy work load in the CC Secretariat. N. A. Bulganin was appointed USSR Military Minister, with Marshals A. M. Vasilevskiy and G. K. Zhukov as first deputies. L. P. Beria took over the USSR Ministry of Internal Affairs, which now combined the work of the former USSR Minister of State Seccrity and the USSR Ministry of Internal Affairs.[98] A. N. Poskrebyshev, who is believed to have been the real impetus behind the Doctors' Plot[99] disappeared.[100] The heads of the navy political administration, who had been appointed personally by Stalin,[101] were removed and L. I. Brezhnev, the future General Secretary, was transferred to replace the chief of the political administration of the navy.[102] The army and navy ministries, split in 1950, were reunited into the Ministry of Defense of the USSR. Under this reorganization, political administrations for the individual service branches were eliminated.[103]

On April 4, Beria's Ministry of Internal Affairs issued a communiqué formally repudiating the Doctors' Plot and stating that the charges were without foundation. This move was one of a whole sequence in which Beria sought to improve his political position. Using his office as chief of the secret police, Beria attempted to gain stronger control over the party and government apparatuses. In fear of this, the other political leaders decided to remove Beria, and he was arrested on July 10. At the same time, the police generals commanding Moscow District, Moscow City, and the Kremlin garrisons were replaced by professional military men.[104] These and other changes appear to indicate that

---

[98] *Pravda*, March 7, 1953.

[99] Bertram Wolfe, p. 5.

[100] Although it was for many years assumed that Poskrebyshev had been executed, it has since been reported that he was merely sent into retirement and died quietly in 1966. See H. Montgomery Hyde, *Stalin: The History of a Dictator* (New York: Popular Library, 1971), p. 242.

[101] Abdurakhman Avtorkhanov, *Stalin and the Soviet Communist Party: A Study in the Technology of Power* (New York: Praeger, 1959), p. 261.

[102] *Pravda*, March 7, 1953.

[103] Petrov, *Stroitel'stvo politorganov*, p. 425, n. 3.

[104] Conquest, *Power and Policy*, p. 332.

the armed forces' leadership may have played a major role in Beria's removal.[105]

On July 16, 1953, the Soviets announced that a meeting of the party organization in the Ministry of Defense had been recently held. At the meeting a report on Beria's removal was made by Colonel General Aleksey Sergeyevich Zheltov, who was referred to for the first time as the head of the political administration of the armed forces.[106] The exact date of Zheltov's appointment is unknown, but it may have come as a reward to the military for its role in Beria's removal, for Zheltov's supervision of the armed forces for the next four years was relatively weak.[107] F. F. Kuznetsov and S. E. Zakharov became deputy chiefs.[108]

Born in 1904 in a worker's family, Zheltov joined the Red Army in 1924. After graduating from the 2nd Moscow Infantry School in 1927, he was appointed commander of a platoon, and then assistant commander of a company. In 1929, he joined the Party. Subsequently, he commanded an infantry company and then a training sub-unit. In 1934, he entered the Military Academy imeni M. V. Frunze, which he successfully completed in 1937. Upon graduation, Zheltov was appointed a division commissar. Completing further military-political courses in 1938, he was made a member of the Military Council of the Volga Military District. From February to August 1941, he was a member of the Military Council of the Far Eastern Front. During the war, Zheltov served as the political representative on the Karel Front (September 1941–July 1942), the 63rd Army (July–September 1942), the Don Front (October 1942), the South Western Front (October 1942–October 1943), and the 3rd Ukrainian Front (October 1943–June 1945). He participated in the battle of Stalingrad, as well as the liberation of the Ukraine, Moldavia, Rumania, Bulgaria, Hungary, Yugoslavia, and Austria. After the war, Zheltov served as Konev's deputy on the Allied Control Commission in Austria and member of the Military Council of the Central Group of of Forces (1945–50). In 1950–51, he was a member of the Military Council of the Turkestan Military District. From January 1951 to April 1953, Zheltov was chief of the Main Cadres Administration of the Soviet Army.

105 For a discussion of the changes, see "Beria Trial Shows Army's Rising Role," by Harry Schwartz in *The New York Times*, December 24, 1953.

106 *The Times* (London), July 17, 1953.

107 Kolkowicz, *The Soviet Army and the Communist Party*, p. 127.

108 After 1953, Kuznetsov was appointed chief of the Main Cadres Administration of the Ministry of Defense (1953–57), chief of the Military-Political Academy imeni V. I. Lenin (1957–59), and a member of the Military Council and chief of the political administration of the Northern Group of Forces (1959–69). In 1969, Kuznetsov entered into retirement. (Prokhorov, ed., *Bol'shaya sovetskaya entsiklopediya*, XIII, 563.)

The Rise and Fall of Marshal Zhukov

A major obstacle to Zheltov's effectiveness as head of the political administration of the armed forces was the appointment of Marshal Zhukov to the post of Deputy Minister of Defense in 1953 and then Minister of Defense in 1955, when Bulganin became the Soviet Premier. Even during World War II, Zhukov made it quite clear that he resented the interference of the political administration in military affairs. On a personal level, he was particularly resentful toward Bulganin and Zheltov, who had both been political officers under Zhukov on the Western Front.[109] From 1953 to 1955, Bulganin was able to limit Zhukov's influence, but as Defense Minister Zhukov reasserted his position.

Under Zhukov's example, professional military leaders began to debate with the Party on three major issues: (1) the Stalinist trend of crediting the Party and Stalin for the military victory in World War II, (2) the stagnation that Stalin had imposed on military thought, and (3) the authority of political officers over the commander. In the first instance, the military leaders sought to win greater praise for their role in the War. This was entwined with the second, which sought to gain for military leaders a freer reign in determining Soviet military doctrine.[110]

The debate on military doctrine concerned Stalin's five so-called "permanently operating factors for victory." These were: stability in the rear, morale of the army, quantity and quality of army divisions, armaments of the army, and organizational and leadership ability of the command personnel. One of the major issues of the debate concerned the factor of surprise, which under Stalin's scheme constituted a "transitory" factor.[111] Various articles by Rotmistrov, Sokolovskiy, and others suggested that surprise had become an extremely important factor in modern warfare.[112] They also suggested that there was a

[109] Janet Zagoria, p. 236.

[110] Commenting on the relationship between historical credit and present-day prestige, one writer noted in 1957: "Another element of maneuver among the military leaders has followed the attempts to restore the credit of Stalin and the improvement of the status of the military, the restoration of due historic credit has begun. But precisely because it is a matter of history, it has become one of politics. For, as has often been observed, in the Soviet Union history is indeed the projection of the present into the past." (Raymond Garthoff. "The Role of the Military in Recent Soviet Politics," *Russian Review*, XVI, No. 2 [April 1957], 19.)

[111] Kenneth R. Whiting, "The Past and Present of Soviet Military Doctrine," *Air University Quarterly Review*, XI, No. 1 (Spring 1959), 48.

[112] *Ibid.*; and Thomas W. Wolfe, *Soviet Power and Europe 1945–1970* (Baltimore: The Johns Hopkins University Press, 1970), p. 60, n. 40.

growing need to study the military doctrines and lessons of foreign capitalist countries.[113] just as Trotsky had once advanced against the Gusev-Frunze group.

Under Zhukov's leadership, the military leaders also sought to lessen the Party's control through the political administration. In September 1955, the role of the political administration was redefined and reduced to emphasis on morale building and indoctrination. At the same time, Zhukov made two moves in attempting to limit further the political administration's effectiveness. First, he re-created under his supervision the political administrations for the Ground Forces, Air Force, Navy, and National Air Defense (PVO strany) in April 1955.[114] Second, he is alleged to have prohibited the political administration from retaining direct contact with the Party Central Committee.[115]

Other moves by Zhukov in the second half of 1955 further curtailed the influence and role of the political administration. The *zampolit* now had less control over the leisure-time activities of the military men. Officers could substitute combat training for political education, and the study of ideology and party history became voluntary. Criticism of the officers' actions was severely limited. On the company level, the *zampolit* was abolished. Many political organs were liquidated; one third in the navy alone. The number of students of the Military-Political Academy and in political preparation courses was sharply reduced.[116]

In the pre-20th CPSU Congress party conferences in the armed forces that started in December 1955, Zhukov again led the military men in an attack on the political apparatus. Of the military elite, it appears that only Marshal Chuykov refrained from severely criticizing the work of the political administration. According to Boris Nicolaevsky, the major line of criticism was that "political propaganda was not specific enough, not sufficiently relevant to military training, and not coordinated with the work of the officers."[117] Whereas the main report of the military district was traditionally delivered by the political officers, it was a mark of the political officer's reduced status that the main reports were given at these conferences by the commanders of the districts.[118] Zhukov's own speech

---

113 Whiting, "Past and Present of Soviet Military Doctrine," p. 49.

114 Petrov, *Stroitel'stvo politorganov*, p. 426.

115 *Ibid.*, p. 435.

116 *Ibid.*, pp. 435–36; and Otto Preston Chaney, Jr., *Zhukov* (Norman: University of Oklahoma Press, 1971), p. 384.

117 Janet Zagoria, p. 236.

118 Nikolai Galay, "Military Representation in the Higher Party Echelons," *Bulletin*, Institute for the Study of the USSR, III, No. 4 (April 1956), 10.

before the Moscow military okrug again emphasized the subordination of the political worker to the commander. Zhukov asserted:

> In the okrug, certain efforts have been made to subject the official activity of commanders to criticism at [party] meetings. Such efforts are reprehensible. Our task is the comprehensive strengthening of the authority of the commanders, giving support to exacting officers and generals.[119]

The 20th Party Congress that followed was clearly a victory for the professional element of the armed forces. At the previous Party Congress, two members of the political administration hierarchy had been elected to candidate membership in the Party Central Committee, namely, Colonel General F. F. Kuznetsov of the army political apparatus and Admiral S. E. Zakharov of the navy political apparatus. No political administration officials were elected to the Party Central Committee at the 20th Party Congress.[120] Kuznetsov was demoted to the Auditing Commission; Zakharov and Zheltov, the new chief of the political administration, were omitted from the Central Committee altogether.[121]

Professional military men fared much better at the 20th Party Congress. In addition to the "political" Marshals Bulganin and Voroshilov, full members of the Central Committee were Konev, Malinovsky, Maskalenko, Sokolovskiy, Vasilevskiy, and Zhukov. Candidate members were Bagramyan, Biryuzov, Budennyy, Chuykov, Yeremenko, Garbatov, Gorshkov, Grechko, Luchinskiy, Nedelin, Timoshenko, and Zhigarev. Moreover, the personal position of Marshal Zhukov significantly improved.

During the Congress, Marshal Zhukov chaired a special meeting for military delegates. Held two days before Khrushchev's famous de-Stalinization speech, the special meeting was ostensibly convoked to mark Soviet Army Day. It is not unlikely, however, as Brzezinski and Huntington have suggested, that Zhukov also used this occasion to win the military's support for de-Stalinization and the rehabilitation of Stalin's military victims.[122] This would explain the great lengths to which Khrushchev went to impugn Stalin's "military genius"

---

[119] Quoted in Merle Fainsod, *How Russia Is Ruled* (Cambridge, Mass.: Harvard University Press, 1963), pp. 483–84.

[120] For a list and analysis of military men (professional and political) elected at the 19th and 20th Party Congresses, see Galay, "Military Representation in the Higher Party Echelons," pp. 6–7.

[121] Conquest, *Power and Policy* , pp. 336–37.

[122] Zbigniew Brzezinski and Samuel P. Huntington, *Political Power: USA/USSR* (New York: Viking Press, 1964), p. 346.

and to credit Soviet military leaders for reversing early war losses. In the so-called Secret Speech to the 20th Party Congress, Khrushchev described Stalin's unwillingness to accept or admit error for military defeats:

> On one occasion after the war, during a meeting of Stalin with members of the Political Bureau, Anastas Ivanovich Mikoyan mentioned that Khrushchev must have been right when he telephoned concerning the Kharkov operation and that it was unfortunate that his suggestion had not been accepted.
>
> You should have seen Stalin's fury! How could it be admitted that he, Stalin, had not been right. He is after all a "genius" and a genius cannot help but be right! Everyone can err, but Stalin considered that he never erred, that he was always right. . . . After the Party Congress we shall probably have to re-evaluate many wartime military operations and to present them in their true light.[123]

Khrushchev went on to note that Stalin's military errors cost many Soviet lives. This situation changed only when the generals were able to take firmer control. In this sense, the generals were ultimately victorious despite Stalin.

Khrushchev also singled out Marshal Zhukiv for praise in stating that Stalin had been particularly degrading toward Zhukov. Of course Khrushchev had defended Zhukov. In the Secret Speech, Khrushchev describes the following incident with regard to Zhukov.

> Stalin was very much interested in the assessment of Comrade Zhukov as a military leader. He asked me often for my opinion of Zhukov. I told him then, "I have known Zhukov for a long time; he is a good general and a good military leader."
>
> After the war Stalin began to tell all kinds of nonsense about Zhukov, among others the following: "You praised Zhukov, but he does not deserve it. It is said that before each operation at the front Zhukov used to behave as follows: He used to take a handful of earth, smell it and say, 'We can begin the attack,' or the opposite, 'The planned operation cannot be carried out,'" I stated at that time, "Comrade Stalin, I do not know who invented this, but it is not true."
>
> It is possible that Stalin himself invented these things for the purpose of minimizing the role and military talents of Marshal Zhukov.[124]

The ultimate mark of the rising influence of the military in general and

---

123 Nikita S. Khrushchev, *The Crimes of the Stalin Era: Special Report to the 20th Congress of the Communist Party of the Soviet Union*, annotated by Boris I. Nicolaevsky (New York: New Leader, 1962), p. S42.

124 *Ibid.*

Zhukov in particular and the declining influence of the political administration was the appointment of Marshal Zhukov as a candidate member of the Party's Central Committee Presidium.[125] In the past, a few "political" generals such as Bulganin and Voroshilov had attained Presidium membership; during the war, A. S. Shcherbakov, the chief of the political administration of the armed forces, had been a member.[126] With Zhukov's appointment, however, this was the first instance of a truly professional military man achieving a position in the Party's highest decision-making body.

It is apparent from events in the next year and a half that Marshal Zhukov viewed his appointment as a signal to open a new campaign for increased military professionalism. In late April 1956, while Khrushchev and Bulganin were in Great Britain, Zhukov assembled senior army political officers for a conference in Moscow. According to Soviet media reports, the main theme of the conference was the need for "radically improving" political work in the armed forces.[127] On April 26, *Krasnaya Zvezda* reported that in his speech Zhukov had urged political officers to put military work above ideological work. Zhukov asserted:

> The task of propaganda consists not only in explaining the theory of Marxism-Leninism, but also in contributing to its practical implementation. The theoretical side of propaganda work must give more space to the problems . . . connected with practical tasks of the troops. . . . A political officer who does not know his military duty cannot cope with the tasks which are set him.[128]

The conflict over the function of political workers in the armed forces appears to have been particularly intense in the first part of 1957. Beginning in February, a draft Instruction for party-political organizations in the armed forces was debated in the Secretariat, twice in the Presidium of the Party CC, in sections of the Party CC, and finally in a specially appointed commission of the Party CC, consisting of Presidium members and candidates A. B. Aristov, N. I. Belyayev, L. I. Brezhnev, P. N. Pospelov, M. A. Suslov, and Ye. A. Furtseva.[129] It was not until April 1957 that it was possible to reach a sufficient consensus to replace the 1947 "Thesis on the Political Organs of the Armed Forces of the USSR,"

---

[125] In 1952, the Central Committee Politburo had been renamed the Presidium, and would be renamed the Politburo in 1966.

[126] Of course, Shcherbakov's influence was derived from more factors than merely his position as head of the political administration. However, that such a high-ranking leader should be appointed to head the political administration was significant.

[127] *The Times* (London), April 27, 1956.

[128] Quoted in Fainsod, *How Russia Is Ruled*, p. 484.

[129] Petrov, *Stroitel'stvo politorganov*, p. 429.

which had given increased authority to political organs, by new "Instructions to the CPSU Organizations in the Soviet Army and Navy." Very little is known about the 1947 Theses because they have never been published in full and their very existence was not made known until June 13, 1957, when they were cited in the navy journal *Sovetskiy Flot*.[130] Similarly, the 1957 Instructions have not been published in full, but there have been several abstracts and commentaries in the Soviet military press. *Krasnaya Zvezda* of May 12, 1957, for example, stated:

> In the Soviet Army the commander guides all combat and political preparations and education of his personnel. The instructions emphasize that Party organizations must be responsible in every way for strengthening the unity of command and the authority of commanders and chiefs.
>
> Political organs and Party organizations must actively support the orders of commanders, protect the authority of the commander, train personnel to obey and execute orders. The Party Central Committee points out in the instructions: "At Party meetings, criticism of orders and decrees of commanders is not permitted." It is necessary to execute strictly these demands of the instructions and to conduct a struggle with those who attempt to undermine the firmness of orders and decrees of a commander.[131]

Therefore, while the Party was formally to retain its paramount role, this abstract indicates that the commander was now to regain responsibility for both military and political training and that the commander would now be free from criticism from his subordinates. In addition, the commander could exempt senior or technical officers from political indoctrination sessions.[132]

As a result of the unsuccessful attempt of the "anti-Party group" to remove Khrushchev in June 1957, Zhukov's status again sharply improved. Having been removed from the Central Committee by a 7 to 4 vote of the Politburo, Khrushchev, with the aid of Zhukov, convoked a meeting of the full Central Committee. Zhukov used his military authority and facilities to bring to Moscow in a short time many of the loyal Khrushchev supporters. He is even reported to have declared in a speech before the full Committee that the army would not allow Khrushchev's removal.[133] When the full Committee voted, Khrushchev

130 Garthoff, "Marshals and the Party," p. 264, n. 4.

131 Quoted in Howard R. Swearer, *The Politics of Succession in the USSR: Materials on Khrushchev's Rise to Leadership* (Boston: Little, Brown, 1964), p. 248.

132 Mackintosh, *Juggernaut*, p. 295.

133 Chaney, p. 399.

was able to retain his position and gain the expulsion of his rivals. As a reward for his support to Khrushchev, Zhukov was promoted to full Presidium membership.

Once the "anti-Party group" was removed, the military, led by Zhukov, posed the only organized threat to Khrushchev's otherwise uninhibited rule. Indeed, Zhukov now spoke publicly on issues that were not traditionally within the scope of military leaders. For example, he was overzealous in his criticism of the "anti-Party group,"[134] a fact which might eventually harm the Party's rule in general. He also opposed Khrushchev's plans for economic decentralization and any attempts by the Party to de-emphasize the heavy-industry sector upon which the military was highly dependent for armaments.[135] "In short," notes Garthoff facetiously, "since military and political strategy must be integrated, Zhukov wanted to do some of the integrating. But so did Khrushchev, and the outcome is well known."[136]

On October 4, 1957, Zhukov was sent on a state visit to Yugoslavia. On October 18, editorials in the Soviet military press began to call for the increased use of criticism and self-criticsm in party meetings within the armed forces.[137] On the next day, Zheltov delivered a speech before the Central Committee Presidium concerning the condition of political work in the armed forces and severely blamed Zhukov for its inferior quality.[138] As the first of Zhukov's accusers, Zheltov re-emerged from the low status to which he had been relegated by Zhukov. The Presidium thereupon noted the need for improving party work in the armed forces.

Zhukov returned from his trip abroad on October 26. In *Pravda*, it was tersely announced that Marshal of the Soviet Union R. Ya. Malinovsky had replaced Zhukov as Minister of Defense. Since Zhukov briefly retained his Presidium membership, there was some speculation that he was moving upward.[139]

On November 3, a *Pravda* article officially announced that Zhukov had been removed from all Central Committee offices at a plenum of the Central Committee. One of the major charges against Zhukov was that he created a personality cult at the expense of party work in the armed forces. According to the Soviet report:

[134] *Ibid.*, pp. 402–3.

[135] Carl A. Linden, *Khrushchev and the Soviet Leadership, 1957–1964* (Baltimore: The Johns Hopkins University Press, 1966), pp. 52–53.

[136] Garthoff, "Marshals and the Party," p. 257.

[137] Kolkowicz, *The Soviet Army and the Communist Party*, pp. 214–15.

[138] Petrov, *Stroitel'stvo politorganov*, p. 434.

[139] *The Times* (London), October 28, 1957.

The plenary meeting of the CPSU Central Committee notes that of late the ex-defense minister Comrade Zhukov has violated the Leninist, party principles of guiding the armed forces, pursued a policy of curtailing the work of party organizations, political organs and military councils, of abolishing the leadership and control of the party, its Central Committee and government over the army and navy.

The plenary meeting of the Central Committee has established that the cult of Comrade Zhukov's personality was cultivated in the Soviet army with his personal participation. With the help of sycophants and flatterers, he was raised to the sky in lectures and reports, in articles, films and pamphlets, and his person and role in the great patriotic war were overglorified.

Thereby, to please Comrade Zhukov, the true history of the war was distorted, the actual state of affairs was presented in a wrong light, the stupendous efforts of the Soviet people were minimized, as well as the valor of all our armed forces, the role of their commanders and political workers, the military skill of the commanders of fronts, armies, fleets, the leading and inspiring role of the Communist Party of the Soviet Union.[140]

The report also observed that Zhukov had misinterpreted the high recognition given to him by the Party. As a consequence, it was charged that Zhukov

... took a wrong view of these high tributes to his services, lost the Communist modesty which Lenin taught us, imagined that he was the sole hero of all the victories achieved by our people and their armed forces under the Communist Party's leadership and began flagrantly violating the Leninist party principles of leadership of the armed forces. In this way Zhukov failed to live up to the party's trust. He proved to be a politically unsound person, inclining to adventurism both in his understanding of the prime objective of the Soviet Union's foreign policy and in his leadership of the Ministry of Defense.[141]

In turn, Zhukov was severely criticized by former friends and opponents in the military elite.[142] The sharpest criticism came from Marshal Konev, a longtime rival of Zhukov. Konev asserted in a *Pravda* article of November 3 that by his erroneous actions Zhukov "lowered Party organizations to the level of purely educational agencies" and consequently "the activity of Party organizations and their independent work were downgraded."[143] Then, after describing Zhukov's

140 Quoted in the *Washington Post and Times Herald*, November 3, 1957.

141 Quoted in *ibid*.

142 For a fuller analysis of the charges against Zhukov, see Paul M. Cocks, "The Purge of Marshal Zhukov," *Slavic Review*, XXII, No. 3 (September 1963), 483–98.

143 Quoted in Swearer, p. 254.

blunders and misrepresentations with regard to World War II, Konev declared:

> During a period when the entire Party and people were waging a struggle
> against the consequences of the cult of an individual, Comrade Zhukov, as an
> exceptionally vain person without Party modesty, used his position as Minister
> of Defense to spread the cult of his personality among the armed forces. He
> ignored the best traditions of Party work in the army and navy, instituted
> blatant rule by administrative fiat and tried to decide all matters personally.
> Criticsm and self-criticism in Party organizations of the armed forces were all
> but abandoned, and a halo of glory and infallibility was artificially created
> around Zhukov's person, with his participation.[144]

In the wake of Zhukov's removal, the party leadership sought to improve
political work in the armed forces. Yet to reaffirm the authority of the political
administration too abruptly would have incurred opposition from the same
military elements upon which Khrushchev had depended for Zhukov's removal.
Khrushchev decided, therefore, to have the new campaign for improved political work carried into effect by a figure who would be more acceptable to his
military supporters. Ironically, then, despite being Zhukov's initial denouncer,
Zheltov fell with his antagonist.[145]

On January 14, 1958, Soviet spokesmen confirmed for Western reporters
that Zheltov had "recently" been replaced as head of the political administration by Colonel General Filipp Ivanovich Golikov.[146] Joining the Party in 1918,
Golikov fought in the Civil War on the side of the Bolsheviks. Up to 1921, he
served in party political work, and then transferred to command posts. In 1931,
he was appointed commander of an infantry regiment and in 1933 commander
of an infantry division in the Volga Military District. In 1939, as commander
of the 6th Army, he participated in the invasion of the western Ukraine. In
July 1940, he became Deputy Chief of the General Staff. At the outset of World
War II, Golikov led a special military delegation to the United States for nego-
tiating Lend-Lease aid. Subsequently, he commanded the 10th Army (after
October 1941), which was one of the seven armies defending Moscow; the 4th

---

144 Quoted in *ibid.*, pp. 255–56.

145 Subsequently, Zheltov headed a section of the CC CPSU (1958–59) and served for twelve
years as head of the Military-Political Academy imeni V. I. Lenin (June 1959–December 1971).
At the end of 1971, he became a consultant for the Group of General Inspectors of the Ministry
of Defense. (*Voyenno-Istoricheskiy Zhurnal*, No. 10 [October 1974], pp. 43–44).

146 Prokhorov, ed., *Bol'shaya sovetskaya entsiklopediya*, VII, 16; and Colonel General A.
Rodimtsev, "In the Service of the Country," *Voyenno-Istoricheskiy Zhurnal*, No. 7 (July 1970)
pp. 43–46.

Shock Army (after February 1942); the Bryansk Front (after April 1942); and the Voronezh Front (after July 1942). Between August and October 1942, he commanded the 1st Guards Army and served as deputy commander of the South Eastern (later Stalingrad) and North Western fronts. In October 1942, he became the commander of the Voronezh Front. In April 1943, Golikov was appointed Deputy People's Commissar of Defense for Cadres. In October 1944, he received the added post of agent of the Council of People's Commissars for the reparation of Soviet citizens. For the two years previous to becoming MPA chief, Golikov was the head of the Military Academy of Armored Troops. At the time of his appointment as political administration chief in January 1958, it was observed that Golikov was not widely known outside the Soviet Union, but that he was the author of a history of World War II, "in which Zhukov's role is only once mentioned, and in which the main credit for the Soviet victory over Germany is ascribed to Stalin's leadership."[147]

It can be said, therefore, that Golikov had several factors in his background which would make him acceptable to the various contending elements. He was a successful military commander and was closely associated with the Stalingrad-related group of military men who came to prominence under Khrushchev.[148] He also had fifteen years of experience in political work in the armed forces. Moreover, as the former chief of personnel, Golikov undoubtedly commanded great loyalty from the leading figures in the political administration hierarchy. Khrushchev probably believed that the appointment of Golikov would satisfy (and thereby win him support from) both the military and the political leaders of the armed forces.

Under these new conditions, a campaign to increase the influence of the Party and the authority of the political officers in the armed forces was launched in 1958. In February, sixty-nine political workers were promoted to the general and admiral ranks.[149] In April, the political administration was renamed the Main Political Administration of the Soviet Army and Navy. In the same month, military councils for the individual service branches were re-established and the deputy chiefs of the political administrations were appointed members of the councils. The post of first deputy head of the political administration or sections was introduced. In August, the staffs of the military councils of districts, groups of forces, fleets, armies, and flotillas were expanded.

---

147 *The Times* (London), January 15, 1958.

148 For an extensive discussion of the Stalingrad Group of military commanders and their relationship to Nikita Khrushchev, see Kolkowicz, *The Soviet Army and the Communist Party*, pp. 574–92.

149 Petrov, *Stroitel'stvo politorganov*, p. 453.

In October, the Central Committee of the Party issued a new set of instructions for political organs in the armed forces, which were designed to raise considerably the authority of the political administration. To ensure their effectiveness the new instructions had passed through an examination of the Party CC Secretariat, the Presidium of the Party CC, as well as a special commission of the Party CC consisting of F. I. Golikov, A. S. Zheltov, N. G. Ignatov, R. Ya. Malinovsky, and M. A. Suslov.[150] The new instructions drew attention to the fact that the Communist Party is the chief source of the Soviet military's power. They also called upon political workers "to strengthen the military power of the Soviet Army and Navy, to ensure the daily and undivided influence of the Party in all life and activity of the armed forces, and to rally the personnel around the Communist Party and the Soviet Government."[151] The political workers were also urged to work for the restoration of "Leninist norms" in military affairs. As summarized in one Soviet source, this meant that the political worker was obliged

> . . . to lead the party organizations . . . to develop the initiative and activity of every party organization in fulfillment of the resolutions and tasks supplied by the Communist Party, to develop criticism and self-criticism in party organizations, and scientifically to scrutinize in the *aktivs* on all sides the military and political training of the troops, to know its condition, and in every way possible to assist in raising its military preparedness.[152]

An important aspect of these new instructions was that the commander was again open to criticism. Moreover, the political workers now regained control over the political training of the troops. Officers' attendance at political education sessions was made mandatory.

In 1959, Golikov introduced a new policy for interchanging military and political personnel. He also made clear that an officer's promotion would depend on political as well as military knowledge. Consequently, opposition to the political administration could result in dismissal or the loss of a promotion. These threats were intensified by the removal of many officers in the wake of Zhukov's ouster, and the appointment of political officers in numerous cases to fill these command posts.

---

[150] *Ibid.*, p. 446.

[151] *Ibid.*, p. 444.

[152] *Ibid.*, p. 445.

3

The Main Political Administration and the Soviet Army and Navy under Khrushchev's Regime

The MPA and the Party-Military Debate: From January 1960 to May 1962

At the 4th Session of the USSR Supreme Soviet, held on January 14, 1960, Nikita Khrushchev observed that in 1955 Soviet armed forces had employed 5,763,000 men, but this figure had been reduced over the next three years to 3,623,000 men. He proposed that this level be further reduced to 2,423,000 men, a reduction of 1,200,000 men. Khrushchev disclaimed the possibility that the reduction of the troop level was an economic necessity or that it would endanger the defense capabilities of the Soviet Union. He said rather:

> Our confidence in the correctness of the proposed measures is based on the fact that the Soviet country is going through a period of unparalleled rough development of the whole national economy. It is based on the indestructible moral-political solidarity of the Soviet public. Soviet scientists, engineers, and workers have insured the possibility of equipping our army with types of weapons, which were hitherto unknown to people: atomic, hydrogen, rocket, and other modern weapons. The development of our economy, the achievements of scientists and technical thought — these have created the conditions for the decision to reduce the armed forces.[1]

Khruschhev next observed that older forms of military methods and equip-

---

[1] N. S. Khrushchev, "Disarmament Is the Path to the Strengthening of Peace and Securing Friendship among Peoples," *O vnesheniy politike Sovetskogo Soyuza, 1960 god (On the Foreign Policy of the Soviet Union, 1960)* (Moscow: State Publishing House for Political Literature, 1961), p. 35.

ment had been made obsolete by the introduction of nuclear weapons and missiles. He stated:

> The military air force and navy have lost their previous importance in view of the modern development of military equipment. This type of armament is not being reduced but replaced. Almost the entire military air force is being replaced by rocket equipment. We have by now sharply cut, and it seems will further reduce and even discontinue, the manufacture of bombers and other obsolete equipment. In the navy, the submarine fleet assumes great importance, while surface ships can no longer play the part they once did. In our country the armed forces have been to a considerable extent transferred to rocket and nuclear arms.[2]

Similarly, Khrushchev asserted that the improved quality of the new weapons appeared to make mass armies obsolete. The new weapons, therefore, permitted troop reduction without endangering defense levels. As he maintained:

> The Central Committee of the Communist Party and the Soviet Government can report to you, comrade deputies, that the arms we now possess are formidable; and those which are, so to speak about to appear, are even more perfect, even more formidable. The arms being designed and, so to speak, in the portfolios of scientists and designers are incredible arms.
>
> All of you, comrade deputies, will probably agree that one cannot now approach the problem of the numerical strength of the army as one did just a few years ago. Suffice it to say that from 1955 the numerical strength of the armed forces in our country has been cut by one-third while its firepower — thanks to the introduction and development of the latest types of modern military equipment — increased many times during the same period.
>
> In our time the defense potential of the country is not determined by the number of our soldiers under arms, by the number of persons in naval uniform. If one is to divert one's attention from the general political and economic factors to which I referred earlier, the defense potential of the country, to a decisive extent, depends on the total firepower and the means of delivery available to the given side.
>
> The proposed reduction will in no way weaken the firepower of our armed forces, and this is the main point.[3]

Khrushchev, moreover, pointed out that under present conditions modern wars

[2] *Ibid.*, p. 36.

[3] *Ibid.*, pp. 36–37.

would little resemble previous wars. In the past, states concentrated their troops along their borders. To invade another state, it was necessary to begin by attacking their troops. Now, however, as Khrushchev observed, missiles made it possible to bypass the border forces and strike directly "the heart of the warring countries."[4]

One consequence of this new method of warfare, suggested Khrushchev, might be the future introduction of a militia army. He revealed that the transformation to a territorial system was once again being studied and considered. In this regard, he noted:

> Looking into the future one can predict that we can have military units formed on the territorial principle. Their personnel will be trained in military matters without an interruption of production, and, when necessary, equipment will make it possible to concentrate troops at the required place on our territory.[5]

In a speech to the same Supreme Soviet, Marshal of the Soviet Union R. Ya. Malinovsky, the USSR Minister of Defense, praised the troop reduction as a "quite sound and timely measure."[6] He also claimed that the Soviet Union possessed a "sufficient" number of nuclear weapons, which he described as "the most effective of all previously existing and present means of warfare,"[7] to ensure Soviet defenses. In these regards, Malinovsky had largely reiterated Khrushchev's position, but his view of wartime operations, while not denigrating missiles, placed a relatively greater stress on the importance of diverse types of troops than did Khrushchev. Malinovsky explained to the Supreme Soviet delegates that:

> The rocket troops of our armed forces are undoubtedly the main type of armed forces. However, we understand that it is not possible to solve all tasks of war by one type of troop. Therefore, preceding from the premise that the successful carrying out of military actions in a modern war are only possible on the basis of a unified use of all means of armed fighting and the combining of the efforts of all types of armed forces, we are retaining at a definite strength and in relevant sound proportions all types of our armed forces whose military operations, as far as their organization and their means of action are concerned, will resemble what took place in the past war.[8]

[4] *Ibid.*, p. 47.

[5] *Ibid.*, p. 53.

[6] Soviet Home Service, January 15, 1960, 1125 GMT, FBIS, *USSR and East Europe*, No. 2 (January 15, 1960), p. 15.

[7] *Ibid.*, p. 14.

[8] *Ibid.*, p. 15.

In this way, Malinovsky contradicted Khrushchev on what would become one of the most sensitive issues in Soviet military affairs over the next few years, namely, the size of the armed forces. The two sides reflected two opposing approaches to the tasks of national defense. Emphasizing reliance on missiles along with troop reduction, the Khrushchev position at the same time maintained greater confidence in the possibilities for peace and in finding shortcuts to national security. Emphasizing a more balanced or unified approach, the Malinovsky stance, on the contrary, expressed greater fear for the possibilities of war and the belief that all means of warfare should be retained.[9]

Quite probably, Khrushchev expected only minor opposition from the military leadership on the troop reduction issue, because the leadership consisted mainly of members of the so-called Stalingrad Group and most of the post-Zhukov military leaders owed their positions — and thereby their loyalty — to him.[10] Indeed, the only military leaders who did not give at least qualified public support to the troop reduction were the two remaining holdovers from the Zhukov era, Marshals Sokolovskiy and Konev. In April 1960, these two were removed from their positions and replaced by members of the Stalingrad Group. Now, all the major posts of the High Command were filled by members of this clique.[11] Consequently, by removing his major opponents, Khrushchev was temporarily able to secure the support of his already generally loyal military chiefs.

Another major step in the Party's attempt to limit military opposition to troop reduction and to reassert party authority over the military was the 4th All-Army Conference of Secretaries of Party Organizations held in Moscow from May 11 to May 14, 1960.[12] Participating in the conference were three Central Committee Presidium members: L. I. Brezhnev, N. G. Ignatov, and M. A. Suslov.

[9] Matthew P. Gallagher, "Military Manpower: A Case Study," *Problems of Communism*, XIII, No. 3 (May–June 1964), 54.

[10] Roman Kolkowicz, *The Soviet Army and the Communist Party: Institutions in Conflict* (Santa Monica, Calif.: Rand, 1966), p. 244. "Stalingrad Group" refers to the bloc of top military leaders who had in common the fact that they all served on the Stalingrad Front. This group retained its close personal ties after the war. In addition, Khrushchev, who also served on the Stalingrad Front as a political officer, developed close ties with the group and installed many of the group in the armed forces' highest positions after he became First Secretary of the CPSU.

[11] Raymond L. Garthoff, *Soviet Military Policy: A Historical Analysis* (New York: Praeger, 1966), p. 55.

[12] For a short summary of the four All-Army Conferences, see "All-Army Conference of Secretaries of Party Organizations," *Kommunist Vooruzhennykh Sil*, No. 7 (April 1973), pp. 81–85. The three previous conferences were held in 1925, 1928, and 1931. The fifth and latest conference was convened in March 1973.

A total of 214 persons spoke at the conference, including Marshal Malinovsky, whose speech was entitled "On the Task of the Further Development and Improvement in the Combat Readiness of the Armed Forces," and Marshal Golikov,[13] who delivered an address, "On the State and Further Tasks of Party Work in the Armed Forces." Brezhnev's speech was not published and only vague summaries of the main reports by Malinovsky and Golikov appeared in the military press.[14] From the meager evidence available, however, it is possible to identify two major concerns of the conference.

First, the conference sought a reorganization and intensification of party work in the armed forces. The objective was "to reform the structure of army and navy party organizations, to heighten the role of primary organizations, and to bring them closer to the personnel.[15] Companies and battalions were given the rights of shop organizations, while the regimental bureau obtained the rights of party committees.

Secondly, the newly intensified political work was to emphasize the technical aspects of military affairs. In addition to such common activities as indoctrinational work, criticism and self-criticism, and competition, the resolution of the conference stated that the basic attention of the party organizations in the armed forces

> . . . is to be focused on the greatest possible rise in the vigilance and combat readiness of the troops, and a correct combination of military, political, technical, and other kinds and branches of arms, the new equipment and arms, as well as the new methods and means of combat.[16]

Consequently, while political work was intensified, it was being used more and more to raise the combat effectiveness of troops and to strengthen discipline.

In sum, a number of important changes had taken place in the first part of 1960. First, Khrushchev had introduced a new military doctrine based on nuclear weapons and troop reduction. Second, he had removed his main military antagonists, Marshals Sokolovskiy and Konev. Third, general party activity in the military was intensified. Fourth, the new activity attempted to take into account

---

13 Golikov was appointed marshal on May 8, 1960.

14 Michel Tatu, *Power in the Kremlin. From Khrushchev to Kosygin* (New York: Viking Press, 1972), p. 75.

15 Yu. P. Petrov, *Stroitel'stvo politorganov, partiynykh i komsomol'skikh organizatsiy armii i flota (1918–1968) (The Construction of Political Organs and Party and Komsomol Organizations in the Army and Navy [1918–1968])* (Moscow: Voyenizdat, 1968), p. 461.

16 "All-Army Conference of Secretaries of Party Organizations," p. 85.

the complexity of shifting to nuclear weaponry and the political worker was supposed to give greater support to purely professional matters. The last two factors contain elements of contradiction — to increase party work and authority, but to subordinate this work and authority to professional military interests — and indeed appear to represent a compromise between the Party and loyal military leaders.

The balance between the political and military branches was disrupted, however, by the U-2 Affair of May 1960. On May 1, a U.S. reconnaissance plane was shot down over Soviet territory and the pilot was captured. Ignorant of the latter fact, the U.S. State Department issued a weak cover story claiming that the flight was for weather research purposes. Subsequently, Khrushchev revealed that in addition to the pilot the plane's photographic equipment had been captured, but he seggested that President Eisenhower, with whom he was supposed to meet in a summit conference on May 16, probably knew nothing about the flight. However, Eisenhower responded with the public admission that the United States had indeed been overflying the Soviet Union with his full knowledge.

Military spokesmen, especially Malinovsky, used this opportunity as an excuse to heap criticism on the "belligerent policies" of the United States, and thereby indirectly on Khrushchev's attempts at Soviet-American détente. Détente had been a natural consequence of troop reductions and Khrushchev's emphasis on economic competition with the West. Malinovsky now asserted that U.S. intentions were becoming increasingly belligerent. On May 31, for example, Malinovsky expressed his belief that the imperialists "are only waiting for a favorable opportunity to attack the Soviet Union and the other socialist countries, and the only thing that stops them is the risk of the total destruction if imperial ism."[17] Quite clearly, the implication was that the Soviet Union could not reduce any of its forces at the very time when the imperialist threat was growing more dangerous.

Against this background, Khrushchev set forth some suggestions in January 1961 at a CPSU Central Committee plenum toward a proposal for allocating greater resources for agricultural production. He warned of "dangerous consequences" if the Soviet economy could not satisfy the rising consumer demand for goods. As he noted:

> The growth of real wages will continue in the future, consequently the population's demand for foodstuffs and consumer goods will increase as well, and this is in accordance with our policy. Therefore, we must do everything possible to see that our economy constantly satisfies the rapidly growing needs of the

[17] Quoted in Tatu, p. 78.

population; otherwise there may be a discrepancy between the purchaser's potential and satisfying their demands, which is fraught with serious consequences.[18]

He also criticized those who overemphasized industrial production at the expense of consumer production. The need was for uniform economic development. He asserted:

> And now some of our comrades have developed an appetite to give the country more metal. That is a praiseworthy desire, providing no harm is done to other branches of the national economy. But if more metal is produced while other branches lag, their expansion will be slowed down. Thus, not enough bread, butter, and other food products will be produced. It will not be a one-sided development. . . .
>
> Let us then not get carried away and thus permit disproportions in the development of the economy. It is essential that all branches of the national economy develop uniformly, that agriculture not lag in its development, that the production of consumer goods and agricultural produce advance more rapidly than the growing requirements of the people.[19]

It appears that Khrushchev's January 1961 proposals were intended more as trial balloons than as firm commitments to a policy. The plenum itself adopted only a few of the specific points of Khrushchev's program and was silent on many other key points.[20] From January to October, when the 22nd Party Congress convened, there was much debate on the issue of resource allocations. The military leadership was very interested in this debate, because Khrushchev was proposing a shift away from heavy industry production, which historically benefited at the expense of the other economic sectors, to a more even approach. The military were concerned that a reduction in the growth rate of the heavy industry branch would necessarily affect military capabilities.

The military, therefore, was one group which tended to withhold support from Khrushchev's program. Some merely omitted reference to the program; others emphasized the need for heavy industry. Armed Forces Day, February 23, 1961, provided the first major opportunity for the military leaders to express their opinions publicly. In their speeches, Marshals Malinovsky,[21] Grechko,[22]

---

[18] Soviet Home Service, January 20, 1961, 1620 GMT, FBIS, *USSR and East Europe*, No. 5 (January 24, 1961), p. 5.

[19] *Ibid.*, p. 9.

[20] Carl A. Linden, *Khrushchev and the Soviet Leadership, 1957–1964* (Baltimore: The Johns Hopkins University Press, 1966), p. 107.

[21] *Pravda*, February 23, 1961.

[22] *Krasnaya Zvezda*, February 23, 1961.

and Moskalenko[23] stressed four principal themes: (1) the socialist system was becoming the dominant and decisive factor of society; (2) wars are not fatalistically inevitable; (3) the USSR will maintain its military capabilities at the "necessary level"; and (4) the Soviet Union is militarily the strongest country in the world. In his article, Marshal Yakubovskiy was one who reminded the reader that heavy industry is "the leading factor in the economy and the basis for the strengthening of the defense capability in our country."[24]

Three events occurred in this period which hindered Khrushchev's plan for troop reductions and economic reform. The first was the American-supported Bay of Pigs invasion of Cuba on April 17. Then, in neither the Vienna Summit between Khrushchev and President Kennedy in June nor in the Berlin Crisis of June and July, were the Soviets able to wring concessions from the United States based merely on threats. The invasion of Cuba was supposedly proof of imperialism's belligerent designs and the latter two created a crisis atmosphere with the potential for a direct Soviet-American confrontation.

Under these pressures, Khrushchev began to retreat from his former proposals and programs. In a speech on June 22, Khrushchev modified his position on Soviet military requirements. While rocket weapons retained their primary importance, he now asserted that "the strengthening of the defense of the Soviet Union depends on the perfecting of all branches of forces of our armed forces."[25] On July 8, Khrushchev announced an increase of 3 billion rubles in defense spending and the suspension of troop reductions.[26] At the end of August, the draftees who were about to be released from active duty had their terms extended,[27] and the resumption of nuclear testing was announced.[28] Quite naturally, the military leaders were giving wholehearted support for increasing the size of the armed forces. On the same day that Khrushchev announced the suspension of troop reductions, for example, Marshal Malinovsky urged that contemporary requirements necessitated the equipping of "all sorts and kinds of troops with contemporary fighting technology."[29]

The MPA sought to offset the concessions granted to the military leadership. In particular, it launched a campaign during this period for "one-man command

---

[23] *Sovetskaya Rossiya*, February 23, 1961.

[24] *Neues Deutschland*, February 23, 1961.

[25] *Pravda*, June 22, 1961.

[26] *Ibid.*, July 9, 1961.

[27] *Ibid.*, August 30, 1961.

[28] *Ibid.*, August 31, 1961.

[29] *Krasnaya Zvezda*, July 8, 1961.

on a party basis" and the interchangeability of military and political personnel.[30] "One-man command on a party basis" appears to be a euphemism for saying that the commander must be more dependent on the political worker. The ultimate objective was the replacement of commanders by the deputy political commander. As Marshal Golikov noted, both lines are closely related to "the increasing role of the party organizations and political organs."[31] It is impossible to estimate the number of instances when commissars were assigned to command positions at this time,[32] but there can be little doubt that any campaign for placing political officers in command positions would be upsetting to the professional military leadership. This would be especially true in a period when professional military spokesmen were contending that nuclear weaponry was making military matters so complex and technical. It is unlikely, in view of the concessions being granted to the professional military in the summer of 1961, that the campaign actually achieved much results.

Indeed, when the 22nd Party Congress convened on October 17, 1961, the trend was clearly in favor of the military. There were 350 military men elected to the 22nd Party Congress, of which 305 had voting rights and 45 were without voting rights.[33] Of this number, 31 were elected as members of the Party Central Committee. In absolute terms, this represented the highest number of military men elected to the Central Committee up to 1961, and as a percentage of total

Proportion of Servicemen in the Central Committee
Elected from the 16th to 22nd Congresses

Congress	Total Membership			Servicemen			Percentage of Total
	Full	Alt.	Total	Full	Alt.	Total	
16th (1930)	70	67	137	2	3	5	3.5
17th (1934)	71	68	139	3	5	8	6.0
18th (1939)	71	68	139	9	6	15	10.7
19th (1952)	125	111	236	6	20	26	11.0
20th (1956)	133	122	255	8	12	20	7.8
22nd (1961)	175	155	330	14	17	31	9.5

Source: Nikolai Galay, "The Soviet Armed Forces and the Twenty-Second Party Congress," *Bulletin*, Institute for the Study of the USSR (January1962), p. 7.

[30] See articles by Marshal Golikov in *ibid.*, July 5, 1961, and *Pravda*, October 9, 1961.

[31] *Pravda*, October 9, 1961.

[32] In his report to the 22nd Party Congress, Golikov vaguely referred to the fact that "many" such interchanges had taken place. *Ibid.*, October 30, 1961.

[33] *Ibid.*, October 22, 1961.

membership showed an increase over 1956.[34] The lone member from the political administration was Marshal Golikov, who was elected to full membership. Theoretically, this gave Golikov equal ranking with the highest of the professional military men, because no military men were elected to the Party Presidium.

In his report to the Congress, Marshal Malinovsky noted that there would be a danger of war as long as imperialism (i.e., capitalism) continued to exist, although such wars were not fatalistically inevitable.[35] However, "if it nevertheless should be unleashed by the imperialist aggressors," and the Minister of Defense, modern war would "inescapably assume the character of a rocket-nuclear war, that is, a war in which the main striking force will be nuclear arms, and the basic means of delivering these to their objective are rockets."[36] He went on to explain that this military doctrine did not imply a declining importance for conventional forces. On the continuing importance of the mass army, for example, he made the observation:

> Despite the fact that in a future war the decisive place will belong to rocket-nuclear weapons, we nevertheless arrive at the conclusion that the final victory over the aggressor can be achieved only as the result of the joint action of all types of armed forces. This is why we are giving the necessary attention to the improvement of all types of weapons, teaching the troops to wield them skillfully and to achieve a decisive victory over the aggressor.
>
> We also consider that in modern conditions the future world war will be conducted, despite huge losses, by mass multimillion-strong armed forces.[37]

With regard to party-political matters, Malinovsky stressed the political reliability of Soviet officers and implied thereby that the officer was worthy of the Party's trust. He stated:

> Our command cadres, all of the officer corps of the Soviet armed forces — this is a select detachment of the sons of the Soviet people, politically mature, highly trained in military-political and technical affairs, boundlessly devoted to the cause of the party and capable at any moment to fulfill their duty for the defense of the beloved homeland.

[34] For a complete listing of the military men elected to the 22nd Party Congress and their positions, see Appendix A.

[35] *XXII s'yezd Kommunisticheskoy partii Sovetskogo Soyuza: Stenograficheskiy otchet (22nd Congress of the Communist Party of the Soviet Union: Stenographic Record)* (Moscow: State Publishing House for Political Literature, 1962), p. 110.

[36] *Ibid.*, p. 111.

[37] *Ibid.*, p. 112.

Our Soviet officer — this is the representative of the Party and Government in the army and navy, this is the commander with single command [*komandir-yedinonachal'nik*], and his order is law for subordinates. At the same time, he is also the solicitous educator of his subordinates and champion of the ideas of the party. It is significant that the proportion of all communists and komsomols among officers, generals, and admirals constitute almost 90 percent.[38]

Also, in a notable passage, Malinovsky discussed what he considered to be the importance of the reforms implemented after Zhukov's removal. The emphasis in the passage is that the reforms *radically improved* the Party's political work in the armed forces. Malinovsky stated:

. . . a very important role in strengthening the army and navy was played by the resolutions, adopted in 1957 by the October Plenum of the CC CPSU, which laid down measures for intensifying the leadership by the Party of the Armed Forces and for a *radical improvement* in party-political work. As a result of the October Plenum and subsequent resolutions of the CC CPSU, the Leninist principle of the leadership of the Armed Forces was completely restored, the role of the political organs and party organizations in the troops was raised, the connection of the army with the people was strengthened, and party-political work with personnel was *significantly improved*.[39]

Consequently, the statements of the MPA head appear to suggest that he differed strongly with Malinovsky on the issues of the 1957 reforms and one-man command. With regard to the 1957 reforms, Marshal Golikov maintained that the reforms had not merely improved party-political work, but had effectively strengthened and enhanced the *authority* of the political organs. According to Golikov, the October plenum resolutions made it possible

. . . radically to correct the conditions in the army, in proper time to restore the Leninist party principles of the leadership of the armed forces, to *enhance the role and authority* of party organizations, political organs, and military soviets, effectively to *strengthen one-man command on a party basis* [*na partiynoy osnove yedinonachaliya*], to raise the role of the community, and so *intensify party authority* in all aspects of the life of troops.[40]

It appears that Malinovsky, who argued that the plenum had improved

[38] *Ibid.*, p. 119. In another place, he gives the more exact figure of 82 percent. See p. 120.
[39] *Ibid.*, p. 120. Italics added.
[40] *Pravda*, October 30, 1961. Italics added.

party work, and Golikov, who argued that it had intensified party authority, were expressing quite contrary opinions. As Malinovsky used the term, the "improvement" of party work was vague and almost meaningless; it implied only that the quality of the party-political work had been raised. Golikov, on the other hand, contended that the authority of the political workers had actually been raised.

This contrast in approach was further emphasized by the diverse description given to the principle of one-man command. As already noted, Malinovsky referred to the Soviet officer as the "commander with single authority" *(komandir-yedinonachal'nik)* whose decree is law for his subordinates. In the previously cited passage from Golikov's speech, the emphasis is on the idea of "one-man command on a party basis" *(na partiynoy osnove yedinonachalya)*. In effect, this phrase suggests the opposite of one-man command, because it stresses that the commander must rely heavily on political workers and party organizations. Indeed, as Golikov himself observed in his report to the Congress:

> In our Soviet sense, one-man command requires from every commander a party and state approach to entrusted affairs, the skill firmly and consistently to implement in action the policy of the Communist Party, *basing himself in all his work on party organizations* and on the forces of the community.[41]

Furthermore, Golikov also praised the act of interchanging political and command personnel, whereby in effect the political officers are appointed to command positions. The Minister of Defense remained silent on the issue of interchange, neither advocating nor criticizing, and presumably believing that the less attention given to it, the better for the professional military.

In the months after the 22nd Party Congress, the debate between the political administration and the professional military spokesmen continued unabated. For example, a three-part series of articles in *Krasnaya Zvezda* in February 1962 stressed the historical importance of the Party's leadership over the armed forces in both political and strategic matters.[42] In a February issue of *Kommunist Vooruzhennykh Sil (Communist of the Armed Forces)*, the official organ of the MPA, an unsigned article accused political workers of many shortcomings, including the charge that not enough time was being given to strengthening one-man command and the commanders' authority.[43] The MPA responded in

[41] *Ibid.* Italics added.

[42] *Krasnaya Zvezda*, February 7, 14, and 16, 1962.

[43] "To Improve the Organizational and Political-Education Work for Strengthening Military Discipline," *Kommunist Vooruzhennykh Sil*, No. 3 (February 1962), p. 37.

an issue of the following month and countercharged that serious shortcomings had been found in the political work of the Defense Ministry's central apparatus. Among these shortcoming, it was charged that:

- favorable conditions for radically improving ideological-political education were being poorly used;

- progressive experiences were poorly summarized;

- theoretical interviews and conferences were not being conducted;

- half of the members did not comprehend the organized forms of political studies;

- criticism and self-criticism were being obstructed;

- insufficient emphasis was being given to the questions of party construction and the increasing role of the Party;

- political lectures were becoming too formalized.[44]

Between late December 1961 and early May 1962, articles began to appear in the Soviet press which rehabilitated several of Stalin's 1937 purge victims. Favorable articles discussed the careers of Tukhachevskiy,[45] Yakir,[46] Kork,[47] Gamarnik,[48] Eydeman,[49] and Blyukher.[50] While some of these purge victime had previously been rehabilitated in the Soviet press,[51] the timing of this new round of articles stressed the important role of these military leaders in the development of the Soviet armed forces and sought to glorify the military establishment. Even the articles on Gamarnik, the former head of the political administration in the armed forces, should be viewed in the same manner, because it extols Gamarnik's virtues not just as a loyal party member, but also as a fighter for military readiness who shot himself rather than approve Stalin's repression

[44] "On the Work of the Party Committee of the Organization Staff and Rear Administration of the Ministry of Defense of the USSR," *Kommunist Vooruzhennykh Sil*, No. 5 (March 1962), pp. 55–57.

[45] *Izvestiya*, December 24, 1961, and *Krasnaya Zvezda*, March 24, 1962.

[46] *Izvestiya*, February 6, 1962.

[47] *Krasnaya Zvezda*, April 5, 1962.

[48] *Ibid.*, April 13, 1962.

[49] *Ibid.*, May 10, 1962.

[50] *Izvestiya*, May 11, 1962.

[51] See Samuel A. Oppenheim, "Rehabilitation in the Post-Stalinist Soviet Union," *Western Political Quarterly*, XX, No. 1 (March 1967), 97–115, esp. pp. 112–14.

of the military. In the context of the debate during this period between the professional military and political administration leaders, these articles appear to have been an attempt by the professional leaders to reassert their own importance.

Then in May 1962, two articles printed in the Soviet press again stressed the need for developing all branches of military service. In one article, Marshal Malinovsky declared that "victory in a contemporary war can be secured only with the combined efforts of all branches of the armed forces and types of troops."[52] In another article on Soviet military doctrine, Colonel I. Sidel'nikov similarly declared:

> The decisive role of rocket-nuclear weapons in a war does not lessen the significance of other types of weapons. The complete and decisive victory over the imperialist aggressors can be attained only as a result of the combined, well-coordinated, and decisive acts of all branches of the armed forces and types of troops. The rocket-nuclear war will be waged by massive, multimillion-strong armies.[53]

Malinovsky's article, however, included a curious element which, according to one American source, "had no known precedent in Soviet public utterances."[54] After criticizing the large military expenditures in the American budget, which "absorb a large part of the state budget, enrich the monopolists, exhaust the economy, and impoverish the mass of people," Malinovsky asserted that conversely Soviet military expenditures were "absolutely necessary and the people completely encouraged them."[55] In the Soviet system, he then contended, military expenditures could not be exaggerated beyond actual needs:

> To this one must add that expenditures in defense with us are strictly regulated. In the Soviet State, there cannot be an exaggeration of military expenditures; all measures for strengthening the defensive power our state conducts within the limits called forth by the actual requirements for defense of the Soviet Union and the fraternal socialist countries from the aggression of the countries of imperialism.[56]

[52] Marshal of the Soviet Union R. Ya. Malinovsky, "The Program of the CPSU and the Question of Strengthening the Armed Forces of the USSR," *Kommunist*, No. 7 (May 1962), p. 19.

[53] *Krasnaya Zvezda*, May 11, 1962.

[54] Gallagher, "Military Manpower," p. 57.

[55] Malinovsky, "The Program of the CPSU and the Question of Strengthening the Armed Forces of the USSR," p. 17.

[56] *Ibid.*

Why was this issue raised by Malinovsky? Of course, he was denying that these expenditures could be exaggerated, but even the denial is interesting. The probable explanation seems to be that Malinovsky was criticizing those who might seek to employ an economic argument against his demand for developing all military branches. He was asserting that larger conventional forces were not an unnecessarily exaggerated expenditure, but an actual requirement.

The Appointment of Yepishev

In a terse back-page report of May 22, 1962, the Soviet press announced that Marshal of the Soviet Union F. I. Golikov had been relieved of his duties "for reasons of health." In his place, the Soviet Council of Ministers had appointed A. A. Yepishev and at the same time promoted Yepishev several grades to the rank of general of the army.[57] An announcement in *Krasnaya Zvezda* on this date also described Yepishev as the new MPA head and carried the official decree of May 11, which promoted Yepishev to his new rank.[58] Apparently, while the official announcement was not made until May 22, Yepishev had been appointed the new head of the MPA by May 11 at the latest.

Less direct evidence suggests that the appointment may have come even earlier. At the 22nd Party Congress, Golikov had been appointed a full member of the Party Central Committee. It is consequently not unlikely that his removal would have had to have the approval of a Central Committee plenum, the last of which had been hastily convened in April.[59] In the latter part of April, Yepishev, then Ambassador to Yugoslavia, was recalled to Moscow. On April 25, Yepishev was elected by the Supreme Soviet to the committee for drafting a new state constitution; he was the only "ambassador" so elected.[60] On May 1, Golikov was absent from the traditional May Day Parade to Red Square. These bits of evidence seem to suggest that the decision to appoint Yepishev may actually have taken place in the latter half of April. Why then did the official announcement of May 22 infer that Yepishev had been appointed on May 11?

But this was not the only delay. If Yepishev was appointed on May 11 as the Soviet press suggests in its report on May 22, why was this fact not made

[57] *Pravda*, May 22, 1962.

[58] *Krasnaya Zvezda*, May 22, 1962.

[59] Nikolai Galay, "Appointment of New Political Commander Strengthens Khrushchev's Control over Training of Soviet Armed Forces," *Analysis of Current Developments in the Soviet Union*, No. 236 (July 24, 1962) p. 2.

[60] Tatu, p. 237.

public until the later date? Two obituaries carried in *Krasnaya Zvezda* between these dates — for Deputy Chief of the General Staff General Gusev[61] and Deputy Commander-in-Chief of the Navy Admiral Golovko[62] — indicate that the highest-ranking MPA official to receive public notice for these eleven days was Golikov's deputy, Colonel P. I. Yefimov. Since the official ranking of names in Soviet announcements may on occasion reflect some political significance, it is noteworthy that Yefimov's signature on the obituaries was well down the list of names. The signature of neither Golikov nor Yepishev occupied the fourth position, the position usually reserved for the head of the MPA. These opportunities, as numerous precedents show, would have been just as favorable for a public announcement without fanfare as the back-page announcements of May 22, if there had not been other undefined factors.

Actually, there are three questions involved here: (1) Why was Golikov removed? (2) Why was the announcement not made immediately? (3) Why was Yepishev selected to replace Golikov?

From the evidence suggested so far, it can be readily seen that there existed a serious debate among professional military and political administration leaders and that the debate had grown increasingly belligerent and public since the 22nd Party Congress in October 1961. The apex of the antagonism was reached in April 1962, when the Central Committee directed the MPA to call a meeting of the chief political personnel in the armed forces. At the meeting, the political officers were bitterly chastised for their political shortcomings.[63] This meeting may have been an indication that the party elites no longer had confidence in Golikov's leadership and that a cleansing of the MPA was in order. The result was Golikov's removal and an intensification of MPA work to eliminate deficiencies in the political administration.

While this in itself is probably enough to explain the fall of Golikov, Michael Tatu adds speculation that the removal may have been occasioned by the Cuban Missile Crisis. In regard to the question of when the decision was probably taken to install missiles in Cuba, Tatu claims:

> According to Khrushchev (speech of December 12, 1962), it was in August that the Russians and Cubans agreed, through the meditation of Che Guevara

[61] *Krasnaya Zvezda*, May 11, 1962.

[62] *Ibid.*, May 18, 1962.

[63] Major General A. Bukov, "The Organizational Work of Party Organs — [They Must Be Made to Function] on the Level of the Party Requirement," *Kommunist Vooruzhennykh Sil*, No. 10 (May 1962), pp. 22–28.

during his visit to Moscow, on the installation of thermonuclear rockets in Cuba. It is quite possible that the formal agreements were concluded on that date, but the real decision, with everything it entailed in the way of preparations and plans, had certainly been taken earlier by Moscow — *probably in April 1962*, to judge from the diplomatic situation and certain changes in the Soviet General Staff.[64]

On the diplomatic front, Khrushchev held meetings with two high-ranking Cuban officials on April 28 and May 5, in which he may have made preliminary soundings.

Moreover, in April, in addition to Golikov, Marshal I. S. Konev was removed from the command of Soviet forces in East Germany and Marshal K. S. Moskalenko was replaced as Deputy Minister of Defense and chief of the Strategic Missile Forces by Marshal S. S. Biryuzov. As with Golikov, the announcement of Moskalenko's removal was delayed and not made public until July. Tatu then suggests the following sequence of events:

> . . . contemplating the futility of all previous efforts to obtain a settlement on Berlin, Khrushchev devised a new means of pressure on the United States — the shipment of nuclear missiles to Cuba. The matter may have been discussed at the formal Party Presidium held on the occasion of the Supreme Soviet session between April 22 and 25 and this may have heightened the difficulties of that agitated period. It is safe to assume that Moskalenko opposed the plan, and Golikov probably did too, hence their resignation.[65]

Another noteworthy item pointed out by Tatu is that both Golikov and Moskalenko seemed to have regained influence in November, that is, after the missile crisis occurred. Thus, Golikov and Moskalenko (1) were removed from their positions in April, (2) had the recognition of their removals delayed, and (3) returned to favor in November.

Based on the material previously presented and Tatu's speculations, it is now possible to summarize four factors which might help to explain the delay in announcing Golikov's removal and Yepishev's appointment.

1. It is quite possible that, as Tatu said, Golikov opposed the placement of missiles in Cuba. This would account for certain similarities with Moskalenko.

2. Golikov may have been removed as a concession to the military in return for their gradually granting support to Khrushchev's plan for installing missiles

[64] Tatu, p. 233. Italics added.
[65] *Ibid.*, p. 238.

in Cuba. This would have been a reasonable demand from the professional military in light of the proceeding debate.

3. Whether connected with the Cuban missile issue or not, there may have been considerable debate and bargaining between party and professional military, as well as among party elites with regard to naming a new MPA head. In terms of the ongoing personal power conflicts among Soviet leaders, both are entirely probable. For the naming of a new MPA head is important not only for party-military relations, but also for the power struggles among party elites.

4. There may have been considerable opposition to the naming of Yepishev, personally, as the new MPA head. Clearly, Yepishev's background was such that his appointment must have stirred some controversy among Soviet leaders. Therefore, the delay may have been the result of opposition from an important segment of opinion, which had to be won over before the announcement.

Each element has its own merit, but none at present appears to be more compelling causes than the others. Nor are all four totally exclusive of each other. Indeed, it may very well have been that all four factors — Golikov's opposition to installing missiles in Cuba, a concession for military support, a general debate on the new MPA head, a personal debate with regard to Yepishev — so interacted as to cause the delay.

A. A. Yepishev: A Political Biographical Sketch

Alexey Alexeyevich Yepishev (sometimes spelled Epishev)[66] was born of Russian parents in May 1908. From 1923 to 1927, Yepishev was employed in various positions in the fishing industry. In 1927, he was appointed as an instructor in a district committee, and later as head of a department, in the Komsomol. He became a CPSU member in 1929. Between 1930 and 1938, Yepishev served in the Red Army. Having graduated from the Military Academy for Mechanization and Motorization in 1938, he was transferred to party posts.

In 1940, Yepishev was appointed to the cadres department of the Central Committee of the Ukrainian Communist Party (UkrCP). In 1940 and 1941, he

---

[66] Unless otherwise indicated, the biographical material on Yepishev has been drawn from three largely repetitive sources: *Yezhegodnik bol'shoy sovetskoy entsiklopedii, 1962 (Annual of the Great Soviet Encyclopedia, 1962)* (Moscow: Soviet Encyclopedia Publishing House, 1962), pp. 594–95; Robert M. Slusser, "Alexei Alexeevich Yepishev," in George W. Simmonds, ed., *Soviet Leaders* (New York: Thomas Y. Crowell, 1967), pp.141–46; and Andrew I. Lebed, Heinrich E. Schulz, and Stephen S. Taylor, eds., *Who's Who in the USSR, 1965–66* (New York: Scarecrow Press, 1966), p. 954.

served as first secretary of the Kharkov City, and later Oblast, Committee of the UkrCP. When Kharkov was captured by German troops in October 1941, he became a member of the military council of the Stalingrad Front. He also served briefly as a deputy commissar of the Medium Machine Building industry. In February 1943, when the Soviets recaptured Kharkov, Yepishev was again appointed the first secretary of the city's party committee, but the city was reoccupied by the Germans in mid-March. Until 1946, he served on the military councils of various armies.

In 1946, Yepishev again became active in the UkrCP. From 1946 to 1948, he served as cadres secretary of the CC UkrCP. Following an extensive party reorganization in 1948, he was made first secretary of the Odessa Oblast Committee.

In September 1951, Yepishev was called from the Ukraine to become USSR Deputy Minister of State Security. At the 19th CPSU Congress in 1952, he was elected an alternate member of the Party Central Committee. In March 1953, following the death of Stalin, Yepishev was removed from his post in State Security and returned to the Ukraine as first secretary of the Odessa Oblast Committee.

In August 1955, Yepishev was appointed as the Soviet Ambassador to Rumania, where he served for five and a half years. In January 1961, he was transferred to Belgrade, where he served as Soviet Ambassador to Yugoslavia until his recall to Moscow in April 1962. During his two tenures as ambassador, Yepishev was elected to alternate membership in the Party Central Committee by the 20th and 22nd Party Congresses. In recognition for his diplomatic service, he was awarded the Order of the Red Banner of Labor in 1958.

In order to explain Yepishev's rise to prominence, it is necessary now to relate his own career background to the careers and political struggles of the other influential Soviet leaders. The purpose here is to attempt to define the individual leaders, factions, and/or groups responsible for Yepishev's rise. Since promotions among Soviet elites are political acts, technical knowledge or experience cannot sufficiently explain this rise. Hopefully, this information concerning Yepishev will lead to some indications as to why Yepishev was elected to be MPA head in 1962.

In January 1938, Khrushchev was elected Acting First Secretary of the UkrCP. He had been sent to the Ukraine in August 1937 as part of a trio whose objective was to carry out a major purge of the UkrCP. As a result of the purge, it became necessary to recruit and promote many new party members.[67] It was

[67] Mark Frankland, *Khrushchev* (New York: Stein and Day, 1966), pp. 51–53; and Robert S. Sullivant, *Soviet Politics and the Ukraine, 1917–1957* (New York: Columbia University Press, 1962) p. 223. Sullivant notes that under Khrushchev's direction, all of the first secretaries and

at that time, and therefore under Khrushchev, that Yepishev began to move up in the UkrCP. During the early stages of World War II, both Yepishev and Khrushchev served on the military council of the Stalingrad Front, along with that group of military leaders (for example, Malinovsky, Chuykov, Grechko, Moskalenko, Biryuzov, Zakharov, Konev, Krylov, Bagramyan, Golikov, and Yakubovskiy) who would gain the chief military positions under Khrushchev in the 1950's and early 1960's.[68] Then, after the war, Yepishev returned to a high position within the UkrCP, which was again under the administration of Khrushchev. Following Khrushchev's brief fall from favor in mid-1947, Khrushchev's return to favor in late 1947,[69] and the reorganization of 1948, Yepishev was made first secretary in Odessa Oblest.[70]

Quite similar to Yepishev's postwar rise in the Ukraine was the emergence of another young man under Khrushchev, Leonid Ilich Brezhnev. In May 1938, Brezhnev became a secretary of the Dnepropetrovsk Oblast Party Committee. During the war, he served as deputy head of the political administration of the Southern Front. In 1945, Yepishev served under Brezhnev as a political officer.[71] In the first year after the war, Brezhnev was appointed as the first secretary of

---

most of the second secretaries of oblast organizations were replaced. An entirely new slate of government officials, including the Prime Minister, was installed. At the 14th UkrCP Congress of June 1938, only three of eighty-seven Central Committee members had been carried over from previous years. Of the thirteen members of the Politburo, Orgburo, and Secretariat, none had served previously.

[68] For a more complete discussion of the Stalingrad Group of military leaders and their careers, see Kolkowicz, *The Soviet Army and the Communist Party*, pp. 573–92.

[69] Frankland, p. 76; and Sullivant, pp. 255–56. In view of unsatisfactory Ukrainian farm production, L. M. Kaganovich and N. S. Patolichev were sent by Moscow to the Ukraine. Khrushchev was removed as First Secretary of the UkrCP, but was retained in the Ukrainian Politburo and Orgburo, as well as the USSR Politburo. By the end of 1947, production in agriculture rose again to satisfactory levels. In December 1947, Kaganovich was recalled to Moscow and Khrushchev was reappointed First Secretary of the UkrCP.

[70] Curiously, however, the opportunity for further advancement in 1949 fell not to Yepishev, but to one of his subordinates. In December 1949, Khrushchev was called to Moscow and was succeeded by L. G. Melnikov. Melnikov's position as second secretary was taken by O. I. Kirichenko, a secretary of the Odessa Oblast, wherein Yepishev was first secretary. Kirichenko was also appointed to the UkrCP Politburo and Orgburo. Kirichenko's later career suggests quite strongly that he was probably raised on Khrushchev's behest. See Sullivant, p. 275.

[71] J. Malcolm Mackintosh, "The Soviet Military: Influence ou Foreign Policy," *Problems of Communism*, XXII, No. 5 (September–October 1973), 4.

[72] Grey Hodnett, "Leonid Ilyich Brezhnev," in Simmonds, p. 23; and Yaroslav Bilinsky, *The Second Soviet Republic: The Ukraine after World War II* (New Brunswick, N.J.: Rutgers University Press, 1964), pp. 371-72.

the Zaporozh'ye Oblast Party Committee in the southeastern Ukraine. In November 1947, he was promoted to first secretary of the Dnepropetrovsk Oblast Party Committee.[72] It is generally agreed that from these positions the future General Secretary of the CPSU gained close contacts with Khrushchev. In addition, the evidence would appear to suggest that the similarities of positions and their geographical proximity probably also drew Brezhnev and Yepishev into close contact. In itself, this latter item does not mean to imply that Yepishev had or would become a Brezhnev follower. It only suggests that Brezhnev was familiar with Yepishev's work.

Some Western observers of Soviet affairs have come to the conclusion, based on Yepishev's rise in the UkrCP at the time of Khrushchev's secretaryship, that Yepishev's fortune was connected with Khrushchev's rise.[73] However, certain events in Yepishev's career after 1951 appear to contradict this contention.

Since 1946, the Ministry of State Security, which controlled the secret police, had been under the leadership of Y. S. Abakumov, a close associate and longtime henchman of Beria.[74] In September 1951, Yepishev was appointed a deputy minister. In the following month, S. D. Ignat'yev was appointed to replace Abakumov as the State Security chief, with M. Ryumin as one of his deputies.[75] Thus, these were the men in charge of the Soviet secret police in the last two years of Stalin's life when several significant purges were either begun or carried out: the Mingrelian Case in Georgia, the Leningrad Case, and the Doctors' Plot. Quite clearly, the Mingrelian Case was a purge directed against supporters of Beria in Georgia.[76] The Leningrad Case was aimed at earlier appointees of Zhdanov. The Doctors' Plot also appears to have been directed against Beria.

The real leaders behind the purges probably were A. N. Poskrehyshev and Ryumin, and Ignat'yev was just as probably no more than a figurehead.[77] Al-

[73] Nicolai Galay, "Appointment of New Political Commander Strengthens Khrushchev's Control over Training of Soviet Armed Forces," p. 3; Robert Conquest, *Russia After Khrushchev* (New York: Praeger, 1965), p. 180; and *The New York Times*, June 3, 1962.

[74] John A. Armstrong, *The Politics of Totalitarianism: The Communist Party of the Soviet Union from 1934 to the Present* (New York: Random House, 1961), p. 226.

[75] Bertram Wolfe, *Khrushchev and Stalin's Ghost* (New York: Praeger, 1957), p. 195.

[76] Robert Conquest, *Power and Policy in the USSR: The Struggle for Stalin's Succession, 1945–1960* (New York: Harper & Row, 1967), pp. 129–53.

[77] Ronald Hingley, *The Russian Secret Police: Muscovite, Imperial Russian and Soviet Political Security Organizations* (New York: Simon and Schuster, 1970), p. 217; Boris Levytsky, *The Uses of Terror: The Soviet Secret Police, 1917–1970*, trans. H. A. Piehler (New York: Coward, McCann & Geoghegan, 1972), p. 215; and Bertram Wolfe, *Khrushchev and Stalin's Ghost*, p. 5. Poskrebyshev was not officially a secret police chief, but his position as Stalin's personal secretary gave him enormous power to control the activities of the secret police.

though Yepishev's specific role in the purges — if any — is not clear, the timing of his appointments — that is, at the beginning of the purges and when Posk-rebyshev's influence over the Ministry of State Security was at its highest — indicates that Yepishev may have played at least a minor role.

When Stalin died in March 1953, Beria caused an immediate shake-up in the State Security leadership. According to some reports, Poskrebyshev was executed quickly and quietly. Ryumin was arrested and executed a year later.[78] Ignat'yev's role as a figurehead was reflected in the fact that after March 1953 he was not executed, but rather demoted to first secretary of the Bashkirian Province Committee.[79] Likewise, in the wake of Stalin's death, Yepishev was demoted to first secretary of the Odessa Oblast Committee, where he served for two years.

Yepishev's limited personal influence over the next few years appears to be the inverse of Khrushchev's rising influence. On June 12, L. G. Melnikov was expelled from his post and replaced by Kirichenko. In June 1953, Beria himself, Khrushchev's major competitor for influence in the Ukraine, was removed from office and shot. This latter move restored supreme authority over Ukrainian politics to Khrushchev. Therefore, Krushchev largely had a free hand in naming Kirichenko's successor as second secretary of the UkrCP. Instead of selecting Yepishev, Khrushchev chose a relative newcomer to party politics, N. V. Podgorny, who had attained his first job in the party apparatus only in 1950.[80] While it is true that Podgorny's position as first secretary of the Kharkov Oblast Party Committee was a high-level one, Yepishev could now boast a national reputation. In this sense, being passed over for the second secretary position must be considered a rebuke for Yepishev.

Despite Yepishev's apparent decline in prestige, his work throughout the 1950's seems to have brought him into close contact with another prominent personality, M. A. Suslov. In 1947, Suslov was appointed a secretary of the CPSU Central Committee and, later in the same year, became the head of the Agitation and Propaganda Department (Agitprop) of the Secretariat. In September 1947, he took an active part in the founding of the Communist Information Bureau (Cominform), an organization of nine national Communist Parties supposedly created for "the organization of interchange of experience, and if need be, coordination of the activities of the Communist Parties on the basis of mutual agreement."[81] As one of the main Soviet representatives at the Cominform convo-

---

[78] Conquest, *Power and Policy*, pp. 244–46, 447–48.

[79] Levytsky, p. 21.

[80] Grey Hodnett, "Nikolai Viktorovich Podgorny," in Simmonds, p. 79.

[81] "The Formation of the Cominform: Announcement of Establishment of the Cominform,

cation of June 1948, Suslov played a principal part in the expulsion of Yugoslavia from the Communist bloc.[82] In 1949 and 1950, he served as editor-in-
chief of *Pravda*, the official newspaper of the Communist Party, and only formally
retained his membership in the Central Committee Secretariat. In the beginning
of 1951, he began to recover from this "semidisgrace."[83] By this period, therefore,
Suslov had already become active in the two areas which were to become his
specialties: ideology and relations with foreign Communist Parties.

In October 1952, Suslov was named to membership in the enlarged Presidium.[84] With this new prestige (and evidently with Stalin's approval), he
launched a scathing attack in *Pravda* of December 24 against P. N. Fedoseyev.
Through his attack on Fedoseyev, Suslov criticized the economic policies of
N. A. Voznesenskiy, a former Zhdanovite and victim of the Leningrad Affair
in 1950. This act is generally accepted as the opening scene for purges in the
ideological and scientific front and Suslov was probably slated to play a major
part in the purge.[85]

If this is true, it is possible to assume that Suslov would have come in close
contact with Yepishev, who was at the time serving as a deputy minister of State
Security. Indeed, while the concrete evidence is lacking, to assume that Suslov
and Yepishev were working together would explain several factors in Yepishev's
career after the death of Stalin.

In the first place, Suslov was one of the Presidium newcomers eliminated
when Stalin's successors reduced the size of the Presidium following the dictator's death. Suslov was retained, however, as one of the five Central Committee

---

November, 1947," in Robert H. McNeal, ed., *International Relations Among Communists*
(Englewood Cliffs, N.J.: Prentice-Hall, 1967), p. 56. The nine parties were from Yugoslavia,
Bulgaria, Rumania, Hungary, Poland, the Soviet Union, France, Czechoslovakia, and Italy.

[82] Grey Hodnett, "Mikhail Andreevich Suslov," in Simmonds, p. 112.

[83] Janet D. Zagoria, ed., *Power and the Soviet Elite, "The Letter of an Old Bolshevik" and
Other Essays by Boris I. Nicolaevsky* (New York: Praeger, 1965), p. 261.

[84] In his Secret Speech to the 20th Party Congress in 1956, Khrushchev asserted that the enlarging of the Presidium in 1952 was the first step toward a purge of older Presidium members.
He charged: "Stalin evidently had plans to finish off the old members of the Political Bureau.
He often stated that the Political Bureau members should be replaced by new ones. His proposal, after the 19th Congress, concerning the election of 25 persons to the Central Committee
Presidium, was aimed at the removal of the old Political Bureau members and the bringing in of
less experienced persons so that these would extol him in all sorts of ways. We can assume
that this was also a design for the future annihilation of the old Political Bureau members."
(Nikita S. Khrushchev, *The Crimes of the Stalin Era: Special Report to the 20th Congress
of the Communist Party of the Soviet Union*, annotated by Boris I. Nicolaevsky [New York:
New Leader, 1962], p. 863).

[85] See, for example, Janet Zagoria, p. 262.

secretaries. One plausible explanation for this relatively mild decline in stature is that his intended purge victims were probably not high-ranking political officials of the post-Stalin regime. Assuming that Suslov worked closely with Yepishev might explain why the latter also suffered only a mild decline in position after March 1953.[86]

Secondly, following the fall of Malenkov, Suslov regained his Presidium post in June 1955. A year earlier, he had been elected chairman of the Supreme Soviet's Foreign Affairs Committee. While the foreign affairs post is weak in itself, Suslov's reappointment to the Presidium gave him new authority in the area of Soviet relations with Communist Parties. In the months succeeding Suslov's Presidium appointment, Yepishev was transferred to the ambassadorship in Rumania. As the ambassador to a state with a ruling Communist Party, Yepishev would have worked closely with Suslov for the next seven years.

Thirdly, as a tentative point, it might be suggested that Yepishev's close relationship with Suslov influenced Yepishev's selection as the MPA head. It should be noted that after the 22nd Party Congress in October 1961 and Yepishev's appointment in April–May 1962, Suslov had become involved in several debates with Khrushchev or his supporters. In one dispute, Suslov openly debated the activities of ideologists under Stalin with L. F. Il'ichev, Khrushchev's ideological assistant.[87] In another, Suslov appears to have resisted attempts by Khrushchev in March 1962 to shift greater allocations to the agricultural sector of the economy.[88] It may very well be, therefore, as Robert Slusser has maintained, that Yepishev's appointment was one element in the factional struggles against Khrushchev.[89]

In this way, it may be possible to hypothesize that the delay in announcing Yepishev's appointment might have been the result of opposition to the appointment from Khrushchev. Similarly, the professional military men may have at

---

[86] One bit of indirect evidence for this view is that one of the deputies of State Security serving with Yepishev was not demoted, but actually promoted as Beria's successor. This was Ivan Serov, who had once served under Khrushchev as the head of the Ukrainian secret police. Myron Rush, *Political Succession in the USSR* (New York: Columbia University Press, 1965), p. 54; Hingley, p. 225; and Levytsky, pp. 230–31. This seems to suggest that Khrushchev had the power in March 1953 to save a loyal supporter in the secret police, if he so desired. Therefore, Yepishev's demotion points to a weak relationship at the time between Khrushchev and Yepishev.

[87] Linden, pp. 134–38.

[88] Tatu, pp. 214–17, esp. p. 216.

[89] Robert M. Slusser, "America, China, and the Hydra-Headed Opposition: The Dynamics of Soviet Foreign Policy," in Peter H. Juviler and Henry W. Morton, eds., *Soviet Policy-Making: Studies of Communism in Transition* (New York: Praeger, 1967), p. 217.

least initially opposed Yepishev, but finally compromised with a qualified acceptance of his nomination.

However, in order to give a more definitive description of Yepishev's role among the factions and groups, it is necessary to examine Yepishev's activities over the next two years, that is, until Khrushchev's ouster.

Summary

In review, this chapter has sought to highlight the main themes of the political-military debates as they occurred in the first two years of the 1960's. As a result of his perception of the postwar "revolution in military affairs," Khrushchev proposed troop reduction and greater reliance on nuclear weapons. Perhaps unexpectedly from Khrushchev's standpoint, the opposition from the professional military was more than anticipated. The professional military leadership, while accepting the idea of greater emphasis on nuclear weaponry, clung to the large-army concept and resisted proposals for troop reduction. Since the MPA head, Marshal Golikov, was unable or unwilling to control the oppositional voices, he was removed.

In May 1962, A. A. Yepishev was appointed to be Golikov's successor. It appears that Yepishev took over his duties after considerable debate and delay. In the context of the time, it seems highly probable that Yepishev was appointed to reassert control over the professional military for party figures. But for which party figures? This is the question. As the chapter has sought to suggest, Yepishev has sometimes wrongly been described as a Khrushchev man. The evidence presented here, however, does not support this contention. Rather, Yepishev was perhaps closer in sympathy with the line laid down by Suslov and other conservatives, and it was probably through Suslov's influence that Yepishev was appointed and retained in office over the last two years of Khrushchev's regime.

The next chapter will examine the period between Yepishev's appointment and Khrushchev's ouster. Particular attention will be given to the relationship between Khrushchev and Yepishev's MPA in order to examine further the suggestion that Yepishev was not appointed as a "Khrushchev man," as well as to the relationship between the professional military and Yepishev's MPA in order to assess the degree of political control exerted by Yepishev over military affairs.

4

Political-Military Rifts in the Period Leading to the Ouster of Khrushchev

The Impact of the Cuban Missile Crisis on Internal Political-Military Debates

In May 1962, *Kommunist Vooruzhennykh Sil* carried an article by Colonel General N. A. Lomov, a professor at the Soviet General Staff Academy and a doctor of military sciences, wherein the author appeared to be calling for the end of the party-military debates. Lomov noted first of all that Soviet military doctrine is formed "under the leadership of the Central Committee of the Party, under its direct control, and on the basis of the theoretical and methodological principles of Marxism-Leninism."[1] He went further to observe, however, that professional military men also contribute a large share in formulating the Soviet Union's military view of the world. He stated:

> The formation of our military view of the world takes place in a creative atmosphere, is accompanied by a struggle of opinions, and is the result of the common efforts of theorists and practitioners of military affairs. Thanks to this, there was drawn up those unified theoretical views, on the basis of which was carried out a broad state program for training the country and the armed forces to defend the Motherland.[2]

Immediately thereafter, quoting Frunze, Lomov maintained that a fundamental factor in the superiority of Soviet military doctrine over imperialist doctrine lay "not only in a common political ideology, but also a unity of views on

[1] Colonel General N. Lomov, "On Soviet Military Doctrine," *Kommunist Vooruzhennykh Sil,* No. 10 (May 1962), p. 12.

[2] *Ibid.*

the character of military tasks confronting the republic, the methods of their resolution, and the methods of combat training for troops."[3] Basically, Lomov's theme was that Soviet military policies should be formulated and implemented through the combined efforts of political and military leaders.

Demonstrating a similar conciliatory tone, Minister of Defense Malinovsky chose in June 1962, the same month in which tensions in Europe were growing high,[4] to criticize the activities of professional military and political administration leaders of the armed forces. In the first instance, Malinovsky observed that "the chief link in the educational work and the guarantee of its success is the education of the leaders, the educators themselves."[5] He then declared that, unless the leaders improved their treatment of persons and never forgot criticism, self-criticism, and self-education, they would lack the moral right to hold a high post. He also indicated, however, that there were some military leaders who did not fulfill these qualifications. According to Malinovsky:

> Leaders who are not self-critical, give themselves airs in guiding, have too high an opinion of their indispensability and infallibility, think that everything is permitted to them and that everything is possible, inflict great harm to the education of troops. Such generals, admirals, and officers, taking complete advantage of their allotted rights, forget about their obligations to the state and the people; they indulge in nonsense [*ochkovtiratel'stvom*], are divorced from the masses, have failed to keep pace with life, and therefore their military qualities are not high. Of course, such people are not many, but they are encountered here and there.[6]

Subsequently, Malinovsky turned his attention to party-political work in the armed forces. He criticized command and political officials for their weak con-

[3] *Ibid.*

[4] In June and July 1962, Soviet pressures for a German treaty gradually grew stronger. On June 7, 1962, a meeting of Warsaw Pact countries approved talks with the United States, but also implied that the Communist countries would soon sign separate treaties with East Germany. Tensions in Berlin and Germany were consequently quite high. Trying to regain some control over the situation, Khrushchev, through a meeting of Soviet Ambassador to the United States A. Dobrynin with U.S. Attorney General Robert Kennedy, informed President John Kennedy that the Soviets would reduce tensions in Germany and Southeast Asia until at least after the November 1962 elections. William Hyland and Richard Wallace Shryock, *The Fall of Khrushchev* (New York: Funk and Wagnalls, 1968), pp. 46–47.

[5] Marshal of the Soviet Union R. Ya. Malinovsky, "Urgent Questions in the Education of Personnel in the Armed Forces of the USSR," *Kommunist Vooruzhennykh Sil,* No. 11 (June 1962), p. 4.

[6] *Ibid.*, p. 6.

trol over komsomol work and the meager assistance they give to the combat and political training of komsomol members in the armed forces.[7] He also chastised commanders and political workers for not concerning themselves sufficiently with the service activities, living conditions, and everyday lives of young officers. He cited as an example the fact that Officers' Houses was more interested in making profits than in satisfying the political, technical, and cultural needs of officers, particularly young officers.[8] His most scathing charges, however, were made with regard to the quality and content of political instruction, which Malinovsky seems to have characterized as generally inappropriate for modern circumstances. The Minister of Defense maintained:

> The improved political and cultured level of troop personnel is not always taken into consideration by commanders, political workers, and party organizations in their educational work.
>
> It is known that political instruction is the basic form of political and military education of the line and sergeant staff of our armed forces. The content and methodology of their instruction must correspond with the improved level of the general educational training of personnel. However, unfortunately, in a number of units and formations political instruction is conducted on a low level and does not satisfy modern demands. Sometimes the leader of a group arrives at lessons with poor preparation, sloppily dressed, and conducts it boringly, with methods of tiresome wordiness. Such a leader often clumsily and unconvincingly argues to the soldiers that the socialist system is better than the capitalist. But the soldiers are themselves convinced of this, know it, and do not doubt it. Such lessons, tiresome and trite, are a burden on the soldiers and do not evoke interest, and they hardly keep from going to sleep at them.
>
> It is necessary to raise the quality of political instruction. They must be not only deep in their content but also interesting in form. Officers, the leaders of groups are obliged to be ardent propagandists of the ideas of Marxism-Leninism, possess certain oratorical talents, master cultural speech, and be educated in the areas of technology, politics, literature, and art. As you know, the political lessons of troops serves in its way as an extension of their school education, where they mastered the bases of a number of social sciences and where they were taught by qualified teachers.[9]

Based on these observations, Malinovsky drew the conclusion and made the suggestion that:

[7] *Ibid.*, p. 14.
[8] *Ibid.*, p. 7.
[9] *Ibid.*, p. 9.

> ... it would be expedient for the Main Political Administration of the Soviet Army and Navy, the military councils of the branches of the armed forces, the military districts, groups of forces, fleets and political administrations to think out methods for the decisive improvement of the content of political lessons, and to make them effectively the basic form of education of soldiers, sailors, sergeants, and senior officers.[10]

While it is true that Malinovsky criticized the political instruction in the armed forces, this does not alter the fact that it was generally a conciliatory article. It must be stressed that Malinovsky addressed his remarks and criticisms to command and political personnel alike. In this sense, the article was directed against neither sector in particular, but at both.

As in the case of Lomov and Malinovsky, Yepishev's first tasks as MPA head seemed also to emphasize a conciliatory theme. In one of his initaial acts, Yepishev presided over an all-army conference whose stated purpose was to improve the mode of life of troops.[11] In this way, Yepishev gave his approval to proposals for overcoming many deficiencies, such as those enumerated also by Malinovsky.

If this was indeed an earnest effort by the new MPA head to be conciliatory, it was short-lived. Toward the middle of June, the MPA initiated a series of moves to expose shortcomings in the military, beginning with the military academies. On June 12, Lieutenant General M. Kalashnik, a deputy head of the MPA, criticized the military academies for their deficiencies in the ideological aspects of the soldiers' education.[12] Then, the MPA journal *Kommunist Vooruzhennykh Sil* reported a meeting of the political administration officials wherein military academies were chastised for "many essential defects and omissions" in ideological-educational work and for giving careless treatment to "the question of raising the ideological content of lectures."[13] Furthermore, the meeting pointed out that the military academies did not give sufficient attention to criticism and self-criticism and to the mistakes of individuals. As the report stated:

> In the struggle for raising the qualities and activities of educational work, still

[10] *Ibid.*

[11] See *Krasnaya Zvezda*, June 4–9, 1962. Perhaps it was a sign of the uncertainty surrounding Yepishev's authority, but Malinovsky was not a member of the conference presidium. Malinovsky's subordinate, A. A. Grechko, then First Deputy Minister of Defense, was the highest-ranking military officer. See *Ibid.*, June 5, 1962.

[12] *Ibid.*, June 12, 1962.

[13] "To Improve Party Work in Academies and Institutions," *Kommunist Vooruzhennykh Sil*, No. 12 (June 1962), p. 41.

poorly used is the powerful weapon of criticism and self-criticism. The faceless-ness of criticism and the lack of keenness in the appraisal of negative phenomena is the particular character for a number of party organizations of departments.[14]

Another article in the "Lecture and Consultation" section of the same journal issue also praised the "weapon of criticism and self-criticism." Concerned with the principle of one-man command, the article maintained that criticism and self-criticism are among the tools a commander needs in order to be a successful leader. The author of the article, a colonel and a candidate of historical sciences, observed:

> One-man command in the Soviet armed forces is formed and strengthened *on a party basis.* This means that every officer, general, and admiral must put the policy of the Party firmly into practice, always and in everything, display a party approach to matters, daily show exactingness with themselves and their subordinates, strongly lean on the party organizations, skillfully make use of the weapon of criticism for the elimination of defects, constantly strengthen the connection with the masses, and combine exactingness to subordinates with a fatherly care for them. Without this commanders cannot successfully guide subdivisions, units, and ships.[15]

In August, *Kommunist Vooruzhennykh Sil* reported on a meeting of secre-taries of political organs in the main and central administrations of the Ministry of Defense. The focus of attention at the meeting was the activities of political organs in the highest levels of the ground forces. Two of the major accusations made against the political organs were that they "poorly directed the attention of communists in the systematic follow-up of the directives of the Minister of Defense and the head of the Main Political Administration on developing and guiding socialist competition"[16] and "did not display the necessary activity and persistence in fulfilling the demands of the 22nd Congress of the CPSU on the basic improvement of ideological work."[17] Yepishev also revealed that studies of the political organs of the other staffs and administrations had similarly con-

---

[14] *Ibid.,* p. 42.

[15] Colonel M. Timofeyechev, "One-Man Command Is a Major Principle of the Construction of the Soviet Armed Forces," *Kommunist Vooruzhennykh Sil,* No. 12 (June 1962), p. 46. Italics added.

[16] "On the Work of Party Committees and Party Organizations of the Staffs and Administra-tions of the Ground Forces," *Kommunist Vooruzhennykh Sil,* No. 15 (August 1962), p. 39.

[17] *Ibid.,* p. 40.

cluded that their organizational and political work "does not for the present meet the requirement of the 22nd Congress of the CPSU."[18]

In October 1962, MPA functionaries from all branches of the armed forces again convened in a meeting. In addition to Yepishev and Malinovsky, participants included Marshals of the Soviet Union M. V. Zakharov, K. S. Moskalenko, V. D. Sokolovskiy, and S. K. Timoshenko. While the exact date of the meeting is unknown, Malinovsky's speech at the conference was published on October 25.[19] As reported in the press, Malinovsky seemed to imply that present political workers lacked the type of educational background necessary to conduct the proper political work in the armed forces. What the political workers need to fulfill their role, said Malinovsky, is a better technical knowledge of modern combat weapons. As he stated:

[18] *Ibid.*, p. 41.

[19] It is well to recall that in context October 25 occurred in the middle of the so-called Cuban Missile Crisis. On October 22, President John Kennedy had announced that the United States had initiated a blockade of Cuba and the Soviets responded in an official statement the following day that ". . . in embarking on such a venture, the United States of America is taking a step towards the unleasing of a world thermonuclear war." (David L. Larson, ed., *The "Cuban Crisis" of 1962* [Boston: Houghton Mifflin, 1963], Document 18, p. 50.) Then, on October 24, in a meeting with the president of Westinghouse International, William Knox, Khrushchev threatened that the missiles and attack planes in Cuba might be used against the United States and that Soviet submarines might start sinking American ships. (Elie Abel, *The Missile Crisis* [New York: J. B. Lippincott, 1966], p. 151.) Certain signs point at this time to the fact that Khrushchev may have been under great pressures. One example, but an obscure point, of the political infighting took place in the Ukraine on October 25. On that date, a small city in the Kirovograd Oblast named Khrushchev was renamed Kremges. Quite clearly, this change at the height of the crisis (at any time, but especially now) could not have occurred without the backing of some high party official or officials. It represented a deliberate slap at the party head during a critical moment (Hyland and Shryock p. 58.) On October 26, a secret message from Khrushchev to John Kennedy proposed to halt Soviet arms shipments to Cuba and to destroy those already in Cuba, if the United States would remove its blockade and promise not to invade Cuba. ("Messages Exchanged by President Kennedy and Chairman Khrushchev During the Cuban Missile Crisis of October 1962," *Department of State Bulletin*, LXIX, No. 1795 [November 19, 1973], 642.) However, a formal message, also broadcast over Moscow radio, included American withdrawal from Turkey as an additional demand. (*Ibid.*, p. 646.) Ignoring the formal message, President Kennedy accepted the compromise solution in Khrushchev's secret letter. If one accepts the secret letter as coming from Khrushchev personally — and this is generally done — then the addition of Turkey could have been the result of pressure put on Khrushchev to seek a *quid pro quo*. Indeed, *Krasnaya Zvezda* on October 27, 1962, suggested that the U.S. precedent could possibly justify Soviet movement against American bases near the frontiers of the Soviet Union.

For a more detailed, comparative analysis of the party, government, and military newspapers during the days of the crisis, see Roman Kolkowicz, *Conflicts in Soviet Party-Military Relations, 1962–63* (Santa Monica, Calif.: Rand, 1963), pp. 11–15.

We must all realize that without a high level of technical training for all personnel and without the knowledge of the principles of physics and mathematics the skilled utilization of modern combat weapons is impossible. *This holds equally true for political workers.* If they do not know combat equipment to the necessary degree, they cannot objectively conduct political-educational work among personnel.[20]

The difference between this and Malinovsky's article of June is that the latter one more particularly singled out the political workers for criticism of their educational deficiencies. In the previous article, Malinovsky had made his remarks with regard to all types of leaders.

In the October speech, Malinovsky also scored the use of criticism and self-criticism by some political organs. The Minister of Defense argued that criticism and self-criticism constitute a "sharp weapon" to be employed sensibly and then only when it "is principled and helps us strengthen our armed forces." Another practice of the political workers criticized by Malinovsky was the superficial guidance given by higher staffs and political organs to deficient units.

An article by Yepishev in an October issue of *Kommunist Vooruzhennykh Sil* further added to the growing rift between the political administration in the armed forces and the professional military. Yepishev noted that the beneficial impact of party resolutions is manifested not only "in the steady growth of the maturity of military cadres," but also in the strengthening of "one-man command on a party basis."[21] Therefore, an "indispensable condition for the implementation of one-man command" derives from "the constant support given to commanders in party and komsomol organizations."[22] He also pointed out that "a tested expedient" for overcoming "distortions of one-man command" is criticism and self-criticism.[23]

Next, Yepishev disparaged the "old, artificial division of ideological and organizational work"[24] practiced by some officers. What the officers do not understand, explained Yepishev, is that "the ideological education of servicemen and the organization of them in the successful determination of problems confronting the military is an indivisible process."[25] Too often one encounters propa-

---

[20] *Krasnaya Zvezda*, October 25, 1962. Italics added.

[21] General of the Army A. A. Yepishev, "To Put Firmly into Practice the Policy of the Party in the Armed Forces," *Kommunist Vooruzhennykh Sil*, No. 19 (October 1962), p. 7.

[22] *Ibid.*, p. 9.

[23] *Ibid.*

[24] *Ibid.*, p. 12.

[25] *Ibid.*

gandists who consider their task to be not more than to read lectures and speeches. In order to overcome such deficiencies, the MPA head recommended the further improvement of the activities of party organizations, because deficiencies arise only when "there is no true struggle for the progressive role of every communist, irreconcilability with shortcomings, and principled criticism and self-criticism."[26]

Coming during the tense atmosphere of the Cuban Missile Crisis, these articles further tended to underline the seriousness of the debate between the professional and political military elements that had been steadily growing since June. Perhaps then, as a result of the added pressures of the crisis and the divisiveness it had created among the Soviet leaders, some prominent figures concluded that the time was ripe to reassert party authority over the armed forces. Moreover, the evidence in the post-crisis period suggests that even some of the leading members of the professional military shared this view.

On November 6, 1962, *Pravda* reprinted a speech by A. N. Kosygin, in which Kosygin praised Khrushchev's actions with regard to the Cuban situation as well as the "mutual concessions" made to end the crisis. He revealed, however, that there were "some people" who did not approve of the concessions.[27] While Kosygin may have in part been pointing to Chinese opposition to the Soviet-American agreement,[28] it is also likely that some of the opposition may have been internal, especially from the professional military.[29]

This interpretation is partially supported by a newspaper interview given by Marshal of the Soviet Union V. I. Chuykov on November 17. A major facet of the interview was the emphasis Chuykov placed on the dominant role of the Party in military affairs.[30] In order to lend authority to his arguments, Chuykov cited an exchange of telegrams between Stalin and Lenin which had not been previously revealed. The telegram from Stalin to Lenin asserted that "diplomacy sometimes successfully wrecks the results of our military successes." Lenin is reported by Chuykov to have replied in a telegram to Stalin that "our diplomacy . . . is under the command of the Central Committee and never wrecks our successes." Furthermore, Chuykov also asserted, with regard to more recent

[26] *Ibid.*, p. 13.

[27] Kolkowicz, *Conflicts in Soviet Party-Military Relations, 1962–63*, p. 16.

[28] For a discussion of Chinese views and actions concerning the Cuban Missile Crisis, see William E. Griffith, *The Sino-Soviet Rift* (Cambridge, Mass.: M.I.T. Press, 1964), pp. 60–66.

[29] Between November 8 and December 7, 1962, Kosygin appears to have fallen from First Deputy Prime Minister to merely Deputy Prime Minister. However, this decline was not connected with his November 6 speech, but rather with a defeat in the economic arena. (Tatu, pp. 283–288.)

[30] *Krasnaya Zvezda*, November 17, 1962.

events, that there are "some comrades" who did not understand "the opinions, conclusions, and advanced policies" of the Party. From the context of the time in which the interview was given — that is, immediately after the Cuban crisis — there is little doubt that Chuykov was using this thinly disguised method to criticize the opposition of some military men to the recent Soviet-American agreement.

In late November a pamphlet ascribed to Malinovsky was published.[31] A major emphasis in the pamphlet was that "military doctrine is developed and determined by the political leadership of the state."[32] Citing Khrushchev's January 1960 speech, the pamphlet, moreover, highly praised the personal role of Khrushchev in developing Soviet military doctrine. However, it maintained that as a result of the Cuban crisis "real reasons exist which force the government and the Communist party to strengthen the armed forces."[33]

Subsequently, in a foreign policy report to the USSR Supreme Soviet on December 12, Khrushchev again noted that there were some who had opposed the Soviet-American agreement by which the Soviet Union removed its missiles from Cuba. According to Khrushchev, "there are some who say that the United States allegedly compelled us to yield on certain points."[34] This was true, stated Khrushchev, but the United States had also been compelled to make concessions. And such "is exactly the policy of peaceful coexistence."[35] He questioned for the opposition whether there was a reasonable alternative:

> We are satisfied with such an outcome of the developments in the Caribbean area; without question all other peoples which stand on the positions of peaceful coexistence are also satisfied. This has made it possible for them to live and work in conditions of peace.
>
> Now let us imagine for a minute what could have happened, had we emulated the die-hard politicians and refused to make a mutual concession. This would be like the two goats of the folk tale who met on a footbridge and, having locked horns, refused to make way for each other.

[31] In analyzing this pamphlet, Thomas Wolfe has suggested that, while Malinovsky may have voluntarily signed it, it was probably not written by him. Thomas W. Wolfe, *Role of the Soviet Military in Decision-Making and Soviet Politics* (Santa Monica, Calif.: Rand, 1963), p. 13.

[32] Quoted in *ibid.*, p. 12.

[33] Quoted in Carl A. Linden, *Khrushchev and the Soviet Leadership, 1957–1964* (Baltimore: The Johns Hopkins University Press, 1966), p. 157.

[34] N. S. Khrushchev, *The Present International Situation and the Foreign Policy of the Soviet Union* (New York: Crosscurrents Press, 1963), p. 17.

[35] *Ibid.*, p. 18.

> As is known, both clashed into the chasms. But is this a reasonable course for human beings?[36]

And, with even more vivid detail, he observed in another place in the report:

> And what would have happened, had we, during the events over Cuba, failed to display due restraint but heeded the shrill promptings of the "ultra-revolutionaries"? We would have entered a period of a new world war, a thermonuclear war. Of course, our vast country would have held out, but tens upon tens of millions of people would have perished. As to Cuba — it probably would have simply ceased to exist as a result of a thermonuclear war. Other countries densely populated and lacking broad expanses, who were involved in the conflict, would have completely perished too.[37]

Conversely, pointed out Khrushchev, the policy followed by the Soviet Union had prevented a thermonuclear war, saved Cuba, and won an American pledge not to invade Cuba in the future.

In sum, while the evidence is sketchy, the Cuban Missile Crisis appears to have split the professional military establishment into two groups. One group adhered more closely to the Party's official line and accepted more readily the "mutual concessions" interpretation of the Soviet-American agreement. Moreover, this group appears to have been more alert to the dangers of the growing political-military conflicts within the armed forces. The second group seems to have opposed the party line and viewed the agreement as a capitulation in the face of U.S. aggressiveness. While it perhaps recognized the growing political-military rift, this group was less willing to submit itself to the party line. In this way, the Cuban Missile Crisis had not only exacerbated the rift between the military and political factions in the Soviet Union, but also divided the professional military into two conflicting subgroups.

The strained relationships were reflected in several of the articles written by professional military men to commemorate the twentieth anniversary of the battle of Stalingrad. The articles were divided on the issue of assigning credit for the victory to military leadership or to the political leadership in general and Khrushchev in particular. As noted by Kolkowicz, Marshals Rotmistrov, Voronov, and Kazakov preferred to emphasize the major part played by the military.[38]

---

[36] *Ibid.*

[37] *Ibid.*, p. 28.

[38] Kolkowicz, *Conflicts in Soviet Party-Military Relations, 1962–63*, p. 23. For the articles of the marshals, see, respectively, *Krasnaya Zvezda*, January 16, 1963; *Pravda*, January 31, 1963; and *Izvestiya*, February 1, 1963.

On the other hand, Khrushchev's dominant role was given greater stress in articles by Marshals Biryuzov, Chuykov, and Yeremenko.[39] Marshal Malinovsky's article for the occasion not only denied that any one individual was responsible for devising the victory plan, but also credited the heretofore condemned Marshal G. K. Zhukov with a partial role.[40]

There were other significant signs that at least some professional military leaders were attempting to demand greater recognition for the importance of the armed forces to Soviet society, for January–February 1963 was another period in which the military press launched one of its rehabilitation campaigns. Again, the press printed favorable articles on victims of the 1937 purges. Marshals Yegorov, Yakir, and Tukhachevskiy were praised in these articles as great military leaders, true Communists, and victims of monstrous slanders.[41]

The MPA's Independent Line

Faced with these oblique challenges, the spokesmen of the political administration in the armed forces responded with a renewed effort in February to reassert the authority of the Party in military affairs. On February 12, there began the first of a three-part series, "The Armed Forces of the USSR in the Contemporary Stage." Written by a candidate of the philosophical sciences and entitled "The Army of the All-National State," the first part defined the class character and functions of the Soviet Army, but contained essentially nothing new or noteworthy.[42] The second article in the series stressed the important functions played by the Party in preparing the Soviet armed forces to fight a future war, in which missile-nuclear weapons would assume the decisive role. Somewhat surprisingly for a political administration publication, however, it also observed that a complete victory could be achieved "only as a result of the combined operations by all types of armed forces and all branches of the services."[43] The third article, authored by three candidates of the historical sciences, went the furthest of the series in emphasizing party dominance. The authors contended that "only the

[39] See, respectively, *Politicheskoye Samoobrazovaniye*, No. 2 (February 1963), pp. 33–41; *Krasnaya Zvezda*, February 2, 1963; and *Pravda*, January 27, 1963.

[40] *Pravda*, February 2, 1963.

[41] In the order named, see the articles in *Krasnaya Zvezda*, January 6 and 20 and February 16, 1963.

[42] *Ibid.*, February 12, 1963.

[43] *Ibid.*, February 15, 1963.

Party, relying in all its activities on the Marxist-Leninist science in conformity with natural social laws, is capable of correctly resolving all the problems connected with the defense of the socialist homeland, military construction, and the theoretical and practical military affairs."[44] They also maintained that party authority should continue to grow in the present era. In their words:

> In contemporary historical conditions, the demands of the leading and guiding influence of the Party in the cause of strengthening the defense potential of the Soviet state and the power of our armed forces are still growing.
>
> The rising leadership role of the Party in the armed forces in the contemporary stage declares first of all the general conformity of the period of the spread of the construction of the communist community, which, as is explained in the Program of the CPSU, "is characterized by the further growth of the role and importance of the Communist Party, as the guiding and directing force of Soviet society."

Moreover, "only the collective wisdom and enormous political experience of the Party and its Leninist Central Committee" could be expected to solve the problems of preventing war and keeping aggressors in check. Specifically, the authors pointed to Khrushchev's speech to the 4th Session of the Supreme Soviet in January 1960 and noted that the policies expressed therein "underlaid contemporary Soviet military doctrine."

At the conclusion of the article, the three authors praised the rising party influence, which had resulted in the fact that 90 percent of the officers holding the rank equivalent to company commander were Communists. In addition, the Party was said to have consolidated one-man command on a "party basis," even though constant improvement was possible. They stated:

> Thanks to the growth of the political maturity of our command cadres, one-man command on a party basis has consolidated. Commanders with single authority consistently put the policy of the Party and Government into practice, actively participate in party-political work, and combine a high degree of exactingness to subordinates with a fatherly care for them. Together with this, it is necessary also in the future to improve the education of the educators, that is, the command-leaders.[45]

Also in February 1963, Yepishev published two articles concerning the authority of the Party over military matters, one in a party newspaper and one

[44] *Ibid.*, February 20, 1963.

[45] *Ibid.*

in a historical journal. The newspaper article repeated the often cited assertions that the leadership of the Communist Party constitutes "the main source" of the armed forces' strength. One "striking illustration" of this, argued Yepishev, was the fact that so many soldiers in World War II requested party membership as they went into battle. He also invoked the example of Lenin to emphasize the importance of MPA work for modern conditions. As the MPA head noted:

> Proceeding from the Marxist thesis of the enormous role of the morale factor in contemporary war, V. I. Lenin and the Party highly appraised the activity of communists and party organizations in the army and attached exceptional significance to party-political work, as one of the decisive factors of the high combat capability of troops.[46]

In another place in the article, referring to a more recent time framework, he reiterated this close relationship between political work and Soviet fighting capability, stating:

> Formed on the basis of directives of the Party, contemporary Soviet military doctrine gives the opportunity for military cadres purposefully and on a scientific basis to construct the whole process for the education of troops and to raise their combat readiness.
>
> Our armed forces, equipped with rocket-nuclear weapons and staffed with the best troops in the world, who are limitlessly devoted to their people, party, and government, are ready at any moment to defend the construction of communism in the country of the Soviets.

Like the newspaper article, Yepishev's journal article emphasized the theme of party dominance over the armed forces. He noted that "only the Communist Party was capable of creating the armed organization of the socialist state and completely carrying out the leadership of it."[47] He also repeated the claim of the third article in the series "The Armed Forces of the USSR in the Contemporary Stage" with regard to the relevance of the Party for the period of communist construction. Yepishev maintained that "now, in the period of developing communist construction, still greatly increasing is the role and significance of the Communist Party as the leading and directing force of Soviet society."[48]

[46] *Pravda*, February 22, 1963.

[47] General of the Army A. A. Yepishev, "The Increasing Role of the CPSU in the Leadership of the Armed Forces," *Voprosy Istorii*, No. 2 (February 1963), p. 3.

[48] *Ibid.*, p. 8.

However, the journal article contained two startling passages for a work by the head of the MPA. First, it enumerated a list of "prominent military chiefs" who had been educated and promoted to leadership posts by the Party. The unusual aspect of this alphabetical listing was the fact that the eleventh entry was Marshal G. K. Zhukov.[49] While it is true that in his February 1 *Pravda* article Malinovsky had given mild recognition to the heretofore condemned Zhukov, Yepishev's reference went even further in describing Zhukov as one of the "prominent military chiefs." Although Yepishev subsequently criticized the personality cult of Zhukov and praised the October 1957 plenum for overcoming it, his inclusion of Zhukov's name with the other "approved" military leaders requires some explanation. To phrase it another way: Why did the head of the MPA favorably cite one of the most extreme opponents of the MPA? One possible explanation is that this reference was closely connected with and set the stage for Yepishev's support for the demands of the traditionalist wing of the professional military that appeared later in the article and constituted the second surprising item in the article.

With the journal article, Yepishev made clear his own position on the issue of the size of the armed forces. As noted earlier, Khrushchev had proposed in January 1960 a movement toward troop reduction. Like the *Krasnaya Zvezda* article by a political administration spokesman on February 15, however, Yepishev supported the alternative proposition, namely, that it is necessary to develop "all branches of the armed forces and all types of troops."[50] With regard to mass armies, he declared:

> The practice of contemporary wars testifies to the fact that the reasoning of some theoreticians on the necessity for the renunciation of the creation of mass armies and on the replacement of men by technology has turned out to be groundless. The popular masses with weapon in hand in a field of battle and the popular masses at the rear, where are created the material means for conducting the armed struggle, are the decisive force, determining the course and outcome of contemporary wars. With the increasing role and significance of technology in contemporary war is also increasing the role and importance of the popular masses and the role of the mass armies.[51]

Within the context of the speeches given by professional military spokesmen,

49 *Ibid.*, p. 7.
50 *Ibid.*, p. 11.
51 *Ibid.*, p. 10.

Yepishev's remarks suggest that he sided with the military on this issue. The speeches of professional military men on Soviet Armed Forces Day (February 23) emphasized the importance of "rocket-nuclear" weapons and generally acknowledged in the speeches that such weapons formed the basis for all branches of services.[52] Malinovsky's reference to the ground forces, moreover, implied a potential major role in the future.

> In many ways, our ground forces have been transformed. In a numerical regard, for recent years they were significantly curtailed, and at the same time their combat capabilities were increased by far. The basis of the combat power of the ground forces has now become rockets of an operational-tactical type.[53]

Yepishev's views on the need for a mass army conflicted with the position of Khrushchev. In a pre-election speech in late February, Khrushchev reiterated his confidence in rocket-nuclear weapons as the major weapon of a future world war. He contended to his audience that if a new war were to be launched "it would end in complete failure *on the very first day of the war.*"[54] This seems to imply that since the enemy would be quickly defeated, there would be little reason to maintain a larger army than at present. Actually, the only significant modification of his earlier policy made at this time was related to the issue of resource allocation. Herein Khrushchev stated that because of the international situation and the failure to reach a disarmament agreement with the United States it would be necessary to allocate greater expenditures for defense appropriations. As explained by Khrushchev:

> ... life dictates the necessity to spend enormous sums for maintaining our military power at the proper height. This, of course, reduces and cannot not reduce the possibility of obtaining direct blessings for the people. But in this one has to proceed in order to defend the gains of the October Revolution, the gains of socialism, and to prevent the imperialists from attacking our homeland and from launching a general war.

[52] See the interview of Marshal Biryuzov, Moscow Domestic Service, February 21, 1963, 1550 GMT, FBIS, *USSR and East Europe*, No. 38 (February 25, 1963), pp. CC21–CC25; speech of Marshal Rotmistrov, Moscow Domestic Service, February 23, 1963, 1545 GMT, FBIS, *USSR and East Europe*, No. 30 (February 26, 1963) pp. CC18–CC23; Marshal Yakubovskiy's article from *Neues Deutschland* of February 22, 1963, translated in FBIS, *USSR and East Europe*, No. 39 (February 26, 1963), pp. CC7–CC14; and Marshal Yeremenko's article from *Narodna Armiia* of February 23, 1963, translated in FBIS, *USSR and East Europe*, No. 40 (February 27, 1963), pp. CC11–CC14.

[55] *Pravda*, February 23, 1963.

[54] *Ibid.*, February 28, 1963. Italics added.

> This is why, when available resources are assessed, we must sensibly take into account the needs of the peace economy and the needs of defense, and so to balance one and the other in order to prevent one side from being over-emphasized. I think that no one with a sober mind will reproach the Central Committee of our Party and the Soviet Goveriment in that they follow such a policy.[55]

Rather, as Khrushchev went on to note, the Central Committee and the Soviet Government would be severely criticized if they failed to allocate the necessary funds for defense.

If not from the head of the Party, then from where did Yepishev receive the political support necessary to advocate such an obviously anti-Khrushchev policy and still retain his position? It seem that Yepishev's declaration in favor of mass armies should be viewed in the context of the various challenges to Khrushchev's leadership being advanced in early 1963 by several of the major conservative political figures.[56] As one Western observer of Soviet affairs has noted, the winter months of 1962–63 "were among the most troubled of the Khrushchev era."[57] The political opposition on a number of issues was so strong, according to rumors in Moscow, that at the February meeting of the Presidium "Khrushchev had found himself in the minority and that his resignation had even been considered."[58] Among the policies adopted at this time apparently without Khrushchev's approval were: (1) a re-Stalinization in art and literature, (2) conciliatory moves toward China and Albania, (3) a stiffening of the line against revisionism, (4) greater emphasis on heavy industry as announced in Khrushchev's February 28 speech, and (5) a recentralization of economic planning and a renewed emphasis on military-related production under a new Supreme Council to be headed by D. F. Ustinov, a renowned exponent of heavy industry.[59]

It is also noteworthy that the leading conservative figures opposing Khrushchev were F. R. Kozlov, apparently the second most powerful political figure since 1960, and Suslov. Of the two, Koslov was the more important, but Suslov gave vital support, especially on re-Stalinization of art and literature and appeasement toward China. It is possible to conjecture, therefore, that Yepishev's support for the ground forces in February 1963 was another feature of the conserva-

[55] *Ibid.*

[56] They were conservative in the sense that they generally supported the orthodox policies of the past and resisted the changes that Khrushchev was attempting to introduce.

[57] Tatu, p. 298.

[58] *Ibid.*, p. 312.

[59] *Ibid.*, pp. 312–40; and Linden, pp. 158–73.

tive opposition to Khrushchev. Similarly, Yepishev's inclusion of Zhukov in the *Voprosy Istorii* article can be explained as an indication of displeasure with Khrushchev, rather than an approval of Zhukov himself.

In March 1963 the *Kommunist Vooruzhennykh Sil* printed an article by a political administration spokesman which praised the concept of the mass army. According to the author, a colonel and candidate of the philosophical sciences, "the increased role of the masses in the achievements of victory is one of the most important regulations of contemporary war."[60] From this, he reasoned that mass armies retain their extremely important function.

> The increased role of the popular masses in contemporary war depends also on the fact that it requires a mass army. It is known that in the first world war the belligerent states mobilized 70 million men, and in the second 110 of the 210 million of the adult population of these states (without colonies). In the event of the beginning of a third world war, it, in spite of the broad use of rocket-nuclear weapons and the diversity of military technology, will be conducted with mass, million-strong armies and in the enormous spaces of the planet. Such armies are used in the first day of the war, so that the coalition will be readily rushed to reach its strategic and military-political aims in as short a time as possible.[61]

Moreover, this article repeated the list of "prominent military chiefs" who had been educated and promoted by the Party that had appeared in Yepishev's *Voprosy Istorii* article. And, as in the original alphabetical listing, Marshal Zhukov's name occupied the eleventh spot.[62]

It should be emphasized that the MPA's support for the mass-army concept, and thereby for the traditionalist wing of the professional military, in no way altered its views on the issue of party dominance over the military in areas of decision making and policy formulation. As already noted, the same articles by political administration spokesmen who approved mass armies also stressed party leadership in military matters. Further signs also existed.

On February 17, 1963, the Party Central Committee approved a new thesis on political organs and instructions to party organizations in the armed forces. The new thesis and instructions reaffirmed several points that the Central Committee had previously ratified in August 1960. Primary party organizations were

[60] Colonel M. Skirido, "The Role of the Popular Masses and the Person in Contemporary War," *Kommunist Vooruzhennykh Sil*, No. 5 (March 1963), p. 9. Italicized in the original.
[61] *Ibid.*, p. 10.
[62] *Ibid.*, p. 16.

created in regiments, battalions, flotillas, companies, and squadrons. They further stated:

> . . . regiments, on ships, and their equivalent units, on faculties of military academies and higher military colleges, numbering above 75 communists, with the permission of the political sections of the sections of the army, the political administrations of districts, groups of forces, and fleets can be created party committees with the right of party organizations of battalions, flotillas, and their equivalent subdivisions with the rights of primary party organizations.[63]

In addition to the structural aspects, the new thesis and instructions "emphasized the leading role of the Communist Party in the armed forces, the significance of party-political work, [and] the role of political organs."[64]

To this was added the fact that an unsigned article in a March issue of *Kommunist Vooruzhennykh Sil* gave a detailed breakdown of a ten-hour lesson to be conducted by political workers on the theme of the Party's leading role in the armed forces. In this article, it was noted once more that one-man command in the armed forces is carried out "on a party basis."[65] The article also pointed out that the political lesson sought to characterize the Party as the dominant factor in military construction. It should be taught, indicated the article, that "only the Party — the chief and directing force of Soviet society, armed with Marxist-Leninist theory — can successfully guide all of the enormous and complicated affairs of military construction."[66] Moreover, as one part of the lesson should make clear, party leadership is displayed first and foremost in the fact that "all questions of the defense of our homeland, the construction of the army and navy, and military practice and military theory are decided in exact accordance with the ideology and policies of the CPSU and on the basis of its resolutions and statutes."[67] In sum, the theme of the article was that only the Party had the capability of formulating the correct doctrines and instituting the appropriate activities for the Soviet armed forces. The importance of the article was re-enforced by the fact that it was presented as an authoritative outline for poli-

---

63 Quoted in Yu. P. Petrov, *Stroitel'stvo politorganov, partiynykh i komsomol'skikh organizatsiy armii i flota (1918–1968) (The Construction of Political Organs and Party and Komsomol Organizations in the Army and Navy [1918–1968])* (Moscow: Voyenizdat, 1968), p. 493.

64 *Ibid.*, pp. 493–94.

65 "The CPSU is the Organizer and Leader of the Soviet People in the Construction of Communism," *Kommunist Vooruzhennykh Sil*, No. 6 (March 1963), p. 71.

66 *Ibid.*, p. 73.

67 *Ibid.*

tical instructions to all servicemen, rather than merely as a personal essay.

Despite the numerous and serious challenges to his personal leadership in 1963, Khrushchev appears to have made a comeback, or at least initiated the moves toward a political comeback, in mid-March. At that time, Marshal Zakharov, probably one of the leading military figures of the post-Cuban crisis opposition to Khrushchev and an outspoken critic of the political organs in the armed forces, was removed from his post as Chief of the General Staff. Subsequently, marshals more favorable to Khrushchev were promoted to key positions. On March 28, Biryuzov was named as Zakharov's successor.[68] In the following two weeks, Beloborodov was appointed the head of the Moscow Military District,[69] and Krylov was made the chief of the Strategic Missile Forces.[70]

Similar moves were made in the political sphere in these months. First, Khrushchev's chief political rival, Frol Kozlov, fell ill and was swept from the scene. His last public appearance occurred on April 10. There were also signs that Suslov's position had slightly slipped. When Khrushchev delivered an important speech toward the end of April, Suslov, a full Presidium member, was not seated among the Presidium members at the table with Khrushchev, but was relegated to a position among the alternate Presidium members.[71] Conversely, two figures favorable to Khrushchev at this time, Brezhnev and Podgorny, were promoted in June to secretaryships in the Central Committee while retaining their Presidium memberships.

Generally speaking, therefore, by mid-June Khrushchev had successfully reasserted his personal authority and was able to quiet, if not silence, most of the major voices of opposition.

The new situation was reflected in the fact that MPA spokesmen temporarily refrained from giving public support for the mass-armies concept. Articles and speeches of the political administration officials now tended to advocate positions more consistent with the propositions advanced by Khrushchev in January 1960. For example, the second of the April issues of *Kommunist Vooruzhennykh Sil* published an article by Colonel S. Baranov, a professor at the Lenin Military-Political Academy, which asserted that a future world war

> . . . will be a war fought with missiles and nuclear weapons, which will give it a fantastically destructive nature. In this war, the initial period will be of particular significance. . . . The imperialists should know that if they unleash a

[68] *Krasnaya Zvezda*, March 28, 1963.

[69] *Ibid.*, April 30, 1963.

[70] *Ibid.*, May 31, 1963.

[71] Tatu, p. 346.

war our armed forces will deal a lightning-swift destructive blow in order to turn and rout the enemy on the first day of the war.[72]

Criticism of Ideological Work in the Armed Forces

Another sign of the new situation was the change in attitude expressed by Colonel General N. A. Lomov. As noted at the beginning of this chapter, Lomov had credited military men in May 1962 with a share in formulating the Soviet Union's military view of the world.[73] Just one year later, however, Lomov wrote in his book *Soviet Military Doctrine* that "the foundations of military doctrine are determined by the country's political leadership, since it alone is competent [*pravomochno i kompetentno*] to solves the problems of military construction."[74] While this was not an unusual statement for an MPA spokesman, its importance rests in its contrast with the earlier statement by the same person and serves to emphasize the changes that had taken place between the two dates.

Then, in June, the Central Committee convened a party plenum, whose main

[72] Colonel S. Baranov, "CPSU Leadership Is the Fundamental Basis for Soviet Military Construction" *Kommunist Vooruzhennykh Sil*, No. 8 (April 1963), p. 19.

At this time the Party also took steps to gain closer control over the Strategic Missile Forces by modifying the existing relationship between the MPA and the political administration of the rocket forces. As one Soviet writer noted, the Party Central Committee had discussed the question of improving party-political work in the rocket forces as early as March. The Central Committee ordered the MPA "to intensify its work, to raise its ideological content, and tightly to coordinate it with military training." (See Petrov, *Stroitel'stvo politorganov*, p. 486.) However, within a brief time the Central Committee appears to have reversed itself and determined that the MPA "could not cope with the management of these problems." *(Ibid.)* Consequently, on April 4, the Party Central Committee adopted a resolution which created a new and separate political administration for the Strategic Missile Forces. In the words of the resolution "On the Creation of the Political Administration of the Rocket Forces," it was decided: "To adopt the proposal of the Minister of Defense of the USSR and the Main Political Administration of the Soviet Army and Navy on the creation of a political administration of rocket forces and abolish in connection with this the administration of the political organs of the rocket forces of the Main Political Administration." (*KPSS o Vooruzhennykh Silakh Sovetskogo Soyuza. Dokumenty 1917–1968* [*The CPSU on the Armed Forces of the Soviet Union. Documents 1917–1968*] [Moscow: Voyenizdat, 1969], p. 367.) It is noteworthy that this lessening of the MPA's influence over the Strategic Missile Forces should come at the very time when Yepishev and the MPA were supporting the mass-armies concept. However, there is no concrete evidence that this was even a minor cause of the separation.

[73] See above, p. 95.

[74] Colonel General N. A. Lomov, *Sovetskaya voyennaya doktrina (Soviet Military Doctrine)* (Moscow: "Znaniye" Publishing House, 1963), p. 5.

topic of concern was ideology. In his report to the plenum, Yepishev began by defining the importance of party-political work in the modern Soviet armed forces. According to Yepishev, a high level of political work positively enhances Soviet defense power

> ... for the power of the Soviet armed forces depends not only on the first-class military technology, but first of all on the people who, in perfecting the mastery of its technology, are educated in the unfading ideas of Marxism-Leninism. The further improvement of all ideological work and the new criteria in evaluating our activities for forming the moral-combat qualities of personnel is a task of primary importance for all military soviets, commanders, political organs, party and komsomol organizations of the army and navy.
>
> The decisive conditions for the unrelenting increasing material and spiritual strength of our army and navy is the constant concern of the Party and its Central Committee on the party-political work and the ideological education of Soviet troops.[75]

The MPA head also pointed out that serious consideration was being given to creating "a more orderly system of Marxist-Leninist training of officers, generals, and admirals, which would provide for them a consistent and deep study of all the component parts of Marxism-Leninism, creatively developing Soviet military science and perfecting the leadership of troops."[76] He also made note of the fact that one area of the officer's training requiring re-examination was "the utilization of the time allotted in educational plans of military-educational institutions on the study of social sciences."[77]

In a speech delivered to the graduates of military academies less than a week after Yepishev's plenum report, Malinovsky conversely stressed the important effects that modern technological changes have had on the combat training of Soviet soldiers. As a result of these innovations, observed Malinovsky, "man must now have considerably more knowledge and skill than in the past years."[78]

[75] *Plenum Tsentral'nogo Komiteta Kommunisticheskoy partii Sovetskogo Soyuza, 18–21 iyunya 1963 goda: Stenograficheskiy otchet (Plenum of the Central Committee of the Communist Party of the Soviet Union, 18–21 June 1963: Stenographic Record)* (Moscow: State Publishing House for Political Literature, 1964), p. 186. A summarized text of Yepishev's report was printed also in *Pravda*, June 21, 1963. For a brief summary of the plenum's decisions, see "To Bring into Operation All Means of Ideological Work," *Kommunist Vooruzhennykh Sil*, No. 14 (July 1963). pp. 9–12.

[76] *Ibid.*, p. 189.

[77] *Ibid.*, p. 190.

[78] *Pravda*, June 27, 1963.

The Minister of Defense also said that "there can be no success in the training and education of troops and in their combat activity without the strict observation of the Leninist principles of one-man command."[79]

Two weeks later, Malinovsky published another and more direct attack on ideological work in the armed forces. He openly admitted that "we are not doing everything" to combat Western ideology and "that in this connection there is still a very primitive approach in our country and that the necessary militant spirit and sharpness are lacking."[80] The consequences of these shortcomings have been manifested in many ways in the Soviet soldiers. Malinovsky maintained:

> Even in our military circles we sometimes meet people who are not willing to work honestly to fulfill their duties as soldiers and citizens of the USSR. We have not gotten rid of parasites, time-servers, swindlers, drunkards, bureaucrats, and heartless functionaries. That there are remnants of the past in the consciousness and behavior of people is one of the most important reasons for gross violations of military discipline.

He also criticized the lack of enthusiasm in some units for military history and traditions, a situation which had developed where "indifferent people with cold hearts and souls" were admitted to propaganda work, and the lack of attention to the fight against red-tapism, stagnation, formalism, and bureaucratism in socialist competition.

Like Yepishev's report to the June plenum, Malinovsky's article recognized a need to improve the system of Marxist-Leninist training of military cadres, but the concrete application of the principle suggested by the two leaders was different. Whereas the MPA head stressed the need for improving social studies and allocating more time to political studies, the Minister of Defense argued for the necessity of overcoming "the alienation of propaganda and theoretical studies from the concrete tasks, from life, and from our practical work." The latter also noted that the center of attention should be shifted away from the structured study of political theory to the private study of theory. After this criticism of political training, Malinovsky further asserted:

> We should no longer put up with sluggishness and slowness in improving the forms and methods of the political training of the soldiers. Thus, for example, there has been talk for a long time about the necessity of radically improving the system of political training of the personnel and sergeants. Yet

[79] *Ibid.*

[80] *Krasnaya Zvezda*, July 5, 1963.

there have been no decisive improvements in this sector .Although in some places new and more efficient methods are being adopted in conducting political training the contents of this training still do not correspond fully to the enhanced requirements of our time. In some places conservatism is manifesting itself as well as adherence to the old recalcitrant forms.[81]

Malinovsky then laid the blame for these deficiencies on "the leading organs," that is, the MPA itself.

Perhaps because of these strong attacks on the officials of the MPA in June and July, Malinovsky went out of his way to be very complimentary to the Party in general and Khrushchev in particular. In the speech to the military graduates, Malinovsky referred to Khrushchev as the "Supreme Commander-in-Chief" of the Soviet armed forces.[82] Even though Malinovsky had once previously, at the 22nd Party Congress, referred to Khrushchev by this title, its usage was extremely rare. In an almost equally rare move for the Minister of Defense, he maintained in his July article that ideological work must be radically improved in order to consolidate further one-man command on a party basis.[83]

Throughout the remainder of 1963, ideological education of the Soviet soldier was one of the most prevalent themes in Soviet political-military writings. The June plenum's resolutions and speeches were constantly cited to illustrate the need for improving ideological work among the troops. [84] Whatever the effect of this campaign to improve the ideological level of the lower ranks, its effect among the officers appears to have been extremely poor. One political administration spokesman observed toward the end of the summer, for example, that:

Serious defects still exist in the ideological and political training of military personnel, particularly officers, in certain units and formations. In a number

[81] *Ibid.*

[82] *Pravda*, June 27, 1963. For Malinovsky to give such a reference only tended to underline Malinovsky's own subordination to Khrushchev in both a formal and an actual sense.

[83] *Krasnaya Zvezda*, July 5, 1963.

[84] Among the many articles and speeches on this theme, see Yepishev's article in *Izvestiya*, July 7, 1963; V. Platkovskiy, "Marxist-Leninist Ideology Is a Powerful Weapon in the Struggle for Communism," *Kommunist Vooruzhennykh Sil*, No. 14 (July 1963), pp. 13–22; Yepishev, "To Conduct Ideological Work Actively, Offensively, and Effectively," *Kommunist Vooruzhennykh Sil*, No. 15 (August 1963), pp. 10–22; Admiral V. Grishanov, "To Instill a Communist Attitude in Military Service," *Kommunist Vooruzhennykh Sil*, No. 17 (September 1963), pp. 18–24; Colonel D. Grishin and Captain 1st Rank F. Sinenko, "The Development of the Leninist Principles of Military Construction in the Program of the CPSU," *Kommunist Vooruzhennykh Sil*, No. 23 (December 1963), pp. 8–16; and Colonel General M. Kalashnik, "The Meaning of Ideological Work Is in Action," *Kommunist Vooruzhennyh Sil*, No. 24 (December 1963), pp. 8–16.

of cases, the tenets of the CPSU Program are being demonstrated with insufficient convincingness. Sufficient attention is not always devoted to problems of proletarian internationalism and socialist patriotism. Generals and senior officers still rarely give talks and lectures in subunits. Independent study of Marxist-Leninist theory by officers, which constitutes the primary method of ideological and theoretical strengthening of military cadres, is frequently poorly organized. Lectures, talks, discussions on theory are rather formalistic and therefore do not have any great influence on increasing troop combat readiness and on strengthening military discipline.[85]

In October, recognizing the weakness in the system of political training in the armed forces, the Central Committee convened an assembly of ideological workers in the army and navy for the purpose of introducing improvements. According to the *Krasnaya Zvezda* report on the assembly, Yepishev again emphasized the fact that "many shortcomings" existed in political work and noted that this applied to work with officers as well as with the lower ranks.[86] In a long speech to the assembly, Malinovsky appears to have enthusiastically endorsed Yepishev's observation. The Minister of Defense declared that ideological activity had entered into a "new stage" as a result of the June plenum resolutions. He also asserted that Marxist-Leninist ideas are "the true and indispensable compass for the resolution of all questions of military theory and practice, the urgent problems of military preparedness, and strengthening the discipline and education of troops."[87] Malinovsky furthermore advised commanders and commanding staffs in the army and navy that they should perfect their skills "to analyze phenomena and facts *from a Marxist-Leninist position*, to think creatively, and to determine the greatest effective paths for the resolution of practical tasks."[88]

As a result of this assembly (together with the reorganization of the MPA in April), the MPA "began to give improved organizational and ideological work in the army and navy," claims one Soviet source. Political workers were urged to supervise more closely the various activities of officers and generals. In this way, it was maintained, the elimination of expressed shortcomings and the exchange of positive experiences were given added impetus.[89]

---

[85] A. Iovlev, "Demands of the 22nd Congress of the Party and the Program of the CPSU on Military Cadres," *Kommunist Vooruzhennykh Sil*, No. 15 (August 1963), p. 45.

[86] *Krasnaya Zvezda*, November 1, 1963.

[87] *Ibid.*

[88] *Ibid.* Italics added.

[89] Petrov, *Stroitel'stvo politorganov*, p. 487.

Ideological Preparation Versus
Technical Training

In a speech to a Central Committee plenum on December 13, Khrushchev once again asserted his intention to reduce the size of the Soviet armed forces and the allocation for military expenditures. He phrased his justification for these acts in terms of the need for peaceful development and disarmament. As the First Secretary of the CPSU observed:

> . . . the Soviet Union proposes to compete not in preparations for war, but in the field of peace. We are against the arms race and do not want to pour oil on the flame. The Soviet Union is confident that there is a more realistic approach to living on one planet with states of different social systems. We would want to think that the understanding of this will also take hold among the statesmen of Western states and that they will submit to the command of the times and the requirements of the people — to start with disarmament.
>
> On its side, the Soviet Union will not relax its efforts in the struggle for the attainment of this goal.[90]

Immediately following this proposition, Khrushchev stated:

> I want to announce to the plenum of the Central Committee that we are now considering the possibility of a slightly further reduction of the numbers of our armed forces.
>
> Bearing such in mind, I will put forth in the forthcoming session of the Supreme Soviet of the USSR a proposal to reduce slightly the military expenditures in the budget for next year — 1964.[91]

Four days later, at the third session of the Supreme Soviet of the USSR, Minister of Finance V. F. Garbuzov revealed that the Soviet Government planned to reduce armed forces expenditures by 600 million rubles. Official allocations,[92] therefore, were set at 13.3 billion rubles and represented a decline from 16.1 percent of the total budget in 1963 to a proposed 14.6 percent in 1964.[93]

[90] *Pravda*, December 15, 1963.

[91] *Ibid.*

[92] While officially announced expenditures are generally considered to be unreliable indicators of Soviet military spending, they do have importance politically and psychologically within the Soviet context. Consequently, the amount may not be exact, but it is a clear sign that the regime has ascribed a lower status to the military budget.

[93] *Pravda*, December 17, 1963.

While the spokesmen for the professional military grudgingly gave their approval to the budget reduction,[94] they generally chose to remain silent on the issue of troop reduction.[95] The strongest, most direct opposition to the troop reduction proposal came from Marshal Chuykov. Although Chuykov had been one of the Party's and, therein, Khrushchev's most ardent supporters in the aftermath of the Cuban Missile Crisis in 1962, his position on troop reduction was probably determined by the fact that his command would be most severely weakened by any decrease in the size of the armed forces. Instead of attacking the idea of troop reduction directly, Chuykov emphasized the need for continuing to maintain a large army. Writing in the government newspaper *Izvestiya* on December 22, Chuykov asserted that the victory in a future world war "can be achieved only by means of the joint actions of all types of armed forces," and concluded consequently that "in modern conditions the ground forces continue to be not only a mandatory but also a most important integral part of the armed forces."[96]

Significantly, spokesmen for the MPA had mixed reactions to the troop reduction proposal. For example, one article in *Kommunist Vooruzhennykh Sil* by a colonel and candidate of historical sciences, although not approaching the issue directly, referred to the ground troops as playing an important role but only as a supplement to the rocket troops.[97] At the opposite extreme was Professor N. A. Lomov, whose two-part *Krasnaya Zvezda* article in early January 1964 clearly supported the mass-army concept. In the first part, Lomov noted that the use of rocket-nuclear weapons might greatly shorten the time needed to achieve wartime objectives, but he also qualified this proposition by pointing out that a world war could possibly become prolonged. According to Lomov:

> . . . it is absolutely clear that, subject to the conditions at the beginning of the war, the armed struggle will be not only to the death, but will not be confined merely to thrusts of nuclear weapons. It could be dragged out and require a protracted and maximum effort of all forces of the army and navy as a whole.[98]

[94] See, for example, the article "In the Leninist Path" by Marshal Grechko in *Krasnaya Zvezda*, December 22, 1963.

[95] Matthew Gallagher pointed out that the few comments made by military men on troop reduction were noncommittal and were printed in foreign press articles, not domestic ones. (Matthew P. Gallagher, "Military Manpower: A Case Study," *Problems of Communism*, XIII, No. 3 [May–June 1964], 62, n. 26.)

[96] Quoted in *ibid.*, p. 61. See also Thomas Wolfe, *Soviet Strategy at the Crossroads* (Cambridge, Mass.: Harvard University Press, 1964), p. 150.

[97] Colonel P. Derevyanko, "Some Features of the Contemporary Revolution in Military Affairs," *Kommunist Vooruzhennykh Sil*, No. 1 (January 1964), p. 20.

[98] *Krasnaya Zvezda*, January 7, 1964.

This point was expanded upon in the second part of the series, so that:

> Winning a victory in the meeting with a strong opponents requires the efforts of a multimillion-strong modern army. *This determines the content of one of the most important principled theses of Soviet military doctrine, which consists in the fact that for the winning of a final victory over the aggressor, it is necessary to have the united effort of all types of armed forces, relying on the decisive role of rocket-nuclear weapons.*[99]

He also maintained that a frequent type of action that the military may be expected to encounter in a future war might be "battles of a large scale."

In February 1964, Malinovsky and Yepishev jointly presided over a conference of Soviet writers wherein the main topic of discussion was "the military-patriotic theme in literature and art."[100] The military press summary of the conference indicated that Yepishev's speech was most directly concerned with the need for improving the stress and presentation of the heroic theme in military writings, a theme in which over the first few years of his administration Yepishev was very deeply interested.[101] A similar theme was addressed by Malinovsky, but he also reiterated the idea that victory in a war launched by the imperialists "can be achieved only as a result of the jointly organized actions of all branches of the armed forces."[102]

Throughout most of the remaining part of 1964, discussions in the political-military press tended to concern themselves with two interrelated issues: the education of political and professional officers and the effect of the postwar technical revolution on military affairs. It was an often cited assertion in the Soviet press that the appearance of nuclear weapons after World War II revolutionized military affairs.[103] Some Soviet spokesmen writing at this time took notice that nuclear weapons were making it possible, among other things, to bypass the enemy's

[99] *Ibid.*, January 10, 1964. Italics in original.

[100] *Ibid.*, February 9, 1964.

[101] See, for example, Yepishev, "To Put Firmly into Practice the Policy of the Party in the Armed Forces," p. 8; General Yepishev's article in *Krasnaya Zvezda*, December 1, 1962; Yepishev, "Military History Is a Very Important Part of Ideological Work," *Voyenno-Istoricheskiy Zhurnal*, No. 1 (January 1963), pp. 3–7; Yepishev, "To Conduct Ideological Work Actively, Offensively, and Effectively," pp. 17–18; Yepishev's report to the June 1963 Central Committee plenum in *Plenum Tsentral'nogo Komiteta . . . 18–21 iyunya 1963 goda*, pp. 191–92; and the report of Yepishev's speech to the All-Army Assembly of Ideological Workers in *Krasnaya Zvezda*, November 1, 1963.

[102] *Krasnaya Zvezda*, February 9, 1964.

[103] See Lomov's article in *Krasnaya Zvezda*, January 7, 1964; Derevyanko, "Some Features of the Contemporary Revolution in Military Affairs," *passim*; Colonel I. Kuzmin, "The Struggle

advance troops and strike directly at his rear installations, to cross the oceans and reach the once geographically invulnerable United States, to destroy swiftly the densely populated centers of countries and indeed annihilate many of the smaller ones, and — from the viewpoint of Khrushchev and the modernist wing of the professional military — to reduce the size of the Soviet standing army. In addition to these factors, the Soviets discussed at great length the effect of the enormous changes of the nuclear era on the soldier and the officer. Such discussions clearly admitted that the greater complexity in the operations and equipment of the contemporary period required a higher level of technical expertise among military personnel. However, the transformation of this requirement into concrete military-educational activities caused considerable debate.

The problems of concretizing the transformation were enormous, yet fundamental. It meant that the Soviet political and military leadership would have to contend with such issues as: (1) the relative importance of ideological training in an era when the importance of technical training was rising by great leaps, (2) with the importance of technical requirements in mind, the amount of time to be devoted to political indoctrination, when such time had to be subtracted from that which might have gone for technical training, (3) the ability (and feasibility) of political workers to maintain positions of leadership, especially in units requiring a high degree of technical expertise, and (4) the apathy of the officer with a high level of technical education toward political-educational activities.

While there had always been in the Soviet armed forces a conflict between the need for political indoctrination and the need for professional training — and the historical development of this conflict has already been noted in previous pages of this study — it again received a significant degree of attention in the aftermath of the June 1963 plenum of the Party Central Committee on ideological matters.

During this discussion, Soviet spokesmen agreed on the propositions that the Communist Party constituted the main source of leadership in military matters (whether solely or in consultation with professional military men) and that the Party's political line should be the motivating principle of military construction. It was also widely remarked that the Party consequently had the right and duty to educate servicemen in the Communist ideology. This right derived from its

of the New with the Old in the Development of Military Affairs," *Kommunist Vooruzhennykh Sil*, No. 8 (April 1964), pp. 40–45; Lieutenant General I. Lipodayev, Colonel P. Galochkin, and Lieutenant Colonel A. Tarasov, "The Revolution in Military Affairs and Some Questions of Party-Political Work," *Kommunist Vooruzhennykh Sil*, No. 19 (October 1964), pp. 8–16.

claim to be the vanguard of the workingman's just and historically determined struggle and the Soviet armed forces were considered to be its instrument for promoting and protecting socialist gains.[104] Moreover, it had the duty because Communist ideology is the vehicle through which is revealed to the Soviet soldier the correctness of his historical mission and, thereby, his consciousness and constancy during battle are strengthened, especially under the severe strains of nuclear engagements. As Professor Lomov stated in his article of January 10:

> The quality of the officer personnel of the armed forces is determined by their Marxist-Leninist concept of the world. It is this very concept which creates a scientific basis for the correct understanding of social features and for a scientific analysis of the laws of the armed struggle and the development trends in military matters. The Marxist-Leninist concept of the world represents the basis for the conviction in the justness of our cause, for the unprecedented moral steadfastness of the Soviet serviceman. It is the ideological basis of their high military discipline.[105]

In his July 1964 speech to graduates of military academies, Khrushchev attempted to rectify the common misunderstanding among some of the Soviet people that the morale factor is not important in the nuclear era. He maintained:

> We now often depict officers in white dressing gowns at a control panel; such a commander sits and presses buttons and in this way supposedly "commands" troops. But we, the military, well know what contemporary military operations will present.
>
> A contemporary war with the use of rocket-nuclear weapons demands from the troops high moral-political and military qualities. Now, as never before, it is necessary for servicemen to have endurance and determination, and organization and discipline.[106]

For these reasons, as one group of Soviet military writers noted, a major item in party-political work "always has been and will be the formation in troops of the steadfast conviction in the rightness and victory of our cause."[107]

---

104 "The Great Revolutionary Force of the Present," *Kommunist Vooruzhennykh Sil*, No. 7 (April 1964), pp. 13–14; and N. Ponomarev, "The Crisis of Bourgeois Theories of War and Peace," *Kommunist Vooruzhennykh Sil*, No. 16 (August 1964), pp. 9–17, *passim*.

105 *Krasnaya Zvezda*, January 10, 1964.

106 *Pravda*, July 9, 1964.

107 Lipodayev, Galochkin, and Tarasov, "Revolution in Military Affairs and Some Questions of Party-Political Work," p. 9.

The recognition of the need for ideological conviction in troops called forth another question: Is it more important to be ideologically prepared or to be technically trained? Of course, the optimum situation would be to do both and slight neither. On this political administration and professional military men were in agreement. However, under the finite limitations of time, both sides asserted the importance of their own sphere and argued that more time should be allowed for it. Neither the political administration nor the professional military appeared to be particularly averse to the other's domain, but then again neither would allow their own sector to be de-emphasized for the benefit of the other.

For its part, the professional military leadership demonstrated a deep awareness for the political administration's obligation to instill in servicemen a strong, politically oriented consciousness in peacetime before a war can begin. From the standpoint of the professional military, this is necessary, for the Party's ideology forms much of the justification for the military policies implemented by, and the comformity required from, the servicemen.[108]

For its part, the political administration leadership was quite well acquainted with the growing complexity in military matters and the time necessary to train soldiers in the use of new weapons. Yet its formal reason for being is to enhance the political level of the servicemen. Consequently, MPA spokesmen tended to stress three factors: first, that the man is more important than the weapons; second, that ideological consciousness is an essential element in the superiority of the Soviet soldier over his counterpart in the imperialist countries; and third, that one-man command on a party basis is a fundamental principle of the Soviet armed forces.

On the first point, the importance of the individual, Marshal F. I. Golikov, a former head of the MPA, observed in September 1964 that, while the Soviet art of war had changed radically in recent years, it still remained true that "in any war victory in the final analyses depends on the condition of the spirit of those who shed blood on the battlefield."[109] From this followed the Soviet contention that the man, not the weapon, would be the decisive factor in a future war, for to assert otherwise would grant the enemy moral equality and/or military superiority and, from a more pragmatic viewpoint, eliminate the MPA's chief reason for being.

In order to prevent this from happening, MPA spokesmen stressed that the higher the level of ideological training, the higher will be the level of Soviet

[108] As Marshal Grechko observed in April 1964: "The entire system of political work among the troops proceeds from the fact that the decisive role is retained by man, the soldier clearly realizing his tasks and ready in the name of the fatherland to accomplish a feat and to sacrifice himself." (*Izvestiya*, April 17, 1964.)

[109] *Krasnaya Zvezda*, September 20, 1964.

military superiority. As Yepishev stated in an article of August 1964, "Marxism-Leninism, the ideas of communism, our social and constitutional system, and the moral-political unity of the Soviet people are the basis and the source of the moral spirit of our armed forces." Subsequently, relating this to Soviet superiority, he claimed:

> The high moral spirit, selfless dedication to the cause of communism, and the consciousness of the historic justice of the cause which is guarded by the Soviet armed forces augmented by the might of the most modern rocket-nuclear weapons make our army invincible. The communist ideological integrity of the Soviet soldiers constitutes our invisible superiority over all the possible adversaries[110]

Another step in inhibiting the decline of the MPA's importance in the nuclear era was the stress placed by MPA spokesmen on the concept of "one-man command on a party basis." Whatever the appeal of such a concept for the dialectician's mind, it is too contradictory to implement concretly. One-man command" asserts the unquestioned authority of the military commander, but "on a party basis" obliges the military commander to seek approval for his actions from the political authorities and to submit his actions to criticism by his unit's party organization. Still, in 1964, MPA officials, continued to argue that one-man command "involves strengthening party-political work" — that is, one-man command on a party basis.[111]

Despite the division between the political administration and the professional military on institutional interests, there was one important factor against which the political administration and the majority of the professional military officials had aligned in common cause. This was the emergence of the military-technical expert, who tended generally to be apathetic in the light of party appeals to engage more actively in political-military matters. The usual rule for political-military propagandists was to stress the idea that agitational and political-educational work had to be the responsibility of all Communists and that no Communists, regardless of rank or position, should be indifferent to this demand.[112] Still, the military "technocrat" possessed a specialized training and performed a needed function. As a result, he had to be tolerated and to a degree pampered.

110 *Izvestiya*, August 9, 1964.

111 Marshal F. Golikov in *Krasnaya Zvezda*, September 20, 1964; and A. A. Yepishev, "The Education of the Soldier-Citizen," *Kommunist* (March 1964), p. 64.

112 Colonel General P. Lukashin, "Political Organs Are the Organizers and Leaders of Ideological Work," *Kommunist Vooruzhennykh Sil*, No. 11 (May 1964), p. 30.

At the same time, professional military men attacked those political administration officers who, like their professional military counterpart, had specialized in their own field and overlooked the complementary side. In such cases, a political worker could not help, it was argued, but be grossly unfamiliar with the equipment used and the activities performed by the men whom he was supposed to be leading. Commenting on this fact in March 1964, Minister of Defense Malinovsky observed:

> Everyone concurs that it is impossible to rely on the success and activity of party-political work if the people organizing it superficially understand the character and nature of contemporary fighting, if they poorly know the new technology and arms, and if they have serious gaps in their tactical training. A political worker, poorly trained in military matters, reduces his activity to sheer enlightenment and is forced to operate only with general appeals and slogans. It is impossible to teach swimming and be afraid to get one's feet wet. Such a person may not be able to note a gross shortcoming in the education of troops and overlook many new and positive things that are born in combat. In a word, he will carry out affairs in isolation from the lives of the soldiers and the problems which they are resolving. In order not to tolerate this, it is necessary for the political leaders, with a feeling of high party responsibility, to expand and deepen their military-technical training and keep abreast of the demands of military science and practice.[113]

Summary

In review, this chapter began to illustrate the dual nature of the problems faced by the MPA in the exercise of political control. Because of its unique position, the MPA is both a spokesman for the professional military and a spokesman for the Party. Thus, in 1963–64, Yepishev and the MPA gave their support to the mass-army concept in apparent opposition to Khrushchev's military policies. Indeed, as late as August 1964, Yepishev's *Izvestiya* article criticized "some bourgeois military theoreticians" who still retain "the hope, which was buried by the experience of World War II, that it is now possible to wage wars with the help of small armies well equipped with nuclear weapons and that, consequently, the role of man boils down to pressing the necessary buttons."[114] Quite clearly,

[113] *Krasnaya Zvezda*, March 3, 1964.

[114] *Izvestiya*, August 9, 1964. As noted earlier, Khrushchev's July 1964 speech to the military academy graduates also criticized the image of the "button pushers." However, the contexts of the two were radically different. Khrushchev was attempting to indicate the continuing importance of the morale factor, whereas Yepishev was referring to the mass-army concept.

this was a "hope" shared also by Khrushchev, so that Yepishev was also declaring his opposition to Khrushchev's military concepts.

At the same time, Yepishev and the MPA were adamant in their contention that the Party must be the guiding force in military construction. Yepishev's opposition to Khrushchev on the issue of mass armies did not mean that he had come under the influence of the professional military. In essence, then, it would appear that Yepishev favored the dominance of the Party — though not necessarily Khrushchev personally — over the professional military.

The next chapter of the study will examine the impact of Khrushchev's ouster on the MPA and political-military matters. Two of the basic questions to be investigated therein will be: What was the role and character of the MPA under the new collective leadership? Were there any significant differences in the role and character of the MPA under the new regime as compared to its role and character under Khrushchev?

5

Political-Military Problems
in the Early Years of the
Collective Leadership

The Removal of Khrushchev: As Seen
from the Viewpoint of the Military

As noted previously, it is extremely rare for public Soviet pronouncements to give recognition to the existence in peacetime of a Supreme Commander-in-Chief. According to the Soviet Constitution, Article 49, Sections 1 and m, the Presidium of the USSR Supreme Soviet "appoints and removes the high command of the U.S.S.R." and "in the intervals between sessions of the Supreme Soviet of the U.S.S.R. proclaim a state of war in the event of an armed attack on the U.S.S.R. . . ."[1] Beyond these general functions, nothing is indicated with regard to a Supreme Commander. However, in the famous volume on Soviet military strategy edited by Marshal V. D. Sokolovskiy and published in mid-1962, it was implied that wartime leadership would be invested in a Supreme Commander:

> All leadership of the country and Armed Forces in wartime will be implemented by the Central Committee of the Communist Party of the Soviet Union, possibly with the organization of a higher agency of leadership for the country and the Armed Forces. This higher agency of leadership may be delegated the same powers the State Defense Committee held during the Great Patriotic War, and be headed by the First Secretary of the Central Committee of the Communist Party of the Soviet Union and head of the government to whom the functions

1 U.S. Congress. House of Representatives. Committee on Internal Security. *The Theory and Practice of Communism in 1971.* Appendix II. 92nd Cong., 1st Sess. (Washington, D.C.: Government Printing Office, 1971), p. 348.

of Supreme Commander-in-Chief of all the Armed Forces may be assigned.[2]

While the official decree appointing Khrushchev to this position has never been published, Malinovsky had acknowledged as early as the 22nd Party Congress that Khrushchev was the Supreme Commander of the Soviet armed forces. He also reiterated that fact in his July 1963 speech to military academy graduates.

In the first months of 1964, Khrushchev's position as Supreme Commander-in-Chief was twice reaffirmed. The first was in Yepishev's March *Kommunist* article, which noted that an enormous influence in the further development and strengthening of the Soviet armed forces had been personally made by "the First Secretary of the CC CPSU, Chairman of the Council of Ministers of the USSR, and Supreme Commander Comrade N. S. Khrushchev."[3] Then the armed forces greeting to Khrushchev on his seventieth birthday on April 17 repeated the very same phrasing.[4]

While these formal recognitions of Khrushchev's position coming so close together in March–April 1964 might suggest that Khrushchev had become unassailable, Malinovsky's personal greeting on the occasion of Khrushchev's birthday injected a note of mild opposition. Despite his reference twice before to Khrushchev as the Supreme Commander, Malinovsky did not make this claim in April 1964, an omission emphasized by its inclusion in the armed forces greeting. Moreover, Malinovsky took this opportunity to assert the view that the professional military should perform an important role in the formulation of military policy and from the context implied that to do otherwise would be a manifestation of the personality cult. In the words of the Minister of Defense:

> A very important condition of the successful resolution of the tasks of military construction was provided by the liquidation by the Central Committee of the Party of everything alien to the Marxist-Leninist stratum which accumulated in the sphere of military policy during the period of the personality cult. The CC of the Party rejected the lifeless canons and dogmas widespread under Stalin and did away with the underestimation of Lenin's military heritage, and reinstated Lenin's principles for the resolution of the problems of military construction. *Before deciding these or other questions*, members of the Central Committee make a detailed study of the state of affairs in the army and navy, the

[2] Marshal of the Soviet Union V. D. Sokolovskiy, *Voyennaya strategiya (Military Strategy)* (Moscow: Voyenizdat, 1962), pp. 428–29. While the 1963 edition of this work carries the paragraph (p. 474), the 1968 edition deletes the final (and obvious) reference to Khrushchev (p. 434).

[3] A. A. Yepishev, "The Education of the Soldier-Citizen," *Kommunist* (March 1964), pp. 64–65.

[4] *Krasnaya Zvezda*, April 18, 1964.

urgent tasks in strengthening the defense potential of the country, and the urgent problems of developing military affairs, *and consult* with the leading military cadres.[5]

The all-military greeting that recognized Khrushchev as Supreme Commander was printed the day after Malinovsky's own mildly independent stand. This suggests a direct relationship between the two. It is possible that the restatement of Khrushchev as Supreme Commander was forced on the military to counteract Malinovsky's position and to demonstrate that the First Secretary was in control of the professional military.

Indeed, there were several signs in mid and late 1964 of Khrushchev's belief that he had firm control over the professional military. In a speech to military academy graduates on July 8, Khrushchev assured the graduates that "lately there has been a mitigation [*smyagcheniye*] of tensions in the international environment."[6] Then, in addressing the Supreme Soviet on July 13, he outlined a plan for increasing personal wages and consumer production. According to Khrushchev, the wage increase had been planned for 1962 but had to be postponed for various reasons, especially by the need in 1962 to increase defense allocations. The wage increase, said the CPSU First Secretary, was:

> . . . one of the next important measures envisaged by the Party for further uplifting the prosperity of the Soviet people. Measures, of which it was a question in previous sessions and was intended to pass earlier, in 1962, but then for some reasons of external and internal order, we were obliged to postpone their implementation temporarily.
>
> An international situation arising at this time forced us to take some measures for strengthening the defense of the country, in connection with which it was necessary to increase the allocation of funds for those purposes. And this found the full approval of the Soviet people.[7]

The implication herein seems to be that the international situation no longer required the increased defense allocations and that these expenditures could be shifted to other economic spheres, including wage increases and consumer production. Indeed, Khrushchev went on to note that "not all leaders have truly understood how important it is to increase constantly the output of consumer goods." It was his view that the situation presented an opportunity "to devote

[5] *Pravda*, April 17, 1964. Italics added.

[6] *Ibid.*, July 9, 1964.

[7] *Pravda*, July 14, 1964.

more resources to the development of the production of consumer goods items."

In the next three months, Khrushchev gave heavy emphasis to the theme of peaceful competition with capitalism. For example, he declared in a speech in early September in conjunction with the signing of a Soviet-Czechoslovakian statement:

> The forces of peace and socialism can maintain peace on earth and prevent a thermonuclear war. We are confident that in peaceful competition with capitalism, socialism will win a victory. In conditions of peace, socialism demonstrates its decisive advantages over capitalism, and therefore the victory of socialism and communism is assured.[8]

Similarly, toward the end of the same month, Khrushchev asserted before the World Forum of Youth:

> To seize power is not enough; it must be held. The main thing, however, is to be able to wield power in order to build a new society and to demonstrate the advantages of the socialist system over the capitalist. But this can be done only by the constructive labor of people in competition, in economic competition. Therefore, the main item in the resolution of the question "Who will win" is this — economic competition, economic competition. I will repeat a third time — economic competition.[9]

As slogans, these utterances would have had little effect on the attitude of the professional military toward Khrushchev. But it appears that Khrushchev was intending to go beyond mere slogan making and to transform these statements into actual programs. On October 2, the Soviet press summarized a speech by Khrushchev wherein Khrushchev was suggesting the reversal of Soviet economic priorities as they existed since the mid-1920's.

> In compiling the long-range plans for the next period, emphasized Comrade N. S. Khrushchev, it is necessary to be guided by the fact that the chief task of this plan is the further raising of the living standard of the people. If in the period of the first five-year plan in the postwar years we laid the fundamental stress on the developing of heavy industry as the basis of raising the economy of the whole country and strengthening its defense potential, then now, when we have powerful industries and when the defense of the country is found to

[8] *Ibid.*, September 5, 1964.
[9] *Ibid.*, September 22, 1964.
[10] *Sovetskaya Rossiya*, October 2, 1964. See also *The New York Times*, October 2, 1964.

be at the appropriate level, the Party sees the tasks of more rapidly developing the branches producing consumer goods.[10]

The general conflict between Khrushchev and professional military men on the possibility of making cutbacks in military spending was abundantly demonstrated in the September debate over the particular issue of the usefulness of tanks in modern warfare. In his speech before the World Forum of Youth, Khrushchev adopted a position that in a future war tanks would essentially be useless. Describing a military exercise he had recently reviewed, Khrushchev declared to the Forum delegates:

> Let me also tell you this. I have lived through two wars, even three: the first world imperialist war, the civil war, and the second world war. In these wars tanks were the terror of the field. But now, let me tell you in secret: when I walked onto the training field and observed as the tanks began to attack and the anti-tank artillery struck these tanks, I was sick. As you know, we spend money making tanks. And if, as they say, God save us, a war breaks out, these tanks will burn even before reaching the line indicated by the command.[11]

Conversely, military writers ascribed an important role for tanks in contemporary wars. For example, the Order of the Day issued by Marshal Malinovsky for Tank Day (September 13) noted:

> The modern tank troops are capable of withstanding successfully the striking force of a nuclear explosion, of inflicting powerful blows, and of carrying on swift military actions to a considerable depth. Today they are the decisive force of the land forces for the maximum utilization of the results of nuclear blows at the enemy and the conclusion of its rout in collaboration with other troops within the shortest possible time.[12]

Likewise, Colonel General of Tank Forces V. I. Zhdanov, who would soon die in a plane crash with Marshal Biryuzov, observed on Tank Day:

> The Soviet Union is in the avantgarde of all progressive mankind in the

[11] *Pravda*, September 12, 1964.

[12] Moscow Domestic Service, September 12, 1964, 2130 GMT, FBIS, *USSR and East Europe*, No. 179 (September 14, 1964), p. CC3. Interestingly, neither this nor the following paragraph, which credited Khrushchev with giving daily attention and practical advice and instructions to the development of the tank forces, appeared in the version printed in *Krasnaya Zvezda*, September 13, 1964.

struggle for peace. The powerful Soviet armed forces play an important role in
securing these tasks, and in this is counted the tank troops.[13]

While the issue of tanks in modern warfare was only a single element in the
larger conflict, it did vividly demonstrate Khrushchev's determination to carry
into effect the reductions proposed in December 1963. In view of such signs, the
professional military were apparently not inclined to come to Khrushchev's aid
in the political power struggle of October 1964, as they had once done in 1957.

On October 13, Khrushchev was called to Moscow by members of the Party
Presidium. Following scathing criticism by Suslov (so it is rumored and generally believed), Khrushchev was informed of his removal. On the following day,
Khrushchev was brought before the Central Committee, but unlike the 1957
episode the Central Committee could not or would not reverse the Presidium
decision. On October 16, the Soviet press carried the official announcement
that by his own request Khrushchev had been relieved of his duties as First Secretary "in view of his advanced age and the deterioration of his health."[14] The
press informed the Soviet public that Khrushchev's duties as First Secretary of
the CPSU would be taken over by L. I. Brezhnev and Khrushchev's position as
Chairman of the Council of Ministers would be assumed by A. N. Kosygin.

There is no evidence that the professional military played a significant and
direct role in Khrushchev's removal. Nor is there evidence that the military bloc
in the Central Committee made any effort, as they had in 1957, to come to
Khrushchev's rescue. There is indeed some question as to the extent to which
the professional military were aware of Khrushchev's fate. While most of the
chief military leaders (Malinovsky, Biryuzov, Chuykov, Grechko, Konev, Moskalenko, and Sokolovskiy) were in Moscow to attend a reception for Polish
visitors, two (Bagramyan and Yeremenko) were in Riga on October 13 to commemorate the twentieth anniversary of the liberation of Latvia.[15] As members
of the Central Committee, these two marshals would naturally be expected to
attend the plenum which removed Khrushchev. However, their absence from
Moscow at this crucial point dispels any suggestion that the entire military elite
was informed of impending events.

In this respect, it is also interesting to compare two articles written by profes-
sional military men that appeared in print on October 14. The first by Marshal
Konev, to commemorate the twentieth anniversary of the liberation of the
Ukraine, made absolutely no mention of Khrushchev's role in the Ukraine during

[13] *Krasnaya Zvezda*, September 13, 1964.

[14] *Pravda*, October 16, 1964.

[15] Tatu, p. 419.

the war.[16] The second by Marshal Biryuzov, also to commemorate the Ukrainian liberation, praised the important and influential role of Khrushchev.[17]

An article by Yepishev was also published on October 14. Its content was similar to that of Biryuzov's article. In addition to his praise for Khrushchev, the MPA head referred to Khrushchev as "our direct leader" at the front during the war.[18]

One possibility strongly suggested by the absence from Moscow of Bagramyan and Yeremenko and the articles of Biryuzov and Yepishev is that the military men were not wholly informed of the plans to remove Khrushchev until the Central Committee meeting on October 14. This would not be unexpected, for, quite obviously, the plot to oust Khrushchev had to be a well-guarded secret. Moreover, it would be consistent with the fact that at least one Presidium member, Podgorny, was apparently not informed of the intent to remove Khrushchev.[19] Therefore, while Malinovsky, as the highest-ranking military figure, might be expected to have had prior knowledge, even this cannot be certain. The most that can be said with assurance is that, in the light of their opposition to Khrushchev's proposals for reductions, the military were fully prepared to acquiesce in the decision of the political leadership.

Similarly, the October 14 article by Yepishev tends to indicate that he was not forewarned about the conspiracy against Khrushchev. Even if one were to assume, as this study has suggested, that Yepishev had opposed Khrushchev on a number of key issues and that Yepishev was more closely connected with Suslov, Khrushchev's chief detractor, than with Khrushchev himself, it would not necessarily follow that Yepishev would have had to have prior knowledge of the Presidium's action. As already noted, the plot was a well-guarded secret known only to a very few. Thus, as in the case of the military men, Yepishev was not informed of the plot beforehand. However, this did not hinder Yepishev from being a very important figure in the new leadership's conflicts with the professional military after Khrushchev's fall.

The Military Versus the Collective Leadership

Several times in the first few days after Khrushchev's fall, the new regime re-

[16] *Pravda*, October 14, 1964.

[17] *Krasnaya Zvezda*, October 14, 1964.

[18] *Komsomolskaya Pravda*, October 14, 1964.

[19] William Hyland and Richard Wallace Shryock, *The Fall of Khrushchev* (New York: Funk and Wagnalls, 1968), pp. 181–82.

assured the professional military that measures necessary to strengthen the country's defense potential would be carried out.[20] Yet on the first occasion for the new regime to present its policy line, the forty-seventh anniversary of the Bolshevik Revolution on November 7, 1964, it struck a generally moderate tone. In his speech, Brezhnev condemned the "subjectivism and arbitrary decisions" that had led to failures in developing the economy and expressed his support for scientific planning and economic incentives for workers. He assured his audience that the Soviet Union possessed "the mighty weapons" to ensure the security of the USSR and other socialist countries. With regard to foreign affairs, he not only stated that "the general line of the foreign policy of the Soviet Union, defined by the latest Congresses and its Program, is consistent and unchanged," but also declared:

> The Soviet Union has been pursuing and is pursuing the Leninist policy of peaceful coexistence of states with different social systems. It is aimed at preventing a world thermonuclear war, settling disputes among states by negotiations, respecting the rights of every nation to select for itself its social and state system and decide for itself the questions of internal development of its country.
>
> The policy of peaceful coexistence provides a basis for mutual understanding and the development of mutually profitable cooperation of countries regardless of the differences in their social system. . . .
>
> Soviet people sincerely desire that the incipient relaxation of international tensions will continue and that solutions will be found for the basic international problems on which depend the peace and security of nations.[21]

Referring particularly to the United States, Brezhnev declared that "the Soviet Union is ready to develop Soviet-American relations in the interests of our nations and in the interests of strengthening peace." He also remarked that most Americans "cherish the interests of peace" and are "tired of the 'cold war.' "

However, at the November parade in Red Square, Minister of Defense Malinovsky took more of a hard line against the United States, which he referred to as the head of the imperialist quarter. Then, when called upon to make a toast at the post-parade reception for dignitaries, Malinovsky stated that the Soviet

[20] See Kosygin in *Pravda*, October 20, 1964; and the editorial in *Krasnaya Zvezda*, October 23, 1964.

[21] *Pravda*, November 7, 1964. In the omission represented by the ellipses, Brezhnev reminded his listeners that the atmosphere of peaceful coexistence also "promotes the success of the national liberation struggle and the attainment of the revolutionary goals of nations."

Union "shall not do as the U.S. defense secretary, who threatens to destroy the Soviet Union at any moment."[22] This view of the United States was inconsistent with the tone set by Brezhnev. Was this an unpremeditated slip due to Malinovsky's drunkenness or was it an indirect attempt to stake out the military's claims for a continuing military buildup? Whatever the real cause, the new regime's concern to avoid appearing anti-American was emphasized by two actions. First, the account of the toast in *Pravda* on November 8 deleted Malinovsky's reference to U.S. hostile intentions. Second, Kosygin attempted to soften the effect of the statement in a conversation with Ambassador Foy D. Kohler.

In an effort to improve his personal authority over the professional military, Malinovsky sought and won political concurrence to reappoint Marshal Zakharov as Chief of the General Staff. As described earlier, Marshal Zakharov, a close follower of Malinovsky and a severe critic of both Khrushchev and the political administration in the armed forces, had been replaced by Marshal Biryuzov in March 1963. However, on October 19, Biryuzov was killed in a plane crash in Yugoslavia. Khrushchev's ouster, therefore, gave Malinovsky the opportunity to reappoint Zakharov.[23]

On November 16, the political leadership offset this act by promoting Yepishev to full membership in the Party Central Committee.[24] Until this promotion, which recognized Yepishev, at least formally, as the political equal of the Minister of Defense and other top professional militarymen, Yepishev's position under the new regime appears to have been uncertain. During the first critical days after Khrushchev's fall, Yepishev had been sent to Belgrade to be part of the military delegation escorting Biryuzov's body back to Moscow. Consequently, instead of standing guard over the armed forces during this crucial period as one might expect from the MPA head, Yepishev was out of the country. It seems possible to conclude from this that Yepishev's status was under discussion.

Who might have opposed Yepishev? Judging from Malinovsky's assertions of independence, it is not unlikely that certain professional military leaders considered this an opportune time to seek Yepishev's removal. In view of his past opposition to MPA interference in military affairs, it is probable that Zakharov

[22] Quoted in the *New York Herald Tribune* (International Edition), November 9, 1964.

[23] Despite being highly favorable for Malinovsky, the timing of Biryuzov's death with Khrushchev's removal appears to be merely a coincidence. The present writer has found no concrete evidence that Biryuzov's death might have been arranged as a political bargain for Malinovsky's support for the new regime.

[24] Yaroslav Bilinsky, *Changes in the Central Committee: Communist Party of the Soviet Union, Union, 1961-1966* (Denver, Colo.: University of Denver, 1967), p. 5.

would have been one of the chief military advocates of Yepishev's removal. The situation was complicated by the fact that Yepishev's apparent protector, Suslov, briefly fell ill at this time and had to be hospitalized.[25]

Moreover, it cannot be discounted that opposition to Yepishev's retention may have come from some of the moderate political leaders, who disagreed with Yepishev's views on the large army and the large budgetary expenditures required by such a force.[26] The strength of this faction was demonstrated by the reduction in the military's official expenditures announced in December 1964. A year previous, Khrushchev had stated that military expenditures for 1964 would be set at 13.3 billion rubles, and on December 9, 1964, Kosygin revealed that this amount would be further reduced to 12.8 billion rubles in 1965.[27]

In sum, while some professional military men may have opposed Yepishev for his views on party dominance, others would have given him strong approval for his views on the large army. And while some political leaders may have opposed him for the economic implications of his views on the need for large armies, others would have strongly desired to retain him for his position on party

[25] *The New York Times*, October 26, 1964. Suslov was listed fourth in official Soviet rankings at this time. However, his illness set in shortly after Khrushchev's ouster, as noted by the fact that he was unable to attend Biryuzov's funeral.

[26] It is generally agreed among Western observers that the problem of the Soviet economy was a very important, if not the most important, factor in Khrushchev's downfall. In the third party program, adopted in 1961, it had been predicted by Khrushchev that by 1970 the Soviet Union would surpass the United States in per capita production and that by 1980 the Soviet Union would have built the material and technical basis of communism. (*Programma Kommunisticheskoy partii Sovetskogo Soyuza* [*Program of the Communist Party of the Soviet Union*] (Moscow: State Publishing House for Political Literature, 1973), pp. 65–66. However, such targets would have been difficult for the Soviet economy, even if growth rates had not been falling in the early 1960's. From 1950 to 1958, the annual growth rates of Soviet gross national product (GNP) averaged 6–7 percent, but fell to 4–5 percent between 1959 and 1964. One estimate shows the following decline: 4.5 percent in 1959; 5.1 percent in 1960; 6.3 percent in 1961; 3.3 percent in 1962; and 2.2 percent in 1963. (Stanley H. Cohn, "General Growth Performance of the Soviet Economy," in U.S. Congress. Joint Economic Committee. Subcommittee on Foreign Economic Policy. *Economic Performance and the Military Burden in the Soviet Union* [Washington, D.C.: Government Printing Office, 1970], p. 9. See also Gertrude E. Schroeder, "Soviet Economic Reform at an Impasse," *Problems of Communism*, XX, No. 4 [July–August 1970], 36; and Theodore Frankel, "Economic Reform: A Tentative Appraisal," *Problems of Communism*, XVI, No. 3 [May–June 1967], 30). Because of the lower growth rates between 1959 and 1964, Soviet economists estimated that the Soviet national income fell 41 billion rubles below what it might have been if the higher GNP growth rate had prevailed. (T. Khachaturov, "Increase of the Effactiveness of Capital Investment and the Scientific Bases of Its Determination," *Voprosy Ekonomiki*, No. 2 [February 1966], p. 8.)

[27] *Pravda*, December 10, 1964.

control of military affairs. Therefore, through whatever combination of support, Yepishev retained his MPA post and was even promoted in political status.

In the few remaining months of 1964 after Khrushchev's ouster, the MPA stressed in its meetings and publications the theme of collective leadership. For example, a *Krasnaya Zvezda* report on accountability and election meetings of party organs in the armed forces in late October noted that "collectivity in the work of party organs" received serious attention. The report also expressed the view that "collectivity is a supreme principle in party leadership" and that collectivity requires a "comprehensive development of criticism and self-criticism."[28] Then, in December, a similar theme was the subject of a *Kommunist Vooruzhennykh Sil* article. The author, a vice-admiral, reiterated the need for collectivity of party organs[29] and the right of party members to criticize deficiencies[30] and also singled out the naval organs and administration for having "serious shortcomings."[31] While noting that "communists are imbued with care for strengthening one-man command," the vice-admiral maintained that commanders should "daily and skillfully lean upon party organizations."[32]

Then an article in the year's final issue of *Kommunist Vooruzhennykh Sil* called for a further intensification of ideological work by political organs. Written by a deputy head of the MPA, the article observed that plans and programs of political study in 1965 would "envisage a thorough study by troops of Marxist-Leninist theory."[33] The author sought to justify an increase in the emphasis on ideological work in stating that the "ideological education of troops is an integral component of the communist education of the people, determining the conditions for the intensification of the moral potential of the Soviet armed forces which in the condition of rocket-nuclear war will play an immeasurably greater role than in wars of past times."[34] He also singled out the engineer-technical staff as a group needing special attention. According to the deputy head of the MPA, the military officials "are successfully overcoming," but have not yet eliminated, "the erroneous notion existing among some engineers and technicians that sup-

[28] *Krasnaya Zvezda*, October 24, 1964.

[29] Vice-Admiral S. Averchuk, "Collectivity of Leadership Is the Indispensable Condition of Normal Activity of Party Organizations," *Kommunist Vooruzhennykh Sil*, No. 23 (December 23, 1964), pp. 18–29, esp. ɪp. 22.

[30] *Ibid.*, pp. 20, 24.

[31] *Ibid.*, pp. 19, 23.

[32] *Ibid.*, pp. 19–20.

[33] Colonel General M. Kalashnik, "To Raise the Activity of Ideological Work," *Kommunist Vooruzhennykh Sil*, No. 24 (December 1964), p. 7.

[34] *Ibid.*, p. 3.

posedly their business is work only with technology and not with people."[35]
In this way, the author reminded military officials that they must give more
attention to ideological matters and not concentrate solely on military-technical
questions.

At the same time, there appeared several articles by MPA officials that clearly
emphasized the hard-line views of the professional military. Particular stress was
given to the international role of the Soviet Union. In the discussion of this role,
it was maintained that Soviet power, economic and military, not only safeguarded
the socialist system but also promoted the national liberation movement. On the
latter point, Colonel S. Lukonin, a candidate of philosophical sciences, declared
that it was Soviet military power which "deters the bellicose ardor of the imperialists and does not give them the possibility to utilize the weapons of massive
striking capability against liberation movements."[36] A comparable line was asserted with regard to internal Soviet development. Again it was claimed that
only a powerful military force could safeguard the gains of the Soviet Union as
well as other peace-loving nations. According to one MPA spokesman holding
the candidate of historical sciences degree:

> One of the most important conditions for the successful fulfillment of the plans
> of communist construction is the reliable protection of the state interests of the
> Soviet Union and the strengthening of the defense potential. There is no for-
> getting that every step of the Soviet people forward and every achievement of
> the socialist system provokes anger in the camp of the imperialists, who are
> leading feverish preparations for a rocket-nuclear war against the USSR and
> other coutries of socialism. This demands from the Communist Party and the
> people unremitting vigilance and constant preparation for a resolute rebuff to
> the aggressor.
>
> Strengthening the defense potential of the Soviet Union and the perfection
> of its armed forces is a straight line and an important influence in the general
> struggle for the construction of communist society and in the cause of the
> consolidation of the security of all freedom-loving peoples of the world.[37]

The argument in favor of strengthening the Soviet armed forces also formed
the basic theme of a study lesson for servicemen drawn up by the MPA in November. The instruction outline called for political workers to inform soldiers that:

[35] *Ibid.*, p. 4.

[36] Colonel S. Lukonin, "The Character of Our Epoch and the General Line of the World
Communist Movement," *Kommunist Vooruzhennykh Sil*, No. 21, (November 1964), p. 22.

[37] Colonel A. Karelin, "Marxism-Leninism on the Regularity of the Construction of Socialism
and Communism," *Kommunist Vooruzhennykh Sil*, No. 23 (December 1964), p. 17

> In recent years the threat of a new imperialist attack on the Soviet Union and
> other countries of the socialist camp has dictated and will dictate the necessity
> of further strengthening the defensive power of our homeland. The Commu-
> nist Party and the Soviet Government took tireless care that the army and navy
> possessed very modern arms and that their fire power excelled the fire power
> of the people of the capitalist army.[38]

Furthermore, the political worker was required by the lesson to point out to the
servicemen that all types of weapons, not merely the new ones, would be needed
to achieve a military victory. According to the outline, "it is important to recall
for the soldiers also that for the achievement of victory in contemporary war
will be needed the skillful application not only of new arms but also without
exception *all* the types of weapons found in the army and navy."[39]

Fundamentally, therefore, the MPA favored the continuation of party dominance over the professional military, but its spokesmen appeared to oppose any
party actions that might lessen the strength of the armed forces or slight any
branch of the army and navy.

Aside from Malinovsky's November 7 anti-American outburst and possible
opposition in some circles to Yepishev's retention, the professional military leaders generally adopted a wait-and-see position with regard to the new political
regime. Like other observers, Soviet and non-Soviet alike, the professional military were uncertain of the course to be followed by the new collective leadership,
whose only major point of agreement appeared to have been its opposition to
Khrushchev's arbitrary and subjective methods. Even the reduction in official
military expenditures seems to have created no significant ill-will. This reduction was probably offset in the minds of military men by the increased emphasis
given to heavy industry by the new regime and by increases in the hidden por-
tions of the military budget.

Then, in late January, an article by two military writers took exception with
some of the ideas that had prevailed under Khrushchev. First, the authors replied
to the observation of several propagandists that "certain comrades" have reduced
all opinions on war and peace to "the possibility of preventing a world war in the
present age." The authors maintained that in view of actual facts "he who sees
only the possibility of preventing a world war and does not want to see the danger
that such a war could be unleashed by imperialism, grossly ignores objective

---

[38] Colonel B. Kolyshkin, "Different Knowledge and the Skillful Application of Technology
and Weapons — The Patriotic Duty of Soviet Troops and a Very Important Condition for Victory in Contemporary War," *Kommunist Vooruzhennykh Sil*, No. 21 (November 1964), p. 78.

[39] *Ibid.*, p. 79. Italics in original.

reality." Subsequently, the writers commented on the issue of formulating military doctrine. Whereas under Khrushchev the Party was credited as the dominant factor in formulating military doctrine, the writers contended that contemporary Soviet military doctrine had been "elaborated through the collective efforts of the leading party, state, and military cadres and of those active on the military-scientific front." A third point of opposition to the Khrushchevian scheme was the authors' argument that even with rocket-nuclear weapons "victory over an aggressor can be achieved [only] by the combined efforts of all types of armed forces and by the skillful use of all other means of armed struggle."[40]

An even clearer expression of disillusionment with arbitrary methods of military leadership sometimes employed by the political leaders was given by Marshal Zakharov in early February. Zakharov said that Soviet leadership must take a scientific approach to decision making and resolutely avoid all manifestations of subjectivism, especially in military construction. He pointed to the Stalinist personality cult and reminded the reader of the effect it had had when it disregarded professional military opinion. The Chief of the General Staff maintained:

> The Soviet people remember very well the great damage done to military building by the subjectivism that thrived during Stalin's personality cult.
> It is known that during the prewar years, along with the socialist building, our people created all the necessary possibilities to repel an aggressor. Ideology and practice of the personality cult, however, hindered us from exploring these possibilities in the way which the objective conditions demanded. The situation during the personality cult was such that the collective opinion of leading party and state workers as well as that of prominent military theoreticians and practitioners was disregarded. Conclusions and recommendations of Soviet military scientists were frequently rejected, although based on profound analysis of military affairs and of the laws of armed struggle.[41]

Still further, Zakharov noted that the role of military men went beyond recommendations on doctrine into the formulation of concrete combat, educational, and personnel decisions. According to Zekharov, military officers have the responsibility to "work out the plans for the combat perfecting of all types of armed forces and service branches, and furnish concrete recommendations and instructions concerning the problems of their organizational structure, their training, their education, the distribution and use of cadres, and so forth." This amounted to a striking assertion, for it would mean that one-man command had indeed been implemented. Since there is no reason to believe that one-man com-

---

[40] Major General K. Bochkarev and Colonel I. Sidel'nikov in *Krasnaya Zvezda*, January 21, 1965.
[41] *Krasnaya Zvezda*, February 4, 1965.

mand had been introduced even briefly and since he did not state directly and positively that the Party and MPA had no role in forming these plans, the statement must not be accepted literally, but should be regarded as a means of emphasizing the role of professional military men. Even in this sense, however, it was a bold assertion for a professional military spokesman, because it clearly minimized the role of the Party and the MPA.

Zakharov's article was followed two days later by another article which challenged the basic concepts of Khrushchev. The author, Colonel General S. Shtemenko, rejected the position that a nuclear war must necessarily be very short. Shtemenko claimed that the United States was "primarily banking on a sudden first blow," but that Soviet doctrine "does not confine the entire war to such a blow." Despite its "recognized military-technical superiority," the Soviet Army should not assume that it would have "an easy and speedy victory." Rather, pointed out the colonel general, "under certain conditions the war can become prolonged and demand extremely tense efforts from the people and the army." Consequently, it followed that, while the ground forces were no longer the decisive factor in war, final victory required the contribution of "all types of armed forces."[42]

Shtemenko also broached the topic of a possible limited war. Under Khrushchev it was generally, but not entirely, agreed that, as noted in Sokolovskiy's work on military strategy, any armed conflict between nuclear powers would "develop, *inevitably*, into a general war."[43] However, while at the same disclaiming any Soviet approval for limited wars, Shtemenko maintained that "Soviet military doctrine does not exclude such wars."[44]

The Soviet attitude toward limited wars was shortly to receive a strong testing, for on February 7 the United States began a series of bombing raids on North Vietnam. Since late November 1964, the Soviet leadership had been giving warnings that the Soviets would render "necessary assistance" if North Vietnam were to be attacked.[45] In February 1965, Kosygin traveled to Hanoi, most likely to demonstrate the new regime's increasing concern for the welfare of its socialist

[42] *Nedelya*, No. 6, January 31–February 6, 1965, FBIS, *USSR and East Europe*, No. 28 (February 11, 1965), p. CC3.

[43] Sokolovskiy, p. 299. Italics added. For further discussion of relevant views and dissenting opinion, see also Thomas Wolfe, *Soviet Strategy at the Crossroads*, pp. 118–24.

[44] *Nedelya*, No. 6, Janary 31–February 6, 1965, FBIS, *USSR and East Europe*, No. 28 (February 11, 1965), p. CC4.

[45] *Izvestiya*, November 28, December 1, 4, 5, 9, and 10, 1964; *Pravda*, January 5, 1964; *Krasnaya Zvezda*, January 8, 1965; *Pravda*, January 8 and 23 and February 3, 1965. All of these references were cited in Daniel S. Papp, "The Soviet Perception of the Goals of and Constrains on American Policy toward Vietnam, June 1964–December 1965" (unpublished Ph.D. dissertation, University of Miami, 1973), pp. 149, 151, 170.

ally. He was present in North Vietnam when the initial raids occurred. During his visit, Kosygin reiterated that the Soviet Union would extend to North Vietnam any assistance that it might need.[46]

In an Armed Forces Day speech, Malinovsky took note of the official Soviet warning that "the USSR would not remain indifferent toward ensuring the security of a fraternal, socialist country, and would give it the necessary aid and support."[47] He declared that the U.S. imperialists had not drawn the "proper conclusions" from this warning, because "the fire which the Pentagon is playing with in Vietnam threatens to kindle the flames of a big war."[48] He then further warned that the Soviet Union "places at the service of socialist interests and social progress its entire might, including nuclear rockets."[49]

Of the many important repercussions from the U.S. bombing, one of the most significant concerned its impact on the debate with regard to Soviet military power. One line expressed by Sokolovskiy, perhaps unwillingly, contended that Soviet might was already sufficient to meet Soviet needs. In an interview given on February 17, Sokolovskiy asserted that the USSR has "more than enough nuclear means to rout any aggressor." Sokolovskiy stated that Soviet foreign policy "is aimed at strengthening peace and not building up nuclear potential." As proof of this fact, he pointed to the 500-million-ruble reduction in military spending,[50] as well as the fact that Soviet armed forces numbered only 2,423,000 — that is, the level to which Khrushchev had planned to reduce. He even noted that "a certain further reduction in manpower is possible."[51]

Other military leaders argued in favor of further developing Soviet military power. Marshal Chuykov, for example, contended that imperialist powers were increasing their stocks of thermonuclear weapons and preparing to strike at the socialist camp. In light of this, argued Chuykov, "the greater our capability of taming an aggressor, the more guarantees there are for a prolonged peace on earth."[52] Moreover, Marshal Krylov reminded the readers of the trade unions'

[46] *Izvestiya*, February 9, 1965.

[47] Moscow Domestic Service, February 22, 1965, 1430 GMT, FBIS, *USSR and East Europe*, No. 35 (February 23, 1965), p. CC6.

[48] *Ibid.*

[49] *Ibid.*, p. CC4.

[50] TASS International Service, February 17, 1965, 0957 GMT, FBIS, *USSR and East Europe*, No. 32 (February 17, 1965), p. BB1.

[51] *Ibid.*, p. BB2. For a further discussion of this line, see n. 56 of this chapter.

[52] *Komsomolskaya Pravda*, February 23, 1964, FBIS, *USSR and East Europe*, No. 38 (February 26, 1965), p. CC4.

newspaper *Trud* that final victory "can only be won as the result of combined actions of all arms of the armed forces."[53]

The hard-line position of the latter group received indirect support from the gradual escalation of U.S. bombing raids against North Vietnam on March 2. Here again was "concrete evidence" of the "aggressiveness" of the imperialist camp, led by the United States. The lesson to be learned, argued some professional military men, was that the Soviet Union must not relax in defense preparations and vigilance. This view was shared by some MPA spokesmen, one of whom maintained that "the Soviet armed forces have been and remain a liberation army ready to come to the aid of people who have become victims of imperialist aggression" and therefore that "the Soviet armed forces must be developed so as to correspond fully to their great international liberating role."[54]

On March 18, an article by a candidate of military sciences, Colonel I. Larionov, on the length of a future war also called for the further buildup of the armed forces. Larionov noted that the Soviet Union must prepare not only for a fast-moving war but also a protracted war. Larionov criticized an argument allegedly sometimes heard "among servicemen" that victory could be achieved by a single rocket strike. He contended, rather, that victory would have to be the result of a "united effort" of all branches and types of armed forces.[55] The argument for a "united effort" was reiterated in an article jointly authored by Sokolovskiy and Cherednichenko, who also observed that a new world war would require "very large armed forces."[56] Then an article in the authoritative party journal *Kommunist* by Marshal Rotmistrov claimed that as a result of "aggressive imperial-

[53] *Trud,* February 21, 1965, FBIS, *USSR and East Europe,* No. 37 (February 25, 1965), p. CC11.

[54] Colonel Ye. Sulimov, "Fundamentals and Principles of Soviet Military Development During the Period of Transition from Socialism to Communism," *Kommunist Vooruzhennykh Sil,* No. 4 (February 1965), p. 14.

[55] *Krasnaya Zvedza,* March 18, 1965.

[56] Marshal of the Soviet Union V. D. Sokolovskiy and Major General M. I. Cherednichenko, "Some Problems of Soviet Military Development in the Postwar Period," *Voyenno-Istoricheskiy Zhurnal,* No. 3 (March 1965), p. 11. Differences with Sokolovskiy's February 17 interview, wherein he implied the possibility of further troop reductions, are apparent. This indicates several alternatives: (1) on February 17 Sokolovskiy was giving his own opinion, but was persuaded by subsequent events and arguments to alter his previous stance, (2) on February 17 he was not expressing his own view but one politically forced upon him, or (3) on February 17 he was giving his own view but was forced to acquiese to the majority opinion of professional military men who generally took a hard line. Whatever the case, however, the change does emphasize that the hard line was increasingly gaining greater importance and that professional military men were in a freer position to assert their views.

ism," being exemplified in Vietnam, the Communist Party and Soviet people would be compelled "to raise continuously the military power of our homeland, to develop the national economy, and to strengthen all other areas of state construction of the USSR with a view to increasing its defense potential."[57]

The Expressed Views of and the Divisions Within the MPA During the Early Period of Collective Leadership

In the first few months after Khrushchev's removal, the professional military seemed content to follow a wait-and-see policy with regard to the new collective leadership. Because it was a "collective" leadership, the political figures and types were not always in agreement on the correct path to pursue. In due course, the professional military used this fact as an opportunity to assert its independent views on a number of fundamental issues: that the Soviet Union, especially Soviet military power, plays an important role in international developments; that the Soviet armed forces need to be strengthened; that a future war might be a prolonged war; that Soviet military leaders should be consulted in the formulation of military doctrine; and that military commanders should take increasing authority over all aspects of military activity.

In mid-February, an article by an MPA spokesman and candidate of historical sciences, strongly reaffirmed the principle of party authority over the armed forces. The writer noted that in contemporary conditions the leadership of the Party must not lessen, but must grow "still greater." While noting that one-man command is a basic military principle, the writer also pointed out that one-man command must be implemented "on a party basis." He also observed that the commander with single authority must develop a party-like attitude toward criticism and self-criticism. One concession made to the professional military was that theoreticians and practitioners of military affairs were included with the Party and the Party Central Committee in the group which "collectively elaborated" Soviet military doctrine.[58]

Similarly, a February issue of *Kommunist Vooruzhennykh Sil* carried two articles which asserted party supremacy. The first, concerned chiefly with World War II, declared that contemporary conditions were characterized by "the fur-

---

[57] Marshal of Armored Troops P. Rotmistrov, "The Leadership of the Party Is the Source of the Power of the Soviet Army and Navy," *Kommunist*, No. 4 (March 1965), p. 23.

[58] V. Karamyshev in *Krasnaya Zvezda*, February 12, 1965.

ther increasing role of party leadership of the armed forces."[59] The second dealt with the party work in the armed forces and emphasized criticism and self-criticism as an important "weapon" in the struggle against shortcomings.[60]

On March 11, an unsigned editorial article in the military newspaper *Krasnaya Zvezda* again urged the use of the "weapon" of criticism and self-criticism. According to the article, only the orders and instructions of commanders and political chiefs were beyond criticism. Outside of this, all Communists of any rank were open to criticism. While noting that many who criticize shortcomings were themselves subsequently made the target of unjust criticism, the article went on to declare that there is nothing in military affairs which can justify the stifling of criticism at any level.[61]

Kommunist Vooruzhennykh Sil reminded its readers in an April issue that "the main source of Soviet military construction is the leadership of the Communist Party over the armed forces" and "the Party has taken care and is taking care of improving the role and influence of party organizations in the army and navy."[62] Signed by the first deputy head of the MPA, the article also noted that the only type of leadership "approved by the Central Committee" was "one-man command on a party basis."[63]

Having asserted the dominant position of the Party in military matters in such forceful terms, MPA spokesmen began to take a more active role in the discussions raised by professional military men.[64] An article in a June issue of

[59] Colonel V. Glazachev and Colonel Ye. Nikitin, "The Party — The Organizer of Our Victory over Fascism," *Kommunist Vooruzhennykh Sil*, No. 3 (February 1965), p. 18.

[60] Colonel General N. Nachinkin, "For Greater Efficiency in Party Work," *Kommunist Vooruzhennykh Sil*, No. 3 (February 1965), p. 33.

[61] *Krasnaya Zvezda*, March 11, 1965.

[62] Colonel General P. Yefimov, "The Party Directs Us on the Leninist Path to Victory," *Kommunist Vooruzhennykh Sil*, No. 8 (April 1965), p. 17.

[63] *Ibid.*, pp. 17–18.

[64] It must be kept in mind that at this time the political leadership was engaged in the discussion and/or debate of several key issues with more or less direct bearing on military matters. One concerned Soviet policy toward Vietnam, as well as Soviet policy toward the PRC in the light of U.S. actions in Vietnam. Because of their commitment of support to Vietnam, some Soviet circles sought to achieve a more united effort with China. (See the remarks of Kosygin and Mikoyan to U.S. businessman Cyrus Eaton as reported in *The New York Times*, May 25 and 28, 1965.) Another important issue was concerned with economic priorities. Speaking on the forthcoming five-year plan, Kosygin commented that despite "some doubts" it would be necessary to raise the living standard more rapidly. (A. N. Kosygin, "Raising the Scientific Validity of Plans Is the Most Important Task of Planning Organs," *Planovoye Khozyaystvo*, No. 4 [April 1965], p. 6.) Then in a May 22 speech in Azerbaijan, Podgorny noted that the living standard of the people is always under the Party's constant care. However, more clearly

Kommunist Vooruzhennykh Sil by a candidate of philosophical sciences, Major General K. Bochkarev, reviewed one MPA position on the character and type of wars in the contemporary epoch. According to their "socio-political" content, explained Bochkarev, there are two types of wars: just and unjust. A war between two imperialist forces would make the war wholly unjust, but a war between an imperialist force and a "progressive" force would be unjust for the former and just for the latter.[65] A second classification of wars characterized wars according to the "means, methods, and scale of military activity." Since the imperialists by nature disregard the interests of the people and the demands of social progress, explained Bochkarev, it cannot be expected that the imperialists will employ any standards of self-restraint.[66] However, just aims will have a "definite influence" on the methods of the progressive side, so that when militarily possible the progressive side will avoid extremes.[67] This in no way implied in Bochkarev's view that the progressive side had an obligation to refrain from using nuclear weapons, for the "peace-loving peoples" here the right to use "all the power of contemporary weapons for the purpose of self-defense and the suppression of aggression."[68]

Bochkarev asserted that "the most typical" form of war for the contemporary epoch is the war of imperialists against "peoples and countries struggling for their social and national liberation or upholding the gains of freedom and independence and their right to construct a new society,"[69] but he also observed that a war between the two social systems is still a possibility. Describing its nature and scope, he stated that a war between the two social systems

---

than Kosygin, Podgorny maintained that for the sake of this living standard some de-emphasis on heavy industry and defense potential would have to be permitted. There was a "fully justified" time, pointed out Podgorny, "when the Soviet people deliberately accepted some material restrictions in the interest of priority development of heavy industry and the strengthening of defense potential." Now, however, social wealth has grown to the point where "the increasing cultural and domestic requirements of workingmen are better supplied." (*Pravda*, May 22, 1965.) Contrarily, Suslov took the position two weeks later that it was still necessary for the people to make sacrifices. While noting that an improvement in the Soviet people's life would be most desirable, Suslov argued that "objective reality" continued to demand large defense expenditures (*Pravda*, June 5, 1965).

[65] Major General K. Bochkarev, "On the Character and Types of Wars in the Contemporary Epoch," *Kommunist Vooruzhennykh Sil*, No. 11 (June 1965), p. 10. Such a definition does not, of course, admit for a war between two "progressive" forces.

[66] *Ibid.*

[67] *Ibid.*, p. 11.

[68] *Ibid.*

[69] *Ibid.*, p. 13.

> . . . would be a decisive armed conflict of two systems. According to its socio-political essence, it would be a class war, monstrously criminal, extremely reactionary on the side of the imperialist power and very just on the side of the countries of socialism. According to its scale, it would inevitably assume a universal scope, and the chief and decisive technical means of waging it would be the rocket-nuclear weapon.[70]

Addressing the issue of limited wars, Bochkarev noted that local wars "bear in themselves the real possibility of developing into world nuclear wars."[71] He argued that a "chain reaction" might develop if the imperialists use nuclear weapons in some part of the world. Therefore, "a 'local' nuclear adventure of the imperialists may acquire a global scale."[72]

Bochkarev's comments were supplemented in the same issue of *Kommunist Vooruzhennykh Sil* by an article which among other things speculated on the origins and modes of a future war between the two systems. The author of the article, Colonel V. Glazov, observed that the war might begin with a "direct assault" on the Soviet Union by means of nuclear weapons or it might develop out of a local, originally non-nuclear war.[73] Nor does Glazov rule out other possibilities. Still, he is even more concerned with the methods of fighting to be used. In this regard, Glazov quite clearly leaned toward the "combined arms" concept of fighting. While he granted that nuclear weapons had an extremely important role, he also observed that "the powerful nuclear blows will create conditions for the prompt and full completion of the rest of the adversary by the fire and blows of tanks, artillery, aviation, and motorized troops."[74] He concluded, therefore, that combat training must include instructions for conventional warfare.

Although he did not become involved in the specific issues of the discussion, Brezhnev's July 3, 1965, address to the graduates of the military academies expressed favor for the military line over the consumer line. Brezhnev noted that "there is still in prospect much to do for resolving the urgent problems of further perfecting the economy and raising the living standard of our people," but he declared that defense-related matters were at present even more important. Khrushchev's successor as First Secretary of the CPSU stated:

[70] *Ibid.*

[71] *Ibid.*, p. 17.

[72] *Ibid.*

[73] Colonel V. Glazov, "The Regularity of the Developmeut and Changes of Modes of Armed Struggle," *Kommunist Vooruzhennykh Sil*, No. 11 (June 1965), p. 50.

[74] *Ibid.*

In the face of the dangerous underhand plottings of the enemies of peace, concern for further strengthening the defense of our homeland and consolidating
the safety of the entire socialist commonwealth acquires paramount significance.
Historical experience teaches us: that the stronger our army is and the higher
our vigilance is, then the more firm is the peace on our borders and the more
firm is the peace on our planet. This we learned well.[75]

Yet Brezhnev reminded the professional military that "the strength of our
army is not only in powerful weapons, but first of all in people."[76] From the party-
political viewpoint, the implication of this contention is that the commander must
not downgrade the political side of the serviceman's training. Another implication is that the need for military-technical knowledge cannot be used to justify
a weakening of political work. Since people are more important than weapons,
it follows that the political training of servicemen continues to be extremely
important. In particular for the commander, as Brezhnev noted, it means that
one-man command must be built "on a party basis." Brezhnev stated:

One-man command in the Soviet army is built on a party basis. This means
that the commander must in his work constantly rely upon party and komsomol
organizations and make use in full measure of their mobilizing forces and
authority and their creative activity for raising the combat readiness of units
and ships. Party-political work is an important inherent part of the activity
of the Soviet officer.[77]

The importance of people over weapons was also the theme of an article in
Kommunist Vooruzhennykh Sil by Colonel A. Milovidov, a candidate of philoso-
sophical sciences. As the MPA spokesman observed, "deeply wrong are those
who see in the revolution in military affairs precisely only one of its sides — the
technical." Milovidov contended rather that "transformations in military affairs
are inseparable from the ideological conviction of troops, and from their moral-
psychological qualities, knowledge, and style of thinking."[78] He also pointed
out that ideological education is necessary, for it provides the framework within
which the individual will act. It "gives the actions of people a purposefulness,
a readiness to overcome any difficulties on the path of achieving a high aim, and
a confidence in victory."[79]

[75] *Pravda*, July 4, 1965.

[76] *Ibid.*

[77] *Ibid.*

[78] Colonel A. Milovidov, "The Revolution in Military Affairs and the Spiritual Strength of
Troops," *Kommunist Vooruzhennykh Sil*, No. 13 (July 1965), p. 8.

[79] *Ibid.*, p. 9.

In September, Minister of Defense Malinovsky also published two articles that dealt extensively with the importance of the individual in military affairs. In *Sovetskiy Patriot,* the organ of the Central Committee of the Voluntary Society for Assisting the Army, Air Force, and Navy (DOSAAF), he directly refuted the reasoning "sometimes heard" that modern weapons have demoted man to a secondary role. According to Malinovsky, Soviet military doctrine "has always stressed that technology and man are two objective factors of waging an armed struggle and that the appearance of new and numerous weapons and complex technology still raises the role of man as the most important factor determining the course and outcome of a war."[80] In the second September article, dealing specifically with the professional qualities of command personnel, the Minister of Defense emphasized the need for ideological conviction in each soldier since "the actions of even one person can lead to far-reaching consequences." Like Milovidov, therefore, Malinovsky believed that the ideologically convinced individual "will not abandon himself to despair and will not panic in the most difficult situation."[81]

However, unlike Milovidov and even Brezhnev, Malinovsky went beyond the need for ideological conviction. While noting that "ideological conviction and stern belief in the historical inevitable downfall of imperialism has increased and is increasing our moral forces" and that "belief in the victory of communist ideals has been and is a well of lofty action, selflessness, and heroism of Soviet soldiers," Malinovsky maintained that this was not enough to win battles. Conviction must be applied practically. The heart of the soldier must "be filled with only pure feelings and motives so that it directs the soldiers to maintain outstanding steadfastness and persistence in achieving a given goal, and our goal is victory."[82] And victory, it was argued, would ultimately rest with the best technically prepared army. As the Minister of Defense contended:

> But victory in the field of battle against a strong enemy does not come by itself. People thoroughly trained for this win it. This is why from every soldier is demanded not only high technical training, but also corresponding moral-psychological hardening, physical endurance, and the ability successfully to use his weapon in very difficult and unexpected military conditions.[83]

One consequence of this difference was reflected in Malinovsky's interpretation of one-man command. In the second of the September articles, Malinovsky

---

[80] *Sovetskiy Patriot,* September 19, 1965.

[81] *Krasnaya Zvezda,* September 24, 1965.

[82] *Sovetskiy Patriot,* September 19, 1965.

[83] *Ibid.*

noted that the commander should rely on party organizations, but he adamantly asserted that only the commander can be responsible for the combat, organizational, and moral-political condition of the men under his command.[84]

Another article in September returned to the issue discussed in June by Bochkarev and Glazov. The article by a candidate of philosophical sciences, Lieutenant Colonel Ye. Rybkin, questioned the validity in the nuclear era of Lenin's (i.e., Clausewitz's) dictum on war as a continuation of politics. In addition to attacking several American writers, Rybkin sharply criticized two Soviet writers, N. Nikolskiy and N. Talenskiy, who maintained, respectively, that "the possibility of a victory in world thermonuclear war as a means of attaining the political goals of states" has disappeared and that "there is no more dangerous illusion than the notion that thermonuclear war still can serve as an instrument of politics, that it is possible to achieve political goals using nuclear weapons and be spared oneself, and that it is possible to find acceptable forms of nuclear war."[85] He admitted that such a world war would be highly destructive. Despite this, however, he asserted that "to maintain that a victory in war is generally impossible would be not only false theoretically but also perilous from a political point of view."[86] One consequence of such a view, if it were to be accepted, would be that it would lead "to moral disarmament, disbelief in victory, fatalism, and passivity."[87] Therefore, argued the MPA spokesman, while the destructive capability of war "limited [it] as a weapon of politics," neither the possibility of the imperialists unleashing war nor the possibility of a Soviet victory should be discounted.[88]

Similarly, Colonel I. Sidel'nikov wrote in the military press about the "occasionally arising opinion" that questioned the need for maintaining large armies and spending large amounts on the armed forces, since thermonuclear war can be prevented. According to Sidel'nikov, such reasoning "has in mind only the possibility of preventing a war and forgets or fails to observe another thing — the presence of a serious danger at the beginning of a world war." He also claimed that due to the threat of imperialist military adventures "our state is forced to strengthen its defense potential, spend large amounts on the equipment and maintenance of the army and navy, and firmly preserve military superiority

[84] *Krasnaya Zvezda*, September 24, 1965.

[85] Lieutenant Colonel Ye. Rybkin, "On the Essence of World Rocket-Nuclear War," *Kommunist Vooruzhennykh Sil*, No. 17 (September 1965), p. 55.

[86] *Ibid.*

[87] *Ibid.*, p. 56.

[88] *Ibid.*

over the imperialist countries."[89] The type of armed forces advocated by Sidel'nikov was one in which all branches were fully developed.[90]

Writing in the October issue of *Kommunist Vooruzhennykh Sil*, Colonel General M. Kalashnik, deputy head of the MPA, also protested that insufficient attention was being given to the struggle between the two opposing social systems. Like Rybkin and Sidel'nikov, Kalashnik pointed out that past Soviet propaganda had given somewhat of a "one-sided interpretation" to peaceful coexistence and the possibilities of preventing war. Conversely, other significant issues received little note. He charged:

> Poorly unmarked were the political, economic, ideological and military diversions of imperialists. Attention was not always focused on the growing military threat, on the fact that peaceful coexistence is a form of irreconcilable class struggle becoming very acute at times and that unremitting vigilance, a thorough readiness and firm resolution to fight the enemy with all means available to us, to disrupt the aggressive plans of the atomic maniacs, and to bind their hands are necessary for the defense of peace.

He then warned that these deficiencies "could only demagnetize the insufficiently prepared section of our people and engender in them pacifist sentiments."[91]

In subsequent writings of MPA representatives, the concept of war as a continuation of politics and the possibility of victory for the socialist forces remained a dominant theme.[92] However, some MPA spokesmen found it necessary to take

[89] *Krasnaya Zvezda*, September 22, 1965.

[90] Sidel'nikov admonished those spokesmen who supported a particular type of military development to the disadvantage of another type. As he stated in his evaluation of what determines a country's defense potential:

"Some people are repeating the thesis which was popular at one time — that if the political and social factors are disregarded, the country's defense potential is not determined by the number of men which we have under arms, but by firepower and the existence of nuclear weapons and the means of delivering them to the target. Referring to the Marxist-Leninist proposition regarding the decisive role of the people in social development, other people take the line that a state's defense potential and the outcome of a possible world war are not determined by firepower or nuclear weapons but by superiority in human resources — in the number of troops. It is not difficult to note that both these assertions reflect a one-sided and, hence, also an incorrect approach to the determination of a country's defense potential." *(Ibid.)*

[91] Colonel General M. Kalashnik, "To Arm Each Soldier with the Communist View of the World," *Kommunist Vooruzhennykh Sil*, No. 20 (October 1965), p. 19.

[92] See, for example, Colonel General N. Lomov, "The Influence of Soviet Military Doctrine in the Development of Military Art," *Kommunist Vooruzhennykh Sil*, No. 21 (November 1965), pp. 17–18; Colonel S. Malyanchikov, "Character and Features of Rocket-Nuclear War,"

issue at the same time with the emphasis placed on technical training by Malinovsky's September 19 article in *Sovetskiy Patriot* and subsequently by some of
their own colleagues.[93] Indeed it seems quite clear from the views expressed by
some MPA spokesmen that there had been a lax attitude toward party-political
work and that in some quarters professional aspects, especially technical training, were being given disproportionately more attention than deemed appropriate. For example, Colonel A. Babakov, a candidate of historical sciences, reminded his readers in an October issue of *Kommunist Vooruzhennykh Sil* that
still valid in 1965 is the directive requiring the policies of military departments
to be passed "on the exact basis of general directives issued by the Party in the
person of the Central Committee and under its immediate control."[94] He also
asserted that, instead of declining, the role of the Party in leading the armed
forces would continue to grow because "at the present stage the problems of
military construction have become considerably more complicated" and "the
circle of economic, political, scientific, and strictly speaking military problems,
which the Party is called on to resolve in strengthening the defense of the country,
has expanded by far."[95] Then another writer forcefully pointed out for the professional military men that there are limits to their authority, stating that "under
present conditions a correct estimate of the capabilities of the military is not only
a military, but a political question."[96]

The laxity in ideological work was thoroughly discussed in an all-army meeting on ideological questions held in October 1965. The major speech of the conference was delivered by M. Kalashnik.[97] In his already cited October article in
Kommunist Vooruzhennykh Sil, which was possibly derived from his confer-

---

Kommunist Vooruzhennykh Sil, No. 21 (November 1965), p. 70; and V. Rybnikov and
Colonel A. Babakov in *Krasnaya Zvezda*, December 7, 1965.

[93] "To Know Perfectly, to Protect, and to Apply Skillfully Military Technology and Weapons,"
Kommunist Vooruzhennykh Sil, No. 21 (November 1965), pp. 74–79; Colonel M. Timofey-
chev, "Man, Technology, Discipline," *Kommunist Vooruzhennykh Sil*, No. 22 (November
1965), pp. 37–41; and Colonel A. Bulatov and Colonel I. Lyutov, "Perfect Knowledge of
Technology Is a Very Important Factor of Constant Preparedness," *Kommunist Vooruzhennykh
Sil*, No. 23 (December 1965), pp. 18–22.

[94] Colonel A. Babakov, "The Growing Role of the CPSU in the Development of Soviet Society,"
Kommunist Vooruzhennykh Sil, No. 19 (October 1965), p. 19.

[95] *Ibid.*, p. 15.

[96] Lieutenant Colonel G. Talyatnikov, "Capability and Reality in Combat," *Kommunist
Vooruzhennykh Sil*, No. 24 (December 1965), p. 41.

[97] Yu. P. Petrov, *Stroitel'stvo politorganov, partiynykh i komsomol'skikh organizatsiy armii
i flota(1918–1968) (The Construction of Political Organs and Party and Komsomol Organizations in the Army and Navy [1918–1968])* (Moscow: Voyenizdat, 1968), p. 500.

ence speech, Kalashnik described the opposition of professional and even political workers to party-political education. The deputy head of the MPA charged:

> Not with all commanders, political chiefs, or in all party organizations are problems of ideological work at the focus of attention. Sometimes new complicated military equipment and weapons have begun to overshadow people and to move aside into second place the education of people. Training is sometimes counterposed to ideological-political and moral preparation of troops. . . . A part of the leaders have even proposed to reduce sharply in the study plans items politically related to the theme of the scientific, Marxist-Leninist view of the world.[98]

According to Kalashnik, technical training continues to be very important, but it would be beneficial to recall that the enemy soldier will also be well-trained technically. Indeed, it was stressed that "the advantage of the Soviet soldier consists in the fact that his deep technical knowledge is matched by communist idealism."[99] Similarly, an MPA spokesman, Colonel A. Milovidov, writing on the need to struggle against the influence of bourgeois ideology, asserted that victory in a rocket-nuclear war will be won by the side which is strong, "not only in weapons and combat equipment, but also in moral spirit and communist consciousness."[100] Also, two MPA spokesmen, writing on the ideological training of Soviet officers, observed in a January 1966 issue of *Kommunist Vooruzhennykh Sil*:

> Ideological conviction is the wings of man. It raises him to greater work, gives him strength, and helps to overcome all possible difficulties and to achieve success. The higher the ideological training of people is, then the more fruitful and practical activities are.[101]

The spokesmen of the MPA who inclined more toward the professional military side did not at this time directly take issue with the argument for ideological training. Rather, the issues receiving most of their attention were the danger of the international situation[102] and a resultant argument favoring in-

---

[98] Kalashnik, "To Arm Each Soldier with the Communist View of the World," p. 16.

[99] *Ibid.*, p. 17.

[100] *Krasnaya Zvezda*, December 24, 1965.

[101] Colonel I. Grishin and Colonel A. Likhovoy, "Party Care for the Ideological Training of Officers," *Kommunist Vooruzhennykh Sil*, No. 1 (January 1966), p. 30.

[102] See, for example, Yepishev's article on militant revanchism in *Izvestia*, January 19, 1966; and also Lieutenant Colonel N. Ponamarev, "Adventurism of Military-Political Concepts of Imperialism," *Kommunist Vooruzhennykh Sil*, No. 1 (January 1966), pp. 42–48.

creased allocations for defense spending. Reminding their readers that the continued existence of imperialism means that war also continues to be a possible instrument of politics, two MPA writers observed that a war between the two systems "will inevitably assume a general and global character and will be waged by rocket-nuclear weapons."[103] Another pointed out that the course and outsome of such a war will be determined "before all and mostly" by what the Soviet economy "gives and is capable of giving for war before its beginning, in peacetime, in the process of military construction."[104] Along this same line, a colonel and doctor of philosophical sciences declared:

> In conditions of rocket-nuclear war, it will be very difficult or generally impossible in a short time to resolve problems of mass production of new equipment and its mastery by troops. Now for the production of the newest arms is needed more *time*, reserves, and qualified working hands. . . . On the strength of this, winning and keeping military-technical supremacy over the likely enemy today, still in peacetime, has a decisive importance.[105]

Bowing to the pressures of this argument, the party leadership decided in December 1965 to raise its announced defense allocation for 1965 by 5 percent. Military expenditures for the new year were to be set at 13.4 billion rubles, which was officially described as 12.8 percent of the entire Soviet budget.[106]

The 23rd CPSU Congress and Its Aftermath

Based upon the evidence presented herein, it is possible to summarize several basic propositions that seem to have gained general support after Khrushchev's downfall. First, the new regime gave more stress to a growing imperialist danger, especially from the United States, which was described as preparing for war against the progressive forces, including the Soviet Union. Second, the leadership also heavily stressed the Soviet's international role — that is, the role of the Soviet Union to support, protect, and foster anti-imperialist movements. Third,

[103] V. Rybnikov and Colonel A. Babakov in *Krasnaya Zvezda*, December 7, 1965.

[104] Colonel P. Trifonenko, "The Objective Laws of War and the Principles of the Military Art," *Kommunist Vooruzhennykh Sil*, No. 1 (January 1966), p. 12.

[105] Colonel I. Grudinin, "The Factor of Time in Contemporary War," *Kommunist Vooruzhennykh Sil*, No. 3 (February 1966), p. 41. Italics in original.

[106] See the budgetary report of USSR Finance Minister V. F. Garbuzov in *Pravda*, December 8, 1965.

Soviet spokesmen emphasized the need, in light of the foregoing, to improve the vigilance and combat readiness of Soviet forces.

In general, professional military and political-military elites were in agreement that vigilance and combat readiness required the all-round development of all branches of the armed forces and increased military expenditures. Like most of the party leadership, both military groups opposed any restrictions, such as increases in consumer allocations, which would detract from its military buildup. On the type of training needed for combat readiness, however, there was less than full agreement. Quite naturally, professional military men tended to stress the need for technical training. Within the MPA, there was divided opinion: one side stressed the need first of all for ideological training and conviction; the other side sympathized with the professional military's argument for the primacy of technical training.

Yet even with this difference of opinion on training, all MPA officials supported the view of the Party's leading role in military matters. As Yepishev pointed out shortly before the 23rd Party Congress, "the leadership of the Party in the armed forces is the fundamental basis of our military construction, the decisive source of the might of the army and navy, and their world-historical victory."[107]

This generally harder line developed after Khrushchev's downfall was again manifested in the speeches and decisions of the 23rd Party Congress, which was held in Moscow from March 29 to April 8, 1966. In the Central Committee report delivered by Brezhnev, it was maintained that "international tension has intensified" and "the military danger, aroused by the aggressive acts of the imperialists, and first of all by the USA, has increased."[108] Also the Resolution adopted by the Congress stated:

> The correlation of forces in the world arena continues to change in favor of socialism, the worker, and the national liberation movement. Together with this, the period under review is characterized by increasing imperialist aggression and activities by reactionaries. The deepening of the general crisis of capitalism and the intensification of its contradictions are reenforcing the adventurism of imperialism, its danger for people, the cause of peace, and socialist progress. Imperialism more and more often endeavors to look for a way out in

[107] General of the Army A. A. Yepishev, "Communists of the Army and Navy Before the Congress of the Dear Party," *Kommunist Vooruzhennykh Sil*, No. 6 (March 1966), p. 24.

[108] L. I. Brezhnev, "Report of the Central Committee of the CPSU to the 23rd Congress of the Communist Party of the Soviet Union," in *XXIII s"yezd Kommunisticheskoy partii Sovetskogo Soyuza: Stenograficheskiy otchet (23rd Congress of the Communist Party of the Soviet Union: Stenographic Record)* (Moscow: State Publishing House for Political Literature, 1966), I, 39.

military provocations, diverse kinds of conspiracies, and direct military intervention.[109]

Despite the "aggressive policy of imperialism," Brezhnev advocated the peaceful coexistence of states with different social systems. As defined by Brezhnev, peaceful coexistence is "a form of class struggle between socialism and capitalism," but wherein the Soviet Union "consistently comes out in favor of a proposal for normal, peaceful relations with capitalist countries, for resolving controversial interstate questions by means of negotiations, and not by means of war."[110] At the same time, the General Secretary[111] clearly advised that peacefull coexistence should not be taken to apply outside of U.S.-Soviet relations. He declared:

> It stands to reason that there can be no peaceful coexistence where the question is the internal processes of class and national liberation struggle in capitalist countries or in colonies. The principle of peaceful coexistence is not applicable to relations between oppressors and the oppressed, and between colonialists and the victims of colonial oppression.[112]

Following from this position, Brezhnev advocated that the USSR has the international duty to support liberation struggles, since such struggles are clearly connected to the success of world socialism and the international working class.[113] As Kosygin likewise pointed out in his report to the 23rd Congress:

> The revolutionary achievements of our people and other people would find themselves threatened if they were not directly and indirectly shielded by the enormous military power of the countries of the socialist society and in the first instance by the Soviet Union. And if the imperialists now and then fear to act as they would like, then it is only because they well know what risk this entails for them.[114]

[109] "Resolution of the 23rd Congress of the Communist Party of the Soviet Union on the Report of the Central Committee of the CPSU," in *ibid.*, II, 303.

[110] Brezhnev, "Report of the Central Committee of the CPSU to the 23 Congress," p. 44.

[111] According to changes introduced at the 23rd Party Congress, the title of the chief party secretary was changed from First Secretary back to General Secretary, as it had been under Stalin. Similarly, the title of Politburo of the Central Committee replaced the title Presidium, which had been in use under Khrushchev. See "Resolution of the 23rd Congress of the Communist Party of the Soviet Union on the Partial Changes in the Statutes of the CPSU," in *ibid.*, II, 319–20.

[112] Brezhnev, "Report of the Central Committee of the CPSU to the 23rd Congress," p. 44.

[113] *Ibid.*, p. 38.

[114] A. N. Kosygin, "Directives of the 23rd Congress of the CPSU for the Five-Year Plan of the Development of the National Economy of the USSR," in *ibid.*, II, 64.

The political leaders furthermore concluded that the international situation required untiring military vigilance. Thus they deemed it necessary "to ensure the further development of the defense industry and the perfection of rocket-nuclear weapons and all other types of equipment."[115] Consequently, on behalf of the Party Central Committee, Brezhnev promised the delegates to the Party Congress:

> The Party will in the future and in every possible way strengthen the defense potential of the Soviet Union, increase the power of the armed forces of the USSR, and maintain such a level of military preparedness of troops which will reliably ensure the peaceful labor of the Soviet people.[116]

In view of the hard line displayed by the political leadership one might expect that there would be a significant increase in the representation of professional military men elected to the 23rd Party Congress and by the Congress to higher party posts. However, no such increase occurred. Of the 4,943 delegates elected to the 23rd Party Congress, 352 were military men, who thereby accounted for 7.1 percent of the delegates elected.[117] In terms of numbers, this was only two more than were elected to the 22nd Party Congress. Thirty-two of the 352 were in turn elected by the 23rd Congress to membership in the Party Central Committee, constituting 8.9 percent of that body, a decrease of 0.6 percent as compared with the 22nd Congress.

	Proportion of Servicemen in the Central Committees Elected by the 22nd and 23rd Party Congresses						
	Total Membership			Servicemen			Percentage
Congress	Full	Alt.	Total	Full	Alt.	Total	of Total
22nd (1961)	175	155	330	14	17	31	9.5
23rd (1966)	195	165	360	14	18	32	8.9

Source: For the statistics on the 22nd Party Congress, see above, p. 77. For the membership of the Central Committee elected at the 23rd Party Congress, see *XXIII s"yezd Kommunisticheskoy partii Sovetskogo Soyuza: Stenograficheskiy otchet*, II, 383–88.

At the 23rd Party Congress, three MPA officials were elected to the Party Central Committee. Yepishev was made a full member. Two others were elected

[115] Brezhnev, "Report of the Central Committee of the CPSU to the 23rd Congress," p. 93.
[116] *Ibid*.
[117] See the report of I. V. Kapitanov in *ibid*., I, 379, 283.

to alternate membership: K. S. Grushevoy and I. A. Lavrenov. (A fourth MPA official, S. P. Vasyagin, was elected to the Central Auditing Commission.) Consequently, a breakdown of professional and political-military representation elected to the Party Central Committee by the 23rd Congress illustrates that 91 percent were professional military men and only 9 percent were political-military officials.

Proportion of Professional and Political-Military
Men Elected by the 23rd Party Congress
to the Party Central Committee

Classification	Full	Alt.	Total	Percentage of Military	Percentage of CC
Total Membership	195	165	360		100.0
Military	14	18	32	100	8.9
Professional	13	16	29	91	8.06
Political	1	2	3	9	0.83

Despite the imbalance in favor of the professional military men in the military representation, it is noteworthy that while three MPA officials were elected in 1966, only one (Golikov) had been elected to Central Committee membership in 1961. Therefore, a total of three does represent a sizable gain for the MPA in 1966. As a full CC member, Yepishev's political status was formally equal to that of the highest professional military leaders. It is also noteworthy, however, that the two alternate members of the new Central Committee from the MPA were not the first deputy and one of the several deputies, but rather the political heads of the Moscow Military District and of the rocket troops. In other words, it appears that one criterion for the increased MPA representation was not standing within the MPA hierarchy but rather the military importance of the unit.

It has already been pointed out that the hard line taken by the political leadership at the 23rd Party Congress was not unexpected and generally confirmed the pre-Congress line. The same was true of the speeches delivered by the heads of the professional military and political-military men.

In his speech to the Congress, Minister of Defense Malinovsky warned that the imperialists "have not abandoned the wild idea of obliterating the socialist countries by force."[118] It followed that in pursuing its "Leninist peace-loving course" the Party must take into account "the growing aggressiveness of the

[118] *Ibid.*, I, 409.

imperialist states headed by the USA."[119] This meant that the Soviet Union must undertake as its chief task "to raise with unrelenting persistence the military might of the army and navy and their readiness to crush any enemy if war is forced on us."[120] At the same time, the Minister of Defense reiterated the proposition of the political and the political-military leadership that Soviet might consists not only of its weapons but also "in the force of spirit of its troop personnel, in their selfless devotion to their people and loyalty to the ideas of the Communist Party."[121] And as proof of the improving ideological-political level in the higher military ranks, Malinovsky noted that about 93 percent of all officers, generals, and admirals were Communists or Komsomols.[122]

Like Malinovsky, Yepishev did not mention the policy of peaceful coexistence in his speech to the 23rd Party Congress. Both apparently agreed on the necessity to stress the danger from the West and on the desirability of underplaying the possibility of normal relations with the West. Indeed, in emphasizing the "piratical acts" of the United States in Vietnam, Yepishev claimed that "thousands of our people and the personnel of entire units" were expressing their readiness to serve as volunteers in Vietnam.[123] Yet it was not the military, but the ideological struggle with the West that drew Yepishev's main concern. According to the MPA head, the West was "counting on the ideological diversion and on the moral and psychological decomposition of the Soviet people" in an attempt to "blow up Russia from inside."[124] Therefore, in addition to raising military might, said Yepishev, It is necessary to perfect the education of Soviet people, especially the youth, "in the spirit of preparedness to withstand the ideological onslaught of the apologists of imperialism."[125]

---

[119] *Ibid.*, p.. 411

[120] *Ibid.*

[121] *Ibid.*, p. 414.

[122] *Ibid.*, p. 415.

[123] *Ibid.*, p. 548.

[124] *Ibid.*, p. 550.

[125] *Ibid.* In part, the emphasis on ideology and indoctrination stressed at the Congress by not only Yepishev but many other speakers was the result of several incidents deemed anti-Soviet by the Soviet leadership. For example, in late February, Andrey W. Sinyavskiy and Yuri M. Daniel were arrested, charged with publishing anti-Soviet works abroad, and sentenced respectively to seven and five years of hard labor. (*The New York Times*, April 18, 1966.) Also an article in the second 1966 issue of *Novyy Mir* by V. Kardin challenged several of the traditions and legends of the military. He alleged that there were no salvos from the *Aurora* in November 1917, nor were there any battles at Pskov or Narva on February 23, 1918 — the battles for which the Soviets celebrate Armed Forces Day. (Wolfgang Leonhard, "Politics and Ideology in the Post-Khrushchev Era," in Alexander Dallin and Thomas B. Larson, ed., *Soviet Politics Since Khrushchev* [Englewood Cliffs, N.J.: Prentice-Hall, 1963], p. 52.)

In sum, Yepishev was in total agreement with the concern of the Congress for combating ideological diversion. He also appeared to be in full agreement with the Party's assertion that combating this diversion would require a strengthening of the role of the Party in Soviet society.

In the months following the Congress, much attention in MPA writings was given to the Party's role in society. One lesson drawn up for study in military seminars dealt with the topic "The 23rd Congress of the CPSU on Improving Political and Organizational Activities of the Party in the Contemporary Stage of Communist Construction" and another closely related topic proposed for discussion was "the 23rd Congress of the CPSU on the Further Increasing of the Leading Role of the CPSU in Communist Construction." Several articles on these topics were also published in *Kommunist Vooruzhennykh Sil*.[126]

In addition, specific attention was also given to party affairs in the armed forces. In order to improve party-political authority and strengthen political-educational activities connected with instilling ideological conviction, many MPA writers stressed the need for eliminating the shortcomings which had been allowed to creep into party organizations and practices in the armed forces.

It was charged that in many instances lessons of political workers were conducted in an uninteresting manner, so that there was little inducement among soldiers for debates and creative discussions.[127] It was also noted that the formalistic approach to party-political work by some propagandists ineffectively and poorly influenced the troops to fulfill their service duties.[128] or to raise their ideological level.[129] Another accusation was that primary party organizations in the armed forces took little interest in the military training of troops.[130] Furthermore, it was readily admitted that these shortcomings could be traced largely to defects in the political workers themselves. As one article in *Kommunist Vooruzhennykh Sil* noted:

---

[126] See, for example, Colonel V. Yakushkin, "Leninist Vanguard of the Soviet People," *Kommunist Vooruzhennykh Sil*, No. 9 (May 1966), pp. 7–15; Major General A. Milovidov, "The Party of the Revolutionary Transformation of Society," *Kommunist Vooruzhennykh Sil*, No. 15 (August 1966), pp. 8–16; and A. Klimov, "The Political and Organizational Activity of the CPSU in the Contemporary Stage," *Kommunist Vooruzhennykh Sil*, No. 18 (September 1966), pp. 7–15.

[127] Major General S. Ilin, "Party Enlightenment in the New Educational Year," *Kommunist Vooruzhennykh Sil*, No. 19 (October 1966), p. 25.

[128] Major General G. Sredin, "Ideological Work Is a High Activity," *Kommunist Vooruzhennykh Sil*, No. 5 (August 1966), p. 19.

[129] Colonel General M. Kalashnik, "Ideological Work Is the Affair of All Communists," *Kommunist Vooruzhennykh Sil*, No. 21 (November 1966), p. 9.

[130] Lieutenant General F. Mazhayev, "Primary Party Organizations and Political Sections," *Kommunist Vooruzhennykh Sil*, No. 17 (September 1966), p. 17.

> Generally, when talk turns to the shortcomings in idealogical-theoretical studies, some officers allude to being very busy at work. Among them, they forget that political self-education is an indispensable condition for success in work. And one ought to study not because somebody demands and controls, but by inner inclination resulting from the demands of life. If you do not have a craving for knowledge, it means there are also no true qualities of a political worker.[131]

Many political workers lacked this craving for knowledge, pointed out the article. As a result, it was maintained that "sections of categories of political staffs are learning extremely unsatisfactorily" and that "this especially concerns the deputy commanders of companies, battalions, and regiments for political affairs and also deputy heads of political organs."[132]

The depth of these shortcomings and the degree of importance attached to overcoming them was reflected in the issuance by the Party Central Committee of a new decree with regard to party-political work in the armed forces on January 21, 1967. Entitled "On Measures for the Improvement of Party-Political Work in the Soviet Army and Navy," the new decree observed that the Soviet armed forces had attained "a qualitatively new stage in its development" and that consequently the political organs and party organizations in the armed forces would be expected to improve their level of work. However, to achieve this task would require the elimination of the "substantial shortcomings" that had developed in party-political work. The defects alluded to by the new decree included the following:

> In the work with personnel insufficiently taken into account are the revitalized demands for moral-political training of soldiers in connection with the appearance of rocket-nuclear weapons, the large-scale changes in the organization of troops, and also the growth of the general educational and cultural level of soldiers.
>
> In a number of cases, party organizations tolerated unscrupulousness in appraising the factors of careless attitude for work, complacency, and conceit of sections of communists.
>
> Insufficiently actively are begun the necessary methods for improving the party leadership of the komsomol, raising the level of work of komsomol organizations with army youths and securing the excellence of members of the VLKSM in fulfilling official functions and personal conduct.
>
> In ideological work with personnel, they still have not overcome the elements

[131] Colonel V. Komissarov and Colonel G. Marusov, "[A Requirement] for the Political Worker Is [to Have] High Professional Preparedness," *Kommunist Vooruzhennykh Sil*, No. 13 (June 1966), p. 42.

[132] *Ibid*, p. 43.

of formalism. In a number of units and formations, political lessons with the line and sergeant staff, lessons for Marxist-Leninst preparedness with officers, and also mass-political measures are conducted on a low level and do not render the necessary influence on the consciousness and conduct of soldiers. They do not give the needed important education to soldiers on the spirit of hatred for imperialism — the worst enemy of the workingman.[133]

The Central Committee decree then resolved that it was the obligation of the Ministry of Defense, the MPA, and other party-political organs "to eliminate the shortcomings noted in the present decision" and "to raise party-political work in the armed forces of the USSR to the level required" by the 23rd Party Congress.[134] In order to meet these obligations, party-political organs were required by the new decree:

> To improve political and organizational work with the masses of troops, concentrating on the basic effort for the further rise of the military preparedness of the armed forces.
>   To secure a rising level and activity of political work. To educate the troops in the spirit of high idealistic conviction and selfless devotion to the socialist homeland, the cause of communism, proletarian internationalism, and combat collaboration with the armies of fraternal countries. To intensify the propaganda for revolutionary and combat traditions of the Soviet people, the Communist Party, and the armed forces, and the successes of our country in communist construction. More persistently to direct the work for exposing bourgeois ideology and for educating personnel in the spirit of high vigilance and class hatred for imperialism. To give particular attention to raising the quality and activity of the Marxist-Leninist training of officers and the political lessons for soldiers, sailors, sergeants, and seniors. Not one soldier should be left outside constant political influence. . . . On the basis of work for strengthening military discipline to lay down the further improvement of political-educational work for all categories of servicemen, raising the exactingness of commanders and political chiefs of all degrees with subordinates, maintaining in every troop unit a steadfast regulation of order, and securing excellence in work and personal conduct first and foremost of communists and komsomols.[135]

"Special significance" was also attached to raising the activities and fighting

---

[133] *KPSS o Vooruzhennykh Silakh Sovetskogo Soyuza. Dokumenty 1917–1968 (The CPSU on the Armed Forces of the Soviet Union. Documents 1917–1968)* (Moscow: Voyenizdat, 1969), p. 415.
[134] *Ibid.*, pp. 415–16.
[135] *Ibid.*, p. 416.

spirit of all primary party organizations in the armed forces. According to the new decree, primary party organizations were obliged

> ... to improve work for instilling in communists idealism, irreconcilability to shortcomings, high moral qualities, and responsibility for raising its party and official duties and for the status of affairs in their organizations and in the Party as a whole; to expand their ties with the masses of servicemen and to develop their activity in resolving the tasks combat and political preparedness. In every possible way, to stimulate the criticism and self-criticism of shortcomings in the work of party organizations and also in the conduct and relations with the affairs of every communist.[136]

This was followed by a general demand from the Central Committee for all political organs in the armed forces to perfect further the style and methods of their activities. As the decree noted, all political organs in the armed forces would be required

> ... to concentrate the basic improvement on the active organizational work in the masses of servicemen. Constantly to realize the concrete leadership of the party and komsomol organizations, to go more greatly into the questions of the problem and placement of military personnel, to study deeply the status of affairs in units and subunits, to disclose at the proper time and principally to appraise shortcomings and to make arrangements for their removal, operationally to determine urgent problems, and to notice and disseminate all new and progressive events that occur in the life of the troops. Systematically, to educate the party aktivs and to train commanders and political workers in practical party-political work.[137]

Summary

As suggested by the evidence presented in this chapter, it appears that neither the professional military nor the political-military leadership in the armed forces were well informed beforehand of the fate which would befall Khrushchev in October 1964. Yet, while neither group actively participated in Khrushchev's ouster, both had reason to acquiesce in his passing. Therefore, Khrushchev could find little support in either group.

With Khrushchev's removal, Malinovsky pushed for a harder line in Soviet

[136] *Ibid.*, p. 417.
[137] *Ibid.*

foreign as well as military policy. However, the new collective leadership was quick to gain control over the situation and to restrain the professional military leaders. One measure of this control was the retention of Yepishev as MPA head and his promoton to full membership in the CPSU Central Committee.

Throughout the period from Khrushchev's removal to the new Central Committee decree on party-political work in the armed forces promulgated in January 1967, the spokesmen of the MPA generally emphasized the hard-line policy. They constantly depicted a growing imperialist threat even in the early months of the new regime, when the political leadership was taking a softer, more conciliatory line in foreign affairs. They advocated increased Soviet support for national liberation movements. Also they continuously stressed the need for vigilance and combat readiness.

At the same time, the MPA demonstrated constant concern for the supremacy of the Party in military policy formulation and for the influence of party-political organs in the armed forces over the implementation of military decisions. On behalf of the political leadership, the MPA asserted that the complexity of contemporary military affairs required the continuation of party leadership and proceeded to define for the professional military some of the basic military tenets. In this role, the MPA under Yepishev was not just the spokesman for "the Party" or "the military," for its positions on the various issues came to be closely identified with those subgroups of the Party and the military which advocated such hard-line stands as: (1) recognition of a growing imperialist threat, (2) a more aggressive third-world policy, (3) the need for greater efforts toward vigilance and combat readiness, (4) the development of all branches and types of arms and services, and (5) higher budgetary allocations for the armed forces.

The major weakness of the political administration in the armed forces during the period under examination was that it sometimes grew lax in its attitude toward ideological work and not infrequently allowed technical training to take precedence over ideological training. Then in January 1967, after months of self-criticism within the MPA, the Central Committee enacted a new decree on party-political work in the armed forces. Though not original in its exhortations, the new decree forcefully enumerated many MPA defects and commanded the MPA to rectify them. An important instrument in this regard undoubtedly was the Central Committee's urging for the MPA officers to become more deeply involved in the placement of military personnel, for this would give the MPA greater leverage in implementing the new decree. Together with its increased representation in the Party Central Committee since the 23rd Party Congress, it would appear that the MPA had become a more influential organization. It also followed that the higher the prestige of the MPA, then the more emphasis could be placed on the hard-line policies and stands enumerated in the previous paragraph.

The next chapter of the study will seek to examine the effects, if any, of this increased MPA prestige in the period highlighted by the appointment of a new Ministry of Defense and the Warsaw Pact invasion of Czechoslovakia.

6

The Emergence of the Hard-Line Policy under Political Control

The Appointment of Grechko as Minister of Defense

The CPSU is constantly concerned with efforts to legitimize its position as the sole political authority in the Soviet Union. According to the third party program, adopted in 1961, the CPSU is "the conscious exponent of the class movement of the proletariat."[1] It theoretically follows, therefore, that the Party embodies the best qualities of leadership. Indeed, the third party program asserts:

> The Party is the brain, the honor and the conscience of our epoch and the Soviet people, as they accomplish great revolutionary transformations. It looks penetratingly into the future, opens before the people scientifically based roads along which to advance, arouses titanic energy in the masses, and leads them to the accomplishment of great tasks.[2]

From the evidence already presented, it is equally apparent that the Party believes its authority should extend over the Soviet armed forces. This is the reason not only for the existence of the MPA as set down in official pronouncements but also for Khrushchev's appointment as the Supreme Commander-in-Chief of the armed forces. Yet a clear and public definition of the relationship in wartime between the political and military leadership has never been made. Under Stalin, the State Defense Committee had taken over the control of mili-

---

[1] *Programma Kommunisticheskoy partii Sovetskogo Soyuza (Program of the Communist Party of the Soviet Union)* (Moscow: State Publishing House for Political Literature, 1973), p. 9.
[2] *Ibid.*, p. 136.

tary matters, but this body was disbanded at the end of the war. In Sokolovskiy's work on military strategy in mid-1962, it was noted that in wartime an agency similar to the State Defense Committee might again be created and presided over by the Party's First Secretary and head of the government (written when Khrushchev combined these offices, Sokolovskiy's implications had been that these offices would be held by a single individual) who would function as the Supreme Commander.[3]

Still, the professional military leaders have on many occasions, though often obliquely, asserted their right to take part in the formulation of Soviet military doctrine and strategic planning. For example, it is sometimes pointed out by professional military spokesmen that Western military leaders have a vital role in deciding military questions. Quite probably, the point being made by these spokesmen concerns the proposition that the importance of including professional military men in decision making is recognized even by the Western political leaders and that the Soviet Union should do likewise. One example of this type of argument appeared in print while the 23rd Congress was being held and was probably intended to influence any decision the Congress might make.[4]

In January 1967, the political leadership responded to these arguments with a particularly strong statement of political supremacy in military matters. According to an article in *Krasnaya Zvezda* by Major General V. Zemskov, "both World War I and World War II demonstrated that the leadership of an armed struggle could not be left in the hands of the military command alone."[5] The author, while noting that "politicians and strategists *jointly solve* the problems of war and supplement one another,"[6] also maintained that "with respect to their destructive properties, modern weapons are such that the political leadership cannot let them escape its control." Commenting further on the effects of the revolution in military equipment, Zemskov suggested that the Soviet Union was in the process of creating a supreme organ for wartime leadership, but he left little doubt that the "single military-political organ" would be within the tight control of the Party.[7]

[3] See above, pp. 129–30.

[4] Marshal of the Soviet Union V. Sokolovskiy and Major General M. Cherednichenko, "On Contemporary Military Strategy," *Kommunist Vooruzhennykh Sil*, No. 7 (April 1966), pp. 62–63.

[5] *Krasnaya Zvezda*, January 5, 1967.

[6] *Ibid.*, Italics added.

[7] Zemskov described the "supreme governmental military-political organs" in several Western countries: the U.S. National Defense Council (headed by the U.S. President), the defense committee headed by the French President, and the defense committee headed by the West German

This issue of control over the armed forces again stirred considerable debate when Minister of Defense Malinovsky died on March 31 from "cancer of the pancreas with extensive metastases."[8] Under pressures from the professional military leadership, one political faction favored the appointment of a professional military figure as Malinovsky's successor. Yet the evidence suggests that another political faction, desiring to strengthen party control over the armed forces, pressured for the appointment of a successor who would be more subservient to the Party's wishes than professional military men had sometimes proven to be. Rumors circulating in Moscow during early April indicated that this group favored the appointment of D. F. Ustinov, a CPSU Central Committee secretary and alternate Politburo member, who was a civilian but had extensive experience in administering the defense industry.[9]

In the course of the debate, a strongly worded article calling for strict political control over military matters appeared in the military press. The author, candidate of historical sciences Colonel A. Babin, made four points in response to the question: "Why does the leading role of the CPSU in military construction and in the USSR Armed Forces increase in the present stage of social development, and how does it manifest itself?" First, in view of the "extremely complicated and responsible tasks" connected with a future war, Babin noted:

> . . . only Marxist-Leninist parties are capable of successfully resolving these tasks, of working out scientifically substantiated tactics and strategy in regard to a possible world war, and of equipping the masses with a correct understanding of the causes of its outbreak, its class character, its course and outcome, and its possible consequences.[10]

Second, "only under the leadership of the Party and its Central Committee, which headed all matters of the country's defense," was it possible to correlate correctly the development and construction among the various types of armed forces, to align military organizational structure with the demands of the revolution in military affairs, to direct military-scientific thought, to carry out the

---

Chancellor. (*Ibid.*, p. CC4.) It is a striking point, furthermore, that in comparison to Sokolovskiy and Cherednichenko, Zemskov totally de-emphasizes the role of professional military men in military policy formulation.

[8] *Krasnaya Zvezda*, April 1, 1967.

[9] Raymond H. Anderson's report in *The New York Times*, April 13, 1967. For a similar report by the Yugoslavian media, see Tanjug International Service, April 6, 1967, 2103 GMT, FBIS, *USSR and East Europe*, No. 68 (April 7, 1967), p. CC1.

[10] *Krasnaya Zvezda*, April 6, 1967.

training and preliminary preparations of military cadres, to work out a "profoundly scientific, comprehensive, and profoundly substantiated" military doctrine, and to determine the chief direction and tasks for further development of military sciences. Third, in order "to supply all the newest types of weapons and matériel to the army and navy and to establish the firm military superiority of the Soviet state over the imperialist aggressive states," it is necessary for the Party to work out "a correct military-economic and military-technical policy, the most expedient organization and location of military production," and to determine "properly substantiated proportions concerning the manufacture of the various types of weapons and matériel conforming to the interests of the reliable defense of the country." Fourth, the Party must ensure the moral-political superiority of the Soviet armed forces over the armies of the imperialist aggressors, since "victory over the enemy will be won not by weapons and matériel alone, no matter how formidable and powerful, but by the people who skillfully and masterfully operate these weapons and possess unsurpassed moral and fighting qualities."

Babin also listed several tasks for further improving party-political work in the armed forces, two of which were: "to enhance the role and importance of the deputy commanders for political affairs" and "to strengthen in every possible manner single-man command and the authority of military leaders . . . who in all their activities rely on the party organizations."

In sum, therefore, Babin's theme was quite closely in agreement with the theme of Major General V. Zemskov's January 5 article, namely, that military leadership cannot be left in the hands of the military command alone and that the Party must maintain the primary position with regard to military matters. The appearance of Babin's article at this particular time, when the discussion of a new Defense Minister was taking place, seems to point to and emphasize the intent of some political leaders to exert greater control over the professional military leadership.

After twelve days of debate and despite the aforementioned pressures for greater control, Marshal A. A. Grechko was appointed Minister of Defense on April 12. Born to Ukrainian peasants on October 17, 1903, Andrey Antonovich Grechko[11] joined the Red Army at the age of sixteen and served in the 1st Cavalry Army in the Civil War. Rising in the ranks primarily in the cavalry, he graduated from cavalry school in 1926 and joined the Party in 1928. Completing the Military Academy imeni M. V. Frunze in 1936, he was appointed commander of a regiment and, subsequently, chief of staff of a division. In 1941, he

[11] A. M. Prokhorov, ed., *Bol'shaya sovetskaya entsiklopediya* (*The Great Soviet Encyclopedia*) (3rd ed.; Moscow: Soviet Encyclopedia Publishing House, 1971), VII, 319.

graduated from the Military Academy of the General Staff. During World War II, Grechko commanded the 34th Cavalry Division, and after January 1942 the 5th Cavalry Corps on the Southern Front. Between April and August 1942, he commanded the 12th Army, waging defensive battles in the Donbass and the North Caucasus. From September to December 1942, he was commander of the 47th and 18th armies in the Novorossiysk and Taupse Directions. During January–October 1943, he served as commander of the 56th Army, participating in the liberation of the North Caucasus. In October 1943, he became deputy commander of the 1st Ukrainian Front. From December 1943 to the end of the war, he commanded the 1st Guards Army, taking part in the liberation of the Ukraine, Poland, and Czechoslovakia.

In the postwar period, Grechko served as commander of the Kiev Military District (1945–53) and commander of the Group of Soviet Forces in Germany (1953–57). Promoted to marshal of the Soviet Union in 1955, Grechko held positions both during and after the war which brought him in close contact with Khrushchev and it is commonly believed that Khrushchev was mainly responsible for Grechko's advancement within the military. In November 1957, following the removal of Zhukov, Grechko was appointed First Deputy Minister of Defense (until April 1967) and commander-in-chief of the Soviet Ground Forces. From July 1960 to July 1967, he served as the commander-in-chief of the Joint Armed Forces of the Warsaw Pact. A candidate member of the CC CPSU between 1952 and 1961, Grechko became a full member at the 22nd Party Congress.

At the same time, several other promotions were made. I. I. Yakubovskiy and S. L. Sokolov were appointed First Deputy Ministers of Defense and were promoted, respectively, to marshal of the Soviet Union and general of the army. In addition, I. G. Pavlovskiy was appointed a deputy minister and promoted to general of the army. All three had in common the fact that they had been commanders of military districts at the time of their appointments: Yakubovskiy in Kiev, Sokolov in Leningrad, and Pavlovskiy in the Far East.[12]

The appointment of Grechko and the promotion of the other professional military men was somewhat of a victory for the proponents of professionalism in military matters and a defeat for the advocates of tighter control over the armed forces. The appointment of Ustinov as Minister of Defense, if such was indeed contemplated by the political leadership, could have significantly curtailed the ability of profesional military men to manage their own affairs. Especially with his expertise in the defense industry, Ustinov would have been able to exert greater party control over military matters through a strict control of

[12] *Krasnaya Zvezda*, April 14, 1967.

military allocations. It is possible, therefore, that the support of Ustinov —
though himself not noted for a soft or pro-consumer line — may have come from
party members who desired to decrease the defense budget.

Still, the appointment of Grechko was less than a total victory for the professional military men. The choice of Grechko, a moderate in comparison to some
of his more extremist colleagues, indicated that the political leadership was attempting to depoliticize the position as much as possible.

The appointment of Grechko had a mixed effect on the stature of Yepishev
and the MPA. The appointment of Ustinov, a high party official with extensive
knowledge of military affairs, would probably have led to a diminution of influence for Yepishev and the MPA. As a civilian Minister of Defense, Ustinov
would have introduced another and very powerful instrument of party control
over the armed forces. In time, it is likely that this new instrument would become
the rival of the MPA for party-political authority in the armed forces. Conversely, the appointment of Grechko, while it gave added prestige to the professional element, also in the long run added to the influence of the MPA by
eliminating a potential party-political rivalry.

Moreover, an analysis of Grechko's past articles and speeches suggests that
his appointment might have received MPA support.[13] Although such a suggestion is quite hypothetical and lacks concrete evidence, it can be inferred from
several factors. First, there does not appear to have been at this time a single
fundamental issue over which Grechko and Yepishev differed. Second, with the
ouster of Khrushchev, Yepishev became a major spokesman for that faction of
the Party and armed forces which advocated the all-round development of the
Soviet armed forces through greater defense allocations, the improvement of all
branches of the military services, and greater emphasis on military training.
Third. in addition to being in close sympathy with this faction, Grechko had not
demonstrated that he was to any significant degree opposed to Yepishev's efforts
to maintain party control over the armed forces. In view of such commonality
of perspective, it would not be unexpected that the MPA favored Grechko's
appointment, especially as opposed to the appointment of Ustinov or a more
radical professional military man. Moreover, the commonality between Grechko
and Yepishev continued to grow in subsequent years as Grechko showed a
marked preference for deferring to party-political authorities and a hard-line
foreign policy prospered.

The triumph of the hard-line policy preferred by the professional military
was signified in various pronouncements made after Grechko's appointment.

---

[13] For a representative article, containing all of the elements alluded to below and made shortly
before Malinovsky's death, see Marshal of the Soviet Union A. Grechko, "50th Anniversary of
the Soviet Armed Forces," *Voyenno-Istoricheskiy Zhurnal*, No. 2 (February 1968), pp. 3–14.

The most important of these was the "Theses of the Central Committee of the CPSU" issued in June 1967 to commemorate the fiftieth anniversary of the Bolshivik Revolution. According to the Theses, "the formation of the world socialist system and the strengthening of the economic and defense power of the Soviet Union changed the correlation of forces in the world arena in favor of socialism."[14] Consequently, because of the union of the socialist countries with all anti-imperialist countries, "imperialism ceased to dominate in the world arena."[15] This means that a new world war can be prevented, stated the Theses, which went on to warn, however, that "while imperialism exists, the threat of predatory wars remains."[16] Pointing to imperialist "aggressions" against Vietnam, Cuba, and the "freedom-loving Arab peoples," the Theses attempted to justify the large expenditures for a military buildup in the Soviet Union. As the Theses stated:

> Consistently defending peace and international security, the Soviet state has maintained and will in the future maintain its defense potential at a very high level. Our armed forces possess all kinds of contemporary military equipment, including also rocket-nuclear weapons. On defense are spent large funds, but the Soviet people understand that this is necessary. The socialist revolution, as taught by Marx and Lenin, must be able to defend itself and to oppose the aggressions of the class enemy with invincible military power.[17]

MPA spokesmen substantially agreed with the hard-line policy advocated by the Theses. For example, an article in the June issue of *Kommunist Vooruzhennykh Sil* recommended for study noted that "strengthening the defense potential of the country and raising the power of the Soviet armed forces has always been a paramount concern of the CPSU."[18] The following month another article acknowledged the obligation of the Party "to secure the further development of the defense industry, the perfection of rocket-nuclear weapons and all other types of equipment."[19] Similarly, Yepishev urged the Soviet armed forces to maintain a high state of combat readiness, because the Soviet people must

[14] "50th Anniversary of the Great October Socialist Revolution: Theses of the Central Committee of the CPSU," in *KPSS v rezolyutsiyakh i resheniyakh s"yezdov, konferentsiy i plenumov TsK* (*The CPSU in Resolutions and Decisions of Congresses, Conferences, and Plenums of the CC.*), IX (Moscow: State Publishing House for Political Literature, 1972), 306.

[15] *Ibid.*, p. 339.

[16] *Ibid.*

[17] *Ibid.*

[18] Lieutenant Colonel A. Bunyayev, "Marxist-Leninist Lesson on the Party and Its Development in Contemporary Conditions," *Kommunist Vooruzhennykh Sil*, No. 12 (June 1967), p. 75.

[19] Colonel Ye. Sulimov, "Soviet Military Construction in the Contemporary Stage," *Kommunist Vooruzhennykh Sil*, No. 14 (July 1967), p. 45.

... live and work under conditions where the imperialists increasingly aggravate the international situation, expanding the war in Vietnam, fanning a hotbed of aggression in the Near East, intensifying their machinations against the national liberation and revolutionary movements, and hatching most evil plans of attacking the Soviet Union and other socialist countries.[20]

Military buildup also received considerable attention in the various speeches in early November. In a report to the joint jubilee meeting of the Party Central Committee, the USSR Supreme Soviet, and the RSFSR Supreme Soviet on November 3–4, 1967, General Secretary Brezhnev asserted, in a description more reminiscent of the Khrushchev period than the present, that a modern world war "could lead to the loss of hundreds of millions of lives, the annihilation of whole countries, and the contamination of the surface and atmosphere of the earth."[21] However, the intended effort was quite different than Khrushchev's. Whereas Khrushchev used the image of destruction to justify arms control and disarmament measures, Brezhnev was employing it to justify a greater military buildup. Brezhnev asserted in his report that "imperialism gives rise to aggressive wars and from it today originates the threat of world thermonuclear conflict."[22] Such circumstances, observed the General Secretary, require the spending of "enormous funds" on the arms race and the creation of "weapons of mass extermination" and prevent "the greatest possibilities uncovered by science and technology" from being used "for the liquidation of hunger, poverty, and disease."[23] Furthermore, "the aggressive nature of imperialism" was alleged by Brezhnev to require that "the peaceful policy of the Soviet Union fortify itself with an invincible defensive power."[24]

Leading professional military spokesmen reaffirmed the General Secretary's position. For example, invoking the authority of Lenin, Minister of Defense Grechko declared that "the armed defense of the country of the soviets must be prepared at length and seriously" and that "the army must have good technical combat equipment and arms because even the best army and people, most devoted to the revolution, would be immediately annihilated by the enemy if they were

[20] *Krasnaya Zvezda*, July 22, 1967. Adding a criticism of German revanchism, the same observation can be found in General of the Army A. A. Yepishev, "50th Anniversary of the Soviet State," *Voyenno-Istoricheskiy Zhurnal*, No. 10 (October 1967), p. 15.

[21] L. I. Brezhnev, *Leninskim kursom: Rechi i stat'i* (*On the Leninist Course: Speeches and Articles*) (Moscow: State Publishing House for Political Literature, 1970), II, 126.

[22] *Ibid.*, p. 108.

[23] *Ibid.*

[24] *Ibid.*, p. 128.

not sufficiently armed."[25] Also invoking the authority of Marx and Lenin, Marshal Zakharov stated that the socialist revolution "must be able to defend itself and ought to oppose the aggression of the class enemy with invincible military power."[26]

Yet one of the strongest statements in the latter part of 1967 in favor of military construction was made by the head of the MPA. First, Yepishev noted that it was necessary to have "large reserves of modern weapons and other military equipment built up during peacetime." Second, he maintained that "increased significance" must be given to basic research "in those fields of science and technology which exert a decisive influence upon strengthening the scientific-technical potential and increasing the defense ability of the country and the fighting ability of the army and navy." Third, the MPA head observed that modern conditions necessitate keeping the country's military capability and readiness "at a level which at the very beginning of an eventual war would make it possible to solve successfully complicated and important strategic problems and inflict a decisive blow upon the aggressor."[27]

Writing a week later in *Krasnaya Zvezda*, Colonel G. Kravchenko, a professor and doctor of economic sciences, reaffirmed that creating the material basis for modern armed forces would require "great efforts and expenditures." Kravchenko cited the "Theses of the Central Committee of the CPSU" with regard to the proposition that "large funds are spent for defense, but the Soviet people understand that this is necessary." Then, like Yepishev, Kravchenko emphasized the importance of peacetime preparations for war. He pointed out:

> Many new aspects have appeared at present in the ties and correlations of the economy and the combat might of the army and navy. At the present time, the strength of military-economic potential is not just determined by the level of development of the production forces and the capabilities of industry and agriculture to produce everything necessary to wage a war, it is also determined by those reserves and stores of rocket-nuclear weapons, means of control, and other material means which were already produced in peacetime. The importance of the most rational deployment of industrial centers has also increased. The requirements have grown for the mobility of the national economy and the viability of industrial installations.[28]

[25] *Krasnaya Zvezda*, November 3, 1967.

[26] Marshal of the Soviet Union M. Zakharov, "The Development of the Military Organization of the Socialist State," *Kommunist Vooruzhennykh Sil*, No. 21 (November 1967), p. 30.

[27] *Krasnaya Zvezda*, November 30, 1967.

[28] *Ibid.*, December 8, 1967.

Soon thereafter, a professional military spokesman, writing on military superiority, claimed that "in war it is the stronger who is victorious." Rear Admiral V. Andreyev, a doctor and professor of naval sciences, explained further that military superiority has two aspects: quantity and quality. As he noted, "the quantity of troops, arms, and military-technical equipment always directly influences the course and issue of combat actions." It was also noted, however, that one must not forget the qualitative side. In the latter regard, science and technology require constant attention. Andreyev observed:

> The process of creating and perfecting new weapons is a continuous process based on the achievements and discoveries of science and technology. Bearing this in mind, one can say that the struggle for the *superiority of the forces on the battlefield begins in the laboratories of scientists and design bureaus.*[29]

As a consequence, the writer maintained, "armed struggle requires a high standard of training and mastery on the part of the fighting men."

Generally speaking, therefore, 1967 ended with the MPA and the professional military in agreement on the issues facing the armed forces. This unity of outlook was soon affected by events in Czechoslovakia and would not resurface until mid-1969.

The Invasion of Czechoslovakia: Yepishev Becomes a Leading Advocate of Suppressing Ideological Deviation by Armed Force

Under attack from party and non-party people and despite an apparent effort by Brezhnev to save him, Antonin Novotny was forced to resign as Party Secretary of the Czechoslovak Communist Party on January 5, 1968.[30] He was replaced by Alexander Dubcek, who has been described as "a sort of compromise candidate, a run-of-the-mill Party functionary who had kept out of trouble — all in all a rather unlikely candidate for the role of national hero which events were later to thrust upon him."[31] Soon after his appointment, Dubcek was informed by General Vachav Prchlik, the head of the political administration of the Czechoslovak armed forces, that a military coup on behalf of Novotny was

---

[29] *Ibid.*, December 13, 1967. Italics in original.

[30] Richard Lowenthal, "The Sparrow in the Cage," Part I, *Encounter,* XXXII, No. 1 (January 1969), 94; see also *The New York Times,* January 6, 1968.

[31] Foy D. Kohler, *Understanding the Russians: A Citizen's Primer* (New York: Harper & Row, 1970), p. 220.

being plotted. Presented with the evidence of the coup at a meeting of the Czechoslovak Presidium, Novotny squashed the plan. As a result, Prchlik was promoted on February 19 to head of the Czechoslovak Central Committee's department for state administration, whose duty it was to oversee the entire security, judicial, and military apparatus.[32] Appointed to replace Prchik as head of the political administration of the Czechoslovak armed forces was Major General Egyd Pepich. Justifying the action of Prchlik and setting the line for the military, Pepich declared shortly after his appointment in a newspaper interview that the Czechoslovak armed forces would not be used as a tool of factions to enforce policies. He stated in reference to the coup:

> To put it frankly: the army, as an instrument of power designed to serve the defense of the country, is not meant to be used to interfere with discussions within the party. On the other hand, each member of the army's party organization is entitled to participate actively in discussions and debates of the party. The matters discussed at the CC meetings were primarily the CC's affair, the party's affair. The Main Political Administration strictly observed this principle.[33]

The initial Soviet reaction to Dubcek's reformist regime was quite cautious in view of the fact that the Czechoslovak party leadership appeared to be in full control of the reform movement.[34] Brezhnev, for example, in a speech at a Leningrad party conference in mid-February took the position that:

> There is not and cannot be any question now of the leadership of the communist movement from any one center. Every party determines its own political course without assistance and completely independently.[35]

Even in the numerous speeches by military figures to commemorate the occasion of the fiftieth anniversary of the founding of the Soviet armed forces, there was no direct expression of displeasure with events in Czechoslovakia. The

[32] Harry Schwartz, *Prague's 200 Days: The Struggle for Democracy in Czechoslovakia* (New York: Praeger, 1969), pp. 92–93. Prchlik replaced Miroslav Mamula, a staunch supporter of Novotny and a principal mainspring of the planned coup.

[33] *Obrana lidu*, February 26, 1968, cited in Robin Alison Remington, ed., *Winter in Prague: Documents on Czechoslovak Communism in Crisis* (Cambridge, Mass.: M.I.T. Press, 1969), p. 50.

[34] Thomas W. Wolfe, *Soviet Power and Europe, 1945–1970* (Baltimore: The Johns Hopkins University Press, 1970), p. 361.

[35] *Leningradskaya Pravda*, February 16, 1968, quoted in the section of documents in *Studies in Comparative Communism*, I, Nos. 1–2 (July–October 1968), 171.

only possible evidence of such displeasure was the vague exhortations, frequently made in the past, for greater unity among Warsaw Pact members.

Concern among Soviet leaders began to grow in mid-March. On March 20, 1968, Western sources reported a meeting in Moscow between Yepishev and Pepich, Yepishev's counterpart in the Czechoslovak armed forces.[36] While the details of the meeting are not available — indeed the meeting itself has generally been overlooked in Western accounts — it seems likely that Yepishev was attempting to ascertain the effect of Pepich's February 24 statement on the political reliability of the Czechoslovak armed forces. Then, on March 23, two days after Novotny's forced resignation from his government post, an emergency meeting of Warsaw Pact members (excluding Rumania) was convoked. It is apparent that the Dubcek regime was given warnings to control the country's internal situation.[37]

Even more serious misgivings about the Czechoslovak situation were felt in Moscow during the first week of April, when the Czechoslovak Party Central Committee, following a week-long meeting and debate, removed many old conservative (that is, pro-Soviet) members from their party and government posts, replacing them with outspoken reformists,[38] and adopted a reformist "Action Program." In addition to specific proposals for greater participation in political decision making, greater freedom of assembly and speech, and greater personal security, the "Action Program" also adopted the following as its guiding democratic principle:

> The main task is to reform the whole political system so that it will permit the dynamic development of socialist relations, the combination of a broad democracy with a scientific, highly qualified stabilization of social relations and the maintenance of social discipline.
>
> The basic structure of the political system must at the same time provide firm guarantees against a return to the old methods of subjectivism and high-handedness from a position of power.[39]

While these condemnations of the old order were undoubtedly upsetting to the Soviet leaders, they probably perceived an equal danger in the position on foreign policy adopted in the "Action Program." Along with its expression of

36 *The New York Times,* March 29, 1968.

37 Thomas Wolfe, *Soviet Power and Europe,* pp. 362–63.

38 *The New York Times,* April 9, 1968.

39 "Action Program of the Czechoslovak Party," quoted in the section of documents in *Studies in Comparative Communism,* I, Nos. 1–2 (July–October, 1968), 178.

support for the world socialist order and the national liberation movement, the "Action Program" declared that "Czechoslovakia will formulate her own standpoint on fundamental questions on world policy."[40] The implication was that the Czechoslovak leadership could no longer be expected to subordinate itself automatically to the policies and decisions handed down by the Soviet leadership. In sum, therefore, the "Action Program" was probably perceived by the Soviet leadership as a threat not only to internal control by the Czechoslovak Communist Party, but also to the unity of the Warsaw Pact and what was left in 1968 of monolithic communism.

Subsequent actions illustrated the growing concern of the Soviet leadership. On April 23, Yepishev reportedly observed at a meeting that "he did not exclude the possibility that 'a group of faithful Communists' in Czechoslovakia might appeal to the Soviet Union and to other Socialist countries to help safeguard socialism in their country" and that "if this happened 'the Soviet Army is ready to do its duty.' "[41] Though the report was based on secondhand information, it is quite conceivable and in character that Yepishev should have made such a statement. It is necessary here to recall the remark of Yepishev at the 23rd CPSU Congress that "volunteers" were ready to go to Vietnam.[42] Then, on May 6, on his return from a visit to Moscow, Dubcek revealed that "our Soviet comrades expressed their anxiety lest the process of democratization in our country be abused against socialism."[43] Two days later, Marshal Konev arrived in Prague allegedly for the celebration of Czechoslovakia's liberation day.[44] The fact that Konev was a former Warsaw Pact commander might explain his visit but not the timing, since liberation day was not until May 17, that is, nine days after Konev's arrival.

---

[40] *Ibid.*, p. 179.

[41] *Le Monde*, May 4, 1968, cited in *The New York Times*, May 5, 1968.

[42] At the time when they were made, neither the Vietnam nor the Czechoslovak threat was reiterated by other leading Soviet figures. While the Vietnam statement was made publicly and can more easily be discounted as propaganda rather than real intent, the Czechoslovak statement was made to a private audience. Yet it is unlikely at this point that the Soviet leaders had already agreed on the necessity for military intervention. This suggests two possibilities. First, Yepishev may have been expressing his unsupported personal opinion in favor of intervention. Second, Yepishev may have been expressing the opinion of a larger hard-line faction. Whichever is accepted, the fact remains that Yepishev was a very early advocate of militay intervention.

[43] Prague Domestic Service, May 6, 1968, 1830 GMT, FBIS, *East Europe*, No. 90 (May 7, 1968), p. D3.

[44] *Krasnaya Zvezda*, May 9, 1968. The delegation headed by Konev included Marshal Moskalenko, Generals of the Army A. S. Zhadov and D. D. Lelyushenko, Colonel Generals A. I. Rodimtsev, A. I. Pokryshkin, and K. V. Kraynyukov, and General Lieutenant of Aviation I. N. Kozhedub.

Also on May 8, the party chiefs of Bulgaria, Hungary, East Germany, and Poland arrived in Moscow for discussions with Soviet party leaders.[45] On May 17, Kosygin unexpectedly accepted an earlier Czechoslovak invitation and descended on Karlovy Vary for a ten-day "rest." A few hours earlier, an eight-man delegation led by Grechko and Yepishev landed in Prague, as announced only the day before, to hold talks with the Czechoslovak Defense Ministers.[46] In response to inquiries from a Prague radio commentator with regard to the *Le Monde* report on Soviet readiness to intervene in Czechoslovakia, Yepishev is reported to have said: "These are all lies."[47]

On May 25, it was announced that Warsaw Pact troop exercises would be carried out in Czechoslovakia in June under Soviet Marshal Yakubovskiy, Despite the completion of the maneuvers on June 30, Yakubovskiy refused to withdraw Soviet troops from Czechoslovakia territory on the excuse that Czechoslovak troops could not adequately defend their own country.[48] Then a letter from five Warsaw Pact states meeting in Warsaw on July 14–15 pointed out to the Czechoslovak leadership:

> The development of events in your country evokes deep anxiety in us. It is our deep conviction that the offensive of the reactionary forces, backed by imperialism, against your party and the foundations of the social system in the Czechoslovak Socialist Republic threatens to push your country off the road of socialism and that consequently it jeopardizes the interests of the entire Socialist system. . . .
>
> A situation has thus arisen which is absolutely unacceptable for a Socialist country. . . .
>
> It is our conviction that a situation has arisen, in which the threat to the foundations of socialism in Czechoslovakia jeopardizes the common vital interests of other socialist countries.[49]

In a press conference on July 15, General Prchlik scathingly attacked the actions of and relationships within the Warsaw Pact. Prchlik's criticisms are important, for they not only show Czechoslovak disenchantment with the Pact but also reveal the extent of Soviet domination over the Pact. According to Prchlik, the political advisory committee, which is supposed to supervise the Pact, "has so far worked very sporadically, thus failing to implement its func-

45 *Pravda*, May 9, 1968.

46 *The New York Times*, May 18, 1968.

47 *Times* (London), May 18, 1968.

48 *The New York Times*, July 17, 1968.

49 "The Five-Party Letter," quoted in the section of documents in *Studies in Comparative Communism*, I, Nos. 1–2 (July–October), 258, 260, 261.

tion." Prchlik went on to criticize the rise of an anti-Czechoslovak faction among the Warsaw Pact members, and then asserted that the Warsaw Pact members had no legal right to station troops on the territory of other socialist states. Prchlik additionally made several observations and recommendations for the joint command of the Warsaw Pact in response to the interviewer's questions.

> To the group of questions which concern the joint command of the Warsaw Pact itself: So far the situation is that this command is formed by marshals, generals, and officers of the Soviet Army and that the other member armies have only their representatives in this joint command.
>
> These representatives, however, have so far held no responsibilities nor had a hand in making decisions, but rather played a role of liaison organs. This is why our party presented proposals in the past for the creation of the required prerequisites for the joint command to competently discharge its functions. One of these prerequisites is the demand that the allied command also be composed of appropriate specialists of the individual armies and that their incorporation in this command be of such a nature as to enable them to cocreate and to participate in the whole process of learning and deciding, in the whole command system. So far the proper conclusions have not been made.[50]

On July 23, *Krasnaya Zvezda* strongly refuted Prchlik's description of the Warsaw Pact.[51] Two days later, the Central Committee department headed by Prchlik was abolished and he was transferred to other duties. Quite clearly, Prchlik had touched upon too many tender points.

On July 29, Czechoslovak and Soviet leaders met at Cierna, Czechoslovakia, for a four-day conference. This was followed on August 3 with another meeting in Bratislava, Czechoslovakia, by the party leaders of Czechoslovakia, the Soviet Union, Bulgaria, Hungary, East Germany, and Poland. According to the statement issued at the Bratislava meeting, all the participants pledged to cooperate "on the basis of the principles of equality, respect for sovereignty and national independence, territorial integrity, and fraternal mutual assistance and solidarity."[52]

Still, the Czechoslovaks did not cower before the other Warsaw Pact members, as the latter had probably expected. Consequently, on August 17, Soviet military leaders (Grechko, Yepishev, Yakubovskiy, Shtemenko, and others) visited southwestern Poland ostensibly to discuss Warsaw Pact maneuvers,[53]

[50] Quoted in Remington, *Winter in Prague*, pp. 218–19.

[51] *Krasnaya Zvezda*, July 23, 1968.

[52] *Pravda*, August 4, 1968.

[53] *The New York Times*, August 18, 1968. Shtemenko had recently been named the Chief of Staff of the Moscow Pact. See *ibid.*, August 5, 1968.

but their real objective was to prepare for the invasion of Czechoslovakia by Soviet, East German, Polish, and Hungarian troops, which began at 11 P.M. (Central European Time) on August 20.[54]

Shortly after the invasion, the Soviet government news agency TASS announced in an authorized statement that the intervention into Czechoslovakia had taken place because the

> . . . people and government leaders of the Czechoslovak Socialist Republic have asked the Soviet Union and other allied states to render the fraternal Czechoslovak people urgent assistance, including assistance with armed forces. This request was brought about by the threat which has arisen to the socialist system existing in Czechoslovakia and to the statehood established by the constitution, the threat emanating from the counterrevolutionary forces which have entered into collusion with foreign forces hostile to socialism.[55]

Although TASS subsequently released what it described as the text of the appeal "by a group of members of the Central Committee of the Czechoslovak Communist Party, the Government, and the National Assembly,"[56] the Presidium of the Czechoslovak Party released its own official statement, which directly refuted TASS's claim. The Czechoslovak Presidium statement asserted that the Warsaw Pact forces crossed into Czechoslovak territory "without the knowledge of the Presidium of the republic, the President of the National Assembly, the Premier, or the first secretary of the Czechoslovak Communist Party Central Committee." Moreover, the statement denounced the invasion "as contrary not only to the fundamental principles of relations between socialist states but also as a denial of fundamental norms of international law."[57]

In asserting the events leading to the invasion of Czechoslovakia from the viewpoint of Soviet interest groups, there appears to have been significant differences of opinion among Soviet leaders. A statistical analysis of the newspapers of various interest groups by David W. Paul, for example, has drawn the conclusion that the Soviet government bureaucracy probably had "grave doubts" about the invasion. As Paul noted in his survey:

> By mid-August, all the elites except the government were hostile toward the Czechoslovak regime. A majority of the references in *Pravda* were unfavorable

[54] Schwartz, *Prague's 200 Days*, p. 208.

[55] *Pravda*, August 21, 1968.

[56] *Ibid.*, August 22, 1968.

[57] Prague Domestic Service, August 21, 1968, 0050 GMT, FBIS, *East Europe*, No. 164 (August 21, 1968), p. D1.

or even malicious, somewhat less than a majority in *Trud* and *Krasnaia Zvezda*. *Izvestiya* showed an inconsistency . . . , with a large majority of neutral references. The conclusion is that the top ranks of the government bureaucracy, including Premier Kosygin, still held ambivalent feelings toward Czechoslovak leaders and, if we carry the inference further, must have had grave doubts about intervening.[58]

Other Western observers have further suggested that the Soviet professional military leadership may have, at least partially, opposed the invasion. One such observer stressed that the Soviet military foresaw the invasion weakening the power of the Warsaw Pact and the loyalty of the Czechoslovak armed forces.[59] Another interpreted the appointment in early August of General Shtemenko, "Stalin's former chief of staff, degraded two ranks on his master's death" and "widely regarded in Soviet military circles as an incompetent timeserver," as the Warsaw Pact Chief of General Staff to be a sign of professional military opposition and a reflection of "a political decision to reimpose a Stalinist line on the generals."[60]

In view of its overlapping membership with the government and military groups, it follows that the Party, in spite of all its efforts to display a unified front in its negotiations with the Czechoslovak political leaders,[61] was itself divided on its attitude toward the events in Czechoslovakia, but that the dominant party faction was opposed to and believed itself to be threatened by these events.

It was with this dominant party faction that the major MPA officials aligned. As in the case of Piotr Shelest, the first secretary of the Central Committee of the UkrCP,[62] Yepishev and MPA spokesmen most strenuously emphasized the danger of ideological diversion emanating from the West and urged the strong-

---

[58] David W. Paul, "Soviet Foreign Policy and the Invasion of Czechoslovakia: A Theory and a Case Study," *International Studies Quarterly*, XV, No. 2 (June 1971), 194. By official Soviet definition, *Pravda* is the newspaper of the Party, *Trud* of the trade union, *Krasnaya Zvezda* of the armed forces, and *Izvestiya* of the government.

[59] John R. Thomas, "Soviet Foreign Policy and the Military," *Survey*, XVII, No. 3 (Summer 1971), 135.

[60] Robert Conquest, "Czechoslovakia: The Soviet Outlook," *Studies in Comparative Communism*, I, Nos. 1–2 (July–October 1968), 9.

[61] Another major party figure who is generally suggested to have opposed the invasion is Suslov. It is contended that Suslov was involved in attempting to convoke a meeting of world Communist Parties and feared the divisive effect of an invasion on the world Communist movement. The position of Brezhnev remains unclear.

[62] *Pravda*, July 5, 1968; and Kiec Domestic Service, July 6, 1969, 0600 GMT, FBIS, *Soviet Union*, No. 135 (July 11, 1968), pp. B1–B17, esp. pp. B11–B12, B14.

est measures to oppose this subversion. For example, an editorial article in a June issue of *Kommunist Vooruzhennykh Sil* pointed out:

> . . . the contemporary stage of historic development is characterized by a sharp intensification of the ideological struggle between capitalism and socialism. The entire enormous apparatus of anti-communist propaganda is now being aimed at this, to weaken the unity of socialist countries and the international communist movement, to alienate the progressive forces of the present, and to attempt to undermine socialist society from within.[63]

Indeed, the head of the political administration of the Strategic Missile Forces, Colonel General N. K. Yegorov, observed is *Krasnaya Zvezda* that "ideological struggle is now one of the particularly important fronts of class struggle" and warned that "our enemies are hoping to undermine the ideological conviction of the rising generation and sap its loyalty to the glorious traditions of its fathers and grandfathers."[64] As part of its campaign against ideological subversion, *Kommunist Vooruzhennykh Sil* also carried strong attacks on the reformist policies of Social Democratic parties,[65] bourgeois concepts of democracy and freedom,[66] and the attempt by "international reaction" to organize "a counter-revolutionary revolt" in Hungary in 1956.[67]

The fear of liberalizing tendencies in Czechoslovakia and concern for ideological diversion was also reflected in the growing anxiety of the MPA concerning the work of political departments in military academies. In July 1968, the MPA convened a meeting of heads of political departments of military academies to discuss defects in their political work. According to the *Krasnaya Zvezda* report of the meeting various reports and speeches on the work of political departments stressed:

> The style and methods of their work do not always conform to present requirements. Sometimes insufficient attention is given to training cadres in a spirit

[63] "The Ideological Work of Party Organizations," *Kommunist Vooruzhennykh Sil*, No. 11 (June 1968), p. 4.

[64] *Krasnaya Zvezda*, July 14, 1968.

[65] Lieutenant Colonel B. Bogdanov, "Contemporary Social-Reformism and the Struggle of Communist Parties for the Unity of the Working Class," *Kommunist Vooruzhennykh Sil*, No. 10 (May 1968), pp. 29–37.

[66] Lieutenant Colonel M. Yasyukov, "Democracy and the Freedom of People," *Kommunist Vooruzhennykh Sil*, No. 14 (July 1968) pp. 8–16.

[67] Captain 1st Rank M. Ruban, "The Armed Forces of the USSR in the Period of Communist Construction," *Kommunist Vooruzhennykh Sil*, No. 13 (July 1968), p. 79.

of high responsibility and party-mindedness. There is still not enough done to raise the level of teaching social sciences. Sometimes there is a lack of impetus and purposefulness in waging the struggle for ideological content and party-mindedness in teaching. Sometimes there is a weakness in denouncing bourgeois ideology and views which ar alien to us.[68]

Subsequently, the first August issue of *Kommunist Vooruzhennykh Sil* printed two articles also containing strong criticism of political work in military academies. Charging that "imperialism headed by the reactionary circles of the USA . . . is intensifying ideological diversion against the USSR and fraternal socialist countries,"[69] the head of the cadre department of the MPA, Lieutenant General L. Vakhrushev, warned that in some Soviet military academies

> . . . the teaching of social science is still not handled on the necessary level. In lecture and seminar lessons, the study material is not always deeply and organically coordinated with the present and the tasks of the armed forces. Now and then attention is poorly given to the military aspects in the account of separate historical factors. Not everywhere is managed a decisive struggle with manifestations of formalism and pedantry in teaching Marxist-Leninist theory.[70]

Reiterating these points, a deputy head of the political sections of a military academy pointed out that there had been "serious flaws" in the political work of some military institutions. As enumerated by the writer, these flaws included the following:

> Sometimes in lectures on actual problems of the construction of communism, the comprehensive character of the leading role of the Party was insufficiently deeply revealed, and the facts and examples of separate theoretical policies were poorly argued. Sometimes teachers were unnecessarily captivated by history and did not give enough attention to the criticism of bourgeois and reformist falsifications of Marxism-Leninism, and unmasking professional anti-Soviets and anti-communists. The chief and most urgent were not always chosen from the complex of questions, in order by them to focus the attention of audiences. Now and then was observed enthusiasm for general reasoning, instead of deep, detailed, and well-reasoned exposure of themes.[71]

[68]*Krasnaya Zvezda*, July 11, 1968.

[69] Lieutenant General L. Vakhrushev, "Some Questions of the Training and Education of Political Workers," *Kommunist Vooruzhennykh Sil*, No. 16 (August 1968), p. 22.

[70] *Ibid.*, p. 24.

[71] Colonel G. Zhuravlev, "The Political Section of Academies and the Teaching of Social Sciences," *Kommunist Vooruzhennykh Sil*, No. 16 (August 1968), p. 31.

In the period immediately following the invasion of Czechoslovakia the MPA again heightened its efforts to underscore the need for vigilance, especially directing its efforts to Soviet youths and komsomol members. On September 18, for example, deputy MPA head Colonel General I. F. Khalipov took note of the "acute sharpening of the ideological struggle between capitalism and socialism" and warned that the class enemies of socialism "are relying not only on military strength but also on undermining the socialist system from within and on ideological subversion." Pointing to "imperialist intrigues" in Czechoslovakia, Khalipov asserted:

> Bourgeois propaganda makes the corruption of youth one of its main tasks in its subversive activity and tries to poison youthful awareness with the poison of disbelief in the construction of communism, to set young people against the older generation and the Komsomol against the party, and to slander the entire heroic road traveled by our people after the victory of the October Revolution. Enemies would like to see our youth inert, apolitical, and incapable of producing real heroes from their ranks.[72]

A week after Khalipov's article was published, the MPA convened a "theoretical conference" of komsomol workers in the armed forces. In attendance at the conference were Defense Minister Grechko, MPA head Yepishev, and numerous other major MPA officials. The high rank of these military figures gives some indication of the importance attached to the conference and ideological issues. According to the sketchy *Krasnaya Zvezda* summary of the conference, Grechko pointed to "the deteriorating international situation and the aggressive intrigues of the American imperialists and the West German revanchists" as reasons for "further revolutionary vigilance and further efforts by every Soviet soldier to strengthen the defensive might of the motherland."[73]

Again charging that imperialist attempts were being made to undermine the ideological conviction of Soviet youths, an October article in *Kommunist Vooruzhennykh Sil* pointed to the increase of international tensions exemplified by events in Czechoslovakia and declared:

> We do not have a right to underestimate the danger of the ideological diversions of imperialism. Our duty is to expose them and in every way to guard youth against the pernicious influence of bourgeois propaganda.[74]

[72] *Krasnaya Zvezda*, September 15, 1968.

[73] *Ibid.*, September 22, 1968.

[74] A. Klimov, "Communism and Youth," *Kommunist Vooruzhennykh Sil*, No. 19 (October 1968), p. 23.

This was followed with a *Krasnaya Zvezda* article by Yepishev, in which the MPA head again emphasized the importance of ideological struggle against imperialist intrigues. The MPA chief declared:

> The ideological struggle is the sharpest and most uncompromising front of class struggles, and has no room for indifference, passivity, and neutralism. Under present conditions, when the entire enormous apparatus of anticommunist propaganda is aimed at weakening the unity of the socialist countries and slandering the socialist troops' noble international mission, and when all imperialist subversive propaganda centers are striving to undermine socialist society internally, irreconcilable struggle with hostile ideology, decisive unmasking of imperialist plots, and inculcation of patriotism, internationalism, and class hatred for the imperialist acquire special significance.[75]

It was within this context that *Kommunist Vooruzhennykh Sil* announced in its final 1968 issue the intention of the Party Central Committee to convene an all-army meeting of secretaries of party organizations during "the first quarter of the next year." Although the journal was vague about the program of the proposed conference, it stated that "the meeting will discuss in detail the tasks of communism for further improving the military preparedness of the Soviet armed forces" and furthermore that "great creative conversation will take place on the condition and measures for the fulfillment of the demands of the Central Committee of the CPSU on improving party-political work among troops."[76] This meeting would be the fifth such all-army conference of party secretaries to be held in the history of the Soviet armed forces and the first since 1960.

However, the conference was not held in the first quarter of 1969 as announced. Rather, it was consistently postponed and was not actually convened until the first quarter of 1973, four years after its announced date. Such a delay seems to suggest the existence of a severe internal debate among Soviet leaders on some grave issue or issues. It appears furthermore to suggest that some faction (or factions) was proposing to use the conference as a forum for expressing its view, but was encountering significant opposition.

The emphasis of major MPA spokesmen on ideological struggle and vigilance

[75] *Krasnaya Zvezda*, November 24, 1968. Much the same point was made in a political lesson for servicemen drawn up by the MPA after the Czechoslovak invasion. See Lieutenant Colonel T. Kondratkov, "Imperialism Is the Source of Wars. Imperialist Aggressions Headed by the USA Are the Worst Enemies of the Peace and Safety of the Peoples," *Kommunist Vooruzhennykh Sil*, No. 18 (September 1968), p. 73.

[76] "To Meet the All-Army Conference of Secretaries of Party Organizations," *Kommunist Vooruzhennykh Sil*, No. 24 (December 1968), p. 3.

certainly points to the assumption that some MPA leaders wanted to increase the amount of indoctrination work among troops; based upon evidence presented later in this study, this seems to be a safe assumption. In the light of internal Czechoslovakia events, which led to the five-power Communist invasion defined as blatantly illegal by the Czechoslovak party leadership, it would also be logical to assume that MPA officials wanted to overcome any sympathy for liberalization among Soviet troops, especially those of the invasion force who gained first-hand knowledge of actual events in Czechoslovakia. Yet the apparent conflicts and debates within the Soviet elite structure were extremely complex and put various roadblocks in the way of plans for such a large convocation.

Summary

In January 1967, the Party took two steps closely directed toward curtailing the independence of action gained by the professional military during the early period of collective leadership. First, a new Central Committee decree, which significantly raised the influence and prestige of the MPA, was issued. Second, the military leaders were reminded of party dominance in military affairs.

Although these moves temporarily reaffirmed the Party's control over military matters, the death of Defense Minister Malinovsky on March 31, 1967, reopened factional debates within the Party on the issue. While one faction appears to have wanted the appointment of a professional military man as Malinovsky's successor, another faction may have attempted to increase te Party's control over the armed forces by working for the appointment of a civilian Defense Minister. The major objective in contending for a civilian Defense Minister appears to have been the desire of a party faction to gain greater control over the armed forces, particularly over military expenditures, and to redirect funds for consumer production.

Eventually, the faction supporting the appointment of a professional military man as Minister of Defense was victorious. In addition, instead of a reorientation toward greater consumerism, there arose greater emphasis on the imperialist threat, the need for a hard-line foreign policy, greater defense expenditures, and higher combat readiness. Yepishev was not only in substantial agreement with this party-political faction, but also one of its leading spokesmen. Consequently, the MPA came to represent chiefly the hard-line viewpoint.

Opposing the liberalization reforms in Czechoslovakia, Yepishev appears to have been one of the first Soviet leaders to suggest the use of armed forces to fight "ideological subversion." He blamed the counterrevolutionary ideas of the

Western states for the activities in Czechoslovakia, and the MPA emphasized the growing importance of the ideological struggle with, and danger from, the imperialists. From the content of Yepishev's speeches at this time, it would appear that he considered the ideological threat of the West to be even more menacing than the military. This would explain the MPA attempt to convene the conference of secretaries of party organizations and to increase ideological training. Faced with strong opposition from the professional military, the MPA escalated the debate from the relatively minor issue of training to the more important, and historically inflammatory, issue of the method of Soviet command in the armed forces.

The next chapter will survey the temporary divergencies between the political administration and the professional military as a result of their differing perceptions, and their resolutions.

7

Disarmament and a
Series of Related
Factional Conflicts
and Debates

The Disarmament Controversy

An extremely inflammatory issue coming to the front at the same time as the Czechoslovak crisis was concerned with disarmament. By June 1968, the Soviet political leadership had agreed to discuss with the United States the possibility of limiting strategic weapons. Signaling Soviet intent in a speech to the USSR Supreme Soviet on June 27, Foreign Minister A. A. Gromyko stated that "the Soviet Union urges the Western powers possessing nuclear weapons to sit down at a conference table, in a narrow or broad composition, with the participation of other states, and to consider seriously the question of an international convention prohibiting the use of nuclear weapons." He further declared that "our country is ready to affix its signature to such an international document immediately."[1] In calling for an end to the arms race, Gromyko also criticized the opponents of disarmament, stating:

> To the good-for-nothing theoreticians, who try to tell us, as all champions of disarmament, that the latter is an illusion, we reply: by taking such a stand you fall into step with the forces of the most dyed-in-the-wool reaction, weaken the front of struggle against it.[2]

[1] *Pravda*, June 28, 1968.

[2] *Ibid.* While it might with some justification be argued that the "theoreticians" alluded to by Gromyko may have been the Chinese, it is also apparent from the evidence below that the Foreign Minister was equally, if not predominantly, referring to internal opponents.

193

Then, on July 1, 1968, the Soviet Union proposed an official nine-point program for the cessation of the arms race. The second and third points of the proposal concerned, respectively, "measures for the cessation of the production of nuclear weapons and the reduction and elimination of stockpiles" and "restriction and subsequent reduction of vehicles for the delivery of strategic weapons." In the text of the second point, the Soviet Government declared that its willingness to negotiate was based upon the possibility of arriving "at an understanding concerning the whole complex of measures leading to the elimination of nuclear weapons as well as certain individual steps directed towards that end."[3]

The convocation for these discussions was somewhat delayed by the Soviet invasion of Czechoslovakia.[4] It seems quite likely from the timing of these events that Soviet willingness to hold such discussions was more than coincidentally tied to the plans for military action against Czechoslovakia. Since the initiation of talks would cast a favorable light on the Soviet Union within the international community, an expression of willingness to discuss strategic arms limitation was probably intended to offset the ill effects stirred up in international opinion by the invasion. Moreover, it was probably within this context that the Soviet anti-disarmament faction agreed to an initiation of talks.

Once the invasion of Czechoslovakia had taken place, the circumstances and forces working in favor of talks fundamentally changed, even though the Soviet's pro-disarmament faction continued to hold the dominant position. In a speech before the United Nations General Assembly on October 3, the Soviet Foreign Minister reaffirmed Soviet willingness to participate in disarmament talks. Gromyko recalled for the General Assembly that the Soviet Union and the United States had already reached an agreement "on exchanging views concerning the mutual limitation and subsequent reduction of strategic means of delivering of nuclear weapons — both offensive and defensive, including also anti-rocket weapons," and informed the General Assembly that the Soviet Union "is prepared to begin a serious exchange of views on this question."[5] In the same way, the main speech on the anniversary of the Russian Revolution delivered on behalf of the political leadership by Politburo member K. Mazurov acknowledged the readiness of the Soviet Union to negotiate with the United States "on a whole

---

[3] "Memorandum of the Soviet Government Concerning Urgent Measures to Stop the Arms Race and Achieve Disarmament, July 1, 1968," *Documents on Disarmament, 1968* (Washington, D.C.: United States Arms Control and Disarmament Agency, 1969), p. 467.

[4] According to a report of *The New York Times* (December 15, 1968), the announcement of the agreement for the initiation of talks had been scheduled for August 21, 1968, but was delayed by the United States when the invasion occurred.

[5] *Pravda*, October 4, 1968.

range" of disarmament questions.[6] Restating Gromyko's October 3 position on disarmament, a Soviet representative to the United Nations maintained on November 12 that "the Soviet Government is ready, without delay, to undertake a serious exchange of views on this question."[7] The same principle was also reasserted on November 28 by another Soviet representative to the United Nations.[8] In most of these pro-disarmament statements, the speakers stressed the benefits to be derived if allocations and technical capabilities could be shifted from military production to production for the people. In apparent agreement, a book prepared by a collective of authors from the political- and military-economics department of the Military-Political Academy imeni V. I. Lenin even cautioned that military overproduction, if it were allowed to occur, would "have an adverse effect not only on increased production, but also on the strengthening of defense capability."[9] Thus, it was pointed out not once, but twice, that:

> Economic preparation for contemporary war assumes a systematic diversion of an increasing part of the country's social product to military needs. In economic terms, this means a "freezing" of part of the aggregate social product (SOP) and its withdrawal from the country's economic circulation. There are, however, real, objective limits beyond which this part of the SOP may not be increased without sharply disturbing the conditions of reproduction of the social product. Economic laws "rebel" against such scandalous violating of the reproduction conditions, and economic potential will be demolished already in the prewar period.[10]

and that:

> It is necessary to observe definite proportions between the production of armaments and the need for social reproduction of producer and consumer goods. An increase of military consumption beyond permissible limits leads not to a strengthening of the state's military power, but to its weakening and to the inescapable collapse of the economy as a whole and military-economic potential in particular.[11]

[6] *Ibid.*, November 7, 1968.

[7] "Statement by the Soviet Representative (Malik) to the First Committee of the General Assembly, November 12, 1968," *Documents on Disarmament, 1968*, p. 709.

[8] "Statement by the Soviet Representative (Roshchin) to the First Committee of the General Assembly, November 28, 1968," *ibid.*, p. 739.

[9] P. V. Sokolov, ed., *Voyenno-ekonomicheskiye voprosy v kurse politekonomii (Military-Economic Questions in Political-Economic Policy)* (Moscow: Voyenizdat, 1968), p. 243.

[10] *Ibid.*, p. 22.

[11] *Ibid.*, p. 245.

While the pro-disarmament faction continued to hold the dominant political position even after the Czechoslovakian invasion, voices of opposition began to emerge and challenge the desirability of disarmament, especially with regard to a limitation of strategic nuclear weapons. In a September issue of *Kommunist Vooruzhennykh Sil*, one of the spokesmen of the MPA criticized those who believed that disarmament agreements could eliminate the danger of war and assure security.[12] Two issues later, an article by a candidate of historical sciences surveyed the military potential and activities of Western states and concluded with the warning that "the lessons of World War II and the contemporary aggressive and adventurist policy of imperialism" have taught the Soviet people to have "vigilance in relations with the enemy and constant care for strengthening the defense of the country."[13] The final issue of *Kommunist Vooruzhennykh Sil* for 1968 carried an article by Lieutenant Colonel V. Bondarenko, one of the leading Soviet experts on science and technology in military affairs and a leading MPA advocate of the continuous struggle for military-technical superiority. According to Bondarenko, military affairs has "its own logic of development" and "sources external with respect to it (economics, science, and politics) can only assist (or interfere with) this process, which has objectively matured and is spontaneously developing in military affairs itself."[14] Consequently, political leaders are left in a position either to work with objective conditions or to fight against them. As Bondarenko maintained:

> Political organizations and their leaders can only take advantage of this objective process for their political aims (then their activity will expedite and "will organize" the revolutionary transformation in military affairs) or, vice versa, not take advantage of open possibilities (then their activity will lay obstacles to the process of revolutionization of military affairs.)[15]

In sum, the opponents of disarmament were arguing that Soviet leaders should be seeking to improve Soviet military potential even further. Still, the

[12] Colonel Ye. Rybkin, "Critique of Bourgeois Concepts of War and Peace," *Kommunist Vooruzhennykh Sil*, No. 18 (September 1968), pp. 89–90.

[13] Colonel N. Kozlov, "Strengthening the Defense of the Country Is the Cause of the Whole Party and All People," *Kommunist Vooruzhennykh Sil*, No. 20 (October 1968), p. 25.

[14] See, for example, Lieutenant Colonel V. Bondarenko, "Military-Technical Superiority Is a Most Important Factor of the Reliable Defense of the Country," *Kommunist Vooruzhennykh Sil*, No. 17 (September 1966), pp. 7–14.

[15] Lieutenant Colonel V. Bondarenko, "The Contemporary Revolution in Military Affairs and the Combat Preparedness of the Armed Forces," *Kommunist Vooruzhennykh Sil*, No. 24 (December 1968), p. 24.

argument brought the anti-disarmament faction into conflict not only with the pro-disarmament faction but also with those leading MPA officials who were advocating an intensification of indoctrination work in the armed forces.

The Issue of Troop Training

The conflict between the anti-disarmament faction and the advocates of ideological work centered initially on the issue of troop training. As suggested in the previous chapter, the advocates of indoctrination work were at this time attempting to win support for increasing ideological work among servicemen and the proposed meeting of party secretaries in the armed forces was to be a major step in this direction. Conversely, the anti-disarmament faction was most interested in winning support for increasing the time allotted for the scientific-technical training of troops. One of the major spokesmen in this latter regard was again Bondarenko, who asserted in his December 1968 article:

> In conditions of the contemporary revolution in military affairs still more urgent has become Lenin's idea that it is impossible to construct a modern army without science. This is conveyed also in the necessity of raising the general scientific horizon of all servicemen without exception, in the sharp increase in the quantity of scientific research institutions devoting themselves to problems of military construction, and in the deep interest of Soviet military cadres for researching the objective laws of war and armed struggle and without a scientific approach the leadership of troops is simply impossible.[16]

In anticipation of a major victory at the proposed meeting of party secretaries in the armed forces, the MPA advocates of increased ideological work, who appear to have been in the majority despite the efforts of the more technical-minded members such as Bondarenko, stressed the need for strengthening party-political influence in the armed forces. Several articles were published in *Kommunist Vooruzhennykh Sil* in the first two months of 1969, which discussed the importance of party leadership, especially in the armed forces.[17] At a meeting

[16] *Ibid.*, p. 28.

[17] Ye. Bugayev, "The Historical Significance of the Experience of the CPSU in the Construction of Socialism and Communism," *Kommunist Vooruzhennykh Sil*, No. 1 (January 1969), pp. 17–26; General of the Army I. Gussakovskiy, "The Care of the Party for the Training and Education of Military Cadres," *Kommunist Vooruzhennykh Sil*, No. 1 (January 1969), pp. 27–33; Major General V. Kotov, "Party-Political Work in Military Duties," *Kommunist Vooruzhennykh Sil*, No. 1 (January 1969), pp. 44–48; "The Secretary of Party Organizations,"

of high-ranking MPA officials in early February, Yepishev severely criticized military publishers for their lack of fervor in the ideological struggle.[18] Then, in an article in *Izvestiya* that appeared on Soviet Armed Forces Day, Yepishev noted the importance of the proposed party secretaries meeting for ideological work. The MPA head maintained:

> Improving the content and forms of ideological party and organizational work, and increasing its effectiveness, purposefulness, and militancy have always been and will remain the object of the party's unfailing concern. New proof of this is the decision of the CPSU Central Committee on holding the fifth all-army conference of party organization secretaries this year.[19]

At the same time, more and more professional military men began to express their opposition to increasing the time given to ideological work in the armed forces. Of course, the method of opposition was not a direct attack on ideological work, but rather an emphasis on the need for greater professional skills and training time. Marshal Yakubovskiy, for example, pointed out:

> Heightened international tension, the interests of protecting the motherland and socialist and communist gains, and objective processes complicating military matters all demand that Soviet troops persist in improving their skills and be tireless in raising the combat readiness of every unit, ship, and subunit, and of the armed forces as a whole.[20]

It followed from the need for greater skills that the time devoted to party-political work could not be increased. Indeed, the commander of the Soviet Group of Forces in Germany declared that his group already possessed "all the conditions for forming a Marxist-Leninist world outlook in the soldiers."[21] Furthermore, the Commander-in-Chief of the Navy warned in an interview published in *Kommunist Vooruzhennykh Sil* against tampering with the training schedule of troops. Admiral Gorshkov contended:

Kommunist Vooruzhennykh Sil, No. 2 (January 1969), pp. 3–8; "Ideological Work of Party Organizations," *Kommunist Vooruzhennykh Sil*, No. 4 (February 1969), pp. 3–8; "The Party of Lenin Is the Leading and Directing Force in the Struggle for Communism," *Kommunist Vooruzhennykh Sil*, No. 4 (February 1969), pp. 72–79.

[18] *Krasnaya Zvedza*, February 11, 1969.

[19] *Izvestiya*, February 23, 1969.

[20] *Krasnaya Zvedza*, February 23, 1969.

[21] Marshal of the Soviet Union P. K. Koshevoy in *ibid.*, April 5, 1969.

Any mission in the new training year and any maneuver must serve to elevate the combat mastery of the officers and of all personnel and the further rise in the combat activity of the sailors.

In conclusion, I should like to say a few words about the importance of the rhythmicity of combat training and its strictly planned nature. This is an important and serious matter. The combat training plan is a law from which there should be no departure whatsoever. The postponement of one or another mission and the disruption of schedules make for unnecessary confusion, lower the quality of the training, and entail loss of rhythm in the training.[22]

The Principle of Command

Instead of remaining within the bounds of a debate on training, the arguments between the pro-ideological and the pro-technical factions quickly began to escalate into a debate with regard to the Soviet principle of command. In the few years preceding 1969, the conflict between "one-man command" and "one-man command on a party basis" had generally been settled in favor of the former, that is, in favor of the commander. This reflected the post-Khrushchevian willingness of the military to accept the principle of party dominance and, in turn, the willingness of the Party to permit increased professionalism and authority for the commander. In February 1969, *Kommunist Vooruzhennykh Sil* resurrected the whole controversy anew.

In an article recommended by *Kommunist Vooruzhennykh Sil* for use in studying the theme "V. I. Lenin and the CPSU on One-Man Command as One of the Most Important Principles of Soviet Military Construction," candidate of historical sciences Colonel M. Timofeyechev historically surveyed and analyzed the Soviet method of command in the armed forces. The writer maintained not only that one-man command should be conducted "on a party basis," but also that commanders should strengthen party organs and utilize the weapon of criticism and self-criticism. He stated:

> The main feature of one-man command in the Soviet armed forces consists in the fact that it is constructed, strengthened, and developed on a firm party basis. V. I. Lenin noted that a very important feature of Soviet one-man command consists in the fact that Soviet authority nominates to the post of leader with single authority the most deserving representatives of the people, capable of successfully putting into practice the policy of the Party and correctly conveying the

[22] Admiral of the Fleet of the Soviet Union S. G. Gorshkov, "The Fleet in Deep Waters," *Kommunist Vooruzhennykh Sil*, No. 4 (February 1969), p. 31.

will of the working masses.

Consequently, a main item in the concept of one-man command on a party basis is the putting into practice by the commander with single authority, whatever the post he may occupy, of the policy of the Communist Party and the steadfast observance by him in all his activities of the Leninist principles of troop leadership. For every general, admiral, and officer, this means: in all his practical activity to be led by the resolutions of the Party and the government; always and in all things to manifest a party approach to matters; daily to manifest exactingness with themselves and subordinates; firmly to rely on the party organization; skillfully to make use of the weapon of criticism and self-criticism for the elimination of shortcomings; and to combine exactingness to subordinates with a fatherly care for them.

Strengthening one-man command on a party basis presupposes without fail and in every possible way the raising of the role of party organs and party organizations, implementing party authority in all personnel, together with commanders putting into practice the policy of the Party in the armed forces.[23]

In contrast to the MPA preference for "one-man command on a party basis," several professional military men in their Armed Forces Day articles for 1969 emphasized that "one-man command" (and, thereby, not "one-man command on a party basis") is the fundamental principle of Soviet military command. For example, Minister of Defense Grechko stated in *Kommunist*, the chief party journal, that "Lenin regarded the most strict centralization and one-man command as the basic organizational principle of the construction of the Soviet armed forces."[24] Yet the Minister of Defense's reference to "one-man command" was somewhat offset by his comments elsewhere in the same article that "the leadership of the Communist Party over the armed forces is the fundamental basis of military construction" and that in Lenin's time "not one question of the defense of the republic was resolved without the guiding instructions of the Central Committee of the Party."[25]

Representing a more extreme professional viewpoint, the rocket forces commander Marshal N. I. Krylov asserted that "it is an objective necessity and law of development for the Soviet Armed Forces that the commander further strengthen one-man command and improve the method of one-man command in controlling troops' combat action." As defined by Krylov, one-man command is

. . . a system of control in which every subunit, unit, and formation has a com-

[23] Colonel M. Timofeyechev, "A Most Important Principle of Soviet Military Construction," *Kommunist Vooruzhennykh Sil*, No. 4 (February 1969), p. 17.

[24] Marshal of the Soviet Union A. Grechko, "V. I. Lenin and the Construction of the Soviet Armed Forces," *Kommunist*, No. 3 (February 1969), p. 19. Italicized in original.

[25] *Ibid.*, p. 17. The first of these two statements was italicized in the original.

mander who in all his activities proceeds from CPSU and Soviet Government policy and the interests of the people, and who personally carries full responsibility for all aspects of the life and activities of the combat collective that he commands. This form of control over troops primarily answers the requirements of modern warfare, the maintenance of combat capability, and the constant combat readiness of units and subunits, and it is the best way of insuring unity and centralism, maximum strength, flexibility and operational capacity in leadership, and the correct organization of training and education for personnel.[26]

For the rocket forces commander, "reliance on party and Komsomol organizations" means that commanders should require political organs to focus their attention on improving combat readiness, technical training, and fulfillment of military duty.[27] In this sense, the political organs would be little more than tools for the commander.

In March 1969, *Kommunist Vooruzhennykh Sil* published two articles by professional military men, one the commander of the Kiev Military District[28] and the other a candidate of military sciences,[29] both of whom supported the principle of "one-man command," although the latter gave some encouragement to the use of limited criticism and self-criticism.

The Zakharov-Yepishev Debate

These were followed in May by a strong statement from the Chief of the General Staff, Marshal Zakharov, in favor of improving the technical level and increasing the military potential of the armed forces. Thus, Zakharov simultaneously aimed at two opponents; the advocates of disarmament and the advocates of increased party-political work. While admitting that a wartime victory is "conditioned by the state of mind" of the soldier, Zakharov quoted Lenin to the effect that "the one who prevails in war is the one who possesses 'the greatest technical equipment, organization, discipline, and the best machines.' "[30] Similarly, while the Chief of the General Staff observed that "man is the master of equipment," he continued by noting that "the better these technical means that

[26] *Krasnaya Zvedza*, February 20, 1969.

[27] *Ibid.*

[28] Colonel General V. Kulikov, "The Combat Readiness of the Unit and the Party Organization," *Kommunist Vooruzhennykh Sil*, No. 6 (March 1969), p. 28.

[29] Major General V. Voznenko, "On the Basic Principles of the Scientific Leadership for Troops," *Kommunist Vooruzhennykh Sil*, No. 6 (March 1969), pp. 22, 25.

[30] Marshal of the Soviet Union M. V. Zakharov, "On Guard over Socialism and Peace," *Partiynaya Zhizn'*, No. 9 (May 1969), p. 11.

man possesses and knowledgeably utilizes, the more powerful he becomes."[31] It would appear, therefore, that the number and quality would be important for the attainment of victory. Indeed, Zakharov maintained:

> Lenin also exposed the harmful and dangerous views of the "left communists" and the "left" social revolutionaries, who disregarded the military-technical factor. He said that only people who had no concept of modern warfare could wave a cardboard sword. The enemy can destroy the very best army of soldiers and commanders devoted to the revolution if they are not sufficiently armed, and supplied with provisions, he wrote in March 1918. . . .
>
> The pressure of nuclear missile armaments introduces new features into the correlation of moral and material forces in war. But these features lie not in the predominance of the technical factor or lowering of the role of the moral factor, but in the simultaneous increase of their roles.[32]

Earlier in this study, it was noted that appeals to Leninist authority were quite often made as part of contemporary debates. Zakharov's reference to Lenin's struggle against the "leftists" seems to fit this pattern. Yet it remains to be determined against whom Zakharov was invoking Lenin. Certainly, the Chief of the General Staff was pointing to the Chinese Communists, for, in the unquoted portion of the above-cited quotation, he strongly criticized the "notorious thesis that a people's army can 'overcome modern equipment with primitive means' and gain ultimate victory over the armed forces of imperialists."

In light of the conflict on ideological versus technical training, however, it should also be understood as part of the internal debate. The timing of Zakharov's reference to "leftists" seems to suggest that he had in mind the MPA leadership, particularly Yepishev. This interpretation is supported by the fact that Yepishev had published two strongly pro-ideological articles in April 1969, one of which was carried in the party journal *Kommunist* and the other in the MPA journal *Kommunist Vooruzhennykh Sil*.

In contrast to Zakharov, Yepishev had stressed the wartime importance of morale and, therewith, the need for party-political work. According to the MPA head:

> . . . victory will not in itself be attained by equipment, even if it is the most modern, but by a man who is strong of spirit, knows well this equipment, and is able to exhaust its possibilities some day.

[31] *Ibid.,* p. 12.

[32] *Ibid.* Ellipses added. It might be pointed out, however, that as stated by Zakharov the increase of both factors does not necessarily imply that each must grow at the same rate.

Hence, a very important means of forming the high moral-political and psychological steadfastness of troops and resolving all the tasks of raising the combat preparedness of troops always is, and will be, well-adjusted ideological-educational work.[33]

Like Zakharov, but for obviously different reasons, Yepishev called upon Leninist authority to support his urgings for party-political work. "Vladimir Ilich emphasized," noted Yepishev,

. . . that where political work is most thoroughly conducted among the troops, there is no lack of discipline, there its order and spirit are better, and there are greater victories. He repeatedly reminded members of military councils, commissars, and all political workers: "Keep an eye on political work," "Do not relax political work," and he was interested in what was being done "for the improvement of political work."[34]

Yepishev also referred to the proposed fifth all-army conference of secretaries of party organizations announced in late 1968 for the first quarter of 1969. As noted by the MPA head, the conference would be held "in the very near future" (*v blizhaysheye vremya*) and "because of its scope, character, and content, the meeting will, without question, be a very important event in the life of the armed forces." Yepishev further suggested that "one of the chief results of it will be a new upsurge in the activity and fighting spirit of army organizations, an increase of effectiveness of all party-political work, and a reenforcement of its authority on the combat readiness of units, ships, and formations."[35] Yepishev also probably indicated the main direction he expected the conference to take when he revealed that plans were being made for a "considerable expansion" of the ideological-theoretical subjects in the political lessons for privates and sergeants.[36] It seems clear that Yepishev foresaw that conference as a step toward greater MPA authority and influence in military matters.

In the second of his April 1969 articles, Yepishev had again emphasized the importance of ideological-theoretical training.[37] Moreover, along with other leading MPA officials, Yepishev indirectly hinted that some sections of the pro-

[33] General of the Army A. A. Yepishev, "Leninism Is the Basis of the Education of Soviet Troops," *Kommunist*, No. 6 (April 1969), p. 67.

[34] *Ibid.*, p. 63.

[35] *Ibid.*, pp. 65–66.

[36] *Ibid.*, p. 70.

[37] General of the Army A. A. Yepishev, "The Political Organs of the Soviet Army and Navy Are Fifty Years Old," *Kommunist Vooruzhennykh Sil*, No. 7 (April 1969), p. 20.

fessional military might be becoming too independent of party control. First, he reiterated "one-man command on a party basis" as the command principle of the Soviet armed forces. Second, in enumerating many instances when the Party stressed party-political work in the armed forces, Yepishev recalled and dwelled upon the decisions of the October 1957 plenum of the Party Central Committee.[38] In view of the fact that the October plenum had been given little attention in the period since the 23rd Party Congress, and particularly since the partial rehabilitation of Marshal Zhukov in 1966,[39] the mention of the decisions at this time was probably intended as a warning to the military's pro-technical faction of what might happen again if they sought to become too professional and too independent. Furthermore, the first deputy head of the MPA reminded *Kommunist Vooruzhennykh Sil* readers in a May 1969 issue that "bold and just criticism and self-criticism is one of the most important norms of internal party life.[40]

The Debate Subsides with the Need for Unity

These articles marked the climax of the conflict between the MPA and the professional military. The polemics, especially on the part of the MPA, quickly subsided thereafter. Indeed, there was a striking difference between the articles previously cited and the articles written by leading MPA officials in the latter part of May to commemorate the fiftieth anniversary of the "creation of the political administration of the Revvoensovet of the Republic, which completed the formation of the system of political organs in the armed forces of the Soviet Union."[41]

[38] *Ibid.*, p. 15,; see also Colonel General N. Nachinkin, "The Political Organs and Their Role in the Construction and Strengthening of the Soviet Armed Forces," *Voyenno-Istoricheskiy Zhurnal*, No. 5 (May 1969), p. 26.

[39] Although in 1969 Zhukov was not an important figure in debates between the professional military and the political-military leaders, it is interesting that on April 25 *Krasnaya Zvezda* published a favorable review of Zhukov's memoirs, *Vospominaniya i razmyshleniya* (*Reflections and Recollections*). According to his memoirs, Zhukov described Marshal Golikov, former MPA head, as one of the major figures in convincing Stalin that Germany was not planning a war against the Soviet Union in the spring of 1941. See Marshal of the Soviet Union G. K. Zhukov, *Vospominaniya i razmyshleniya* (Moscow: Novosti Press Agency Publishing House, 1974), I, 242, 244.

[40] Colonel General P. Yefimov, "On the Laws of the CPSU and the Education of Communists," *Kommunist Vooruzhennykh Sil*, No. 10 (May 1969), p. 15.

[41] "To the Political Organs, Commanders, and Political Workers of the Soviet Army and Navy," *Kommunist Vooruzhennykh Sil*, No. 12 (June 1969), p. 3; see also above, p. 20

Neither Yepishev's radio broadcast[42] nor his *Pravda* article[43] on this occasion made reference to "one-man command on a party basis," the October 1957 plenum of the Party Central Committee, or criticism and self-criticism. It is also noteworthy that neither the broadcast nor the article referred to the proposed fifth all-army conference of secretaries of party organizations. Similarly, articles by the two highest-ranking deputy heads of the MPA, Colonel M. Kalashnik[44] and Colonel General N. Nachinkin,[45] avoided any mention of these subjects.

The only exception to this general trend was an article in *Krasnaya Zvezda* by the first deputy MPA head, Colonel General P. Yefimov. The writer recalled the fact that the October 1957 plenum had "considerably consolidated" one-man command on a party basis.[46] Still, like his MPA colleagues, Yefimov made no reference to the proposed conference of secretaries.

Subsequently, as shown by a review of *Kommunist Vooruzhennykh Sil* articles for the next few months, mention of these topics was strictly avoided even in historical surveys.[47]

Therefore, at the beginning of May 1969, the leading MPA officials were still looking forward to the party secretaries conference and a major ideological triumph. By the end of the month, however, these hopes had been dashed and the possibility of a party secretaries conference had evaporated. Needless to say, the decision to drop the idea of a party secretaries conference was not made by the MPA (who still wanted to hold it) or by the professional military (who would have lacked the authority to make such a decision). Only the top political leadership could have decided the issue.

It appears, furthermore, to be beyond mere coincidence that the party leadership simultaneously made a decision adversely affecting the professional military. At the end of April, only a few days before the traditional May Day celebration, it was announced that "the CPSU Central Committee and the Council of Ministers of the USSR have found it expedient to hold, beginning with this year, parades of Soviet troops only on November 7."[48] Since the TASS announcement

[42] Moscow Domestic Service, May 26, 1969, 2000 GMT, FBIS, *Soviet Union*, No. 102 (May 27, 1969), pp. E1–E4.

[43] *Pravda*, May 26, 1969.

[44] *Izvestiya*, May 25, 1969.

[45] *Sovetskaya Rossiya*, May 25, 1969.

[46] *Krasnaya Zvezda*, May 25, 1969.

[47] One seeming contradiction to this observation appeared in a June article which asserted that one-man command "is conducted and is developed on a firm party basis." (Colonel A. Babakov, "Leninist Principles of Military Construction," *Kommunist Vooruzhennykh Sil*, No. 11 [June 1969], p. 25.) However, this might be explained by the fact that Babakov's article was signed to press before May 25.

did not indicate, even for ceremonial purposes, that the Ministry of Defense had been instrumental in reaching this decision, it seems possible to conclude that the decision was a move by the party leadership to demonstrate publicly its authority over the armed forces and the military leadership.

In sum, it appears that in May 1969 the top political leadership took steps to assert its authority over both the professional military and the political-military leaderships. As an example of these restrictions, the party leadership deprived each of the military groups of their public displays. This meant that there would be no weapons parade for the professional military and no party secretaries conference for the political-military. Yet there are grounds for believing that the reason for these actions was more than merely to eliminate the petty squabbles of the two military groups.

In 1969, the CPSU desperately needed internal unity. This need arose from three factors. First, the Soviet Union was being sharply challenged, ideologically and militarily, by the Chinese Communists. On March 2 and 15, Soviet and Chinese troops clashed at Damanskiy Island on the Ussuri River. The first encounter lasted only two hours, but the second lasted nine hours and it is believed that several hundred soldiers were killed.[49] Then, at the 9th National Congress of the Chinese Communist Party, the Central Committee report delivered on April 1 by Minister of Defense Lin Piao, who had at this time been named as Mao Tse-tung's successor as leader of the Chinese Communist Party but would soon fall into disgrace, condemned the Soviet party leadership of revisionism and imperialism and appeared to call for the overthrow of the Soviet clique. As Lin Piao accused:

> . . . since Brezhnev came to power, with its baton becoming less and less effective and its difficulties at home and abroad growing more and more serious, the Soviet revisionist renegade clique has been practicing social-imperialism and social-fascism more frantically than ever. Internally, it has stepped up its collusion with U.S. imperialism and its suppression of the revolutionary struggles of the people of various countries, intensified its control over and its exploitation of various East European countries and the People's Republic of Mongolia, intensified its contention with U.S. imperialism over the Middle East and other regions and intensified its threat of aggression against China.[50]

[48] *Krasnaya Zvezda*, April 27, 1969.

[49] For a detailed analysis of the border incidents, based on primary sources, see Thomas W. Robinson, *The Sino-Soviet Border Dispute: Background, Development, and the March 1969 Clashes*, RM-6171-PR (Santa Monica, Calif.: Rand, 1970), pp. 33 ff.

[50] Lin Piao, "Report to the Ninth National Congress of the Communist Party of China," *Current Background*, No. 880 (May 9, 1969), p. 44.

This was followed with the contention:

> ... we firmly believe that the proletariat and the broad masses of the people in the Soviet Union, who have a glorious revolutionary tradition, will certainly rise and overthrow this clique consisting of a handful of renegades.[51]

A second factor requiring internal Soviet unity at this time was the convocation on June 5 of the long-awaited International Conference of Communist and Workers' Parties, which had been fifteen months in preparation. In view of the recent invasion of Czechoslovakia and the cleavages caused in numerous Communist Parties as a result of the Sino-Soviet conflict, the uncertain and potential atmosphere necessitated that the Soviets put forth the appearance of a united front. Seventy-five of the world's eighty-eight Communist Parties were represented at the conference, but among those absent were five of the fourteen ruling Communist Parties, namely, the Chinese, Albanian, North Korean, North Vietnamese, and Yugoslavian. Since a major Soviet objective was to win approval for Soviet actions in Czechoslovakia and support for its arguments with the Chinese Communists,[52] and thereby present a significantly unified world Communist movement under Soviet leadership, it would be helpful if internal Soviet conflicts could be reduced.

The third factor requiring internal Soviet unity concerned the initiation of the Strategic Arms Limitation Talks (SALT), begun in November 1969 in Helsinki, Finland, between the Soviet Union and the United States. As noted earlier, the Soviet invasion of Czechoslovakia in August 1968 had delayed the announcement of the talks. On January 20, 1969, the day of inauguration for President Richard M. Nixon, the head of the Soviet Foreign Ministry press department addressed the problem of disarmament and recalled the favorable reaction of the U.N. General Assembly to the Soviet-American agreement reached in 1968 on "the initiation of talks concerning mutual limitation and subsequent reduction of strategic weapons delivery means, including defensive systems." "For its part," announced Zamyatin, "the Soviet Government considers it necessary to reaffirm that it is ready to begin an exchange of views on

---

[51] *Ibid.*, p. 45.

[52] Despite its efforts, however, the Soviets were unable to win clear approval for the doctrine of limited sovereignty or condemnation of China. The final document adopted on June 17, 1969, made reference to neither China nor Czechoslovakia. See "Tasks at the Present Stage of the Struggle Against Imperialism and United Action of the Communist and Workers' Parties and All Anti-Imperialist Forces," in *Documents Adopted by the International Conference of Communist and Workers' Parties* (Moscow: Novosti Press Agency Publishing House, n.d.), pp. 9–68.

this important issue."[53] Thereafter, two major speeches delivered by Party General Secretary Brezhnev in May and June 1969 were quite restrained with regard to the United States and both speeches stressed the benefits of peaceful coexistence and the solution of problems by negotiations. In a speech on May Day in Moscow's Red Square, Brezhnev made the usual general condemnation of imperialism, but he made no reference to "imperialism headed by the USA." Nor did he refer to "U.S. aggressors in South Vietnam," but only to "imperialist aggressors in South Vietnam."[54] The impression was that Brezhnev was trying to de-emphasize the "aggressiveness" of the United States. Moreover, Brezhnev insisted that the Soviet Union would continue to defend "the Leninist principles of peaceful coexistence of states with different social systems and to advocate the solution of unsolved international problems through negotiations."[55]

Then, in his speech to the International Conference of Communist and Workers' Parties on June 7, although Brezhnev attacked U.S. imperialism, he did so sparingly and in a restrained manner. He also expressed a desire for peaceful coexistence (except in ideological matters) and negotiations. The General Secretary of the CPSU stated:

> Substantiated by V. I. Lenin, the principle of peaceful coexistence of states irrespective of their social system underlies the relations of the Soviet State with the countries of the capitalist world. This principle implies that disputable questions arising among countries must be resolved not by force of arms, not by war, but by peaceful means. . . .
>
> Peaceful coexistence does not apply in the struggle of ideologies; this must be emphasized with all resoluteness. At the same time, it is not reduced simply to the absence of war between socialist and capitalist states. Observance of the principle of peaceful coexistence also opens up broader possibilities for developing relations between them. This is a question of the settlement of international problems at the negotiation table, the coordination of measures for reducing war danger and easing international tensions, and also mutually beneficial economic trade, scientific-technical and cultural ties.[56]

In a news conference on June 19, President Nixon announced that on presi-

[53] *Pravda*, January 21, 1969.

[54] L. I. Brezhnev, *Leninskim kursom: Rechi i stat'i* (*On the Leninist Course: Speeches and Articles*) (Moscow: State Publishing House for Political Literature), II, 360.

[55] *Ibid.*, p. 361.

[56] *Ibid.*, pp. 411–12.

[57] Richard M. Nixon, "President Nixon's News Conference of June 19," *Department of State Bulletin*, LXI, No. 1567 (July 7, 1969), 2.

dential instructions Secretary of State William Rogers suggested July 31 to the Soviets "as the target date for the beginning talks."[57] Referring to the American proposal in a speech before the USSR Supreme Soviet on July 11, Foreign Minister Gromyko observed:

> The Soviet Government has already reported to the Supreme Soviet on its readiness to start the exchange of opinions with the USA on the so-called strategic weapons. The U.S. Government said it was getting ready for such an exchange. The Soviet Government is also ready for this. One should like to hope that both sides will approach the matter with its great importance taken into account.[58]

Because of various delays, the opening of SALT did not take place in Helsinki until November 17. Of the twenty-four Soviet representatives, six were delegates and eighteen were advisers. According to occupation, professional military men accounted for eight of the total representation and for two of the six delegates. Of the four remaining delegates, two were from the Soviet Foreign Ministry and two were closely connected with the radio industry, which is responsible for Soviet radar and radio-control systems.[59]

Main Political Administration
Opposition to SALT

The opposition of some MPA spokesmen to Soviet disarmament proposals was already apparent in late 1968. This MPA subgroup, then characterized broadly by its pro-technical inclination in military affairs, appears initially to have been quite small, because the majority of the leading MPA officials were preoccupied with ideological issues and preparations for the proposed all-army conference of secretaries of party organizations. Toward mid-1969, two factors were at work which tended to win increased support for the MPA's anti-disarmament faction. First, the announced party line in favor of SALT gradually grew more concrete after January and would end in November with the actual commencement of talks. Second, when the political leadership squashed the idea of a secretaries conference for the armed forces, it simultaneously served to remove the major point of conflict between the professional military and the political-military

[58] *Pravda*, July 11, 1969.

[59] For a complete list and occupational breakdown of the Soviet and American representatives, see *The New York Times*, November 21, 1969. For a more detailed examination of the six, Soviet delegates, see *ibid.*, November 12, 1969.

leaderships. Consequently, in mid-1969, the two groups in the military found themselves growing closer together in their opposition to the dominant party faction, which still favored disarmament talks.

From the side of the MPA, the movement toward greater unity with the professional military in opposition to SALT actually began in April. Therefore, while the cancellation of the party secretaries conference was not the direct cause of unity, it certainly gave impetus to it.

In an April issue of *Kommunist Vooruzhennykh Sil*, candidate of philosophical sciences Lieutenant Colonel T. Kondratkov pointed out that Soviet military power had put the United States in an uneasy position. He stated:

> It is no secret that the USA already long ago lost the monopoly and superiority in the newest types of arms and lost former inaccessibility and invulnerability. And now the American imperialists and their partners are forced to be uneasy about their own security, so that they cannot go unpunished for their nuclear blackmail.[60]

The implication of this statement seems to be similar to the warning of Bondarenko in December 1968: arms limitation can only serve to hinder the Soviet position vis-à-vis the United States, whereas the Soviet position could and should grow stronger. Furthermore, Kondratkov questioned the intent of the United States and argued that "the recent decision of the American Government on the deployment of the 'Safeguard' ABM defense system in the USA will signal a new stage of the arms race."[61]

Then, in Yepishev's previously cited April *Kommunist* article, the reader was warned that "the ruling circles of the imperialist states are feverishly preparing for a new world war."[62] He also condemned those "ideologists of imperialism and political and military figures of capitalist states" who have alleged that nuclear war has made obsolete Lenin's dictum of war as the continuation of policy by forceful means. According to Yepishev, a third world war would be "a decisive class collision between two opposite social systems." For the imperialists, such a war would be "the continuation of the criminal, reactionary, and aggres-

---

[60] Leiutenant Colonel T. Kondratkov, "Limited War Is an Instrument of Imperialist Aggression," *Kommunist Vooruzhennykh Sil*, No. 8 (April 1969), p. 25.

[61] *Ibid.*, p. 30.

[62] Yepishev, "Leninism Is the Basis of the Education of Soviet Troops," p. 68. In his speech to the International Conference of Communist and Workers' Parties on June 7, Brezhnev referred to "aggressive" and "moderate" circles in capitalist states, but he did not go so far as to suggest that the "aggressive" circle was also the "ruling" circle. Indeed, it would appear that Brezhnev was making the opposite point. (Brezhnev, *Leninskim kursom*, II, 412.)

sive policy of imperialism," but on the Soviet side it would be "a continuation of the revolutionary policy of freedom and independence of socialist states, of guaranteeing the construction of socialism and communism, and a legitimate and justified counteraction to aggression."[63]

The imperialist threat of war was again emphasized in the May issue of the party-political journal of the armed forces. It was asserted in an article authored by Colonel S. Lukonin, a candidate of philosophical sciences, and Lieutenant Colonel of the Reserves N. Tarasenko that "the danger from the side of the aggressive forces of imperialism is increasing still greater in connection with the revolution in military affairs." In addition to this increasing threat, the authors declared, "in their striving to block the road to revolutionary renewal and to liquidate socialist countries by means of war, the imperialists are beginning to prepare for any adventure."[64] Similarly, a vitriolic article in the July issue, which almost seems to have come directly out of the "hate campaigns" of George Orwell's *1984*, observed that imperialists "are preparing for a new war against the USSR and the other countries of socialism."[65] It was argued, consequently, that the "crazy plans" of the imperialists require a constant hatred for and combat readiness against the enemy. As the author stated:

> In all stages of its heroic history, the Communist Party of our country has considered work for the education of hatred for imperialism as one of the chief tasks. The significance of it in contemporary conditions has increased even more. This is caused first of all by aggravation of international tension and by the increased war danger being stirred up by aggressive actions of the imperialists headed by the USA. . . .
>
> It is absolutely clear that the new war being prepared for by the imperialists will be aimed against the Soviet and the other socialist countries. The aggressors openly announce their crazy plans to abolish the socialist countries by means of war. All of this makes it necessary to intensify the education of Soviet troops

[63] Yepishev, "Leninism Is the Basis of the Education of Soviet Troops," p. 69. The present writer's interpretation of this statement is that despite a third world war the Soviets would continue to strive to guarantee the construction of socialism and communism. This differs quite fundamentally from the interpretation of Anatole Shub (*The New York Times*, April 27, 1969), who has taken the statement to mean that "World War III would 'guarantee the construction of socialism and communism.'" It would appear that Shub's interpretation is based upon a mistranslation of Yepishev.

[64] Colonel S. Lukonin and Lieutenant Colonel of the Reserves N. Tarasenko, "V. I. Lenin on the Defense Function of the Socialist State," *Kommunist Vooruzhennykh Sil*, No. 10 (May 1969), p. 19.

[65] Lieutenant Colonel B. Demin, "Hatred for the Enemy Is an Inherent Aspect of the Patriotism of Soviet Troops," *Kommunist Vooruzhennykh Sil*, No. 13 (July 1969), p. 27.

in a spirit of high vigilance and class hatred for the imperialist aggressors and on this basis support the constant combat readiness of our armed forces.[66]

Another theme closely related to that of the imperialist threat concerned the international duty of the Soviet Union. MPA spokesmen frequently pointed out that the international role and obligations of the Soviet Union were constantly increasing. Colonel A. Babakov, a member of the Department of Marxist-Leninist Philosophy at the Lenin Military-Political Academy and a candidate of historical sciences, maintained, for example, that "in conditions of a changed correlation of forces in the world arena in favor of socialism, the role of our country and our armed forces in rendering economic, political, and military assistance to people fighting for national freedom or asserting their independence increases."[67] Again, another writer claimed:

> Now, in conditions of radical changes in military equipment and weapons, the defensive power of the Soviet Union more than ever comes forward as the decisive guarantee of the defense of all socialist states, as well as the progressive states striving for national liberation, and the guarantee of the defense of peace in the whole world.[68]

Under such conditions, it was claimed that "the utmost strengthening of the defense of the USSR is an objective necessity of the formation and development of socialism and of its development into communism, and a sacred duty of the Party to the people and workers of the whole world."[69]

Clearly, the propositions presented by these articles were being directed against SALT. The increased threat of war and the expanded international duty of the Soviet Union and its armed forces were arguments directed toward strengthening, not curtailing, Soviet military power. However, in the fall of 1969, even stronger statements in favor of a military buildup were made by MPA spokesmen.

In August, a *Kommunist Vooruzhennykh Sil* article by a candidate of philosophical sciences, General of the Army V. Ivanov, claimed that the maintenance of powerful armed forces is the "paramount" concern of a socialist society. "Among the concrete problems resolved in the process of creating a new society,"

---

[66] *Ibid.*, pp. 29–30.

[67] Babakov, "Leninist Principles of Military Construction," p. 29.

[68] Colonel of Engineering A. Klimenko, "The Social Consequences of Scientific-Technical Progress," *Kommunist Vooruzhennykh Sil*, No. 16 (August 1969), p. 28; see also Lukonin and Tarasenko, p. 20.

[69] Babakov, "Leninist Principles of Military Construction," p. 22.

asserted Ivanov, "the task of guaranteeing the security of the socialist state is paramount since on the reliable defense of it depends the fate of all communist construction."[70]

Subsequently, two military writers noted the relationship between the level of military equipment used by an army and the outcome of a war. Writing in *Krasnaya Zvezda*, Professor and (retired) Major General A. Lagovsky cited Leninist authority on the fact that "in modern warfare he who has the greatest equipment, the greatest level of organization, discipline, and the best vehicles is the victor."[71] Using somewhat the same approach, the political head of the newly created Central Asian Military District, Major General K. Maksimov, wrote on November 4:

> Constantly at the center of the CPSU's attention is V. I. Lenin's instruction to the effect that the best army and the people most devoted to the cause of the revolution would be quickly destroyed by the enemy if they were insufficiently armed, equipped, and trained. In recent years economic, scientific, and technological successes have permitted the creation of a qualitatively new material base for equipping the Soviet Army and Navy with the latest arms, including nuclear missiles.[72]

Furthermore, as in Bondarenko's December 1968 article, Ivanov contended that the political leadership should consistently lean on the knowledge and experience of military cadres and utilize the recommendations of military science. He said:

> Military science, revealing the regularity of the development of military affairs and armed struggle, elaborates on their basis recommendations for questions of military construction and the organization of the defense of the country as a whole. And the more the political leadership is guided by the conclusions and instructions of military science, then the more effective and effectual will be accepted their decisions and the greater will be reached the unity of political and military leadership. V. I. Lenin repeatedly emphasized the importance of special knowledge and the role of specialists in the leadership of any matter, including also the defense of the country.[73]

[70] General of the Army V. Ivanov, "The Scientific Principles of the Leadership of the Defense of the Socialist Fatherland," *Kommunist Vooruzhennykh Sil*, No. 16 (August 1969), p. 12.

[71] *Krasnaya Zvezda*, September 25, 1969.

[72] *Kazakhstanskaya Pravda*, November 4, 1969, FBIS, *Soviet Union*, No. 219 (November 12, 1969), p. E3.

[73] Ivanov, "The Scientific Principles of the Leadership of the Defense of the Socialist Fatherland," p. 12.

In late November 1969, an all-army conference of young officers called by the Ministry of Defense[74] was convened in Moscow for the purpose of discussing "important questions concerning the growth of the role, tasks, and responsibility of young officers in raising the quality of combat and political training, in educating personnel and strengthening discipline," as well as questions concerning "the further strengthening of the troops' combat capacity and combat-readiness at the present stage of development of the Soviet armed forces."[75] As compared to earlier debates, the expressed purpose and the speeches delivered by the Minister of Defense and the head of the MPA seem to indicate that by the end of the year the professional military and political-military leaderships were again pursuing a substantially unified objective. In speeches to the conference, both Grechko and Yepishev stressed such propositions as the danger of imperialist aggression, the need for strong Soviet armed forces, the desirability of "one-man command," and the necessity for mutually improving the political and technical training of the troops.[76] It is also a striking point that in both reviews of the international situation, neither Grechko nor Yepishev gave praise, or even mention, to the SALT negotiations, which had begun the previous week.

Once the SALT negotiations had begun, the attention of MPA and professional military spokesmen focused on the "military-industrial complexes" of the Western states. For example, in defining the makeup and assessing the influence of military-industrial complexes, a colonel and candidate of historical sciences wrote in *Kommunist Vooruzhennykh Sil:*

> The leadership of the army has a decisive voice in the distribution of billions of military orders, in which monopolies are incredibly acquired. . . . Receiving enormous and lucrative military orders, the monopolists by all means are preventing the relaxation of international tensions, and are actively supporting the reactionary military clique in its aggressive plans. Because of this thus formed the so-called "military-industrial complex" — the union of the reactionary military clique with the monopolist circles directly interested in the arms race. The military-industrial complex in a number of imperialist countries has turned into "a state in a state" and *exerts a decisive influence* on the decisions not only of the foreign, but also the internal policy of the government.[77]

Then, in the first of a series of articles on the military-industrial complexes

[74] Interview of Lieutenant General I. S. Mednikov, Moscow Domestic Service, December 1, 1969, 1930 GMT, FBIS, *Soviet Union*, No. 232 (December 2, 1969), p. E10.

[75] Marshal Grechko in *Krasnaya Zvezda*, November 27, 1969.

[76] *Ibid.* For Yepishev's speech, see *Krasnaya Zvezda*, November 28, 1969.

[77] Colonel N. Melinikov, "The Bourgeois Army and Policy," *Kommunist Vooruzhennykh Sil*, No. 23 (December 1969), pp. 25–26. Italics added.

of the major imperialist states and "the colossal influence which the military-industrial complexes of these states exert on their foreign and internal politics," it was asserted that this influence "not only has not abated, but is increasing with every day." Colonel General K. Skorobogatkin, the author of the first article of the series, alluded to an enormous and rising U.S. military budget and the resultant fortunes made by American monopolists. "All of this indicates," said Skorobogatkin, "that Washington is taking *new steps* for whipping up military preparations and the arms race."[78] Furthermore, it was maintained that imperialism "is in every possible way intensifying the international situation, continuously unleasing local wars, and strenuously preparing for world thermonuclear war," and as a consequence that "in such conditions, the further strengthening of the military power of the Soviet Union and the entire socialist community is the chief means of averting a new world war."[79] Similarly, the view was expressed by Soviet spokesmen that the huge military buildup of the United States in the 1960's, which was aimed against the Soviet Union and the other socialist states, "obliges us to maintain the defense potential at a very high level."[80]

As with the conference of young officers in late November 1969, the numerous party conferences held by military units in late January and early February 1970 again suggested that by the end of 1969 the professional military and political-military leaderships were pursuing common purposes. In the MPA's announcement of the conferences, it was pointed out that a major obligation of the meetings would be "to discuss the status and measures for further improving the party-political work in the light of the demands of the CPSU CC, for raising the quality of combat and political training, for strengthening discipline, and for intensifying the fighting efficiency and combat readiness of troops."[81] From the terse reports in the central press,[82] the theme of all the

---

[78] *Krasnaya Zvezda,* December 28, 1969. Italics added. Soviet commentators on the U.S. military-industrial complex naturally argued that a military-industrial complex could not possibly develop in a socialist society, because socialist societies do not have a desire for expansionism, an industrial monopolist class greedy for profits from armaments production, or an economy supported by military production. See, for example, Major General Ye. Sulimov's article in *ibid.,* January 15, 1970. Conversely, for a Western examination of the Soviet military-industrial complex, see the several articles in the *Journal of International Affairs,* XXVI, No. 1 (1972).

[79] Colonel G. Khvatkov, "The Problem of War and Peace and the Revolutionary Process," *Kommunist Vooruzhennykh Sil,* No. 1 (January 1970), pp. 33–34.

[80] Colonel M. Ushakov, "V. I. Lenin on the Economic Basis of the Defense Potential of the Country," *Kommunist Vooruzhennykh Sil,* No. 2 (January 1970), p. 37. It was also a theme of the article that the USSR had the economic capacity to support large defense expenditures.

[81] "Party Conferences," *Kommunist Vooruzhennykh Sil,* No. 23 (December 1969), p. 3.

[82] See *Krasnaya Zvezda* for reports on the following conferences: Moscow Antiaircraft District

party conferences seems to have been that party-political work must concentrate its activity on, and be closely linked with, promoting combat readiness. Indeed, a *Krasnaya Zvezda* summary of Yepishev's report to the party conference of the Moscow Military District noted that henceforth the chief consideration of party-political work would be the development of combat readiness and that this work could not be the same with all types of troops. As observed in the report:

> The main thing which distinguishes *present party-political work* is an increasingly concrete and businesslike attitude in the solution of the key problems which determine troops' high combat and mobilization readiness. Fuller consideration is taken for the profound and multi-faceted changes which have occurred in the armed forces in recent years, the tendencies and prospects of their further development, and the peculiar and specific features of types and categories of troops.
>
> *The central place in party-political work is now occupied by* questions linked with further reducing the time required to make troops combat ready, performing combat duty, mastering new equipment, increasing the quality of the field, sea, and air training of personnel, and further tightening military discipline.[83]

Again, in the major military articles and speeches on Soviet Armed Forces Day in February 1970, significant emphasis was given to combat readiness and related issues. Yepishev, for example, stated that "constant high combat readiness" is a daily concern of the Party.[84] Grechko similarly observed that "particularly high vigilance and combat readiness are necessary because of the danger of a sudden nuclear strike."[85] Moreover, like MPA spokesmen before him, Grechko asserted that the strengthening of the defense power of the Soviet armed forces is "the sacred duty of the Party and all Soviet people" and "the most important function of the socialist state."[86] In the same way, USSR Deputy Minis-

---

(January 15, 1970); Belorussian MD and Lenin Military-Political Academy (January 22); Odessa MD and Black Sea Fleet (January 25); Southern Group of Forces (January 28); Group of Forces in Germany (January 29); Ground Forces, North Caucasian MD, and Leningrad Naval Base (January 31); Ministry of Defense and Civil Defense Headquarters, Siberian MD, and Transcaucasian MD (February 1); Strategic Missile Forces, Air Force, and Naval headquarters (February 3); Central Asian MD (February 6); and Moscow MD (February 8)

83 *Ibid.*, February 8, 1970. Italics added. The context of the report implies that the statement was made by Yepishev, but this is not wholly clear.

84 *Ibid.*, February 23, 1970.

85 Marshal of the Soviet Union A. Grechko, "On Guard of Peace and Socialism," *Kommunist*, No. 3 (February 1970), p. 63.

86 *Ibid.*, p. 62.

ter of Defense and Commander-in-Chief of Air Defense Forces Marshal P. F. Batitskiy called upon Leninist authority to justify maintaining military power and combat readiness "on a level insuring the decisive and full defeat of any enemy who dares to encroach on our Motherland."[87]

In the next few months of 1970, points of difference were given less attention, as attention focused on factors indicating cooperation and agreement. First, the large-scale Dvina and Okean military maneuvers held in March and April took up most of the time of the chief military figures. Both professional military and political-military leaders were deeply involved in the preparations and operations connected with the maneuvers. Second, beginning in May, numerous articles were written, speeches given, and meetings held to mark the twenty-fifth anniversary of Germany's defeat in World War II.[88] It was uniformly asserted on these occasions that the Soviet Union had achieved a great victory, but that imperialism had not given up "hopes of 'replaying' the historic battles of the 20th century."

Summary

In May 1969, the party leadership cracked down on both the professional military and the political-military leadership. A need for internal unity arose out of the theoretical and military challenges of the Chinese Communists, the convocation of an International Conference of Communist and Workers' Parties, and the initiation of the strategic arms limitation talks with the United States. Morover, as part of the softer line toward the United States taken by the political leadership when SALT began, it was necessary to restrain the strongly antiimperialist and anti-American declarations of both the MPA and the armed forces spokesmen. Hence, the MPA was denied its conference and the armed forces their military parade on May Day.

As the Czechoslovakian issue subsided and SALT emerged, the conflicts between the professional military and the political-military evaporated. Now, both groups were united in their opposition to any political moves which might hinder the strengthening of Soviet military power. At least in the early stages of

[87] *Sotsialisticheskaya Industriya*, February 22, 1970.

[88] For major articles by professional military men, see Marshal of the Soviet Union A. Grechko, "Great Victory," *Voyenno-Istoricheskiy Zhurnal*, No. 5 (May 1970), pp. 3–13; Marshal of the Soviet Union M. V. Zakharov, "The Historic Victory of the Soviet People and Its Armed Forces," *Voprosy Istorii KPSS*, No. 5 (May 1970), pp. 3–15; and S. Sokolov, "The Immortal Exploit of the Soviet People and Its Army," *Kommunist*, No. 7 (May 1970), pp. 80–90.

SALT, the arguments advanced by the spokesmen of these groups seemed to indicate that the Soviet Union had more to lose by the limitation of armaments than did the United States. Consequently, MPA spokesmen maintained the necessity to achieve high combat readiness and to strengthen the Soviet armed forces to the utmost. These spokesmen also gave considerable attention to the U.S. military-industrial complex, which allegedly had great influence on American policy making and was interested in a continuation of the arms race.

SALT therefore changed the focus of MPA attention. While the improvement of ideological training was still emphasized, there was no longer the indication that ideological training time would be increased at the expense of technical training time. Indeed, as SALT progressed, MPA spokesmen gave more emphasis to the need to improve technical training and specialist qualifications, as well as the necessity for political organizations to work for improving combat readiness.

The next chapter will further illustrate the growing unity of views between the political administration and the professional military.

8

Political and Economic
Considerations in Light
of the 24th CPSU Congress

The 24th CPSU Congress and the
9th Five-Year Plan

Between March 30 and April 9, 1971, 4,963 delegates assembled in Moscow for
the 24th Congress of the CPSU. According to the report of the chairman of the
credentials commission, 4,740 of the delegates had voting rights, while 223 were
granted merely a consultative voice.[1] In total numbers, the representation was an
increase of twenty delegates over the 23rd Party Congress in 1966.

Unlike the stenographic record of the 23rd Party Congress, which specifically
listed 352 military delegates, the stenographic record of the 24th Party Congress
gave no occupational breakdown of the delegates and vaguely stated with regard
to military delegates only that "a large group of servicemen of the Soviet army,
navy, and border-guard units had been elected to the Congress.[2] Therefore, it is
not known how many military delegates were elected to the 24th Party Congress.[3]

The new Central Committee elected by the 24th Party Congress had a total
of 396 representatives, of whom 241 were full members and 155 were alternates.

---

[1] I. V. Kapitonov in *XXIV s"yezd Kommunisticheskoy partii Sovetskogo Soyuza: Stenograficheskiy otchet (24th Congress of the Communist Party of the Soviet Union: Stenographic
Record)* (Moscow: State Publishing House for Political Literature, 1971), I, 331.

[2] *Ibid.*, p. 334.

[3] It has been speculated by one Western observer that the lack of occupational information and
Kapitonov's failure to mention the number of military delegates elected to the 24th Party
Congress indicated an attempt by the political leadership to hide the fact that an excessively
large group of military delegates had been elected to the Congress. See Christian Duevel, "An
Armed Skeleton in the Politburo's Closet?" *Radio Liberty Dispatch*, November 10, 1971.

Consequently, this was the largest Central Committee and the largest number of full members ever elected. Likewise, the total number of military delegates and the number of military delegates elected to full membership were the highest ever. Indeed, the full membership of military men as a percentage of total membership illustrates a sharp increase,

Proportion of Servicemen in the Central Committees Elected
by the 22nd, 23rd, and 24th Party Congresses

	Total Membership			Servicemen			Percentage
Congress	Full	Alt.	Total	Full	Alt.	Total	of Total
22nd (1961)	175	155	330	14	17	31	9.5
23rd (1966)	195	165	360	14	18	32	8.9
24th (1971)	241	155	396	20	13	33	8.3

Source: For the statistics on the 22nd and 23rd Party Congresses, see above, p. 159.
     For the list of full and alternate members of the new Central Committee, see
     *XXIV s"yezd Kommunisticheskoy partii Sovetskogo soyuza: Stenograficheskiy
     otchet*, II, 313–18.

especially after the decline in 1966: 8.0 percent in 1961, 7.2 percent in 1966, and 8.3 percent in 1971. However, the decline of the military representation among alternate members by nearly one third meant that total military representation as a percentage of total Central Committee representation continued to decrease, from 9.5 percent in 1961 and 8.9 percent in 1966 to 8.3 percent in 1971. In sum, therefore, while total military representation as a percentage of total Central Committee representation decreased, full membership of the military as a percentage of total full membership increased. The latter factor is important, because only full members possess the right to vote on matters before the Central Committee.[4]

As did the 23rd Party Congress in 1966, the 24th Party Congress elected three MPA officials to the Party Central Committee. Yepishev was retained as the single full-member from the MPA, and K. S. Grushevoy and P. A. Gorchakov were elected to alternate membership. (By the precedent of the 23rd Congress, a fourth MPA official, S. P. Vasyagin, was re-elected to the Central Auditing Commission by the 24th Congress.) Consequently, since MPA representation remained constant, a breakdown of professional military and political-military representation elected to the Party Central Committee by the 24th Congress

[4] For a list of the military representation in the Central Committee elected by the 24th Party Congress, see Appendix A. For an in-depth analysis of the Party Central Committee as a whole, see Christian Duevel, "The Central Committee and the Central Auditing Commission Elected by the 24th CPSU Congress," *Radio Liberty Research Paper*, No. 46 (1972).

illustrates a decline in MPA representation as a percentage of (1) total representation, (2) total military representation, and (3) full membership of the military.

				Percentage	Percentage
Classification	*Full*	*Alt.*	*Total*	*of Military*	*of CC*
CC	241	155	396		100.0
Military	20	13	33	100	8.3
Professional	19	11	30	91	7.57
Political	1	2	3	9	0.75

Proportion of Professional and Political-Military
Men Elected by the 24th Party Congress
to the Party Central Committee

In addition, whereas the MPA had 7.6 percent of the military's full membership in 1966, it amounted to only 5 percent in 1971.

By occupational breakdown, MPA representations in the Party Central Committee elected in 1966 and 1971 were identical. The MPA head (Yepishev) and the political head of the Moscow Military District (K. S. Grushevoy) were both re-elected in 1971, Lavrenov's successor as political head of the rocket troops (P. A. Gorchakov) was elected to take Lavrenov's slot as an alternate member. In the same way, the political head of the ground forces (Vasyagin) was renamed to his position on the Central Auditing Commission. Thus the only change in MPA representation came about as a result of Lavrenov's death and his position in the Central Committee was taken by his successor in the armed forces. Therefore, it appears that the criterion for election of MPA officials to the Central Committee in 1971, as in 1966, remained the military importance of the unit, rather than the standing of the individual within the MPA.

Contrary to custom, Yepishev did not address the 24th CPSU Congress, so that no MPA report was delivered in 1971. Available evidence does not suggest, however, that the absence of an MPA report reflected disapproval of Yepishev personally. First, Yepishev was re-elected to full membership in the Party Central Committee. Second, whereas Yepishev had been appointed only to the Secretariat of the 23rd CPSU Congress, he was promoted to the Presidium of the 24th CPSU Congress.[5] Although membership in the Presidium of the Con-

---

[5] Marshal Malinovsky was the only military man appointed to the Presidium of the 23rd Party Congress and Yepishev was the only military man appointed to its Secretariat. No military men were on the credentials or editorial commission. (For the list of members of these organs, see *XXIII s"yezd Kommunisticheskoy partii Sovetskogo Soyuza: Stenograficheskiy otchet* [Moscow: State Publishing House for Political Literature, 1966], I, 11–15.) At the 24th CPSU Congress, both Grechko and Yepishev were appointed to the Presidium of the Congress;

gress — not to be confused with membership in the Party's Politburo — is more of a ceremonial position than a decision-making position, it would tend to indicate that Yepishev's fortunes were not on the decline.

The reason for the absence of an MPA report would seem to rest in the general emphasis of the political spokesmen on a cautious, but moderate, foreign policy and a significant preoccupation with internal issues, especially economic development.

On relations with the United States, for example, Party General Secretary Brezhnev observed in "The Report of the Central Committee of the CPSU to the 24th Congress of the Communist Party of the Soviet Union," delivered on March 30, that "the improving of Soviet-American relations would meet the interests of Soviet and American peoples and the interests of consolidating peace." However, in alluding to "the aggressive acts of the USA in diverse regions of the world," Brezhnev also cautioned that "frequent zigzags in American foreign policy, which, apparently, are also connected with some internal policy maneuvers of an expedient nature, complicate the conducting of affairs with the United States." Still, he noted that the Soviet Union proceeds on the belief that "improving relations between the USSR and the USA is possible."[6]

Similarly, a mixture of mild optimism and caution characterized Brezhnev's remarks on disarmament[7] and Soviet relations with West Germany.[8] Despite major strides in these areas, Brezhnev injected the observation that "it is impossible to consider the threat of a new world war as completely eliminated."[9]

On economic matters, Brezhnev asserted that "the chief task" of the new five-year plan would be "to provide for a significant development of the material and cultural levels of the life of the people on the basis of high rates of development of socialist production, raising its effectiveness, scientific-technical progress, and accelerated growth of productivity of labor."[10] Moreover, the General Secretary maintained that the task of raising the standard of living "will determine

---

Yakubovskiy was the only military man on the Secretariat; and Ivanovskiy, the commander of the Moscow Military District, served on the credentials commission. (See *XXIV s"yezd Kommunisticheskoy partii Sovetskogo Soyuza: Stenograficheskiy otchet,* I, 13–24.)

[6] *XXIV s"yezd Kommunisticheskoy partii Sovetskogo Soyuza: Stenograficheskiy otchet,* I, 51.

[7] *Ibid.,* p. 50.

[8] *Ibid.,* pp. 48–49.

[9] *Ibid.,* p. 52.

[10] *Ibid.,* p. 64. The exact same statement also appeared in the economic report of Chairman of the Council of Ministers A. Kosygin, delivered on April 6. See *Ibid.,* II, 16. In both instances, the statement appears in italics in the original.

our activity not only in the impending five years, but also the general orientation of the economic development of the country in the long-term outlook."[11]

Despite these pledges for an improved standard of living,[12] however, both Brezhnev and Kosygin acknowledged that heavy industry would retain its primary position in Soviet economic development. Brezhnev pointed out that increasing consumer production "does not reverse our general line on the accelerated development of the production of the means of production."[13] Likewise, Kosygin observed that "heavy industry has been and remains the foundation of the economic might of the country and the further growth of the people's standard of living."[14]

One of the justifications cited by Brezhnev for a continued emphasis on high growth rates in heavy industry was that "without the development of heavy industry it is impossible to maintain at the necessary level the defense capability which will guarantee the safety of our country and the peaceful labor of our people."[15] Indeed, although under the 8th Five-Year plan (1966–70) 80 billion rubles,[16] or nearly one fourth of all funds available for economic development, had been allocated for defense requirements,[17] the General Secretary seemed to indicate that an even higher level of defense capability would be required. As Brezhnev stated to the delegates of the 24th Party Congress:

> Comrades, everything that is created by the people must be reliably defended. To strengthen the Soviet State means to strengthen also its *armed forces* and to raise the defense capability of our country in every possible way. And as long as we live in a restless world, this task remains as one of the most important.[18]

[11] *Ibid.*, I, 65.

[12] It must be noted additionally that Brezhnev clearly connected these pledges with increased labor productivity, and not increased investment allocations. (*Ibid.*, p. 66.) Furthermore, a Western analysis of the 9th Five-Year Plan has concluded that "the directives placed unusual emphasis on bettering the lot of the consumer, but the figures given imply that the rate of progress planned for the standard of living is somewhat lower than that achieved in 1966–70." (Douglas B. Diamond, "Principle Targets and Central Themes of the Ninth Five-Year Plan," in Norton T. Dodge, ed., *Analysis of the USSR's 24th Party Congress and 9th Five-Year Plan* [Mechanicsville, M.: Cremona Foundation, 1971], pp. 47–48.)

[13] *XXIV s"yezd Kommunisticheskoy partii Sovetskogo Soyuza: Stenograficheskiy otchet*, I, 69.

[14] *Ibid.*, II, 25.

[15] *Ibid.*, I, 70.

[16] *Ibid.*, II, 9.

[17] Theodore Shabad in *The New York Times*, April 8, 1971.

[18] *XXIV s"yezd Kommunisticheskoy parti Sovetskogo Soyuza: Stenograficheskiy otchet*, I. 106. Italics in original.

In sum, the international situation described by the leading political official was mildly optimistic. As a result, the foreign policy advocated was cautious, but moderate, in tone. In internal economic policy, increasing the living standard of the Soviet people was in principle accepted as the main task of the new five-year plan even though heavy industry and defense industry development would in reality retain their dominant positions.

In contrast to the outlook of the political leaders, the international situation described by Minister of Defense Grechko in his report to the 24th CPSU Congress was more menacing and immediately threatening. As depicted by Grechko, Western states headed by the United States were fomenting international tensions, surrounding the Soviet Union with military bases, and unceasingly increasing their combat capability. Disregarding the tragedies of World War II, stated Grechko,

> . . . the forces of reaction are already nurturing plans for the next campaign against the Soviet Union and the other socialist countries, and are attempting anew to unleash a still more destructive war. The increasing aggressiveness of imperialism, the spearhead of which is directed against the Soviet Union, creates tension in the contemporary international situation. In this, the kings of the monopolies of the United States of America set the fashion. They are trying to mobilize in the struggle with the countries of the socialist community the whole arsenal of the political, economic, and military resources of the capitalist world.
>
> The preparations of the imperialists of the USA for aggression have never ended and are today proceeding at an unflagging speed. They have encircled the socialist states by aggressive military-political blocs, have enmeshed the world with a barbed wire of military bases, are continuously building up and perfecting the means of war, and are from year to year increasing allocations for military purposes.[19]

Under such conditions, explained Grechko, the Soviet Union "has been forced to make the necessary defense arrangements and to support its peaceful policy by a reinforcement of defense capability and an increase in the defense potential of the armed forces and their combat readiness."[20] Moreover, in order to underscore that increasing military strength was not only a past policy but also a future concern, the Defense Minister asserted that "the constant strengthening of the armed forces is an objective necessity of the successful construction of socialism and communism."[21]

[19] *Ibid.*, p. 346.
[20] *Ibid.*, p. 348.
[21] *Ibid.*, p. 345.

On the military requirements of the Soviet armed forces, Grechko was even more explicit in a *Krasnaya Zvezda* article written two days before the opening of the 24th Party Congress.[22] He maintained, for example, that "an objective necessity dictated by the interests of the reliable defense of the achievements of socialism and communism is the strengthening and maintenance *at the highest possible level* of the defense of the Soviet State."[23] In this connection, Grechko also stressed the need for consistently improving the material-technical basis of the Soviet armed forces. Reviewing the decisions of the 23rd Party Congress, Grechko noted that "as one of the immediate tasks, the Congress explained the necessity to perfect the production of defense equipment so that the Soviet army and navy were equipped with contemporary means of armaments." Furthermore, he declared that combat readiness, which "in the end is the crown of the combat skill of the troops in peacetime and the guarantee of victory in war," "is, of course, connected first and foremost with the perfection of the material-technical basis of the armed forces."

The first major MPA reaction to and analysis of the 24th Party Congress was an article by Yepishev in the party newspaper *Pravda* a week after the closing of the Congress. In a section on foreign policy, Yepishev's estimate of the international situation was more akin to Grechko's than to Brezhnev's. The MPA head's single reference to the United States was made with regard to the United States as the head of world imperialism and the aggressor in Southeast Asia. There was no mention of peaceful coexistence, the possibility for improving Soviet-American relations, or disarmament negotiations. On internal economic policy, Yepishev acknowledged the Party's intent to give "special attention" to the further growth of the standard of living of the Soviet people, but he also pointed out that this would not lessen the attention given to "the development of heavy industry, including its defense sectors." Moreover, Yepishev quoted from Brezhnev's report to the 24th Party Congress: "as long as we live in a restless world, this task [of strengthening the armed forces] remains as one of the most important."[24]

---

[22] In conjunction with the absence of a report to the 24th Party Congress by Yepishev, the explicitness of Grechko's *Krasnaya Zvezda* article as compared with his Congress report appears to reinforce suggestions that (1) the political leadership was making an effort to avoid giving too much recognition to a hard-line military policy, and (2) Grechko and Yepishev were substantially in agreement on the need for such a line. Consequently, Yepishev's report was eliminated and Grechko's report was toned down. The above-mentioned second point will be further developed below.

[23] *Krasnaya Zvezda*, March 27, 1971. Italics added.

[24] *Ibid.*, April 16, 1971. For the full Brezhnev quotation, as cited also by Yepishev, see above, p. 223. Although Yepishev was quoting Brezhnev, it would seem that their inferences were slightly different. This interpretation is based upon the fact that Brezhnev expressed relatively

Subsequent analysis of the 24th Party Congress in *Kommunist Vooruzhen-nykh Sil* articles was not uniform in interpretations and emphases. Several articles underlined the Soviet desire to raise the living standard of the people.[25] One article even reflected Brezhnev's moderate foreign policy line and stressed the importance of peaceful coexistence and disarmament.[26]

Other articles followed the harder line taken by Grechko and Yepishev. An article by a candidate of historical sciences recommended for study, for example, reviewed Soviet foreign policy, stressing the international duty of the Soviet Union and the continued threat of imperialism, especially the United States.[27] However, unlike the previously cited foreign policy review, there was no mention of peaceful coexistence or disarmament negotiations. Similarly, an article by a candidate of philosophical sciences strongly condemned the consistently aggressive nature of American military-political strategy from the Monroe Doctrine to Nixon's Vietnamization. Treating specifically American policy since Truman, the author argued that the policies of the Nixon administration were a direct continuation of previous policy, and definitely not a new approach.

> President R. Nixon, speaking for the transition from "an era of confrontation to an era of negotiations," amplified still greater the aggressive course of his predecessors. It is impossible not to agree with the American newspaper "The New York World Telegraph and Sun"; "If we died from duplicity, then Washington would be an extinct city."[28]

Again without mentioning peaceful coexistence or disarmament negotiations, another article in the same *Kommunist Vooruzhennykh Sil* examined the international situation and declared:

---

more faith in the possibility for negotiations to settle some Soviet-American problems. Conversely, Yepishev expressed no such belief and stressed only the American threat.

[25] "The Economic Policy of the Party at the Modern Stage. The Growth of the Living Standard of the Soviet People," *Kommunist Vooruzhennykh Sil*, No. 9 (May 1971) pp. 80–85; B. Kommissarov, "The Economic Policy of the Party at the Modern Stage," *Kommunist Vooruzhennykh Sil*, No. 10 (May 1971), pp. 10–17. The first of these articles was a study guide for the lessons and seminars led by political workers in the armed forces.

[26] "The 24th Congress of the CPSU on the International Status of the USSR and the Foreign Policy Activity of the Party," *Kommunist Vooruzhennykh Sil*, No. 9 (May 1971), pp. 75–79, esp. pp. 78–79. This also was a study guide.

[27] A. Shutov, "The Leninist Course of the Foreign Policy of the CPSU," *Kommunist Vooruzhennykh Sil*, No. 9 (May 1971), pp. 22–29, esp. pp. 23, 26.

[28] Colonel A. Migolatev, "The Aggressive Nature of the Military-Political Strategy of American Imperialism," *Kommunist Vooruzhennykh Sil*, No. 10 (May 1971), p. 80.

It is impossible to consider the threat of a new world war as being completely eliminated.

International imperialism and the forces of reaction have never ceased and are today continuing at a mounting pace preparations for a large war and are nurturing plans for a new campaign against the Soviet Union and the other socialist countries.

. . . [An] aggressive course of foreign policy and exaggeration of militarism, which carries in itself the threat of world war, is especially characteristic for the USA.[29]

As might be expected, this latter group of articles concluded that the Party must do everything necessary to strengthen the defense capability of the Soviet armed forces. One candidate of philosophical sciences following this line maintained:

To strengthen the Soviet State means to perfect its armed forces and to raise the defense capability or our country in every possible way. And as long as the real danger of military attack of imperialists exists, this task remains one of the most important.[30]

Moreover, it was stressed that present achievements, though impressive, were not sufficient, because "the contemporary development of military equipment and weapons is characterized by constant quantitative and qualitative changes."[31]

In conjunction with this, MPA spokesmen emphasized the need to relate science and technical knowledge more closely to military activity. In an article shortly before the 24th Party Congress, Yepishev had observed:

The Party is trying to see that the process of perfecting the technical bases of the army is accompanied by a broad introduction of science in all spheres of

---

[29] "The 24th Congress of the CPSU on the Further Strengthening of the Defense Potential of the Country and Raising the Combat Readiness of the Soviet Armed Forces," *Kommunist Vooruzhennykh Sil*, No. 10 (May 1971), p. 72.

[30] E. Strukov, "Urgent Tasks of the Social Policy of the Party," *Kommunist Vooruzhennykh Sil*, No. 10 (May 1971), p. 24. This paraphrase of Brezhnev's statement at the 24th Party Congress (quoted above, p. 223) is more strongly worded and directly anti-imperialist than the original. It would appear that Strukov did not consider the original statement to be clear enough. Whereas Brezhnev wanted "to strengthen," Strukov wanted "to perfect" the Soviet armed forces. And, whereas Brezhnev saw a "restless world," Strukov envisioned "the real danger of military attack of imperialism." The unusualness of this move was underlined by the fact that most Soviet spokesmen were content to quote Brezhnev's statement.

[31] "The 24th Congress of the CPSU on the Further Strengthening of the Defense Potential of the Country and Raising the Combat Readiness of the Soviet Armed Forces," p. 75.

military activity. Today science is becoming one of the most important items of the combat power of the armed forces.[32]

Similarly, the post-Congress study outline on the armed forces noted:

> Readiness for war is inconceivable without deep technical knowledge. Only in skillful hands do military equipment and weapons become threatening to the enemy. This is why we ought to spare neither efforts nor time to study military equipment and weapons, to perfect technical knowledge, and to raise class qualifications.[33]

The emphasis on the technical aspect was also reflected in a new recommendation to political organs for the training of political officers on the company level. According to a *Krasnaya Zvezda* report of an MPA meeting in late May, political organs were instructed "to organize the military-technical training of company political workers so that each of them in the course of study and everyday life possesses the volumes of knowledge, giving him the potential at the necessary moment to fulfill the obligations of commander of the company."[34]

At the same time, MPA spokesmen strongly denied that the broad introduction of science and technology into military matters had resulted in the "convergence" of the armed forces of socialist and capitalist states. In the military newspaper of July 8, 1971, for example, a candidate of historical sciences and assistant professor, Colonel V. Serebryannikov, criticized several Western "bourgeois authors" for disapproving the class-political standard used by socialists to evaluate armies. Serebryannikov contended that similarity in weapons between armies of the opposing social systems was a superficial phenomenon which did not override their essential differences. He stated:

> Indeed, there are rocket-nuclear weapons in the armies of the USA and the USSR. But in the hands of the imperialist army, they play an extremely reactionary role, lay obstacles to progress, and create an unprecedented threat to the lives of hundreds of millions of people. In the hands of the soldiers of the Soviet armed forces, these weapons are used for the protection of a progressive social system, the achievements of the revolutionary and liberation movement, and are a mighty factor deterring an aggressor.
>
> Therefore, outwardly similar processes in the development of armaments

[32] *Pravda*, March 25, 1971.

[33] "The 24th Congress of the CPSU on the Further Strengthening of the Defense Potential of the Country and Raising the Combat Readiness of the Soviet Armed Forces," p. 76.

[34] *Krasnaya Zvezda*, May 30, 1971.

do not change and cannot alter the class-political nature, essence, and predestination of armies.[35]

Secondly, Serebryannikov refuted the contention, attributed to Roman Kolkowicz, that the rapid growth of the engineer-technical education of officers and the increase in the proportion of engineers and technicians in the military had led to a "de-ideologization" of the Soviet armed forces.[36] While acknowledging that engineers and technicians occupied "up to 45 percent of the officer positions," he denied the alleged emergence of Soviet "technocrats," who "supposedly resist being drawn into party-political work and have 'strained relations' with political workers."[37] Serebryannikov maintained:

> Socialist reality and the whole tenor of life of our army and navy objectively leads to the combination in the Soviet military engineer of the qualities of the ideological-political figure and the technical specialist. These aspects are indissoluble; they are interlaced and mutually reinforce one another. Socialist society forms soldiers with high political consciousness and socially active citizens with the strongly pronounced traits of social-political figures.[38]

Thirdly, Serebryannikov rejected the claim of "bourgeois military sociologists" that the scientific-technical revolution has given rise to conflicts between "progressive" and "conservative" military leaders on such issues as new weapons and strategic doctrine. The nature and "predestination" of the Soviet armed forces, asserted the author, preclude the possibility of cleavages on theory and policy. He noted:

> In the Soviet army, united opinions on all basic questions of the theory and policy of the Party, the development of military affairs and military construction, and on the forms and methods of combat actions formed a long time ago

[35] *Ibid.*, July 8, 1971.

[36] In a similar, but more general, approach, candidate of philosophical sciences Colonel K. Payusov condemned those advocates of " 'liberal' or 'intellectual' anti-communism" who envisioned that the rise of the technological intelligentsia would also give rise to a supra-class " 'universal' ideology." (*Ibid.*, September 24, 1971.)

[37] Likewise, in a December 1971 issue of the MPA journal, Yepishev scored the slanders of those bourgeois ideologists who "endeavor in a pseudo-scientific form to suggest to readers the thought of supposedly existing 'contradictions' between the political and the technical structure of our army." (General of the Army A. A. Yepishev, "For the High Effectiveness of Ideological Work," *Kommunist Vooruzhennykh Sil*, No. 23 [December 1971], p. 9.)

[38] *Krasnaya Zvezda*, July 8, 1971.

and exist. Technical "flux" and professional one-sidedness are alien to Soviet officers. In our army, such conflicts by force of its very nature and historical pre-destination are impossible.[39]

At the same time, professional military leaders are more frank with regard to the fact that some of their colleagues "do not keep pace with life and the development of scientific thought."[40] For example, some military leaders were quite slow to introduce into practice the latest scientific developments, especially those pertaining to computer usage.[41] For this reason, MPA spokesmen were constantly concerned with assuring such conservative military leaders that automation does not lessen the role of the commander, but supposedly makes it more important.[42]

The Influence of the 24th Party Congress on Party-Political Work in the Armed Forces

On July 11, 1971, the armed forces newspaper *Krasnaya Zvezda* noted the publication of five new monographs by military men on the topic of the 24th Party Congress.[43] As set down in the introduction to Yepishev's work, the main task assigned to the armed forces by the 24th Congress was "the further strengthening of the combat power of the army and navy and the ensuring of their constant combat readiness for the frustration of the aggressive schemes of imperialism." Moreover, Yepishev observed that all activities and military personnel were

[39] *Ibid.* For a more general treatment of Soviet attitudes on convergence theories, see Leon Goure *et al.*, *Convergence of Communism and Capitalism: The Soviet View* (Coral Gables, Fla.: Center for Advanced International Studies, University of Miami, 1973), *passim*; excerpts of Serebryannikov's and Payusov's articles are printed on pp. 116–17 and pp. 120–22, respectively.

[40] Colonel General N. V. Ogarkov in *Krasnaya Zvezda*, September 3, 1971.

[41] Colonel of Engineering S. Kuts in *ibid.*, September 29, 1971.

[42] Lieutenant Colonel V. Bondarenko, "Scientific-Technical Progress and the Strengthening of the Defense Capability of the Country," *Kommunist Vooruzhennykh Sil*, No. 24 (December 1971), p. 13.

[43] *Krasnaya Zvezda*, July 11, 1971. Two were written by professional military men: Grechko's *Na strazhe mira i stroitel'stva kommunizma* (*On Guard for Peace and the Construction of Communism*) and Yakubovsky's *Voyennoye sodruzhestvo* (*Combat Collaboration*). Two were by leading MPA officials: Yepishev's *Kommunisty armii i flota* (*Communists of the Army and Navy*) and Vasyagin's *Partiya vedet nas k kommunizmu* (*The Party Leads Us to Communism*). The fifth was candidate of economic sciences Colonel S. S. Bartenev's *Pyatiletka velikogo sozidaniya* (*A Five-Year Plan of Great Creation*).

"subordinate to the solution of this task."[44] Similarly, within the text itself, Yepishev asserted:

> . . . the pivotal and determining questions of party-political work in the armed forces have always been and remain, the questions of raising the communist consciousness of personnel, vigilance, and combat readiness. The maintenance of a constantly high combat readiness of troops is the personally important goal of party-political work and the index of its effectiveness and effectualness. In this is our military contribution to the common task of communist construction.[45]

Elaborating on this, Yepishev also noted four ways to make party-political work, concrete and purposeful under contemporary conditions. He explained:

> To construct party-political work concretely and purposefully means, first, to derive from the policy of the CPSU tasks which are determined by the Party and the people at this or that stage of the development of our society. Secondly, to take stock of the concrete-historical military-political and international conditions and tasks arising from them. Thirdly, to take into consideration the peculiarities of the concrete stage in the development of the armed forces, the changes occurring in their technical equipment, social structure, organization, system of training of personnel, and to secure the conformity of the content of party-political work demanded by contemporary war and the tasks of the comprehensive training of troops with the level of combat actions. Fourthly, to conduct party-political work with regard for the peculiarities and character of the tasks being implemented by the specific kinds of armed forces and arm of the service.[46]

The fourth of Yepishev's points was particularly important for party-political work in the armed forces. It emphasized that party-political work had to be approached differently in the various branches of service. Such factors as the revolution in military affairs arising from scientific-technical progress and the extremes of educational levels among servicemen forced the MPA leadership to diversify its party-political work so that it could better take into account the nature of the work done by the various service branches. A reflection of this con-

[44] General of the Army A. A. Yepishev, *Kommunisty armii i flota* (Moscow: Voyenizdat, 1971), p. 3.

[45] *Ibid.*, p. 72.

[46] *Ibid.*, p. 73.

cern was the interjection, begun under the January 1967 decree on party-political work in the armed forces, of political administrations of branches.

Despite these moves to invigorate party-political work in the armed forces and despite previously cited assertions denying the existence of cleavages within the military on party-political work, MPA activities continued by Soviet admission to have serious defects. Generalizing from the type of criticisms made by Soviet spokesmen, it would seem that these shortcomings could be traced to the lack of enthusiasm for party-political work among the political, as well as the professional, element of the armed forces. While Soviet authorities claim that these shortcomings occur only infrequently, their continued existence points not only to a fundamental incompatibility between an extreme form of political indoctrination and scientific-technical progress, but also to the justification for attaching party-political work to combat readiness rather than conducting it as an end in itself.

Broadly speaking, the defects criticized in the Soviet press fell into two groups according to their origin: (1) defects attributable to soldiers who demonstrated little interest in political indoctrination and (2) defects attributable to party-political workers who not only allow the soldiers to be apathetic but also engender superficiality themselves. Within the first group, it was acknowledged in the military newspaper, "we still have quite a number of members and candidate members of the Party who underrate the significance of Marxist-Leninist studies and are not raising their ideological-theoretical level."[47] The apathy of officers in particular was illustrated by the admission of *Kommunist Vooruzhennykh Sil* that in some groups less than half of the members attend lectures. Furthermore, the same article charged that even among those who attend lectures and seminars there is little enthusiasm for independent work. It was stated:

> Unfortunately, sections of officers and communists are still encountered who confine themselves to attendance at lectures and seminars, and do not bother themselves with the independent study of primary sources and party documents. As a rule, such comrades explain their passivity as being excessively busy with work.[48] A detailed study of individual cases, however, shows that the cause is not in some particular difficulty, but in lack of organization and inability, and sometimes unwillingness, to harmonize daily work with concern for their ideological growth.[49]

[47] *Krasnaya Zvezda*, June 30, 1971.

[48] For an example of the complaint that political workers lack sufficient time to carry out their responsibilities, see Major General V. Chupov and Colonel A. Lunichev in *ibid.*, November 26, 1971.

[49] "The Marxist-Leninist Training of Officers [Should Be] at the Level of New Tasks," *Kommunist Vooruzhennykh Sil*, No. 18 (September 1971), p. 7.

Under the second category, some political organs and party organizations in the armed forces were criticized because they "are still poorly taking care of the ideological-theoretical growth of communists, are not demanding enough from those comrades who neglect their political study, and are not giving help to those who need it."[50] In addition, political workers were charged with frequently being unprepared to conduct their lectures and seminars. As a result, some meetings stifled the indoctrination process and suffered from the lack of creativity and flexibility. As one *Krasnaya Zvezda* report complained:

> . . . the role and authority of party conferences and their ideological influence have risen. However, there are still quite a number of such conferences, the educational potential of which is low, and still persisting are cases where naked practicism smothers the political sounding of some questions and where the lively, creative discussion is regulated by an organizational scheme worked out in advance.[51]

Another criticism was that lectures and seminars were often conducted without consideration for the level of preparation and interests of participants.[52] Moreover, in the area of selection for party candidacy, the chief of administration of organizational-party work in the MPA protested that cases are still encountered where party-political officials "approach a question of admittance formally, recommending notoriously unworthy people," who are eventually dropped from candidacy.[53] With proper care, these people would never have been chosen in the first place.

In an attempt to rectify some of these deficiencies, a party conference of leading ideological workers from the various branches, sections, and departments were convened in Moscow on October 13–16, 1971. In attendance were the highest-ranking members of both the MPA and the professional military. Major speeches were delivered by Grechko, Yepishev, Kalashnik, and several lesser figures. According to a summary of the conference activity in the armed forces newspaper, several speakers noted that some individuals were not giving sufficient attention to the study and implementation of the 24th Party Congress decisions and pronouncements. Consequently, it was urged that more emphasis ought to be given to "the significance of profoundly explaining to personnel the questions of increasing the guiding role of the Party in communist construction and strengthening the military power of the Soviet country, and of intensifying

---

50 *Krasnaya Zvezda*, June 30, 1971.

51 *Ibid.*, August 17, 1971.

52 *Ibid.*, October 1, 1971.

53 *Ibid.*, September 21,1971.

the influence of the CPSU as the chief revolutionary force at the present."[54]

In a speech to the conference reprinted in *Kommunist Vooruzhennykh Sil*, Minister of Defense Grechko noted "a certain relaxation of tension" recently in Europe, which had arisen from the fact that "the forces of socialism and democracy are continuously strengthening their position."[55] Again stressing the relationship between a high level of Soviet military power and peace in the world, Grechko asserted that "if the imperialists had believed that they were more powerful than us in a military sense, they would, without a doubt, plunge the world into a new war." He argued that for this reason "the strengthening of the armed forces in every possible way is the chief guarantee of our safety and an important condition for the successful foreign policy activity of the Soviet State."[56]

Subsequently, Grechko defined the elements he considered necessary for success in war. It will depend "first on what level of technical equipment the troops have, and second on who has the stronger moral spirit and which army has the higher military organization and military skill."[57] Claiming that the Soviet Union possessed advantages in all these factors, Grechko nonetheless maintained that these advantages had to be developed persistently. Yet, while acknowledging that "a very important place belongs to party-political and ideological-educational work," Grechko was quite clear on the point that moral spirit could in no way substitute for military hardware. On the relationship between man and equipment, the Minister of Defense stated:

> We frequently talk about the growing role of man and his moral force in achieving victory over the enemy. This is right. But it should always be emphasized that a man can prevail only under the condition that he is armed by the newest equipment and weapons and is able to use them perfectly. One should not leave out of account that, while in the past a shortage of equipment or the inability to wield it could be made up for by the high moral spirit of personnel or the effect of physical forces, now the matter is more complex. Superiority over an opponent in ideological-political considerations must without fail be combined with the equipping of troops with the newest equipment and the skillful possession of them.[58]

Although ideology received somewhat less emphasis, the Minister of Defense

[54] *Ibid.*, October 17, 1971.

[55] Marshal of the Soviet Union A. Grechko, "To Educate Soldiers in a Spirit of High Combat Readiness," *Kommunist Vooruzhennykh Sil*, No. 22 (November 1971), p. 4.

[56] *Ibid.*, p. 5.

[57] *Ibid.*, p. 6.

[58] *Ibid.*, p. 10.

still recognized its importance for the military buildup. Ideological struggle between the two opposing systems had become "particularly acute" and ideological differences continued to be "irreconcilable," pointed out Grechko, even in conditions of peaceful state-to-state relations and negotiations. Consequently, it was still necessary, as noted at the 24th CPSU Congress, to stress that "an irreconcilable offensive struggle against bourgeois and revisionist ideology" remained a chief item in the ideological work of the Party among servicemen. For with greater ideological conviction comes greater military determination and efficiency on the part of the soldier. "It can be said without exaggeration," explained Grechko, "that if we manage to temper well in ideological respects all our officers, generals, and admirals, and to arm them with a deep understanding of the ideas and decisions of the Party and the skill to put them efficiently into practice, then by it we will to a large extent predetermine success in all areas of the life of the army and navy."[59]

In the following issue of *Kommunist Vooruzhennykh Sil,* Yepishev noted the continued preparations for war being made by the imperialists and declared that in consequence:

> It is necessary to educate people and to direct affairs so that our armed forces are ready at any time to repulse the assault of any enemy, wherever it may come from, so that the aggressor in case of an attempt of assault on our country receives an annihilating blow in return, and so that no fortuity has found us by surprise.[60]

As defined by the MPA head, this meant that "questions connected with guaranteeing the constant and reliable combat readiness of troops" would constitute "the chief and basic questions in all of our party-political work."[61] In view of this close connection with combat readiness, Yepishev observed that ideological work had rightly become more attuned with the features of the individual branches of the armed forces and the increased amount of field exercises. Furthermore, Yepishev elaborated several features which ideological work under contemporary conditions was forced to take into account:

> First, all ideological measures and all our efforts must proceed from the necessity of raising its effectiveness, which is manifested in the realization of party resolutions and in the pursuits, deeds, and conduct of people. Second, the fur-

[59] *Ibid.,* p. 13.
[60] Yepishev, "For the High Effectiveness of Ideological Work," p. 5.
[61] *Ibid.,* p. 4.

ther upsurge of ideological work demands its still more accurate scientific organization, the application of concrete criteria for its effectiveness in the matter
of resolving tasks of combat readiness of troops. Third, this work is today being
put into practice in conditions of unceasing "ideological war," which demands
from us a reinforcement of the offensive might of our ideological weapon and
the raising of class principledness, political watchfulness, and vigilance.[62]

Despite these efforts, however, defects in party-political work would continue to exist and eventually be a major reason for the calling of an all-army
conference of party secretaries in March 1973 as part of a massive campaign to
improve party-political work in the armed forces.

Détente or Increasing International Duty: The Influence of the Resource Allocations Debate on Party-Military Affairs

In a September 1971 issue of *Kommunist Vooruzhennykh Sil,* a candidate of
military sciences of high military rank noted that only the powerful armed
forces of socialist states, "leaning on a developed economy. and first of all on
heavy industry," can block the aggressive aspirations of the imperialists.[63] Two
issues later, Colonel A. Kormiltsev, a candidate of economic sciences, observed
that "heavy industry, as before, constitutes the basis of the development of production" and development of the entire national economy, the further growth
of the living standard of workers, and the strengthening of the economic and
defense power of the country."[64] Five days before the opening of the November
1971 plenum of the Party Central Committee, an article in the armed forces
newspaper *Krasnaya Zvezda* took note of the "growing role" that heavy industry
was playing in the development of the material-technical basis of the military
power needed to defend the Soviet Union.[65] At the same time, an article in the
party newspaper *Pravda* declared that Soviet agricultural problems ought to be
traced to deficiencies in the skill of farmers, rather than to a lack of equipment.[66]

[62] *Ibid.,* p. 8.

[63] Major General M. Cherednichenko, "Contemporary War and Economics," *Kommunist
Vooruzhennykh Sil,* No. 18 (September 1971), p. 20.

[64] Colonel A. Kormiltsev, "The Role of the Branches of the National Economy in Centemporary
War," *Kommunist Vooruzhennykh Sil,* No. 20 (October 1971), p. 10.

[65] *Krasnaya Zvezda,* November 17, 1971.

These articles, especially the ones appearing shortly before the November 1971 plenum of the Party Central Committee, seem to indicate that a lively debate on resource allocations was taking place away from the public view. In emphasizing the importance of heavy industry and defense industry, the abovementioned articles were indirectly arguing against greater allocations for agricultural and consumer investments.

There is reason to conjecture that Soviet military leaders desired a larger voice in the determination of resource allocations. Indications of this arose again in a February 1972 article in a Komsomol journal by Minister of Defense Grechko, who invoked the authority and example of Lenin to prove that "only on the basis of unity of political and military leadership" is it possible to achieve the rational distribution of the state's resources.[67] Subsequently, in articles commemorating the fifty-fourth anniversary of the establishment of Soviet Armed Forces Day, both Grechko[68] and Yepishev[69] asserted that a constant strengthening of the armed forces was an "objective necessity."

In addition to their less than optimum economic situation, the Soviet armed forces were also faced with the possibility that the summit negotiations to be held in May 1972 between General Secretary Brezhnev and President Nixon might further restrict Soviet military capability. Under these conditions, but without directly challenging the advisability of peaceful negotiations, the military leadership sought to stress concepts which emphasized the increasing importance of strong armed forces.

In a *Kommunist* article, which appeared during the same month as the so-called Moscow Summit between Brezhnev and Nixon, MPA head Yepishev analyzed the function of armies. According to Yepishev, the armed forces of an imperialist state have two functions. First, they are an instrument for the internal suppression of any popular demonstration or revolutionary movement which might seek to destroy the exploiting system of capitalism and liberate the masses. Second, they are an instrument by which the ruling classes expand control over new areas, export counterrevolution, and suppress national liberation movements.[70] Likewise, explained Yepishev, the Soviet armed forces originally had

[66] *Pravda*, November 17, 1971. See also Christian Duevel, "Heavy Industry Lobby Beaten Off at Central Committee Plenum," *Radio Liberty Dispatch*, November 23, 1971.

[67] Marshal of the Soviet Union A. Grechko, "Soviet Youth in the Defense of the Country," *Molodaya Gvardiya*, No. 2 (February 1972), p. 5.

[68] *Pravda*, February 23, 1972.

[69] *Krasnaya Zvezda*, February 23, 1972.

[70] General of the Army A. A. Yepishev, "The Historic Mission of the Army of the Socialist State," *Kommunist*, No. 7 (May 1972), p. 62.

two functions: to aid in the deposing of Russia's exploiting classes and to secure the state for the construction of socialism.[71]

Superficially, therefore, the imperialist armies and the Red Army of the early years had in common the fact that each had an internal and an external function. More fundamentally, however, Yepishev noted vast differences derived from the opposing content and social orientation of the two types of armies.[72] Based on these differences, as the Soviet Union ceased to need a dictatorship of the proletariat and came to be a "state of the whole people," it was possible for the Soviet army gradually to lose its internal function and to retain only its external function.[73]

Yepishev pointed out, furthermore, that the continuing external function of the Soviet armed forces had not remained static. "In the present epoch, which is characterized by a reinforcement of the position of socialism and the sharp antagonism of the two systems," maintained the MPA head, "there has occurred naturally *a deepening of the external function* of the Soviet armed forces." [74]

According to Soviet professional military and political-military spokesmen, the Soviet armed forces were being called upon increasingly to fulfill four roles: (1) to provide the military defense of the Soviet Union, (2) to provide the military defense of the fraternal socialist community, (3) to create opportunities for and support on behalf of national liberation movements, and (4) to forestall the adventuristic designs of the imperialists, headed by the United States. Accordingly, in its external function, the Soviet armed forces were declared to have not only the passive role of defending socialist gains, but also a more active role of promoting Soviet foreign policy interests. Indeed, General I. Pavlovskiy, Deputy Minister of Defense and Commander of the Ground Forces, clearly asserted in regard to the active role of the armed forces that "further implementation of the foreign policy program formulated by the 24th CPSU Congress will depend, to a large extent, on the defense capability of the Soviet state and the condition of its armed forces."[75]

[71] *Ibid.*, pp. 62–63.

[72] For a similar attempt to contrast the purpose of armies in socialist and "antagonistic" societies, see Marshal of the Soviet Union A. Grechko, "Armed Forces of the Union of Soviet Socialist Republics," *Kommunist*, No. 3 (February 1972), pp. 48–50.

[73] See also *Marxism-Leninism on War and Army* (Moscow: Progress, 1972), p. 221.

[74] Yepishev, "The Historic Mission of the Army of the Socialist State," p. 64. Italics added.

[75] Moscow Domestic Service, July 11, 1972, FBIS, *Soviet Union*, No. 143 (July 24, 1972), p. M1. It might be possible to speculate that this is not only an assertion, but also a warning to the Party. If there had been a leveling off of allocations for military expenditures as suggested by the announced figures, Pavlovskiy may have been arguing here that such leveling would

At this time, military spokesmen also emphasized that the active aspect of the armed forces' external function was significantly increasing. First, it was claimed that the strength of the armed forces had a primary role in curtailing the adventuristic activities of the imperialists. In his November 1971 *Kommunist Vooruzhennykh Sil* article, for example, Marshal Grechko mentioned that the combat might of the Soviet armed forces constituted "a decisive factor in curbing the imperialist aggressors."[76] Elaborating on this point in a book which contained chapters by various leading Soviet personalities, Yepishev noted:

> Imperialism is the chief source of war, and as long as it exists on earth, there also remains a real danger of war, including the danger of the outbreak of a new world war. But now imperialism can no longer unleash wars with impunity. The world has such a material and military force in the person of our army and the armies of other socialist states which is capable of crushing an aggressor if he dares to begin a war. This circumstance deprives imperialists of real hopes for achieving their predatory, gendarmist goals by military means. And if they have not unleashed a world war until now, it is only because they know our military might and fear the inevitable retaliation which might bring them to their downfall.[77]

A mid-1972 article in *Kommunist Vooruzhennykh Sil* similarly stated that "as a specific political instrument of a socialist state, our army is stepping forth as a powerful force capable of restraining imperialist expansion and the exporting of counterrevolution."[78] Furthermore, in advancing the argument for a large, modernized navy, the Commander of the Navy, Admiral of the Fleet S.

---

hinder the Party's foreign policy objectives, since the attainment of these objectives "depends" on military capability.

[76] Grechko, "To Educate Soldiers in a Spirit of High Combat Readiness," p. 5. While Grechko's references to the Soviet armed forces at this time (1972) were made only in general terms, reference made in 1974 would be more explicit and more closely reflective of Yepishev's 1972 position. See Marshal of the Soviet Union A. Grechko, "The Leading Role of the CPSU in Building the Army of a Developed Socialist Society," *Voprosy Istorii KPSS*, No. 5 (May 1974), pp. 30–47.

[77] General of the Army A. A. Yepishev, "In the Leadership of the Party Is Our Invincible Strength," in Colonel S. M. Isachenko, comp., *Armiya bratstva narodov* (*Army of the Brotherhood of Peoples*) (Moscow: Voyenizdat, 1972), p. 36. See also Yepishev's article in *Izvestiya*, May 9, 1972.

[78] D. Volkogonov, "Urgent Questions of Soviet Military Construction in Light of the Resolutions of the 24th Congress of the CPSU," *Kommunist Vooruzhennykh Sil*, No. 11 (June 1972), p. 11.

Gorshkov, contended that "the presence of the Soviet Navy on the oceans is a deterrent to the aggressive designs of international imperialism.[79] This line was then seconded by a study guide prepared by the MPA for the political instruction of soldiers, in which it was stated:

> In an appropriate manner, our navy implements its international mission. In the past three years, Soviet vessels called upon the ports of 60 states of Europe, Asia, Africa, and Latin America. Tens of thousands of sailors visited on shore. All of this contributes to the strengthening of friendship and mutual understanding among peoples and to raising the authority of the Soviet Union.[80]

Another area in which the active aspect of the armed forces' external function was said to be significantly increasing concerned Soviet aid to national liberation movements. Not only did Soviet spokesmen stress the benefits of the military assistance given to other present-day socialist countries during their past struggles for liberation, but they also maintained that the very existence of a strong Soviet Union, rebuffing the "exportation of counterrevolution" by the imperialists, gives continued support to national liberation movements. Yepishev, for example, in his May 1972 *Kommunist* article noted:

> The liberating mission of the Soviet army was most strikingly displayed in the years of the Second World War. Introducing a decisive contribution to the destruction of the military machine of German fascism and Japanese militarism, the armed forces of the USSR by their victories created exceptionally favorable conditions for the growth of the liberation movement, as a result of which the peoples of a number of countries of Europe and Asia chose the path of free development; this path objectively led them to socialism. In these countries, the forces of internal reaction which cooperated with fascism were smashed. Soviet troops prevented the exportation of counterrevolution to these countries, guarding them from foreign intervention. In this is the greatest historical service of the Soviet armed forces to the world socialist system and all of progressive mankind.[81]

In this respect, Yepishev's statement was not unlike that of other spokesmen

[79] *Zolnierz Wolnosei* (Warsaw), July 28, 1972, FBIS, *Soviet Union*, No. 154 (August 8, 1972), p. M2.

[80] "The Soviet Armed Forces, Their Historical Predestination and Organization. Command, Political, and Engineer-Technical Cadres," *Kommunist Vooruzhennykh Sil*, No. 18 (September 1972), p. 73.

[81] Yepishev, "The Historic Mission of the Army of the Socialist State," p. 67.

with regard to the liberating role of the Soviet armed forces.[82] However, the MPA head went beyond this point and urged that the time was ripe for the Soviet Union to become even more directly involved in assisting the national liberation movement. As Yepishev said:

> In contemporary conditions, the opportunities of the Soviet Union to render support to workingmen and to the revolutionary and national-liberation movement have increased still greater. Deterring the aggressive inclinations of imperialism against young developing states, granting the necessary equipment at the request of their governments, and assisting those countries in the training of national cadres, the Soviet state makes an invaluable contribution to the struggle of peoples for freedom and independence.[83]

It appears that the argument of an increased external function for the Soviet armed forces was at least partially prompted by the continuing debate on resource allocations. Consequently, the external function was frequently tied to a need for constantly strengthening the armed forces. For example, a study guide on Soviet war preparations outlined by a candidate of economic sciences declared that "the struggle against the intrigues of the aggressive imperialist forces rests upon a durable material base and an efficient long-term program."[84] Moreover, a *Kommunist Vooruzhennykh Sil* article containing recommended material for Armed Forces Day speeches in 1972 noted that the absence of world war since socialism had become an international system is due "not so much to the political realism of the leaders of the imperialist states, as it is to the economic and defensive power of the states of the Warsaw Pact and to the moral-political unity of our peoples."[85]

While Soviet spokesmen insisted that the Soviet economy had "the firm material base for solving all social tasks and also tasks concerned with strengthening the defense of our country,"[86] they were equally insistent on the proposition that the strengthening of the Soviet armed forces was necessitated solely by foreign threats. In an October 1972 article in *Kommunist*, for example, Mar-

[82] Cf. Grechko, "Armed Forces of the Union of Soviet Socialist Republics," p. 54.

[83] Yepishev, "The Historic Mission of the Army of the Socialist State," p. 67.

[84] Colonel S. Bartenev, "Imperialism Is the Source of Wars. Raising Combat Readiness and Efficiency of the Army and Navy in Every Possible Way Is a Very Important Factor in Deterring Aggressors," *Kommunist Vooruzhennykh Sil*, No. 21 (November 1972), p. 73.

[85] "Faithful Guardian of the Achievements of Socialism," *Kommunist Vooruzhennykh Sil*, No. 2 (January 1972), p. 44.

[86] Volkogonov, "Urgent Questions of Soviet Military Construction in Light of the Resolutions of the 24th Congress of the CPSU," p. 11.

shal Grechko claimed:

> It is known to the entire world that socialist countries threaten no one and intend
> to attack no one. Peace, not war, is necessary for socialist and communist con-
> struction. And if socialist states nevertheless strengthen their military power,
> this is by no means provoked by internal causes of their development, but by
> the intensifying aggressiveness of imperialism and its striving to resolve the
> basic contradiction of the contemporary epoch — the contradiction between
> capitalism and socialism — by means of the annihilation of the world socialist
> system.[87]

Since the Soviet economy had the capacity to strengthen Soviet military
might, it followed, in the arguments of the military spokesmen, that a powerful
armed force should in fact be constructed[88] — even, moreover, in an era of peace
and negotiations with the imperialists. In an article published in the naval journal
shortly before the May 1972 Moscow Summit, for example, Admiral S. Gorshkov observed:

> The basic and solitary means of waging armed conflict between states has always
> been the army and navy, which in peacetime continue to serve as the instrument
> or weapon of their policies. Many examples from history attest to the fact that
> in the age of feudalism and capitalism all problems of foreign policiy were
> always solved on the basis of and taking into account the military might of the
> "negotiating" sides, and that the potential military might of one state or another,
> built up in accordance with its economic capabilities and political orientation,
> permitted it to conduct a policy advantageous to itself to the detriment of other
> states not possessing a corresponding military power.[89]

The 5th All-Army Conference of Secretaries
of Party Organizations, March 27–29, 1973

On January 23, 1973, the armed forces newspaper *Krasnaya Zvezda* announced
that an all-army conference of secretaries of party organizations, the fifth such

[87] Marshal of the Soviet Union A. Grechko, "The Military Cooperation of the Armies of
Socialist States," *Kommunist*, No. 15 (October 1972), p. 35.

[88] See, for example, General of the Army I. Pavlovskiy, "The Economy and the Armed Forces
of the USSR," *Planovoye Khozyaystvo*, No. 2 (February 1973), pp. 20–30.

[89] Admiral of the Fleet S. G. Gorshkov, "Navies in Wars and in Peace," *Morskoy Sbornik*,
No. 2 (February 1972), p. 21.

conference to be convened during the history of the Soviet armed forces, would be held at the end of March 1973.[90] Subsequently, in February, the Party Central Committee issued two new decrees, a "Statute on Political Agencies" and a related "Instructions for the CPSU Organizations in the Soviet Army and Navy,"[91] which were designed, according to Soviet spokesmen, to increase the role and influence of party organizations in all aspects of armed forces life. These actions clearly indicated an increasing concern for party-political work within the armed forces.

On March 27, 130 participants assembled in Moscow for the 5th All-Army Conference of the Secretaries of Party Organizations. Although General Secretary Brezhnev did not attend, Politburo members N. A. Suslov and F. D. Kulakov, Politburo candidate members Yu. V. Andropov, P. N. Demichev, and B. N. Ponomarev, as well as the leading figures of the armed forces, were among those attending.

In view of the recent détente between the Soviet Union and the United States, early speculation among Western observers was that an important task of the conference would be the replacement of the United States with the People's Republic of China as the main "enemy" of the Soviet Union.[92] If this possibility was contemplated, it was never mentioned, either directly or indirectly, in the various reports of the conference.[93]

According to the newspaper accounts, the first meeting of the conference was opened by Yepishev. After presiding over the election of the CPSU Politburo as the honorary presidium of the conference, Yepishev turned the floor over to Suslov, who read the Party Central Committee's greetings to the conference which had been signed by Brezhnev. This was followed by speeches from Grechko and Yepishev.[94]

---

[90] *Krasnaya Zvezda*, January 23, 1972. A more extended announcement appeared in the MPA journal. See "All-Army Conference of Secretaries of Party Organizations," *Kommunist Vooruzhennykh Sil*, No. 4 (February 1973), pp. 3–9. As previously noted, the conference for party organization secretaries had originally been scheduled for early 1969, but was postponed for unexplained reasons. For speculation on the causes of the postponement, see Chapter 7.

[91] Although neither the exact date nor the documents themselves seem to have been published, the documents have been extensively summarized on several occasions. Especially important is Yepishev's article in *Krasnaya Zvezda*, March 2, 1973. See also Colonel General P. Yefimov, "Documents of Great Political Significance," *Kommunist Vooruzhennykh Sil*, No. 7 (April 1973), pp. 16–27. See Appendix B of this study.

[92] *The Wall Street Journal*, January 24, 1973; and the *Washington Post*, March 28, 1973.

[93] Speeches and discussions of the conference were not reprinted in full. They appeared in print only as summary reports. Consequently, if the People's Republic of China was mentioned, the references were all deleted in the public transcripts.

[94] *Krasnaya Zvezda*, March 28, 1973.

The two basic lines stressed at the conference were already evident in the Central Committee's greetings. First, it was reaffirmed that, in spite of the relaxation of tensions, Western "imperialism" continued to be the main threat to and enemy of socialism. According to the greetings of the Central Committee:

> By the efforts of the USSR, the fraternal socialist countries, and the peace-loving forces of mankind has been achieved a noticeable improvement of the international situation. However, the aggressive circles of the capitalist world stubbornly resist the healthy process of relaxation of international tension and intensify the arms race.
>
> History teaches that while imperialism exists, the danger of new aggressive wars remains. Therefore, all possible strengthening of the defense capability of the country of the Soviets and of the combat might of its armed forces always has been and will remain the sacred duty of the Party, of the Soviet government and people.

Second, party organizations were urged to increase their efforts to raise the combat readiness of the troops and to improve the implementation of party policy. Soviet state security demands, said the greetings, that servicemen

> . . . further raise the vigilance and unceasing perfection of the combat readiness of the troops. And this, in its turn, is unthinkable without the all possible improving of party-political work and raising the role and increasing the influence of party organizations on all aspects of the life and activity of troops.
>
> The resolute and consistent implementation by military party organizations of the policy of the CPSU in the army and navy is one of the decisive conditions for successfully fulfilling the tasks assigned to the armed forces of the USSR. In this regard, the raising of the militancy of party organizations and the activism of all communists has specific importance. In this connection, it is important that every party organization should constantly take care of improving ideological work, champion everything new and progressive, have irreconcilable concern for shortcomings, be the initiator of socialist competition for the excellent mastery of equipment and for fulfilling the tasks of combat and political training.[95]

On the issue of the imperialist threat, Grechko, while he recognized the significant achievements of "our peace offensive on the foreign policy front,"

---

[95] "Greetings of the Central Committee of the CPSU to the All-Army Conference of Secretaries of Party Organizations," *Kommunist Vooruzhennykh Sil*, No. 8 (April 1973), pp. 11–12. See also *Krasnaya Zvezda*, March 28, 1973.

observed that "the anti-popular class nature of imperialism" was still unchanged. Consequently, the Minister of Defense warned:

> Imperialism has not reconciled itself to the existence of socialist states and is not preparing to lay down its weapons.
>
> Of course, imperialists are not now resolved to a direct military assault. They well understand that such a step would end in a catastrophe for them. But they are still counting on achieving military superiority, undermining the foundations of international peace, and at a favorable moment resolving the historical dispute between capitalism and socialism by armed means. The imperialist states are not stopping preparations for war, are increasing their military budgets from year to year, and are continuing the arms race.[96]

Like Grechko, Yepishev noted in his speech to the conference that "the explanation of the international situation is an important task of ideological work in contemporary conditions." In the context of the speech, this seems to imply that the masses should not be allowed to receive objective information or be left to draw their own conclusions from the recent East-West détente. "It is necessary not simply to inform the people about these or those international events," asserted Yepishev, "but also resolutely to expose the aggressive intrigues of imperialism, to instill a class hatred toward them, and to form in every soldier a clear understanding of the sources and danger of the outbreak of war and the necessity for vigilance and the constant readiness to repulse aggression." Moreover, in view of an increasingly acute ideological struggle, Yepishev called for "an offensive struggle against bourgeois ideology and revisionism."[97]

Just as striking as the absence of reference to China at the conference was the absence of direct reference to "peaceful coexistence." Neither in the reports of the various speeches and discussions nor in editorials concerning the conference was the term employed.[98] Even Grechko, who praised the "peace" policy of the Soviet

[96] Marshal of the Soviet Union A. Grechko, "Report of the Minister of Defense of the USSR Marshal of the Soviet Union A. A. Grechko," *Kommunist Vooruzhennykh Sil*, No. 8 (April 1973), p. 15. Like the version in *Krasnaya Zvezda*, March 28, 1973, this is a press summary of Grechko's speech.

[97] General of the Army A. A. Yepishev, "Report of the Head of the Main Political Administration of the Soviet Army and Navy General of the Army A. A. Yepishev," *Kommunist Vooruzhennykh Sil*, No. 8 (April 1973), p. 24. Like the version in *Krasnaya Zvezda*, March 28, 1973, this is a press summary of Yepishev's speech. In view of the lack of reference to China during the conference, it is interesting that Yepishev warns against the danger of revisionism, but not against the menace of dogmatism, which is sometimes associated with the Chinese leadership.

[98] *Pravda and Krasnaya Zvezda*, March 27–31, 1973.

Union, did not comment on "peaceful coexistence." This seems to be yet another
indication of Soviet fear of adverse effects resulting from the post-Moscow Summit Soviet propaganda concerning the United States' acceptance of the "peaceful coexistence" principle. Apparently the Soviet leadership was afraid that the
Soviet citizenry was taking the "peaceful" in "peaceful coexistence" too literally.

Based upon this assessment, then, it would appear that the desire to improve
internal controls was the primary reason for convening the conference of party
secretaries in the armed forces. This would explain, therefore, why relatively
more attention was given in the summarized speeches and discussions[99] to the
need for strengthening party-political work and for eliminating organizational
and indoctrinational defects, than to the imperialist threat itself. As the Minister
of Defense stated in his report to the conference:

> The increase of the role of party-political work is explained by the complexity
> of the international situation, the intensification of the struggle on the ideo-
> logical front, and the new demands made on the Soviet armed forces. The
> important tasks set in the resolutions of the 24th Congress of the CPSU for the
> army and navy give rise to the necessity for a further activation of the work of
> army and navy party organizations and the increased influence of communists
> on the masses of troops. In this connection, primary significance attaches to the
> generalization of accumulated experience of party-political work and the dis-
> semination of everything positive that assists the strengthening of our armed
> forces and the raising of its combat readiness. This also composes the chief task
> of the present conference.[100]

In the same way, the MPA head asserted:

> The objective necessity of further raising the levels of ideological work and its
> effectiveness is conditioned by the increase of the importance of the spiritual
> factors as powerful accelerators of communist construction, by the exacerbation
> of the ideological struggle in the world arena, as well as by the complexity of
> the tasks of military construction and the scale and depth of this influence,
> which the scientific-technical revolution exerted and continues to exert on
> military affairs.[101]

[99] In addition to the major speeches by Grechko and Yepishev, *Krasnaya Zvezda* summarized
the reports of numerous lesser military figures on March 28–29, 1973. The March 29 issue also
carried summaries of discussions presided over by the commander and the political head of the
various branches of the armed forces.

[100] Grechko, "Report of the Minister of Defense of the USSR Marshal of the Soviet Union
A. A. Grechko," p. 13.

[101] Yepishev, "Report of the Head of the Main Political Administration of the Soviet Army
and Navy General of the Army A. A. Yepishev," p. 24.

However, the resolution adopted by the conference, like many of the summarized speeches and discussions, indicated that some units lacked "purposefulness and efficiency" in party-political work. Among the specific defects cited were the fact that some party organizations were lax with regard to their influence on training exercises and combat watches, that some party organizations made little effort to overcome the apathy of individual Communists toward combat training and maintenance of combat readiness, and that some party members were themselves displaying bad personal examples.[102] It was pointed out, furthermore, that some party organizations were not making full use of diverse indoctrinational means or making an aggressive attack against bourgeois ideological subversion.[103]

Summary

In the period of the 24th CPSU Congress and its aftermath, a recurring theme was the similarity of views expressed by leading MPA and professional military spokesmen, especially on such issues as opposition to détente, the danger of Western ideological subversion, the growth of heavy industry for defense purposes, the expanding external role of the Soviet armed forces in support of foreign clients, and the importance of improving party-political indoctrination in the armed forces. Indeed, professional military leaders became very fervent in their calls for party leadership of military construction, because political control at this time meant emphasis on those factors which the professional military considered most important and necessary. It was a period in which the professional military seemed to perceive its vital interests to be in danger as a result of party actions and the MPA supported this view.

A situation of unity between the MPA and the professional military historically has not tended to last beyond the solution of the immediate crisis. In the past, such alliances degenerated because the irresolvable conflict of basic interests proved more fundamental or were broken up by a reassertion of party leadership authority. The next chapter will concentrate on the step taken by Brezhnev to regain political control over the armed forces.

---

[102] "Resolution of the 5th All-Army Conference of Secretaries of Party Organizations," *Kommunist Vooruzhennykh Sil*, No. 8 (April 1973), p. 29.

[103] *Ibid.*, p. 32.

9

The Transformation
to Party Leadership
in the Soviet Armed Forces

The Political Significance of Grechko's
Appointment as a Full Member of the
Politburo

On April 27, 1973, the Party Central Committee named three new full members to its Politburo, Chairman of the KGB Yu. V. Andropov, Minister of Foreign Affairs A. A. Gromyko, and Minister of Defense A. A. Grechko.[1] Grechko's appointment marked only the second time in Soviet history that the armed forces were represented in the Politburo, the highest decision-making organ in the Soviet system, by a professional military man. No less noteworthy is that Andropov's appointment marked the first full Politburo membership for the head of the secret police since Beria's execution in 1953. Institutionally, the new promotions added to the prestige of those groups concerned with internal security, foreign policy, and external defense.

The appointment of Andropov, Grechko, and Gromyko reflected various aspects of the policy line taken by the political leadership especially since the May 1972 Moscow Summit. First, Gromyko's appointment indicated Soviet interest in opening wider negotiations with the West, including important trade agreements with the United States. Second, Andropov's appointment illustrated that during the détente period prudent consideration would be given to the need for intensifying internal police controls, as time would demonstrate, both symbolically and actually. This presumably was a forceful warning to dissident

[1] *Pravda*, April 28, 1973. The KGB is the Soviet acronym of the Committee for State Security, that is, the internal security police.

elements that the relaxation of international tensions should not be misconstrued as a more lenient attitude toward internal affairs.

Lastly, Grechko's appointment appears to have been, in part, directed toward reassuring the professional military leadership — and, one might also say, the military's supporters in the defense industry sector — that military construction would not slacken even in an era of disarmament, arms control, and peaceful coexistence.[2] Indeed, a Central Committee resolution adopted likewise on April 27 stated not only that peaceful coexistence had won greater recognition, that a turn from "cold war" to a relaxation of tensions had taken place, and that "the activization of foreign economic and mutually beneficial relations of the USSR" with states of another social system was possible and desirable. The resolution also emphasized that close cooperation with the West in several select areas did not suggest that the external threat had abated, particularly in military matters. Attention was called to "the necessity for constant vigilance and preparedness to give a rebuff to any intrigues of the aggressive, reactionary circles of imperialism."[3] Thus, Grechko's political elevation, as well as those of Andropov and Gromyko, appear to have been due more to political requirements of the system than to the personal importance of the individuals. It underscored the rickety foundation of Communist rule, which requires more stringent internal repression and military preparedness as peaceful contacts with the West increase.

In a major article published in the most authoritative party-theoretical journal shortly after his political elevation, Grechko reaffirmed the commitment of the 24th Party Congress on strengthening the armed forces. He also reassured the various components of the Soviet military-industrial complex that "in the area of raising of defense capability, the chief efforts of the Party are directed toward the creation of a well-developed military-economic base and a powerful armed forces equipped with all contemporary means of struggle."[4] However, when challenged by Western leaders on the size of Soviet defense expenditures, Soviet spokesmen responded that "allegations concerning the growth of the Soviet

[2] Indications of military preoccupation with this are to be found in an article by Lieutenant General I. Zav'yalov (*Krasnaya Zvezda*, April 19, 1973), written just a few days before the announcement of Grechko's appointment. In the article, Zav'yalov observed that the "interconnection of war and the economy" is a "law-governed phenomenon." Soviet doctrine, he said, is based upon "the determining role of the economy and its ever increasing influence on war." Moreover, Zav'yalov, after examining various aspects of the interrelationship, concluded that "in proportion to its development, military affairs make ever increasing demands on the economy."

[3] *Pravda*, April 28, 1973.

[4] Marshal of the Soviet Union A. Grechko, "On Guard over Peace and Socialism," *Kommunist*, No. 7 (May 1973), p. 16.

Union's armed forces do not correspond to the facts," because expenditures for 1970–73 had remained at a constant 17.9 billion rubles per year.[5] Moreover, in September 1973, Minister of Foreign Affairs A. A. Gromyko presented to the U.N. General Assembly a recommendation for a 10 percent reduction of military expenditures for all Security Council members, part of which would be used to aid the developing countries.[6]

Soviet qualifications to the 10 percent reduction clearly indicate that the proposal had no serious intent other than as a propaganda instrument among developing nations and Western arms control advocates. First, the official Soviet military budget of 17.9 billion rubles is far below even the most conservative Western estimates. Thus, without a true picture of Soviet expenditures, Western states could not even seriously consider a percentage reduction. Furthermore, Gromyko stressed that "such a measure requires the participation of all permanent Security Council members without exception." Therefore, even if Western states should agree, the suggestion was bound to be rejected by the PRC, a permanent Security Council member which consistently denounces Soviet arms control and disarmament (ACD) proposals.

Without even a brief, perfunctory pause, the Soviet press demonstrated their lack of serious arms control intent. In the issue of *Kommunist Vooruzhennykh Sil* immediately following Gromyko's reduction proposal, a guide for political lessons in the armed forces instructed political officers to inform servicemen that the Party and Government "are constantly concerned about the further strengthening of the defense capabilities of the country."[7] Indeed, one doctor of philosophical sciences observed that "the strengthening and perfection of its military-technical base is a law-governed principle of socialist army development."[8] Moreover, it was warned that the "objective necessity" of defending socialist gains would be impossible "in the absence of constant renewal and improvements in the material foundation for the military might of the state and its armed forces."[9]

While such statements are hardly unusual in Soviet literature, they had a

[5] Colonel General N. V. Ogarkov in *Krasnaya Zvezda*, July 10, 1973.

[6] *Pravda*, September 23, 1973.

[7] Colonel N. Cherednichenko, "The Requirements of the CPSU and the Soviet Government of the Maintenance of High Vigilance and Constant Combat Readiness of the USSR Armed Forces. Personnel Tasks in the New Training Year," *Kommunist Vooruzhennykh Sil*, No. 20 (October 1973), p. 70.

[8] Colonel A. Timorin, "Leninist Teaching on the Defense of the Socialist Fatherland and the Present," *Kommunist Vooruzhennykh Sil*, No. 22 (November 1973), p. 14.

[9] Lieutenant Colonel A. Gromakov in *Sovetskiy Patriot*, November 21, 1973.

dual purpose. As already noted, they gave a reassurance to military and defense industry personnel that military construction would not be neglected in the era of détente and arms control negotiations. Yet there are indications that the military was forced to fight a rear-guard action against Soviet figures who apparently believed that ACD negotiations should actually be aimed at a de-emphasis on military construction. Therefore, statements on the need for improvements in the military-technical base, which in Soviet parlance mean increasing allocations for the defense sector, must be seen in conjunction with the discussion on the nature of war that simultaneously arose at this time.

In a September 1973 issue of the military history journal, Lieutenant General S. Lototskiy restated the formal Soviet position that, even under conditions of a nuclear missile war, war "remains the continuation of the policy of these or those classes and states since the social and national causes engineering it have not disappeared."[10] Likewise, two prominent political officers noted in a foreign affairs journal that the irrationality of world thermonuclear war to achieve political aims does not nullify war as the continuation of policy, because "as long as the socio-economic soil breeding militarism exists there will be political forces capable of risking the unleashing of a military adventure."[11] Still, Soviet spokesmen made quite clear that the objects of their attacks were not the typically unnamed "bourgeois analysts" or "Western Sovietologists," but other Soviet writers. In one instance, Major General A. Milovidov denounced "some works by Soviet authors," which allegedly "tolerated errors, for example, in the question of the essence and consequences of a nuclear missile war." According to Milovidov, these authors "absolutized the quantitative analysis and arithmetical calculation of the destructive force of nuclear weapons,"[12] rather than concentrating on the West's material preparations for waging war. Subsequently, in a hardline article suggestive of his September 1965 attack on Nikolskiy and Talenskiy, Colonel Ye. Rybkin took the highly unusual approach of criticizing another Soviet spokesman by name. Addressing Western contentions that "the Clausewitzian formula on war as a continuation of policy is inapplicable in our time," Rybkin charged:

> Unfortunately, erroneous opinions of a similar type now and then appear also in the pages of our press. In this respect, one should point to the statements of

[10] Lieutenant General (Ret.) S. Lototskiy, "The Classics of Marxism-Leninism and the Regularity of the Development of Military Art," *Voyenno-Istoricheskiy Zhurnal*, No. 9 (September 1973), p. 5.

[11] P. Zhilin and Y. Rybkin, "Militarism and Contemporary International Relations," *International Affairs* (Moscow), No. 10 (October 1973), p. 29.

[12] *Krasnaya Zvezda*, May 17, 1973.

Comrade A. Bovin on the pages of some periodical publications. Thus, while he correctly confirmed that general nuclear war is unacceptable as a means of achieving a political aim, A. Bovin at the same time tolerates an outstanding methodological error. Criticizing the widely known Clausewitzian formula, the author in a number of his publications for some reason mentions not one word about the Marxist-Leninist definition of war as a continuation of policy and makes no attempt at a scientific analysis of the essence of war.[13]

The military's offensive against budgetary restraints continued into 1974. Rear Admiral V. Shelyag, professor and doctor of philosophical sciences, denied the arguments of some "authors," whose "mathematical calculations" showed that a world nuclear war would bring about "the death of civilization." In his opinion, Soviet nuclear weapons would conversely provide "the means of defeating the aggressor and, consequently, the means of defending civilization."[14] Moreover, it was pointed out that, if it were not for the economic and military power of the USSR, "it would not be possible to establish such a correlation of forces in the world as would hold back the aggression of the imperialists and would contribute to the national liberation struggle of peoples."[15]

At the same time as they were advocating higher defense spending, MPA officials mounted a major effort to protect the armed forces from accusations of developing a military-industrial complex similar to those of capitalist states. They argued that Soviet defense expenditures are caused solely by factors external to the Soviet Union. According to a political study guide, for example, "the military preparations of the capitalist states force the socialist countries to allot necessary means to defense."[16] MPA chief Yepishev likewise asserted that "the threat of a military attack from the imperialist camp alone causes the Soviet state to allocate funds for defense and to maintain the army and navy at a high level of readiness for combat and adequately equipped with the latest weaponry."[17] This position was underscored by professional military men, especially

[13] Colonel Ye. Rybkin, "The Leninist Concept of War and the Present," *Kommunist Vooruzhennykh Sil*, No. 20 (October 1973), p. 26. A. Bovin was then and still is a political commentator for the government newspaper *Izvestiya*.

[14] *Krasnaya Zvezda*, February 7, 1974. See also General of the Army Ye. Mal'tsev in *ibid.*, February 14, 1974.

[15] Colonel V. Rut'kov, "The Leninist Criticism of Militarism and the Present," *Kommunist Vooruzhennykh Sil*, No. 1 (January 1974), p. 15.

[16] Colonel A. Pozmogov, "The Construction of Socialism and Communism in the USSR — The Embodiment of the Ideas of Leninism," *Kommunist Vooruzhennykh Sil*, No. 3 (February 1974) p. 78.

[17] General of the Army A. Yepishev, "Soviet Army's Historic Mission," *Soviet Military Review* (Moscow), No. 2 (February 1974), p. 5.

Minister of Defense Grechko, who wrote in a *Kommunist* article:

> . . . notwithstanding a certain slackening of international tension, the threat of
> war has not been completely eliminated. . . . And if imperialist reaction have
> not till now dared to unleash a new world war, this is hindered, first of all, by
> the growing economic and defensive might of our state and the power of its
> armed forces. In order to establish peace on the whole planet and for the Soviet
> people to build communism tranquilly, it will be necessary in the future to
> strengthen the defense capability of the country and to raise the combat might
> of the army and navy. The aggressive forces must constantly feel that we are
> always on the alert.[18]

The major speeches delivered to commemorate the fifty-sixth anniversary of
the founding of the Soviet armed forces appear to indicate that by February
1974 the Party had sufficiently reassured the professional military on the issue
of military expenditures. While some officers pointed out the necessity for further strengthening the armed forces,[19] most acknowledged that the armed forces
had "everything necessary" to defend the Soviet Union. Indeed, several speakers
observed that the armed forces presently meet "modern requirements," but that
the Party and Government would nonetheless continue to strengthen Soviet defense capabilities.[20]

Conferences and Campaigns

In the fourteen months between March 1974 and May 1975, the Soviet armed
forces held three major conferences and initiated four campaigns based upon
party and/or military decrees. As a whole, these efforts clearly demonstrate the
continued concern of the Soviet leadership that the average Soviet soldier,
despite decades of intense indoctrination, still lacks an appropriate commitment to the attainment of ideological steadfastness and combat efficiency. They
also appear to indicate that the routine devised to motivate soldiers has been
unsatisfactory. As in the economic sector, conferences and campaigns are under-

[18] Marshal of the Soviet Union A. Grechko, "V. I. Lenin and the Armed Forces of the Soviet
State," *Kommunist*, No. 3 (February 1974), p. 23. See also General of the Army S. L. Sokolov,
First Deputy Minister of Defense, *Krasnaya Zvezda*, February 23, 1974.

[19] For example, Marshal of the Soviet Union A. Vasilevskiy, TASS International Service,
February 22, 1974, FBIS, *Soviet Union*, III, No. 38 (February 25, 1974), p. V5.

[20] For example, Marshal of the Soviet Union A. Grechko, *Pravda*, February 23, 1974; and
Chief Marshal of Aviation P. Kutakhov, *Sovetskaya Kultura*, February 22, 1974.

taken for the purpose of eliminating defects, but acknowledged shortcomings persist. A broad assessment seems to point to the fact that a major source of these troubles is the lack of enthusiasm on the part of Soviet youth for the sustained sacrifices required by the Communist commitment to unending intersystemic struggle. This is a particularly acute problem in the military, where command cadres "have been significantly rejuvenated,"[21] so that approximately two thirds of regimental officers are now under the age of thirty.[22] Appropriately, therefore, the first of the major conferences was a meeting of komsomal secretaries.

On March 13, 1974, the All-Army Conference of Komsomol Organization Secretaries convened in Moscow's Great Kremlin Palace. All of the leading professional military and political-military figures were in attendance, attesting to the importance ascribed to this organization. Major speeches were delivered by Grechko, Yepishev, and first secretary of the Komsomol Ye. M. Tyazhelnikov. In a report to the Conference,[23] Grechko applauded the developing relaxation of tensions but also observed that the "positive improvement" must not be permitted "to blunt the revolutionary vigilance of the Soviet people, particularly the soldiers of the armed forces, or stimpuate in them a sense of complacency and carelessness." To meet an alleged Western threat he called for an increased strengthening of the armed forces and the military-economic potential of the country. The Minister of Defense enumerated three reasons behind the rising importance of the armed forces' komsomol. First, a majority of regiments and ships are composed almost entirely of party and komsomol members, and therefore combat readiness to a large degree depends upon the standards of komsomol training. Second, the ratio of komsomol members among officers and especially among platoon and company commanders, who have responsibility for soldier training, has risen.[24] Finally, komsomol responsibility in the area of indoctrination has increased as part of "the intensification of the struggle on the ideological front." MPA chief Yepishev's remarks to the Conference even more clearly suggested that the relaxation of tension and Western thought were having, from the Soviet leadership's viewpoint, a disconcerting effect on the spirit of "unremitting struggle." In calling for an "offensive struggle against the hostile ideol-

---

[21] "To Continue to Perfect Party Work," *Kommunist Vooruzhennykh Sil*, No. 5 (March 1975), p. 6.

[22] General of the Army S. L. Sokolov in *Komsomolskaya Pravda*, May 8, 1975.

[23] Marshal of the Soviet Union A. Grechko in *Krasnaya Zvezda*, March 14, 1974.

[24] In further discussion of the Conference, Lieutenant Colonel Ye. N. Makhov, assistant chief of the MPA for komsomol work, noted that this role is doubly important because some companies and equivalent sub-units lack party organizations or party groups. (*Ibid.*)

ogy," Yepishev emphasized that Soviet youth were a prime target of Western thought.

> We live in a world where the battle of ideas goes on unabated. Bourgeois ideo-
> logists, applying the most varied means, strive to exert influence on the minds
> and hearts of people, especially the younger generation. The purpose of these
> efforts is clear: to try to weaken our society from within, to shatter the Soviet
> people's moral-political unity and, with respect to the Army, to undermine the
> moral spirit of the personnel.[25]

In view of persistent problems related to indoctrination, the CPSU adopted a resolution in August 1974 having significant impact on the armed forces even though it was not directly focused upon the military organization. The decree, entitled "On Work for the Selection and Education of Ideological Cadres in the Belorussian Party Organization," judged that the scope of Communist construction and the nature of the international ideological struggle "are making higher demands on ideological work, and therefore on cadres." The Belorussian CP was consequently instructed to upgrade its selection, placement, and training of cadres involved in ideological work.

It was clearly recognized that this stentorian call for improving ideological work was aimed at a far larger audience than the Belorussian CP. On January 28–29, 1975, therefore, was convened the All-Army Conference of Ideological Workers, described in one editorial as the largest such conference in the post-World War II period.[26] The Conference was attended by all of the top military figures and major speeches were delivered by Grechko, Ponomarev, and Yepishev.[27] Ponomarev, not a military man, concentrated on foreign affairs issues such as détente and the Western economic crisis. While claiming that the capitalist countries are continuing their material preparation for war, Ponomarev maintained that the international situation was increasing the opportunities for anti-Western struggles.[28] Grechko centered his remarks on the assertion that

[25] *Pravda*, August 31, 1974.

[26] *Krasnaya Zvezda*, January 31, 1975.

[27] Interestingly, Soviet references to the Conference speakers appear to imply a definite order of importance, corresponding to their position in the political hierarchy. Grechko, a full Politburo member, has the full title of his speech cited. Ponomarev, a candidate Politburo member, is cited as having delivered "a long speech." Yepishev, a Central Committee member, is described tersely as having "made a speech." See summaries on the Conference in *ibid.*, January 29, 1975, as well as "All-Army Conference of Ideological Workers," *Kommunist Vooruzhennykh Sil*, No. 4 (February 1975), p. 3.

[28] *Krasnaya Zvezda*, January 29, 1975.

the West was using détente as a means to subvert the Soviet system, and consequently there must be "an appreciable increase of the volume and significance of ideological work." Discussing the importance of ideological work, Grechko stated:

> Under conditions of army and navy life, it is one of the most important factors for the successful resolution of literally all tasks. Whether it is the elaboration of new methods of combat action or the introduction of new forms of troop organization, the development of military science or the resolution of concrete questions on military cadres training — the paramount role everywhere belongs to ideological means. Combat and political training, patriotic and international education, the coordination of healthy military collectives, the struggle for a further strengthening of discipline — these and many other features of existence and life in the army and navy to a large degree depend on the state of ideological work, the skill of propagandists, and the breadth of all our cadres' participation in it.[29]

Emphasizing the threat of Western ideological subversion, Yepishev pointed out that strong indoctrinational efforts should be directed toward companies and batteries, because "our ideological influence and effective individual influence is primarily needed here."[30]

In February 1975, the armed forces initiated two new campaigns: one emphasized "socialist competition" and the other stressed criticism from below. As a complement to a campaign oriented toward competition in the economic sphere,[31] a motorized rifle division in the Transbaykal Military District challenged all other military units to a "socialist competition" for increasing combat readiness.[32] Receiving Brezhnev's personal endorsement, this challenge evoked numerous responses from units promising to improve various standards of military expertise. In an attempt to ensure the success of these competitions, the Party issued the resolution "On the State of Criticism and Self-Criticism in the Tambov Oblast Party Organization," which demanded "fuller utilization of the party-tested methods of criticsm and self-criticism for eliminating existing de-

---

[29] *Ibid.*

[30] *Ibid.*

[31] Jointly issued by the CC CPSU, the Council of Ministers, the CC of the Trade Unions, and the CC of the Komsomol, the decree "On the All-Union Socialist Competition" exhorted industrial, construction, and transport workers to fulfill the 1975 economic plan and the 9th Five-Year Plan ahead of schedule. (*Izvestiya*, January 12, 1975.)

[32] *Krasnaya Zvezda*, February 21, 1975.

fects and raising cadres' responsibility for work charged to them."[33] Despite the title of the resolution, this requirement was not meant to be limited to Tambov Oblast. Thus, numerous articles appeared subsequently in the military press urging Soviet soldiers to use criticism and self-criticism in meeting the goals of the socialist competition for combat readiness.

The capstone of these meetings and campaigns was marked in May 1975 with the convening of the All-Army Conference of Army Men with Excellent Results in Combat and Political Training. In the major address to the Conference, Grechko reiterated such themes as the Western military threat, the need for intensifying combat training and ideological indoctrination, and the necessity for improving "socialist competition."[34] In smaller meetings by military services, individual servicemen were singled out for praise for their accomplishments. A particularly noteworthy feature of this conference was the spotlight put on the professional military as opposed to the political-military leaders. For example, the major speech was delivered by Grechko, as expected; however, there is no reference in the Soviet press regarding a speech by Yepishev, although he is listed as being in attendance. This is a major departure from the two previous all-army conferences in March 1974 and January 1975. Also, the summaries of service meetings gave a few descriptive lines on main reports by the service commanders, but only tersely observed that the chief of each service's political administration make some concluding remarks.[35]

The Impact of the Military-Economics Debate on Political and Military Leadership

The speeches of major military spokesmen on the occasion of the fifty-seventh anniversary of the establishment of the Soviet armed forces almost uniformly stressed the continued danger of war, the intensifying efforts of capitalist states to prepare for war, defense of the USSR as an "objective necessity," and party leadership over the armed forces as the decisive conditions for victory.[36] How-

[33] "On the State of Criticism and Self-Criticism in the Tambov Oblast Party Organization," in *Spravochnik partiynogo rabotnika* (*Handbook of the Park Worker*), XV (Moscow: State Publishing House for Political Literature, 1975), 414.

[34] *Krasnaya Zvezda*, May 30, 1975. This issue also carries the list of major military figures in attendance and the summaries of service meetings.

[35] The only exception was in the meeting of the airborne forces, where the political chief made the major presentation while the commander made the concluding remarks.

[36] See, for example, Grechko (*Pravda*, February 19, 1975), Yakubovskiy (*Krasnaya Zvezda*, February 23, 1975), Kulikov (*Komsomolskaya Pravda*, February 23, 1975), Yepishev (*Krasnaya*

ever, division of opinion arose on the issue of weapons procurement. In his *Izvestiya* article, Yepishev asserted that the Soviet armed forces have everything necessary to fulfill their tasks and that the defense industry produces the most modern weapons and equipment "in the required quantities." Conversely, several professional military men presented arguments for the further strengthening of the armed forces. Pavlovskiy argued that, despite the conclusions of some strategic theorists, "unremitting attention" to strengthening the armed forces was required. In his *Krasnaya Zvezda* article, Yakubovskiy emphasized that the recent relaxation of international tension resulted from not only the overall change in the correlation of world forces but also the rise in the economic and military might of the USSR. Accordingly, said Yakubovskiy, there could be no relaxation of efforts to strengthen Soviet military power in the détente era. Moreover, in a *Krasnaya Zvezda* article, Colonel General of Engineering N. Alekseyev, Soviet Deputy Minister of Defense for armaments, quoted Lenin's warnings that in war "the upper hand is gotten by the one who has the greatest equipment, organization, discipline, and the best machines" and that "the very best army and the people most devoted to the cause of revolution will be immediately destroyed by the enemy if they are not armed, supplied with food, and trained to a sufficient degree."

Taking Yepishev's lead, political-military spokesmen continued to argue that military power was already "at the proper level." Assessing Soviet military-economic policy in World War II, Major General S. Baranov, a professor and doctor of historical sciences, pointed out that the CPSU "has always regarded and now regards the creation and strengthening of the economic foundation of the Soviet state's defense potential as one of its most important tasks." This means that the Soviet armed forces "have everything necessary" to destroy an aggressor.[37] Commenting on the nature of a future war, a guide for political instruction observed that the Soviet armed forces "are now provided with a sufficient quantity of all the perfected kinds of weapons and combat equipment, which permit them constantly to maintain combat power at the proper level, to raise combat readiness, and successfully to carry out any missions on the ground, in the air, and at sea."[38] Likewise, in an article for leaders of political lessons,

---

Zvezda, February 19 and 22, 1975; *Izvestiya*, February 22, 1975, and *Sovetskaya Moldaviya*, February 23, 1975), Sokolov (*Sovetskaya Rossiya*, February 22, 1975) Alekseyev (*Krasnaya Zvezda*, February 20, 1975), Ivanovskiy (*Neues Deutschland*, February 21, 1975), Kutakhov (*Trud*, February 23, 1975), and Pavlovskiy (*Sel'skaya Zhizn'*, February 23, 1975).

[37] *Krasnaya Zvezda*, February 27, 1975.

[38] Colonel V. Izmaylov, "The Character and Features of Contemporary War," *Kommunist Vooruzhennykh Sil*, No. 6 (March 1975), p. 73.

Colonel F. Fedchenko contended that the Soviet armed forces "are continuously receiving the most modern types of weapons and combat equipment" and consequently "are at the level of contemporary needs."[39]

At the conference held on April 17–18 to commemorate the thirtieth anniversary of the end of World War II, numerous speakers[40] praised the Soviet contribution to the victory over Nazi Germany. While passing reference was made to the contributions of the members of the "anti-Hitlerite coalition," especially the United States and Great Britain, it was claimed that the "decisive contribution" to the war effort was made by the Soviet people and armed forces.[41] As Minister of Defense Grechko noted in his major report to the conference:

> It is well-known that, at the time of German fascism's unleashing the Second World War, there were in the West no forces capable of countering the aggressive usurpation of the German-fascist army. The Soviet armed forces fulfilled this mission with honor. In a sustained, brutal struggle, they blocked the path of aggression, halted the enemy and then in numerous battles and engagements crushed his primary forces and destroyed the overwhelming part of his military equipment and armaments. This exerted a decisive influence upon the entire course of the Second World War and foreordained its victorious conclusion.

P. N. Fedoseyev, vice-president of the USSR Academy of Sciences, observed, furthermore, that this triumph had a tremendous impact on international communism. Fedoseyev maintained:

> In the course of the war, the class struggle within the national framework of individual captured states deepened and broadened. In a number of European and Asian states, people's democratic, then socialist, revolutions were victorious. The world colonialist system collapsed. Preconditions were created for a radical shift in the correlation of world forces in favor of socialism, for the unification of socialism, the international communist and workers' movement, and the national liberation movement into a single anti-imperialist force, and for the transformation of this force into the determining factor of progress.

[39] Colonel F. Fedchenko, "To Execute the Tasks of Combat Duty and the Performance of Guard and Watch Duty in Our Exemplary Way," *Kommunist Vooruzhennykh Sil*, No. 7 (April 1975), p. 75.

[40] According to Grechko's concluding remarks, there were seventy-four speakers at the conference (*Krasnaya Zvezda*, April 19, 1975).

[41] General of the Army P. I. Batov, chairman of the Soviet War Veterans Committee, in *ibid.*, April 18, 1975. Except for Grechko's concluding statement, the details of major conference speeches are taken from the summaries in this issue of *Krasnaya Zvezda*.

Still, the commonly expressed view posited that the CPSU was not only "the organizer and director" of this triumph, but also the "fundamental basis" of modern Soviet military construction. It was perhaps to underscore the primacy and continuity of party rule that Grechko gave passing reference to the fact of General Secretary Brezhnev's promotion to the four-star general officer rank, "general of the army." Since Brezhnev held only the two stars of a lieutenant general as a political officer in the late 1940's and again in the mid-1950's, and since he has not to this point ever been reported as having been promoted to the three-star rank of colonel general, Grechko's revelation appears to have been a dramatic attempt by Brezhnev to enhance his personal prestige and reaffirm his and the Party's control over military matters.[42] A further significant move occurred on May 8, when the Chairman of the Supreme Soviet, N. V. Podgorny, awarded Brezhnev the "Marshal's Star," hitherto given only to active-duty generals of the army.[43]

Despite Brezhnev's reassertion of authority over the military, the MPA shifted to a more adamantly anti-imperialist line. Yepishev observed in one article that the wartime experience "cautions against the underestimation of the military danger generated by imperialism."[44] In an educational journal, he also warned that "in the countries of capitalism under certain conditions it is possible to find madmen, who are capable of forgetting the lessons of history and challenging common sense."[45] Like Western anti-Communists, criticized Colonel A. Dmitriyev, a candidate of philosophical sciences, "some authors in the USSR" are making the mistake of saying that "nuclear war should not be considered a continuation of politics and its instrument."[46]

[42] Since December 1974, rumors had been circulating in the West concerning Brezhnev's political stability and physical health. Many were speculating that Brezhnev might soon be removed or, at least, be forced to retire. In mid-April 1975, however, his fortunes rose sharply. Coincident with the Grechko revelation, a CC plenum announced on April 16 the retirement of A. N. Shelepin, considered to be a strong Brezhnev rival, "in connection with his health," and the adoption of a foreign policy resolution which gave a strong, personal endorsement to Brezhnev's conduct of foreign policy. (*Pravda*, April 17, 1975.)

[43] *Krasnaya Zvezda*, May 9, 1975. First awarded in November 1974, the Marshal's Star was given only to active-duty commanders. However, the granting of the Marshal's Star to the general of the army did not signify promotion to the military rank of marshal of a service or marshal of the Soviet Union.

[44] *Ibid.*, May 8, 1975.

[45] General of the Army A. A. Yepishev, "To Educate Patriots and Staunch Defenders of the Homeland," *Sovetskaya Pedagogika*, No. 5 (May 1975), pp. 15–16.

[46] Colonel A. Dmitriyev, "Marxist-Leninist Training on War and the Army Is an Important Element of the Scientific World Outlook of Military Cadres," *Kommunist Vooruzhennykh Sil*, No. 13 (July 1975), p. 13.

Political officers argue, on the contrary, that the danger of imperialist nuclear aggression was increasing because of the recent advances in militarism and fascism in capitalist states.[47] The argument was consistently repeated that capitalist aggression could be deterred only through Soviet military power and vigilance.[48] Thus. one source asserted that "a relaxation of tension in the world in many respects depends on the might" of the Soviet and Warsaw Pact armed forces.[49] A guide for political lessons among ensigns and warrant officers explained, moreover, that the Party's objective was not merely parity, but military superiority over the Soviet Union's opponents. "The Party takes care," noted the guide, "that the Soviet army and navy always have qualitative superiority over the armies of our true enemies and have at their disposal modern means for the defense of the Homeland."[50] Furthermore, it was insisted that the Soviet people must make great sacrifices for the sake of heavy military expenditures to meet this goal. Accordingly, one Soviet source stated:

> The Party thoroughly takes into account the requirements of the army and navy for armaments and equipment under modern conditions. And although the armament of the army and navy costs great resources and efforts, the Soviet people have to make these expenditures since it is a matter of the destiny of socialism's achievements and the peace and security of our Homeland and fraternal socialist countries.[51]

Emphasis on the "anti-imperialist" line was again evident in the speeches on the fifty-eighth anniversary of the Soviet armed forces. Particularly strong was the allegation that Western "forces of reaction and aggression" were taking every possible measure in preparation for war against the Soviet Union, including

[47] See, for example, Colonel V. Katerinich, "Activization of Neofascism in the Capitalist World," *Kommunist Vooruzhennykh Sil*, No. 15 (August 1975), p. 73; and V. Mikhaylov and Yu. Khudyakov, "Imperialist Armies and Military Blocs," *Kommunist Vooruzhennykh Sil*, No. 16 (August 1975), p. 70.

[48] See, for example, Colonel A. Timorin, "The Armed Forces of a Mature Socialist Society: Features and Basic Tendencies of Its Development," *Kommunist Vooruzhennykh Sil*, No. 20 (October 1975), p. 21; and Colonel S. Tyushkevich, "The Development of Training on War and the Army in the Experience of the Great Fatherland War," *Kommunist Vooruzhennykh Sil*, No. 22 (November 1975), p. 13.

[49] "Recommendations for a Seminar Lesson," *Kommunist Vooruzhennykh Sil*, No. 21 (November 1975), p. 21.

[50] Colonel V. Mogutov, "The Leading and Directing Force," *Znamenosets*, No. 11 (November 1975), p. 29.

[51] Colonel F. Fedchenko, "To Treat Military Labor Conscientiously and to Protect Military and Public Property," *Kommunist Vooruzhennykh Sil*, No. 23 (December 1975), p. 77.

raising NATO military expenditures and standardizing weapons.[52] Because of this continued threat, it was argued, there must be a "constant concern" for the strengthening of the Soviet armed forces.[53] For example, First Deputy Minister of Defense and Warsaw Pact Commander Yakubovskiy observed:

> Despite the positive improvement in international affairs, the danger of war has not been eliminated. The arms race continues and the reactionary circles are intensifying the ideological struggle against the forces of peace and social progress. A complicated and explosively dangerous situation continues in the Near East. Our Party and the Soviet Government, struggling to resolve the central tasks of the present — the strengthening of peace and security of peoples — manifest constant concern for strengthening the combat might of the army and navy.[54]

Moreover, with the historical example of the difficulties surroundisg post-World War II economic recovery, it was pointed out that even under the most arduous circumstances military buildup can and must continue.[55]

The 25th CPSU Congress

On February 24, 1976, 4,998 delegates assembled in Moscow for the 25th Party Congress. In a reversal of the practice of previous Congresses, delegates at the 25th Congress were not divided into those with voting rights and those with consultative voices; all 4,998 had voting rights. While the ratio of delegates to party members continued the downward trend of recent Congresses (1:2,500 in 1966; 1:2,900 in 1971) to a current 1:3,000, the total number of delegates increased to thirty-five over the previous Congress.[56]

[52] General of the Army A. A. Yepishev, *Sovetskaya Rossiya*, February 23, 1976.

[53] The one major exception to this was General of the Army S. L. Sokolov, First Deputy Minister of Defense, who stated that the CPSU and the Soviet Government "are doing everything necessary" for the armed forces to meet modern demands. (*Pravda*, February 23 1976.)

[54] *Izvestiya*, February 22, 1976. See also Colonel General V. Govorov, commander of the Moscow Military District, *Moskovskaya Pravda*, February 22, 1976; Colonel General S. Belonozhko, commander of the Turkestan Military District, *Pravda Vostoka*, February 22, 1976; and General of the Army Ye. Ivanovskiy, commander of the Group of Soviet Forces in Germany, *Neues Deutschland*, February 23, 1976.

[55] General of the Army S. Kurkotkin, Deputy Minister of Defense, *Sel'skaya Zhizn'*, February 22, 1976; and Lieutenant General M. Popkov, chief of the political administration of the Central Asian Military District, *Sovetskaya Kirgiziya*, February 22, 1976.

[56] I. V. Kapitonov, chairman of the Mandate Commission, *Pravda*, February 28, 1976.

Among the delegates to the 25th Congress, there were 314 servicemen, border guards, and internal troops.[57] The publication of the number of military men marked a return to the 23rd Congress method, which listed 352 military men, and away from the 24th Congress, which listed only "a large group." Using the ratio and figures for the 23rd and 25th Congresses, it is possible to calculate that party membership in the armed forces was approximately 880,000 in 1966 and approximately 942,000 in 1976.[58] However, the military men as a percentage of total delegates declined from 7.1 percent in 1966 to 6.3 percent in 1976. From the 314 military men, 30 were elected to positions in the CC CPSU, thus representing slightly above 7 percent of that body but a decline of 1.3 percent as compared with the 24th CPSU Congress. Most importantly, this decline reflects a drop in

Proportion of Servicemen in the Central Committee Elected
by the 22nd, 23rd, 24th, and 25th Party Congresses

Congress	Total Membership			Servicemen			Percentage of Total
	Full	Alt.	Total	Full	Alt.	Total	
22nd (1961)	175	155	330	14	17	31	9.5
23rd (1966)	195	165	360	14	18	32	8.9
24th (1971)	241	155	396	20	13	33	8.3
25th (1976)	287	139	426	20	10	30	7.0

Source: *Pravda*, March 6, 1976.

alternate membership (those with only a consultative voice in CC matters), whereas full membership (those with voting rights) remained the same as in 1971.[59]

As in the two previous Congresses, the 25th CPSU Congress named three MPA officials out of the total of thirty military men to the Party Central Committee. Yepishev was elected as the sole full CC member from the political administration for the third straight time. To alternate membership were elected K. S. Grushevoy (third time) and P. A. Gorchakov (second time). However, it was in the Central Auditing Commission where the only change occurred. The number of MPA officials increased from one to two: S. P. Vasyagin (third time)

[57] *Ibid.*

[58] Carrying this calculation one step further, using the often-cited Soviet figure that one fifth of all military men are party members, would indicate that the size of the Soviet armed forces, including border guards and internal troops, was 4.4 million in 1966 and 4.71 million in 1976.

[59] For a full list of military representation elected by the 25th CPSU Congress, see Appendix A.

and I. S. Mednikov (first time). Statistically, this means that, in comparison to 1971, MPA membership as a percentage of the military's full CC membership remained at the same 5 percent, but MPA membership as a percentage of the military's alternate CC membership increased from 15 percent in 1971 to 20 percent in 1976.

	Proportion of Professional and Political-Military Men Elected by the 25th Party Congress to the Party Central Committee				
Classification	Full	Alt.	Total	Percentage of Military	Percentage of CC
CC	287	139	426		100.0
Military	20	10	30	100	7.0
Professional	19	8	27	90	6.33
Political	1	2	3	10	0.70

By occupational breakdown, MPA representation in the Party Central Committee elected at the 23rd, 24th, and 25th Party Congresses was identical. At all three Congresses, the MPA head (Yepishev) was elected to the single MPA slot in the full CC membership and the head of the political administration of the Moscow Military District (Grushevoy) and the head of the political administration of the Strategic Missile Forces (Lavrenov in 1966 and Gorchakov in 1971 and 1976) were given the two MPA positions as alternate CC members. The single change in the Party's highest organs over the past three Congresses was the appointment of the head of the political administration of the Group of Soviet Forces in Germany (Mednikov) to the Central Auditing Commission to go along with the thrice-named head of the political administration of the Ground Forces (Vasyagin).

Based upon the actions of the last three Party Congresses, it has been CPSU practice to name MPA officials to the Central Committee because of the military importance of the unit, rather than the standing of the individual within the MPA hierarchy. Thus the first deputy MPA head (G. K. Sredin) and other deputy MPA heads have been passed over in favor of second-level heads of political administrations of services.

In sharp contrast with previous Congresses, the only major speech on foreign policy and military affairs was delivered by General Secretary Brezhnev. There were no speeches by Minister of Foreign Affairs Gromyko, Minister of Defense Grechko, or MPA head Yepishev. Likewise, Chairman of the Council of Ministers Kosygin presented only a few superficial generalities on foreign economic matters. Consequently, an analysis of foreign policy and military aspects of the

25th CPSU Congress must focus its attention primarily on Brezhnev's Accountability Report.[60]

Brezhnev maintained that the principal Soviet line in relations with the West is "the struggle for the affirmation of the principles of peaceful coexistence, for lasting peace, for the lessening and, in the long run, the elemination of the danger of the outbreak of a new world war." Yet Brezhnev was emphatic that peaceful coexistence would not and could not be a neutral policy in support of the status quo or accommodation with the West. The General Secretary stated that détente, the most recent stage in peaceful coexistence,

> does not in the slightest measure abolish, and cannot abolish or alter the laws of class struggle. . . . We make no secret of the fact that we see in détente the way to create more favorable conditions for peaceful socialist and communist construction.

Moreover, Brezhnev reiterated the standard CPSU position that the West has since 1972 acquiesced to the principles of peaceful coexistence not because the majority of Western leaders desire friendly relations or because "imperialism" has lost its militaristic essence. Rather, he observed that the explanation lies in the shift in the correlation of world forces in socialism's favor (usually considered to have occurred in 1969–70), which has forced the capitalist states to confront "reality" and yield to Soviet demands for "peace."

With respect to Soviet-American relations, Brezhnev noted that several events, particularly the end of the Vietnam War and the conclusion of several U.S.–USSR summit agreements, had caused "a turn for the better in our relations with the major power of the capitalist world, the United States of America." He declared further that "there are good prospects for our relations with the USA also in the future." However, these optimistic statements were balanced with warnings that "the generally positive development" of Soviet-American relations is impeded by "influential forces in the USA" who oppose détente (as the Soviets define it), insinuate the danger of a "Soviet threat," agitate for a U.S.–NATO arms buildup, and (in reference to the Jackson Amendment) attempt to interfere in internal Soviet affairs through discriminatory trade measures.

[60] *Pravda*, February 25, 1976. The only Soviet military officer to speak at the 25th Congress was Major General S. G. Kochemasov, commander of a Strategic Missile Forces division. (*Ibid.*, February 29, 1976.) Replete with stock slogans and platitudes, Kochemasov's very brief presentation cannot be considered a major speech. Indeed, such a relatively low-ranking general officer appears to have been chosen expressly to stress the lack of importance attached to the military speech.

In the military arena, Brezhnev's overwhelming emphasis was on arms control and disarmament issues. Noting that "general and complete disarmament" is the Soviet's "ultimate goal," he voiced support for a ban on bacteriological weapons, nonproliferation, a limitation on existing strategic weapons systems, a ban on new weapons systems, a ban on military bases in the Indian Ocean, a reduction of armaments and troops in Central Europe with the present correlation preserved, and a treaty on the non-use of force in international relations. Allegedly, the major obstacle to the completion of such agreements has to this point been the determined effort of NATO leaders to gain "unilateral advantages" in negotiations between the two blocs.

Considering the lack of speeches by Grechko or Yepishev, it is surprising that Brezhnev made only two fleeting references to the Soviet armed forces in his five-hour speech. In the first passage, Brezhnev alluded to the importance of the political and technical training received by servicemen. As the General Secretary stated:

> Young men enter the soldier's family, lacking practical schooling. However, they return from the army as men who have gone through a school of endurance and discipline and have received technical and vocational knowledge and political training.
>
> Our army is educated in the spirit of deep loyalty to the socialist Homeland, the ideas of peace and internationalism, and the ideas of the friendship of peoples. In this regard, the Soviet army differs from the bourgeois army. This is why the Soviet people love their army and are proud of it.

In the second passage, Brezhnev addressed the technical and professional aspects of the armed forces, tersely observing:

> For all these years, the Party devoted the proper attention to strengthening the defense potential of our country and to perfecting the armed forces. We can announce to the Congress that we have done a considerable amount in this area. The fitting out of the armed forces with modern weapons and combat equipment has improved; the quality of combat training and ideological tempering has risen. In general, comrades, the Soviet people can be confident that the fruits of their creative labor are under reliable defense.
>
> No one should doubt that our Party will do everything so that the glorious armed forces of the Soviet Union will henceforth have at their disposal all the necessary weapons for the fulfillment of their responsible task — to be a guard of the Soviet people's peaceful labor and a bulwark of general peace.

Though lacking concrete evidence, one must assume that Brezhnev's moderate tone in foreign policy and military affairs was far from adequate in the military's viewpoint. Not only did Brezhnev describe Soviet-American relations more positively than at his previous two Congresses, but the General Secretary also refrained from any clear support for the "further strengthening" of the Soviet armed forces. Quite obviously, as "aggressive, imperialistic" America, making every effort to pursue the arms race, is a more desirable image as far as the military are concerned. Moreover, the absence of a speech by any top military leader precluded any possibility for the presentation of a harder military line.

Why was there no speech by Minister of Defense Grechko or MPA head Yepishev? In the case of Yepishev, there is the precedent of the 24th CPSU Congress. Although the head of the MPA had spoken at previous Congresses (e.g., Golikov at the 22nd and Yepishev at the 23rd), there was no MPA presentation at the 24th Congress. It might be argued, therefore, that the pattern was broken in 1971 and that the absence of an MPA statement has become the accepted order of business.

Much more meaningful is the absence of a Grechko presentation because of its lack of precedent. Although Grechko died two months later, there is no indication that poor physical health kept him from making a speech. He was extremely active and highly visible at this time.[61] The explanation appears, rather, to derive from a more personalized opposition to Grechko himself. It should be pointed out that, in addition the unprecedented absence of a speech to the Congress by the Minister of Defense, even more surprisingly the Soviet newspapers did not carry a major article or mention a major speech by Grechko on Soviet Armed Forces Day, which fell a few days before the 25th Congress. Indeed, at the major meeting of military officials held at the Central Academic Theater of the Soviet Army on February 20, the featured speaker was General of the Army I. G. Pavlovskiy, Deputy Minister of Defense and Commander-in-

[61] Soviet media photographs clearly show that Grechko attended the sessions of the 25th Congress and sat through the long speeches of the delegates and foreign observers. (See, for example, *Izvestiya*, February 25, 1976) which pictures Grechko during Brezhnev's five-hour-plus speech.) In addition, Soviet newspapers reported numerous Grechko meetings with foreign dignitaries and appearances at official functions throughout February and March with no apparent gap. During the crucial final days of February, *Krasnaya Zvezda* reported Grechko presenting awards to Olympic athletes (February 20, 1976), attending an Armed Forces Day meeting (February 21, 1976), issuing the order of the day for Armed Forces Day (February 22, 1976), presenting awards to military personnel (February 24, 1976), standing at a wreath-laying ceremony (February 26, 1976), and attending the Congress session at which Major General S. G. Kochemasov spoke (February 29, 1976).

Chief of the Ground Forces.[62] Furthermore, the only major speech made by Grechko summarizing events at the 25th Congress was printed in an extremely abridged form by the Soviet press.[63]

These facts seem to point toward two hypotheses, which are not mutually excluding. First, Grechko may have strongly objected to Brezhnev's moderate speech and, in response, prepared a much more hard-line speech, which the political leadership found unsuitable for presentation. If Grechko had been in essential agreement with Brezhnev, his speech would have served to buttress the General Secretary's position. Since many speeches by Soviet delegates had little actual purpose beyond praising Brezhnev's astuteness and wisdom,[64] there is no reason to believe that Brezhnev would shun any laudatory remarks by the Minister of Defense as well.

Secondly, the political leadership may have already decided before the end of February to remove Grechko from the Ministry of Defense. As late as Armed Forces Day in 1976, the speeches of the top military men reflected the fact that Grechko was either unwilling or unable to moderate the public exhortations of his military colleagues for a harder "anti-imperialist" line and for greater military buildup. If Grechko were already slated for retirement, the striking of a Grechko speech would indicate the leadership's displeasure with Grechko and a maneuver in his gradual withdrawal. Moreover, if gradual withdrawal were complicated by the inability of the leadership to find an acceptable replacement, this would explain why neither Yakubovskiy nor Kulikov, both First Deputy Ministers of Defense and the most likely military candidates to succeed Grechko, took Grechko's place as chief military spokesmen at the 25th Party Congress.

The second of these arguments appears to be supported by stronger circumstantial evidence. Given Grechko's close connection with Brezhnev since World War II and Grechko's typical mode of operation since becoming Minister of Defense in 1967, there appears to be slim grounds for assuming that Grechko would directly attack Brezhnev's policies. It is more likely that the political leadership was preparing to remove Grechko and replace him with a more suitable figure as soon as a candidate could be agreed upon.

[62] *Krasnaya Zvezda*, February 21, 1976.

[63] *Ibid.*, March 17, 1976.

[64] While Brezhnev himself stressed the principle of collective leadership, a Brezhnev "cult of personality" was very much in evidence. As a not atypical example, V. I. Prokhorov, head of the Soviet trade unions, described Brezhnev as "an eminent figure of the Leninist type," with "enormous experience, worldly wisdom, fast-growing and astonishingly accurate philosophical observations and generalizations and the knowledge of everything that constitutes the substance of the laboring person's life." (*Pravda*, March 4, 1976.)

The Reassertion of Political Control over the Professional Military Apparatus

In late April 1976, the Soviet press announced the death of two of the Soviet Union's highest-ranking professional military officers. The first was General of the Army S. M. Shtemenko, first deputy chief of the General Staff of the Soviet Armed Forces and chief of staff of the Joint Armed Forces of the Warsaw Pact, who died on April 23, "after a difficult, protracted illness."[65] This was followed by the even more important announcement that on April 26 Marshal of the Soviet Union A. A. Grechko, Minister of Defense, had died "suddenly."[66] By two decrees of the Presidium of the Supreme Soviet dated April 29, D. F. Ustinov was named Minister of Defense with promotion to the military rank of general of the army.

Born in 1908 to a worker's family, Dmitriy Fedorovich Ustinov[67] joined the CPSU in 1927. During the same year, he went to work as a metal worker and then as a machinist. After completing the Leningrad Military-Mechanical Institute in 1934, Ustinov worked until 1941 as an engineering designer for the Scientific Research Institute (NII), chief of a factory bureau for exploitation and experimental work, a deputy chief designer, and director of the Leningrad factory "Bolshevik." Beginning with the war, Ustinov held government posts as People's Commissar for Armaments, attaining the rank of colonel general of engineering-technical services in 1944 (1941–46), and Minister of Armaments (1946–53). Subsequently, he served as Minister of Defense Industries (1953–57), and then deputy chairman (1957–March 1963) and first deputy chairman (March 1963–March 1965) of the Council of Ministers. In the latter capacity, he also served as chairman of the Higher Council of the National Economy (VSNKh).

In March 1965, Ustinov was transferred out of government service and took up a party post in the Secretariat of the CC CPSU, retaining this position until his appointment as Minister of Defense. Elected to full CC membership in 1952, Ustinov was raised to candidate membership in the Party Presidium in March 1965 and renamed to candidate membership in the Party Politburo in April 1966. At the 25th CPSU Congress in March 1976, he was promoted to full Politburo membership.[68]

[65] *Krasnaya Zvezda*, April 25, 1976.

[66] *Ibid.*, April 27, 1976.

[67] For biographical material, see *Yezhegodnik bol'shoy sovetskoy entsiklopedii, 1971* (*Annual of the Great Soviet Encyclopedia, 1971*) (Moscow: Soviet Encyclopedia Publishing House, 1971), p. 634; and *Deputaty Verkovnogo Soveta SSSR. Devyatyy sozyv* (*Deputies of the USSR Supreme Soviet. Ninth Convocation*) (Moscow: n.p., 1974), p. 451.

[68] *Pravda*, March 6, 1976.

In view of the apparent unexpectedness of Grechko's death,[69] the appointment of the first civilian in twenty-one years to head the Ministry of Defense after a mere three days' discussion appears significant. When Malinovsky died as a result of a long illness in 1967, rumors had hinted that Ustinov was being considered for Minister of Defense but after thirteen days Grechko was selected. If indeed, as earlier suggested, Grechko had been slated for removal as far back as February because of the Party's intent to exert greater control over the professional military, the swiftness of Ustinov's appointment indicates the Party's determination to preclude any challenge from the professional military leadership.

Several factors recommended Ustinov as Grechko's successor. Although very little is known in the West about Ustinov's personal views, he obviously has the background in and knowledge of the Soviet defense industry establishment to be able to ensure party control in the increasingly complex area of military economics. Secondly, his acceptability in the top political circles had already been demonstrated by his March 1976 promotion to the Politburo. The appointment of a civilian already in the Politburo — even though at age sixty-eight Ustinov may be considered by the political leadership to be an interim head — defers possible heated debates on the issue of raising a new professional military man to Politburo status, a move not lightly taken in the Soviet system. Thirdly, the selection of a civilian avoided the necessity of choosing from among the possible military candidates, who may have been considered "too professional" for present requirements.

Yet, more surprises followed. On May 9, Soviet newspapers carried a Supreme Soviet decree, dated May 7, which resolved "to award the military rank of Marshal of the Soviet Union to the chairman of the USSR Defense Council, Comrade Leonid Il'ich Brezhnev."[70] Thus Brezhnev formally became at the time of the decree one of the ten highest-ranking military men in the Soviet Union, of whom only three others were in active command positions.[71] A curious aspect of this announcement was the public recognition given to the existence of the

---

[69] As in February and March, Grechko was still highly active in April. For example, just four days before his death he attended ceremonies marking the 106th anniversary of Lenin's birth. (See *ibid.*, April 23, 1976.)

[70] *Izvestiya, Krasnaya Zvezda,* and *Pravda,* May 9, 1976. Moreover, these newspapers carried a large picture of a new statue of Brezhnev unveiled in Dneprodzerzhinsk on May 8, as well as lengthy details on the unveiling ceremony headed by First Secretary of the UkrCP V. V. Shcherbitskiy.

[71] These three are Marshal of the Soviet Union I. I. Yakubovskiy, First Deputy Minister of Defense and Commander-in-Chief of the Joint Armed Forces of the Warsaw Pact; Marshal of the Soviet Union P. F. Batitskiy, Commander of the Air Defense Forces; and Admiral of the Fleet of the Soviet Union S. G. Gorshkov, Commander of the Navy. The remaining six are semi-retired members of the General Inspectorate.

USSR Defense Council and Brezhnev's chairmanship of it. While the Supreme Soviet decree gave no indication of the exact duties or authority of the Defense Council or when Brezhnev became its chairman, it appears to have been a clear sign that Brezhnev is the Supreme Commander of the Soviet armed forces, as well as the supreme state authority over all other non-military war-related matters. In one swift stroke, it was a public demonstration of Brezhnev's personal supremacy over both the military and the government organizations. Indeed, the total supremacy of Brezhnev was reflected in the fact that he was identified in the May 7 Supreme Soviet decree *only* as the chairman of the Defense Council, which supposedly coordinates all party, state, and military functions, rather than as the head of any particular apparatus.

Brezhnev's promotion was followed at the end of July by another Supreme Soviet decree, which resolved "to award to General of the Army Dmitriy Fedorovich Ustinov the military rank of Marshal of the Soviet Union."[72] Thus the highest authorities in military affairs are presently men with unsurpassed rank and with essentially civilian backgrounds, albeit close military ties. A conscious pattern of civilian leadership over military affairs seems to develop if one adds General of the Army Yepishev, whose posts before becoming MPA head in 1962 were in the party and diplomatic service.

Summary

This chapter has shown that détente has had a tremendously unsettling effect on the political control of the Soviet armed forces. At first, the party elites tried to co-opt the leaders of the hierarchies responsible for the armed forces as well as foreign affairs and internal security. However, in the case of the armed forces, this co-optation proved less than successful. Grechko was either unable or unwilling to expunge the demands of the military men for even larger military budgets and even further strengthening of the armed forces. Moreover, the MPA, the organ responsible for party leadership, often sided with the professional military in these arguments.

As a result, the Party was forced to reassert its direct control over the armed forces. "Marshal" Brezhnev's chairmanship of the Defense Council, the highest organ of civilian administration and control over the armed forces, was publicly announced. "Marshal" Ustinov, a government and party official, was placed at the head of the Ministry of Defense. The coinciding of these two events seems

[72] *Krasnaya Zvezda*, July 31, 1976.

to indicate that the CPSU, under pressures from internal advocates who argued for less emphasis on a military hard line during the era of détente, took these steps to demonstrate forcefully and dramatically its determination to control the armed forces.

Yet it seems possible that the very forcefulness of these actions only serves to underscore the uneasiness which the party perceives concerning its ability to control the armed forces, not only on the highest level but also on the level of the common soldier.

Appendix A

Military Representation in the CC CPSU
Elected at the 22nd Congress

Name   Position

Full Members

Bagramyan, I. Kh.	Deputy Minister of Defense; Chief of Rear Services
Biryuzov, S. S.	Deputy Minister of Defense; Commander-in-Chief, Antiaircraft Defense
Chuykov, V. I.	First Deputy Minister of Defense; Commander-in-Chief, Ground Forces
Fokin, V. A.	Commander, Pacific Fleet
Golikov, F. I.	Head of the Main Political Administration of the Army and Navy
Gorshkov, S. G.	First Deputy Minister of Defense; Commander-in-Chief of the Navy
Grechko, A. A.	First Deputy Minister of Defense; Commander-in-Chief, Joint Armed Forces of the Warsaw Pact
Konev, I. S.	Commander-in-Chief, Group of Soviet Forces in Germany
Krylov, N. I.	Commander, Moscow Military District
Malinovsky, R. Ya.	Minister of Defense of the USSR; Commander-in-Chief of the Armed Forces of the USSR
Moskalenko, K. S.	Deputy Minister of Defense; Commander-in-Chief, Strategic Missile Forces
Vershinin, K. A.	Deputy Minister of Defense; Commander-in-Chief, Air Forces
Yakubovskiy, L. I.	First Deputy Commander, Group of Soviet Forces in Germany
Zakharov, M. V.	First Deputy Minister of Defense; Chief of the General Staff of the Army and Navy

Alternates

Batitskiy, P. F.	Commander, Moscow District Air Defense
Budennyy, S. M.	Member of the Military Council of the Ministry of Defense
Chabanenko, A. T.	Commander, Northern Fleet
Getman, A. L.	Commander, Carpathian Military District
Kazakov, M. I.	Commander, Leningrad Military District
Koshevoy, P. K.	Commander, Kiev Military District

Name	Position
Penkovskiy, V. A.	Commander, Belorussian Military District
Pliyev, I. A.	Commander, North Caucasian Military District
Rokossovskiy, K. K.	Deputy Minister of Defense
Rudenko, S. I.	Chief of Staff, Air Forces
Savitskiy, E. Y.	Deputy Commander-in-Chief, Air Forces
Sokolovskiy, V. D.	Formerly Chief of the General Staff of the Army and Navy
Stuchenko, A. T.	Commander, Transcaucasian Military District
Sudets, V. A.	Commander, Strategic Air Forces
Timoshenko, S. K.	Chairman, Committee of War Veterans
Varentsov, S. S.	Commander, Artillery Forces
Yeremenko, A. I.	Deputy Commander-in-Chief, Joint Armed Forces of the Warsaw Pact

Source: *XXII s"yezd Kommunisticheskoy partii Sovetskogo Soyuza: Stenograficheskiy otchet* (*22nd Congress of the Communist Party of the Soviet Union: Stenographic Record*) (Moscow: State Publishing House for Political Literature, 1962), III, 356–60.

Military Representation in the CC CPSU
Elected at the 23rd Congress

Full Members

Bagramyan, I. Kh.	Deputy Minister of Defense; Chief of Rear Services
Batitskiy, P. F.	First Deputy Chief of the General Staff of the Army and Navy
Beloborodov, A. P.	Commander, Moscow Military District
Chuykov, V. I.	Chief of Civil Defense of the USSR
Gorshkov, S. G.	Deputy Minister of Defense; Commander-in-Chief of the Navy
Grechko, A. A.	First Deputy Minister of Defense
Konev, I. S.	General Inspector of the Group of General Inspectors of the Ministry of Defense
Krylov, N. I.	Deputy Minister of Defense; Commander-in-Chief, Strategic Missile Forces
Malinovsky, R. Ya.	Minister of Defense of the USSR
Moskalenko, K. S.	Chief Inspector of the Ministry of Defense
Vershinin, K. A.	Deputy Minister of Defense; Commander-in-Chief, Air Forces
Yakubovskiy, I. I.	Commander, Kiev Military District
Yepishev, A. A.	Head of the Main Political Administration of the Army and Navy
Zakharov, M. V.	First Deputy Minister of Defense; Chief of the General Staff of the Armed Forces

Name	Position

Alternates

Amelko, N. N.	Commander, Pacific Fleet
Budennyy, S. M.	Member of the Presidium of the USSR Supreme Soviet
Getman, A. L.	Chairman, DOSAAF
Grushevoy, K. S.	Head of the Political Administration of the Moscow Military District
Kazakov, M. I.	First Deputy Chief of the General Staff of the Army and Navy; Chief of the Staff of the Joint Armed Forces of the Warsaw Pact
Koshevoy, P. K.	Commander-in-Chief, Group of Soviet Forces in Germany
Lavrenov, I. A.	Head of the Political Administration of Strategic Missile Forces
Lobov, S. M.	Commander, Northern Fleet
Lyashchenko, N. G.	Commander, Turkestan Military District
Maryakhin, S. S.	Commander, Belorussian Military District
Ogarkov, N. V.	Commander, Volga Military District
Penkovskiy, V. A.	Deputy Minister of Defense
Rokossovskiy, K. K.	General Inspector of the Group of General Inspectors of the Ministry of Defense
Sokolov, S. L.	Commander, Leningrad Military District
Sokolovskiy, V. D.	General Inspector of the Group of General Inspectors of the Ministry of Defense
Stuchenko, A. T.	Commander, Transcaucasian Military District
Timoshenko, S. K.	General Inspector of the Group of General Inspectors of the Ministry of Defense
Yeremenko, A. I.	General Inspector of the Group of General Inspectors of the Ministry of Defense

Source: *XXIII s"yezd Kommunisticheskoy partii Sovetskogo Soyuza: Stenograficheskiy otchet (23rd Congress of the Communist Party of the Soviet Union: Stenographic Record)* (Moscow: State Publishing House for Political Literature, 1966), II, 381–623.

Military Representation in the CC CPSU Elected at the 24th Congress

Full Members

Bagramyan, I. Kh.	General Inspector of the Group of General Inspectors of the Ministry of Defense
Batitskiy, P. F.	Deputy Minister of Defense; Commander-in-Chief, Air Defense

Name	Position
Chuykov, V. I.	Chief of Civil Defense of the USSR
Gorshkov, S. G.	Deputy Minister of Defense; Commander-in-Chief of the Navy
Grechko, A. A.	Minister of Defense of the USSR
Ivanovskiy, Ye. F.	Commander, Moscow Military District
Konev, I. S.	General Inspector of the Group of General Inspectors of the Ministry of Defense
Krylov, N. I.	Deputy Minister of Defense; Commander-in-Chief, Strategic Missile Forces
Kulikov, V. G.	Commander-in-Chief, Group of Soviet Forces in Germany
Kutakov, P. S.	Deputy Minister of Defense; Commander-in-Chief, Air Forces
Lyashchenko, N. G.	Commander, Central Asian Military District
Maryakin, S. S.	Deputy Minister of Defense; Chief of Rear Services
Moskalenko, K. S.	Deputy Minister of Defense; General Inspector of the Group of General Inspectors of the Ministry of Defense
Ogarkov, N. V.	First Deputy Chief of Staff of the Army and Navy
Pavlovskiy, I. G.	Deputy Minister of Defense; Commander-in-Chief, Ground Forces
Shavrov, I. Ye.	Commander, Leningrad Military District
Sokolov, S. L.	First Deputy Minister of Defense
Yakubovskiy, I. I.	First Deputy Minister of Detense; Commander-in-Chief, Joint Armed Forces of the Warsaw Pact
Yepishev, A. A.	Head of the Main Political Administration of the Soviet Army and Navy
Zakharov, M. V.	First Deputy Minister of Defense; Chief of the General Staff of the Army and Navy

Alternates

Name	Position
Budennyy, S. M.	Member of the Presidium of the USSR Supreme Soviet
Getman, A. L.	Chairman, DOSAAF
Gorchakov, P. A.	Head of the Political Administration of Strategic Missile Forces
Grushevoy, K. S.	Head of the Political Administration of Moscow Military District
Koldunov, A. I.	Commander, Moscow Air Defense District
Kurkotkin, S. K.	Commander, Transcaucasian Military District
Lobov, S. M.	Commander, Northern Fleet
Mayorov. A. M.	Commander, Central Group of Forces
Okunev, V. V.	On "responsible duty" in the Ministry of Defense
Salmanov, G. I.	Commander, Kiev Military District
Smirnov, N. I.	Commander, Pacific Fleet

Name	Position
Tolubko, V. F.	Commander, Far Eastern Military District
Tret'yak, I. M.	Commander, Belorussian Military District

Source: *XXIV s"yezd Kommunisticheskoy partii Sovetskogo Soyuza: Stenograficheskiy otchet (24th Congress of the Communist Party of the Soviet Union: Stenographic Record)* (Moscow: State Publishing House for Political Literature, 1971), II, 313–18; see also Christian Duevel, "The Central Committee and the Central Auditing Commission Elected by the 24th CPSU Congress" *Radio Liberty Research Paper*, No. 46 (1972), pp. 57–58. While the latter source has some minor inaccuracies, it gives the positions of the military man, which is not found in the Russian source.

Military Representation in the CC CPSU Elected at the 25th Congress

Full Members

Altunin, A. T.	Deputy Minister of Defense; Chief of Civil Defense of the USSR
Bagramyan, I. Kh.	General Inspector of the Group of General Inspectors of the Ministry of Defense
Batitskiy, P. F.	Deputy Minister of Defense; Commasder-in-Chief, National Air Defense
Chuykov, V. I.	General Inspector of the Group of General Inspectors of the Ministry of Defense
Gorshkov, S. G.	Deputy Minister of Defense; Commander-in-Chief of the Navy
Grechko, A. A.	Minister of Defense of the USSR
Ivanovskiy, Ye. F.	Commander, Group of Soviet Forces in Germany
Kulikov, V. G.	First Deputy Minister of Defense; Chief of the General Staff of the Army and Navy
Kurkotkin, S. K.	Deputy Minister of Defense; Chief of Rear Services
Kutakov, P. S.	Deputy Minister of Defense; Commander-in-Chief, Air Forces
Lyashchenko, N. G.	Commander, Central Asian Military District
Moskalenko, K. S.	Chief Inspector of the Group of General Inspectors of the Ministry of Defense
Ogarkov, N. V.	Deputy Minister of Defense
Pavlovskiy, I. G.	Deputy Minister of Defense, Commander-in-Chief, Ground Forces
Petrov, V. I.	Commander, Far Eastern Military District
Sokolov, S. L.	First Deputy Minister of Defense

Name	Position
Tolubko, V. F.	Deputy Minister of Defense; Commander-in-Chief, Strategic Missile Forces
Tret'yak, I. M.	Commander, Belorussian Military District
Yakubovskiy, I. I.	First Deputy Minister of Defense; Commander-in-Chief, Joint Armed Forces of the Warsaw Pact
Yépishev, A. A.	Head of the Main Political Administration of the Soviet Army and Navy

Alternates

Gerasimov, I. A.	Commander, Kiev Military District
Gorchakov, P. A.	Head of the Political Administration of the Strategic Missile Forces
Govorov, V. L.	Commander, Moscow Military District
Gribkov, A. I.	Commander, Leningrad Military District
Grushevoy, K. S.	Head of the Political Administration of the Moscow Military District
Kozlov, M. M.	First Deputy Chief of the General Staff of the Army and Navy
Maslov, V. P.	Commander, Pacific Fleet
Mayorov, A. M.	Commander, Baltic Military District
Pokryshkin, A. I.	Chairman, DOSAAF
Yegorov, G. M.	Commander, Northern Fleet

Source: *Pravda*, March 6, 1976.

Appendix B

As indicated throughout this study, the structure and influence of the political administration of the Soviet Army and Navy have undergone several modifications and even more alterations during its history. It can be readily seen from these fluctuations that the status of the political administration is closely related to the political climate in the state at a given time, as well as the personality of the political administration head. Thus the structure and duties of the political administration change with the political environment, as frequently noted in the text of this study. The purpose here is to describe the present structure and duties of the political administration.

Presently, the instrument of political administration in the armed forces is the Main Political Administration (MPA) of the Soviet Armed Forces (Glavnoye politicheskoye upravleniye Sovetskoy Armii i Voyenno-Morskogo Flota). The MPA has dual subordination to the CPSU Central Committee and the Ministry of Defense. Thus it is simultaneously an arm of the military, structurally paralleling the military apparatus and holding appropriate military ranks, and an arm of the Party, working with the rights of a section of the CC CPSU.

The political administration of the armed forces is divided into four major levels, corresponding to the major subdivisions of the military apparatus. These levels are: (1) the Main Political Administration on the General Staff level, (2) the political administration in the services, (3) the political administrations of military districts, groups of forces, fleets, and air defense districts, and (4) the political sections in various military subdivisions down to the company level. Leadership of the MPA rests in the MPA Bureau, consisting of the head of the MPA (chairman), his deputies, the heads of organizational-party and agitprop administrations, the assistant for the Komsomol, the secretary of the party commission, and the editor of *Krasnaya Zvezda*. Decisions of the Bureau are made by a majority vote. While general directions on party-political work must be signed by both the Minister of Defense and the MPA head, the latter has authority to issue decrees on "current" questions over his own signature.

Because it has both political and professional responsibilities, the duties of the MPA are widely diversified. The MPA carries out party and government resolutions; supervises the political organs as well as the party and komsomol organizations; elaborates the most important points of party construction; generalizes and puts into practice progressive methods; engages in the selection, placement, and education of cadres of political workers; aids in the combat preparation of troops; organizes ideological work; looks after the material well-being, living conditions, and cultural facilities of servicemen; controls the ideological content of military newspapers, journals, and publishing houses; and takes part in the selection, placement, and attestation of officers.

On each level of the political administration, the political organs are broken down into a number of departments. The departments are responsible for the organization and leadership of the various type of party-political work. At the head of the political organs is the political chief, who is responsible for the general operation of the political organ. Other political workers and departments usually included in the political organs are:

- The deputy political chief, who is primarily responsible for implementing the tasks of the political chief and guiding the work of political officers.

- The assistant political chief for komsomol work, who guides party-political work among komsomol members and alternates in the armed forces.

- The instructor for komsomol work, who is picked from the ranks of soldiers and sergeants and is subordinate to the assistant political chief for komsomol work. His primary duty is to organize ideological-educational work among komsomol members in the armed forces.

- The senior instructor for organizational-party work, who is responsible for organizing and guiding party-political work in sub-units.

- The propagandist, who is responsible for organizing theoretical seminars and conferences and guiding the ideological education of military personnel.

- The senior instructor for cultural-mass work, who is responsible for establishing clubs and libraries and other cultural facilities for the education and use of military personnel.

- Other departments may include responsibilities for collecting information, supervising political schools, and publishing propaganda materials.

Training for political officers is conducted at a number of educational institutions, specifically designed for that purpose. In addition to the high-level Military-Political Academy imeni V. I. Lenin, which enrolls students from all of the services to become political officers, there are specialized political schools for each service branch or arm. After four years of training, graduates are awarded the rank of lieutenant. These schools are:

- Donetsk Higher Military-Political Aviation School of Engineering and Communications Troops
- Kiev Higher Naval Political School
- Kurgan Higher Military-Political Aviation School
- Leningrad Higher Military-Political School of the National Air Defense
- Lvov Higher Military-Political School
- Military-Political Department of the Rostov Higher Military Command School
- Novosibirsk Higher Military-Political Combined Arms School
- Simferopol Higher Military-Political Construction School
- Sverdlovsk Higher Military-Political Tank-Artillery School

Index

DATE DUE